Feminist Digital Humanities

TOPICS IN THE DIGITAL HUMANITIES

Humanities computing is redefining basic principles about research and publication. An influx of new, vibrant, and diverse communities of practitioners recognizes that computer applications are subject to continual innovation and reappraisal. This series publishes books that demonstrate the new questions, methods, and results arising in the digital humanities.

Series Editors
Susan Schreibman
For a list of books in the series, please see
our website at www.press.uillinois.edu.

Feminist Digital Humanities

Intersections in Practice

Edited by
LISA MARIE RHODY
AND SUSAN SCHREIBMAN

UNIVERSITY OF ILLINOIS PRESS
Urbana, Chicago, and Springfield

Funding from CUNY Research Foundation and Maastricht
University Library's Open Book Fund made open access
publication possible. The text of this book is licensed
under a Creative Commons Attribution Non Commercial-
No Derivatives 4.0 International License: https://
creativecommons.org/licenses/by-nc-nd/4.0/

Library of Congress Cataloging-in-Publication Data

Names: Rhody, Lisa Marie, editor. | Schreibman, Susan, editor.
Title: Feminist digital humanities : intersections in practice /
    edited by Lisa Marie Rhody and Susan Schreibman.
Description: Urbana : University of Illinois Press, [2025]
    | Series: Topics in the digital humanities | Includes
    bibliographical references and index.
Identifiers: LCCN 2024042366 (print) | LCCN 2024042367
    (ebook) | ISBN 9780252046421 (cloth; alk. paper) |
    ISBN 9780252088506 (paperback; alk. paper) | ISBN
    9780252047732 (ebook)
Subjects: LCSH: Feminist theory. | Digital humanities. |
    Women and technology.
Classification: LCC HQ1190 .F447 2025 (print) | LCC
    HQ1190 (ebook) | DDC 305.4201—dc23/eng/20250210
LC record available at https://lccn.loc.gov/2024042366
LC ebook record available at https://lccn.loc.gov/2024042367

Open Access ISBN 978-0-252-04830-2

Contents

Preface   vii

Acknowledgments   ix

Introduction   *Lisa Marie Rhody and Susan Schreibman*   1

PART I   READINGS

1   Playback Is a Bitch: A Feminist Rationale
for Audiation as a Framework for Theorizing
Digital Tools   *Tanya E. Clement*   17

2   Feminist DH: A Historical Perspective:
Excavating the Lives of Women of the Past
Monika Barget and Susan Schreibman   35

3   Textiles and Technology: Needlework as Data Storage
and Feminist Process   *Jaime Lee Kirtz*   59

PART II   INFRASTRUCTURES

4   Feminist Infrastructure Building
Susan Brown and Laura Mandell   79

5   From Lab to Cooperative: A Feminist Infrastructural
Reimagining   *Jacqueline Wernimont and Nikko L. Stevens*   102

6   Infrastructures for Diversity: Feminist and
Queer Interventions in Nordic Digital Humanities
Jenny Bergenmar, Cecilia Lindhé, and Astrid von Rosen   121

7   Exploring Constellations of Care and
    Professionalization in Black Feminist
    Digital Humanities: A Black Woman Graduate
    Student's Reflection   *Ravynn K. Stringfield*   143

8   Infrapolitics, Archival Infrastructures, and
    Digital Reparative Practices   *Nanna Bonde Thylstrup,
    Daniela Agostinho, Katrine Dirckinck-Holmfeld,
    and Kristin Veel*   159

PART III PEDAGOGIES

9   Walking Away from the Black Box of
    Social Media   *Mark Sample*   181

10 Teaching Feminist Text Analysis   *Lisa Marie Rhody*   198

11 Dismantling the Code: A Liberatory Feminist Pedagogy
    for Teaching Digital Humanities   *Dhanashree Thorat*   220

12 Reparatory Praxis: The Role of Intersectional Feminism
    in Digital Pedagogy   *Andie Silva*   238

Contributors   257

Index   261

Preface

Feminist Digital Humanities: Intersections in Practice grew out of a seren-dipitous conversation between the editors after a session at the Modern Language Association (MLA) Convention in New York in January 2018. Although "feminism" or "feminisms" as a term was much in the news, we wondered what made feminist digital humanities (DH) practice relatively hard to find. We knew that there were, had been, and continued to be feminist DH projects. We were aware of previous and ongoing work to critique, recover, reclaim, decolonialize, and transform DH in terms of theorization, digital collections, algorithmic methods, and labor practices, but what seemed surprising at the time was that seemingly few "announced" themselves as explicitly feminist. Or, if they did, that they were scattered across numerous journals and collections of essays.

Fueled by our curiosity, we began searching databases, journals, and professional profiles. While many scholars mentioned feminism as an area of interest, few of the titles we came across or the keywords and metadata we searched included the terms "feminism" and "digital humanities" together. Could the fear of being relegated to the margins of the field or dismissed as too narrowly focused be one of the reasons why it was so challenging to find feminist DH projects announced as such in conference papers, posters, articles, and grant proposals?[1] It struck us that feminist DH practice was alive and vibrant, but disparate and difficult to find. We thus saw a need for a collection that demonstrated explicit connections between feminist theory and action in digital humanities.

The collection published here is shaped by other impacts, as well. The first is a surge in digital humanities scholarship invested in announcing itself as feminist that was published during the period contributors were writing their chapters.[2] The second is the outsized impact the global pandemic has and continues to have on the lives of women, gender minorities, and feminist scholars. For feminist DH scholars included in this volume and for many who are not, the pandemic served as a prism through which to view the multiple dimensions of precarity that characterize academic labor. The impact has been tangible costs for the invisible burdens many women bear, which are discussed in several of the chapters in this collection in which labor practices and infrastructural concerns surface.

Though COVID-19 is not explicitly the subject in the majority of chapters, its impact on women's personal and professional lives are present in the volume. Women and female-identifying practitioners are not a monolith, and there is no singular experience shared by contributors; however, our anecdotal experience confirms what empirical analyses have claimed to be true. The pandemic created and continues to create additional burdens for women in academe, who shoulder the majority of emotional, administrative, and familial responsibilities. Assembling this volume during the pandemic, we editors, as straight, white women, witnessed how much more is required of colleagues who experience complex intersections of oppression born out of academia's white, male, colonialist legacy. Some contributors had to withdraw while others were invited. Childcare responsibilities, teaching in new online modalities, course revamping, and the general stress of the pandemic delayed, changed, and caused revisions to submissions. The resultant collection is not what we originally imagined: it is stronger. Some of that strength comes from collaborations and contributions that are not immediately visible in the final volume that, nevertheless, helped shape our work. This collection is, therefore, timely and relevant to the field because the work of dismantling systems of oppression, illuminating invisible labor, and lifting silenced voices remains necessary and ongoing.

Notes

1. Nickoal Eichmann-Kalwara, Jeana Jorgensen, and Scott B. Weingart, "Representation at Digital Humanities Conferences (2000–2015)," in *Bodies of Information: Intersectional Feminism and Digital Humanities*, edited by Jacqueline Wernimont and Liz Losh, Debates in the Digital Humanities (Minneapolis: University of Minnesota Press, 2018), https://dhdebates.gc.cuny.edu/read/untitled-4e08b137-aec5-49a4-83c0-38258425f145/section/5dcc1fee-caef-4c10-aa3c-08a9bbf0b68b.

2. Jacqueline Wernimont and Elizabeth Losh, eds., *Bodies of Information: Intersectional Feminism and Digital Humanities*, 2018, https://dhdebates.gc.cuny.edu/projects/bodies-of-information.

Acknowledgments

An edited volume is a necessarily collective and communal effort—especially one that strives to practice feminist values. This volume has benefitted from a generous community of colleagues, partners, contributors, editors, and readers.

We are grateful to the volume's contributors, who collaborated patiently and collegially during what was a profoundly stressful collective experience. Some of our contributors have been with us from the start of the project, while others signed on along the way, when COVID-19 and the varied professional, personal, and medical stresses we were experiencing made it impossible for other contributors to carry their projects forward. Through multiple cycles of revision, cowriting sessions, peer-to-peer feedback, review, and countless discussions of what we mean by "feminist DH," the authors in this volume continued to surprise and humble us with their enthusiasm and commitment to the project. As a result, we believe that, as a whole, the volume produces salient moments of recognition and conversation across and among our various positionalities, experiences, disciplines, and modes of DH practice. The time, energy, emails, drafts, abstracts, and conversations of an extended community of scholars helped to shape our understanding of what feminist DH means, could be, and often leaves out. Thank you to Angel Nieves (who unexpectedly and sadly passed during the editing of this volume), Carmen Kynard, Elizabeth Myers, Elvis Bakaitis, Emily Drabinski, Gabriella Foreman, Hannah Smyth, Jennifer Guiliano, Jennifer Rajchel, Jessica Despain, Julianne Nyhan, Karina van Dalen-Oskam, Kim Gallon, Lauren Klein, Elizabeth Losh, Meredith Broussard, Moya Bailey, Quinn Dombrowski, Roopika Risam, Sara Kerr, Shawn(ta) Smith-Cruz, and Tara McPherson whose conversations informed our collective vision for the volume as it stands, and it is better for it.

We want to express particular appreciation to Filipa Calado, who served as research assistant and whose facilitating of administrative and editorial tasks, copyediting, and citation checking was instrumental. Additionally, we are grateful to the anonymous readers whose particular and holistic comments strengthened the volume.

Thank you to the editorial staff at University of Illinois Press for their assistance at each stage of the project. Dawn Durante, previously senior acquiring editor at University of Illinois Press, offered generous feedback, insights, and encouragement during the developmental stages of the volume. Alison Syring continued to support and shepherd our work throughout the review and editing process.

Work on *Feminist Digital Humanities* has been supported through two PSC-CUNY research grants. Funding from CUNY Research Foundation and Maastricht University Library's Open Book Fund made open access publication possible.

Lisa would also like to thank Julia for letting her ramble during their Saturday morning walks; Evie and Claire for their patience, love, and support; and Jason for his constant love, support, honest feedback, and for teaching her the value of play.

Introduction

LISA MARIE RHODY AND
SUSAN SCHREIBMAN

Feminist Digital Humanities: Intersections in Practice adopts critical and affirmative stances toward the creation, use, integration, and influence of emerging technologies in digital humanities (DH) practice. Providing examples of each contributor's approach to feminist research, teaching, and project design, definitions of feminisms are brought into conversation with DH scholarship. Authors theorize feminist DH practices as sites of possibility for exploring, exposing, and revaluing marginalized forms of knowledge production by enacting new modes and processes of meaning making. As such, the chapters reflect on what it means to be a feminist and a technologist, and how feminist practice intervenes in DH analyses, methodologies, infrastructures, and pedagogies, providing intersectional, critical perspectives to expose inequities that result from normative assumptions. *Feminist Digital Humanities* is informed by and in conversation with voices in feminist scholarship more broadly, and the volume represents solidarity around the authors' commitment to socially informed and infused research. Attuned to the challenges of feminist DH practice, the chapters provide optimistic scholarship, examples, and provocations for future research and teaching. Taken together, this volume demonstrates how feminist lenses attuned to issues of intersectionality and gender can uncover structural inequities and present opportunities for social and intellectual change.

Recognizing that there are multiple feminisms and multiple digital humanities, we, as editors, have not imposed a uniform definition of either. Instead, we have asked chapter authors to articulate their formation of each term in the context of their positionalities as scholars. Individually, some authors may be conflicted about labeling themselves "feminist" (perhaps preferring womanist or liberationist), while others may not describe themselves as "digital humanists." Inclusion in the volume instead coheres around shared feminist values—ethics of care, situated knowledge, and alternative modes of knowledge production, affect, and labor—and ways of doing feminism in DH—critiquing, building, rebuilding, or interrogating and transforming structures of white male privilege.

Feminist DH projects are forging new interpretive strategies, infrastructures, and pedagogies that help confront structural injustice by making the invisible visible. In *Digital Black Feminism*, Catherine Knight Steele, drawing on lessons learned from hip-hop feminism, suggests that her use of the term "Black feminism" is a "generationally specific and historically contingent iteration of Black feminist thought."[1] Steele's acknowledgment of Black feminism as historically situated and contingent, shaped through and transformed by engagements with technology is instructive for us, as well. While feminism is not new to DH, what we mean by feminist DH has changed, as has our understanding of what it means to *do* feminist DH.

Throughlines across the collection focus on the nature of care and carework; issues of gender, technology, access, and exclusion; technology and minoritized forms of knowledge and knowledge production; and the responsibilities we have as (feminist) scholars to our families, our communities, our professions, our students, and ourselves. Claiming DH work as explicitly feminist thus demonstrates a collective, aspirational commitment to and striving for equity that begins in theory and results in action. Through targeted intervention, chapters in this volume demonstrate how historical, infrastructural, and educational systems can be interrupted, creating opportunities for change. Many of the chapters also widen the lens that contributors use to look beyond the North American experience.

DH proves fertile ground for doing feminist scholarship, and chapters in this volume share concerns that build from previous feminist scholarship, which are enacted through technological interventions. Several chapters draw on Judith Butler's *Bodies That Matter: On the Discursive Limits of "Sex"* (1993); bell hooks's *Teaching to Transgress* (1994), and Karen Barad's *Meeting the Universe Halfway: Quantum Physics and the Entanglement of Matter and Meaning* (2007). Their engagement with contemporary feminist, postcolonialist, environmental, and critical race theory resonates throughout the chapters as well, drawing into conversation Donna Haraway's "Cyborg Manifesto" (1991) and *Staying with the Trouble* (2016), Deb Verhoven's "As Luck Would Have It: Serendipity and Solace in Digital Research Infrastructure" (2016), Sarah Ahmed's *Living a Feminist Life* (2017), Safiya Umoja Noble's *Algorithms of Oppression* (2018), Roopika Risam's *New Digital Worlds* (2018), Laura Mandell's "Gender and Cultural Analytics: Finding or Making Stereotypes" (2019), K. Rawson and Trevor Muñoz's "Against Cleaning" (2019), and Ruha Benjamin's *Race after Technology* (2020).[2] The discursive relationship between the authors in this volume and contemporary scholarship extends outward to form connections among the chapters themselves.

This volume participates in a notable surge of interest in, community around, and reimagining of feminist DH practice. As the chapters in this volume make clear, care for and attention to issues of gender and sexuality in DH feminisms are acute. In 2018, when we began discussing this volume, several key books in feminist DH had not yet been published, among them *Feminist in a Software Lab* (2018), *Bodies of Information* (2018), *Data Feminism* (2020), *Gamer Trouble: Feminist Confrontations in Digital Culture* (2020), and *Digital Black Feminisms* (2021). Together, the chapters in *Feminist Digital Humanities* take a complementary approach to these and other current feminist DH scholarship by extending and expanding ongoing conversations, particularly in terms of transformative interventions in both theory and praxis. These interventions have been helped by the rapid transformations in digital technologies that have improved the ease of use of tools for humanities research and teaching, from questioning infrastructural frameworks to excavating individuals heretofore hidden from the historical record.

Women are, and have been, active, innovative, and perceptive practitioners in the field as principal investigators, directors, researchers, encoders, designers, and keypunch operators on DH projects as early as Father Busa's *Index Thomisticus*.[3] As Amy Earhart argues in *Traces of the Old, Uses of the New: The Emergence of Digital Literary Studies*, projects in the 1980s–2000s typically involved recovery projects—whether they were digital editions, journals, archives, or blogs.[4] Early feminist editing and archival recovery projects marked space for female authors in what was a crowded panoply of digital collections centered on white, male authors (e.g., William Blake, Walt Whitman, Herman Melville, and Dante Gabriel Rossetti).[5] They digitized, encoded, and published collections including the Women Writers Project, the Dickinson Electronic Archive, the Orlando Project, the Victorian Women Writers Project, the Early Caribbean Digital Archive, Documenting the American South, Collective Biographies of Women, and the Black Gotham Archive.[6] Feminist DH recovery projects addressed gaps in the scholarly record. Sites like the "Voice of the Shuttle" and the "Women's Studies Database" served as a clearinghouses and repositories for information about feminist studies, including course syllabi, calls for conference proposals, and resources for students, researchers, and instructors.[7] Similarly, feminist initiatives such as FemTechNet, HASTAC Commons, #transformDH, and the Crunk Feminist Collective, many of which are still active, constructed human and digital infrastructures to support collectivity and community around feminist practice in DH.[8]

The chapters in this volume extend the work of early initiatives by signaling new directions or departures, or by responding to changes in technology. They expand our focus from canon formation and representation of women and gender minorities in digital collections to include research infrastructures and sonic interpretations. This shift is also reflected in how we teach digital humanities in formal and informal settings through assignments like disrupting social media algorithms. Feminist pedagogies benefit from the growth in opportunities to learn digital humanities skills like text encoding or text, image, or sound analysis and makes tangible connections between theoretical aspects of feminism, social justice, and race theory and methodology.[9] Doing so creates intersectional throughlines, extending disciplinary concerns by leveraging the technical to present new knowledge.

As the chapters in this volume demonstrate, DH offers rich terrain for feminists to interrogate and challenge existing hierarchies, exploring and implementing new practices through collaboration and care. Its methodological affordances present opportunities to excavate hidden figures and to increase access to resources and knowledge, and to expose, imagine, and implement more desirable social situations, inspiring criticality and creativity. Clear-eyed about technology's potential to produce harm, the authors in this volume "live a feminist life" by bringing theory into practice through their adaptation, construction, development, and production of DH scholarship.[10] While it would be impossible to account for all the ways that feminist theory might be valuable to DH, what has become clear is that feminist DH practice has much to offer in terms of how we move forward as a field at large to meet the ever-growing challenges confronting the humanities in the twenty-first century, including how to represent and interpret the past, build for the future, and prepare future generations to continue our work.

Intersections between chapters offer a glimpse of where feminist DH practice is headed, a point Jaime Lee Kirtz gestures to in her chapter when she notes that feminist methods can be used to investigate fields as seemingly disparate as data science and textile arts and that by investigating their inherent "intertwined" underpinnings we can provide a thread through which to "rethink data," along with the history of DH itself in a "foundationally feminist way." For many authors in the collection, feminist DH creates conditions to elevate and champion alternative modes of knowledge production, proposing gender-conscious methods, means, modes, and processes that enable minoritized forms of knowledge to be uncovered or produced. Across each section, feminist theory is activated as a form of resistance, participating in a tradition of "reading against the grain" or acting, as Ahmed describes it, as "feminist killjoys." Throughout the volume, questions of authority and value in knowledge production are entwined with considerations of space, physical and metaphorical.

Points of Intervention: Readings, Infrastructures, Pedagogies

Contributors to this project were charged with elucidating how they put feminism(s) into digital practice, and the results are varied and innovative. Chapters describe and explore how to create spaces for the production of minoritarian knowledge, for resisting dominant narratives and finding new forms of representation and distribution. What energizes and animates each chapter is authors' engagement with sites and situations in which DH and feminism(s) might be productively enmeshed. The authors in this volume are largely in agreement with Ahmed's assertion that feminism is practiced: consequently, each chapter carefully articulates how feminist thought is actualized *in* and *through* practice. Much feminist DH involves a conscious interplay between theory and action in the service of social impacts that lead to change: change in the ways in which we teach, in the ways in which we define and build infrastructure, and in the ways in which we do research. The volume's twelve chapters are grouped into three sites of intervention where authors explore opportunities for intersectional creativity and critique: Readings, Infrastructures, and Pedagogies. However, while the chapters share values of various feminisms, their interventions into DH practice are located at three sites of resistance to dominant practice.

In Readings, authors operationalize or activate feminist thought through digital praxis or in analytical approaches, methodologies, and interpretive strategies either enabled by or encoded within digital technologies. Chapters in the second site of intervention, Infrastructures, suggest new structures for knowledge creation, publication, access, and sharing that disrupt binaries and challenge the matrix of domination.[11] In Pedagogies, feminist practice engages students in research, preparing future generations to continue to improve upon our work, which is ongoing, hopeful, and constantly transforming.

Readings

The chapters in Readings deploy digital methodologies to revise or refashion dominant narratives of the past as acts of recovery. Feminist practices are manifest through interpretation of corpora, both textual and sonic. Tanya

E. Clement introduces strategies for listening and relistening as a feminist audiation practice in which positionality is foregrounded as an interpretative strategy. Monika Barget and Susan Schreibman demonstrate a need to read data with an awareness of and accounting for absence that utilizes digital methods as archival practice. Jaime Lee Kirtz unpacks the ways methods of production traditionally ascribed to women, such as weaving, can be refashioned into a reading and interpretive strategy. Recovery as feminist practice is necessary to (re)place women's lives, work, and contributions in the historical record. For example, Schreibman and Barget's middle-distance readings of networks of letters reveals women's political influences in World War I Ireland, while Clement's iterative playback and sonic interpretations reformulate female authorship in 1960s America by focusing on Anne Sexton's psychotherapy sessions as a process of often misunderstood self-formation and poetic voice.

Feminist practice leads toward change, and in Readings change manifests in authors' conscious refashioning and redeploying tools and systems of knowledge in, as Kirtz writes, "feminist modes" of understanding. It comes in the form of a renewed or new possibilities of material interchange between feminist practices and canonical archives, as demonstrated in many chapters in the volume, including the ways in which we conduct feminist research in archives that, on the surface, seem to have little to offer, as suggested by Barget and Schreibman. Kirtz troubles the perception of data as immaterial through readings of textile-based data storage in the Tempestry Project and the Knitting Map, wherein data storage and display "not only [are] the textile materialized, but so too are the connections, assumptions, and historical narratives of gender-textile relations." For Barget and Schreibman, recovery involves breaking down the barriers between public and traditional research, while Kirtz resurfaces Indigenous reading and data storage practices to revise feminist media histories. Clement's affective and embodied interpretations, which she names audiation, reinterpret Anne Sexton's negotiation of power and self-representation through the forensic and remediated technologies of capture and playback of audio recordings. For Clement and Kirtz, metaphorical space materializes in physical storage media and through the embodied practice of recording, listening/reading, replaying, and storing. Clement's audiation reclaims for Sexton the embodied act of self-presentation, including the choice not to speak through pauses, and argues for feminist DH to create space for embodied and affective forms of interpretation and meaning making. Similarly, Kirtz points to a feminist tradition in which women use textiles and weaving to create spaces "to identify and critically interrogate the assumptions upon which dominant narratives about expertise, value, work, and ultimately, who gets to have a voice, are founded in DH and beyond," not as an escape from the world, but part of and as an intervention in it. Barget and Schreibman create visible space for women's voices that would otherwise be overlooked in large archival collections using geographic and data visualizations combined with readings that combine macro and micro to find a middle distance. Creating space for Barget and Schreibman means breaking down the barriers between public and traditional academic research methods to elevate the everyday experiences of Irish women during the period of social and political unrest between 1915 and 1923. Where the overrepresentation of male discourse through archival collections of letters often reinscribes lived experience through the lens of "male spheres of influence," Barget and Schreibman alternate between large- and small-scale readings to unearth the everyday conversations and participation of women within political and social discourse.

Infrastructures

Infrastructures addresses how feminist theory and practice alter, reshape, and improve systemic challenges confronting DH, ranging from the conditions of labor (including carework and affective labor) to architectures of knowledge. Here infrastructure is interpreted widely, including human, information, and physical, ranging from experimental DH centers (Wernimont and Stevens), to research architectures (Mandell and Brown; Thylstrup et al.; Bergenmar, Lindhé, and Rosen), to professional networks (Stringfield). Approaching infrastructure-building from a feminist perspective exposes opportunities to refashion architectures of knowledge creation and distribution to be more equitable and inclusive. For example, the availability or absence of infrastructure informs the kinds of research that is possible or the methods we can teach. Increasingly, as more data sources become part of a public infrastructure, DH methods can provide new ways of excavating feminist readings from datasets that at first do not seem amenable to feminist scholarship. Infrastructure for feminist DH has been a site of hopeful struggle. The elusive promise of DH, and humanities computing before that, has been to elevate, expose, and reward the labor history of knowledge production making inclusive, collective, and collaborative scholarly activities more recognizable and valued within traditional forms of acknowledgment and production in the academy. This promise, as the chapters in the Infrastructure section make clear, has been unevenly realized. Whether this is in the feminization of infrastructural maintenance and repair (Brown and Mandell) or the reproductive and affective carework of sociotechnical networks (Stringfield), feminist DH seems, at the most fundamental level, to necessarily concern itself with the hidden infrastructures of knowledge production and repeated recovery of invisibilized labor.

Change comes to fruition through naming and identifying what is possible, even within, as Barad writes (as quoted by Brown and Mandell) technical, social, and political constraints to reveal a "dynamic of possibility." Jacqueline Wernimont and Nikki L. Stevens write of "hopefulness" and "trust" as agents of change in building a DH cooperative. Jenny Bergenmar, Cecilia Lindhé, and Astrid von Rosen describe it as conscious collecting, and Nanna Bonde Thylstrup et al. to intervening in and reimagining infrastructures. Perhaps, above all, we are reminded here, in the words of Ann Balsamo, as quoted by Susan Brown and Laura Mandell, that what we are striving for in a feminist DH practice is not a singular thing "with set boundaries or well-defined edges" but to create "an unfolding set of possibilities" refashioning the social, material, and technological constraints in which we work. Thylstrup et al. find that situating "reparative practice" as an ongoing rather than a finite practice elucidates "the processual, transformative, and quotidian micro-labor of repairing the past into something new," something possible.

Mandell and Brown, drawing on D'Ignazio and Klein's first principle of data feminism—*rethink binaries*—posit feminist DH infrastructures as resisting "in some way, shape, or form, the bifurcation of humanity into m/f."[12] Doing so leads them to imagine feminist DH infrastructures as an ecological arrangement, as opposed to the "stack" previously imagined by Alan Liu in "Toward a Diversity Stack: DH and Diversity as a Technical Problem." Similarly, Bergenmar, Lindhé, and Rosen also reference D'Ignazio and Klein's principles of data feminism—*embrace pluralism* and *consider context*—to avoid what they describe as "epistemic violence," a term borrowed from Gayatri Spivak. To this end, they note that humanities infrastructures designed to archive collections of performing arts were necessarily community-engaged. Their public orientation allows them to "be informed by epistemological and critical interrogations," questioning hierarchies of knowledge and holding space for meaning among the communities the archives are designed to represent. Thylstrup et al. reveal infrastructural resistances through editing shared knowledge projects such as Wikipedia to better represent the presence of queer, trans, and nonbinary people. While infrastructures may be visible or invisible, the authors in this collection agree that infrastructures are ideologically laden, and that feminist DH practice involves making invisible assumptions and incongruities visible: in other words, giving them visible space where questions of authority and value can be exposed and reassessed.

Ravynn K. Stringfield reflects upon her experiences as a doctoral student to call for more robust sociotechnical infrastructures to support academic training and identity-formation for Black women scholars in DH. For doctoral students, and in particular for Black women in graduate programs, the sociotechnical infrastructure of DH professional and research development depends on invisible labor and networks of care enacted in and through technological platforms, and physical and intellectual spaces. The act of self-formation as a digital humanist necessitates participation in online platforms that are both proven to be particularly hostile to BIPOC and at the same time a locus of connection to networks of care, collectivity, and connection. Stringfield considers the challenges that confront Black women in DH to create these sociotechnical support structure. She points to physical and intellectual sites of space-making, such as the Intentionally Digital, Intentionally Black conference (2018), the Equality Lab at William & Mary, and the Race and Social Justice workshop at the DH Summer Institute, that foster an ethic of care that has enabled her academic self-formation, and calls for wider recognition and implementation of space-making practices to better support other Black women doctoral students in their own professional growth.

Brown and Mandell note that for feminists, infrastructure presents a double-edged challenge, where equity depends both on making infrastructure visible, which is inherently disruptive, and equitable access to infrastructure, which depends on reliability and ease of use. Drawing on Deb Verhoeven's definition of "infrapuncture"—an embracing of transformation that is temporal, spatial, and political—Wernimont and Stevens's Nexus cooperative experiments with feminist infrastructures for labor and knowledge production. They consider how the space of the lab reimagined as a labor cooperative might disrupt the reproduction of academic hierarchies that structure who can know, what we know, and how we know. Bergenmar, Lindhé, and Rosen argue that feminist infrastructure takes into consideration what has been discarded as "waste" in order to give space and voice to what has been discarded as invaluable. Beginning and ending with a reflection on conference presentations at Nordic DH conferences, they suggest that we might find an alternative history to feminist and gender studies within disciplinary conferences were there a record of what proposals were discounted from inclusion.

What is absent, repressed, or invisibilized from both our physical and digital infrastructures is as powerful a determinant in the research landscape as what is present, foregrounded, and normative. As the chapters in this section demonstrate, taking a feminist approach to the creation of infrastructure involves interrogation and refashioning of the research architectures we take for granted so as to be more equitable, inclusive, and socially just.

Pedagogies

Finally, in Pedagogies, chapters demonstrate the ways in which feminist theories, pedagogies, and approaches can be activated within DH curricula ranging from course design to professional development. Mark Sample considers what possibilities are available to "walking away" from social media black boxes through a pedagogy of adversarial design; Andie Silva turns toward feminist pedagogy to cultivate "informal spaces that center affect and community as the starting point for equitable DH practice" and to decolonize DH syllabi. Likewise, Dhanashree Thorat reflects on the importance of professional training and teaching that is informed by local knowledge, language, and practices; and Lisa Marie Rhody's pedagogical design attends to the social and situated contexts that often deter women and other marginalized communities in technology from entering the field.

In this section, Sample asks students to consider Ursula Le Guin's short story "The Ones Who Walk Away from Omelas" as a model for reading against the normative forces of social media constructions of happiness through a process he calls "adversarial design." In their assignments, students develop content that is in opposition to users' interests and values, as identified algorithmically by Google, Facebook, and Instagram. Likewise, Rhody's students read against the grain of algorithmic assumptions in text analysis methods by challenging what Mandell describes as the m/f binary, which conflates gender and biologically assigned sex. Activities challenge what it means to "clean" data that removes context and affect or merely stereotypes gender for the sake of statistical and pedagogical ease. Students in Rhody's course consider whether feminist text analysis is inherently reactionary, relegated to calling out harmful methods glossed over by algorithmic ease or if there is opportunity for speculation and change.

Sample, Rhody, Thorat, and Andie Silva consider DH courses as sites of liberatory feminist praxis and approach the DH classroom as a site of transformation through cooperation, collective knowledge production, and attention to the impact of digital methods. Each author resists the reproduction of technological harms to call into question and to transform use of digital media to enact change. Sample's Gender and Technology course forms an intellectual space for students to witness the harms codified through the black boxes of social media—a space that does not exist outside the classroom given the privacy and secrecy of proprietary systems. However, through the creation of adversarial social media campaigns, students began to expose the "cellar" of social media through practices such as filling out forms that prioritize the needs of advertisers over individuals.

Meanwhile, Rhody argues that "computational text analysis courses present opportunities for feminist scholars to create space for cultural critique in the classroom, to cultivate engagement and knowledge creation among students who may not see themselves as welcome contributors to the fields of information and computer science, and to mobilize feminist theory toward social justice." Enjoining students to explore the open-endedness of whether or not there can be such a thing as "feminist text analysis," the course makes space for students to establish a sense of authority in which their lived and academic experiences can be brought to bear on computational methods in order to enact a more justice-oriented approach to computational methods that underpin much of our textually mediated online culture. Thorat considers the decolonialist opportunities that community-engaged DH institutes present through her work directing the DH Winter School in Pune, India. She emphasizes the "importance of theorizing, teaching, and making based on space and place, local histories and sociopolitical conditions" in order to address coloniality, caste, gender, and sexuality through place-based and community-oriented learning. Silva explores how an intersectional feminist framework can be used to develop a classroom environment through care and social action that enables digital literacy and advocacy, citizenship, and activism in concert with one another. She suggests that the radical pivot to virtual and online learning that took place during the COVID-19 epidemic not only exposed and exacerbated existing racial, gender, and economic divides, but also allowed us to think about what a liberatory digital pedagogy might look like. Silva uses the occasion of her Feminist DH pedagogy course to consider the spaces of the DH classroom—online, physical, and ideological—and to reconsider what community-engaged learning practices require, particularly at moments of trauma and crisis.

Taken together, the chapters in this volume form a nexus for research and reflection into the intersections of feminist and DH scholarship, the opening of a dialogue awaiting further iteration.

Notes

1. Lindsey, "Let Me Blow Your Mind," Hip Hop Feminist Futures in Theory and Praxis," qtd. in Steele, *Digital Black Feminism*, 10.

2. A demonstration of the intersectionality of our work, much of the scholarship in this list participates across multiple disciplinary fields.

3. Nyhan, "Gender, Knowledge, and Hierarchy."

4. Earhart, *Traces of the Old, Uses of the New.*

5. "The William Blake Archive"; "The Walt Whitman Archive"; "Herman Melville Electronic Library"; "The Dante Gabriel Rosetti Archive."

6. *Women Writers Project*; Smith, "Dickinson Electronic Archive," https://www.emilydickinson.org/; Brown, Clements, and Grundy, eds., *Orlando*; "Victorian Women Writers Project—Home"; "Early Caribbean Digital Archive"; "Documenting the American South Homepage"; "Collective Biographies of Women"; Peterson, "Black Gotham Archive."

7. Liu, "Voice of the Shuttle (VoS)"; UMD Women's Studies Program, "Women's Studies Database."

8. "FemTechNet"; HASTAC Commons, "Welcome to HASTAC Commons"; Bailey et al., "Reflections on a Movement"; Boylorn et al., "Crunk Feminist Collective."

9. In addition to the chapters in this volume, see, for example, the work of the Pedagogy of the Digitally Oppressed Collective, "Pedagogy of the Digitally Oppressed: Futurities."

10. Ahmed, *Living a Feminist Life*.

11. Collins, *Black Feminist Thought*, 227.

12. D'Ignazio and Klein, *Data Feminism*.

Works Cited

Ahmed, Sara. *Living a Feminist Life*. Durham, NC: Duke University Press, 2016.

Bailey, Moya, Anne Cong-Huyen, Alexis Lothian, and Amanda Phillips. "Reflections on a Movement: #transformDH, Growing Up." In *Debates in the Digital Humanities 2016*, edited by Matthew K. Gold and Lauren F. Klein. Minneapolis: University of Minnesota Press, 2016. https://dhdebates.gc.cuny.edu/read/untitled/section/9cf90340–7aae-4eae-bdda-45b8b4540b6b.

Boylorn, Robin, Brittney Cooper, Susana Morris, Eesha Pandit, Sheri Davis-Faulkner, Chanel Crunkista, and Rachel Raimist. "Crunk Feminist Collective: Where Crunk Meets Conscious and Feminism Meets Cool." March 22, 2021. https://www.crunkfeministcollective.com/.

Brown, Susan, Patricia Clements, and Isobel Grundy, eds. *Orlando: Women's Writing in the British Isles from the Beginnings to the Present*. Cambridge University Press, 2022. Accessed August 3, 2023. https://www.orlando.cambridge.org.

Collins, Patricia Hill. *Black Feminist Thought: Knowledge, Consciousness, and the Politics of Empowerment.* New York: Routledge, 2002.

Criado-Perez, Caroline. *Invisible Women: Data Bias in a World Designed for Men*. New York: Abrams Press, 2019.

"The Dante Gabriel Rosetti Archive." Accessed September 24, 2023. http://www.rossettiarchive.org/.

D'Ignazio, Catherine, and Lauren F. Klein. *Data Feminism*. Strong Ideas Series. Cambridge, MA: MIT Press, 2020.

"Documenting the American South Homepage." Accessed September 24, 2023. https://docsouth.unc.edu/.

Earhart, Amy E. *Traces of the Old, Uses of the New: The Emergence of Digital Literary Studies*. Editorial Theory and Literary Criticism. Ann Arbor: University of Michigan Press, 2015.

"Early Caribbean Digital Archive." Accessed September 24, 2023. https://ecda .northeastern.edu/.

Eichmann-Kalwara, Nickoal, Jeana Jorgensen, and Scott B. Weingart. "Representation at Digital Humanities Conferences (2000–2015)." In *Bodies of Information: Intersectional Feminism and Digital Humanities*, edited by Jacqueline Wernimont and Elizabeth Losh. Debates in the Digital Humanities. Minneapolis: University of Minnesota Press, 2018. https://dhdebates .gc.cuny.edu/read/untitled-4e08b137-aec5–49a4–83c0–38258425f145/ section/5dcc1fee-caef-4c10-aa3c-08a9bbf0b68b.

"FemTechNet." Accessed September 24, 2023. https://www.femtechnet.org/.

HASTAC Commons. "Welcome to HASTAC Commons." February 8, 2022. https://hastac.hcommons.org/.

"Herman Melville Electronic Library." Accessed September 25, 2023. https:// melville.electroniclibrary.org/.

hooks, bell. *Teaching to Transgress: Education as the Practice of Freedom*. New York: Routledge, 1994.

Klein, Lauren F., and Jason Rhody. "A Time Capsule for Future Social Researchers: Lauren Klein—Covid-19 and the Social Sciences." *Social Science Research Council (SSRC)* (blog). Accessed September 25, 2023. https://covid19research .ssrc.org/time-capsule/lauren-klein/.

Lindemann, Hilde. *An Invitation to Feminist Ethics*. 2nd ed. New York: Oxford University Press, 2019.

Lindsey, Treva B. "Let Me Blow Your Mind: Hip Hop Feminist Futures in Theory and Praxis." *Urban Education* 50, no. 1 (January 2015): 52–77. https://doi.org/ 10.1177/0042085914563184.

Liu, Alan. "Voice of the Shuttle (VoS)." September 9, 1994. https://liu.english .ucsb.edu/voice-of-the-shuttle-vos/.

McPherson, Tara. *Feminist in a Software Lab: Difference + Design*. Metalabprojects. Cambridge, MA: Harvard University Press, 2018.

metoo. "Get To Know Us | History & Inception." Accessed September 24, 2023. https://metoomvmt.org/get-to-know-us/history-inception/.

Nyhan, Julianne. "Gender, Knowledge, and Hierarchy: On Busa's Female Punch Card Operators." *Arche Logos* (blog), April 29, 2014. https://archelogos .hypotheses.org/135.

Pedagogy of the Digitally Oppressed Collective. "Pedagogy of the Digitally Oppressed: Futurities, Imaginings, Responsibilities, and Ethics for Anti-Colonial DH Praxis." *Digital Studies/Le Champ Numérique* 10, no. 1 (2021): 20–37.

Peterson, Carla. "Black Gotham Archive." 2011. https://archive.blackgotham archive.org/index.html.

Phillips, Amanda Denise. *Gamer Trouble: Feminist Confrontations in Digital Culture*. New York: New York University Press, 2020.

Smith, Martha Nell, ed. "Dickinson Electronic Archive." University of Maryland, 1996–2023. Accessed August 3, 2023. https://www.emilydickinson.org/.

Steele, Catherine Knight. *Digital Black Feminism*. Critical Cultural Communication. New York: New York University Press, 2021.

UMD Women's Studies Program. "Women's Studies Database." 1992. https://archive.mith.umd.edu/womensstudies/.

"Victorian Women Writers Project—Home." Accessed September 24, 2023. https://webapp1.dlib.indiana.edu/vwwp/welcome.do.

"The Walt Whitman Archive." Accessed September 24, 2023. https://whitman archive.org/.

Wernimont, Jacqueline. "Whence Feminism? Assessing Feminist Interventions in Digital Literary Archives." *Digital Humanities Quarterly* 7, no. 1 (July 1, 2013). https://digitalhumanities.org/dhq/vol/7/1/000156/000156.html.

Wernimont, Jacqueline, and Elizabeth Losh, eds. *Bodies of Information: Intersectional Feminism and Digital Humanities*. Minneapolis: University of Minnesota Press, 2018. https://dhdebates.gc.cuny.edu/projects/bodies-of-information.

"The William Blake Archive." Accessed September 24, 2023. https://www.blakearchive.org.

Women Writers Project. Northeastern University, 1999–2016. Accessed February 29, 2016. https://www.wwp.northeastern.edu.

I

Readings

1

Playback Is a Bitch

A Feminist Rationale for Audiation as a Framework for Theorizing Digital Tools

TANYA E. CLEMENT

I am not a tape. I'm a human being.
—Anne Sexton, "Journal, 1961"

Presumably, our goals when we use digital analysis tools in literary analysis include learning something about the object or subject at hand that we did not previously know. Recognizing what we don't know, however, also means recognizing what we already think we know. Audiation is a concept that provides some insight. In music learning theory, to audiate is to imagine playing a song. Practicing audiation, a musician learns to play a piece by creating a mental model of how she will play a score based on her particular experience of the music. Instead of having a concept or an image in the "mind's eye," audiation is having a concept or a sound in the "mind's ear." This chapter forwards a feminist rationale for using audiation as a theoretical model for literary analysis with digital tools. I use the example of audio presentation and analysis tools, but the concepts I introduce can also apply to using tools for textual, image, or video analysis. In my example—an analysis of audio recordings of the poet Anne Sexton—a digital tool provides a playback experience that is a remediation or a deformation of my audiation or mental model of the object (the recording) and the subject (Anne Sexton's poetry) of interest.[1] Thinking of that mental model as an audiation reorients discussions of playback tools to reflect on *how* scholars perceive literary objects of study rather than *what* scholars perceive, a refocus on how we audiate rather than what we hear.

To clarify how a theory of audiation might play out, I provide a research anecdote for using digital humanities (DH) tools to compare Anne Sexton's therapy text with recordings of her reciting poetry. I have divided the chapter into three parts where I define the therapy text and describe how feminist inquiry helps articulate a rationale for audiation. Karen Barad writes, "Mattering is simultaneously a matter of substance and significance."[2] Likewise, how objects of study are determined is contingent on the modes of determination scholars choose to articulate as meaningful—on what we choose to interrogate as meaning making, as making meaning, as mattering. I demonstrate that (part one) a scholar's positionality matters when initiating analyses with digital tools; that (part two) a focus on multimedia matters when trying to articulate how we understand objects of study for literary study; and that (part three) infrastructure matters because developing tools and systems for representing, accessing, and analyzing objects of interests are issues that concern power negotiations (who and what perspective matters) in knowledge production and digital scholarship.

Positionality Matters: Agential Realism and Anne Sexton's Therapy Text

To forward audiation as a driving concept is to put emphasis on the significant role that positionality plays in why scholars select particular objects and subjects of study as well as how they select tools for analyzing these topics. What scholars value plays a significant role in what and how scholars hear.[3] Barad's notion of "agential realism" serves as an epistemological-ontological-ethical framework for a theory of audiation that is rooted in feminist inquiry and articulates how responsibility and justice can play a key role in scholarship:[4] "An agential realist perspective helps us approach the question, 'How then shall we understand our role in helping constitute who and what come to matter?'"[5] Calling playback "a bitch" purposefully signals how "bitch" has been reclaimed as a term of empowerment within feminist movements and points to the difficulties inherent to articulating the power negotiations behind playback tools that materialize space, time, and bodies and rely on the intersection of gender, race, sexuality, religion, and nationality to engage meaning making. Because listening to Anne Sexton's therapy text through playback tools means I will engage with this text's power-negotiating bitchiness, it also means that I should articulate why I am listening. What do I expect to hear? What am I listening for? What matters to me?

Tapes, journals, and their digital surrogates comprise what I am calling the Sexton therapy text, an intermedia text of analog and digital text, images, and sound. Sexton began her writing career with two books of poetry: *All My Pretty Ones* (1962) and *Live or Die* (1966), for which she won the Pulitzer Prize in 1967. Between completing her first book and starting work on her second, she began seeing her psychiatrist Dr. Martin Orne twice weekly. For therapeutic reasons, Orne recorded the sessions on reel-to-reel tapes to which Sexton would listen in between sessions, writing her responses in a journal after or while listening. Many critics have discussed how the experiences Sexton relayed in therapy influenced what she wrote and how she was received,[6] but none consider how the act of recording, listening, and replaying became a process of self-formation that informs her poetic syntax and imagery.[7]

Using digital tools to determine how the development of Sexton's therapy text influenced her writing is a cacophonous experience that involves listening to and reading text, audio, and images distributed across two physical archives located 2,000 miles apart with different protocols for access.[8] As a researcher it is impossible to have a coherent, embodied playback experience with the therapy text (which for privacy reasons is not online), but that disconnectedness, rooted in the number and type of playback apparatuses involved, accentuates the disjointedness that may have also been Sexton's experience. Listening to herself discussing listening to herself and writing about those discussions in her journal, her own process of audiation was doubly mediated. It is the physical and conceptual dislocation between Sexton's sense of self and Sexton's therapy text alongside the difficulty of accurately representing or productively repositioning that sense of self through poetry that begins my own process of audiation with Sexton's therapy text.

Sexton's evolving understanding of her subjectivity becomes entangled with how she came to understand herself through the recording process. At first, Sexton disapproves of the tapes. She does not like listening to herself as she begins to reexperience the anxieties that inspired the recording process in the first place.[9] Listening to the tapes revealed what Orne called her "hysteria," but she was drawn to listen because they also fed her almost-constant need for approbation. "The thing that upsets me is the affect that the tape has on me," she says on one tape. She explains to Dr. Orne what she hears during her listening sessions: "You love me. I hear it in your voice—your voice is gentle and loving and accepting. I can hear it. You love me. That's what love is. It's a perfect symbol for me."[10] Describing similarly complex feelings about her poetry performances, Sexton notes in an autobiographical piece titled "The Freak Show" in the *American Poetry Review* (1973) that "Some people hope you will do something audacious . . . that you vomit on the stage or go blind, hysterically blind or actually blind."[11] Like her performances, the tapings revealed to Sexton a gendered pathology that entailed a dual positionality in which she was both noteworthy and a "freak."

Even before I listen, I consider playback, in this case, a "bitch." Playback in the digital environment depends on a technical infrastructure, but interpreting what is played back is influenced by audiated models that evolve with the process of each playback. What is important in the instance of Sexton's therapy text is how listening to Sexton listen to herself requires a kind of redoubled reading of her practice and my own. Articulating how a model of the therapy text in my mind's ear is shaped by Sexton's understanding of her own subjectivity compels me to listen to myself listening to Sexton listening—a many-layered mediation that becomes important when considering adding digital tools for presentation and analysis.

Audio Matters: The Taping Apparatus as Material-Discursive Practice

In the context of Sexton's therapy text, I use the term "taping apparatus" to mark the recording experience as a sociotechnical phenomenon that reflects knowledge production and power in particular ways. Calling apparatuses "causal intra-actions through which matter is iteratively and differentially articulated," Barad argues that an apparatus or tool "reconfigure[es] the material-discursive field of possibilities and impossibilities in the ongoing dynamics of intra-activity that is agency."[12] These causal intra-actions might include the original recording and playback devices as well as their more current digital counterparts, but also Dr. Orne's and Sexton's positionalities, the digital environment where the intermedia therapy text is represented and analyzed, and the scholars, like myself, who use these tools. All are implicated in the creation, storage, and playback cycle that continue to produce Sexton's therapy text. Yet, different agential cuts "enact different materialized becomings": my audiation means that I am attuned to how the therapy text invites me to listen to myself listening to Sexton listening to herself.[13] As a result, I am interested in how the taping apparatus as a material-discursive phenomenon involving the varied power negotiations and material restrictions might encourage Sexton to develop a poetics that would resist simple analysis.

Consequently, the taping process becomes a boundary-object. For Sexton, it marks the difference between predictable, generalizable, and routinized language and language that transcends the "real" to become poetic. In 1964, after many years of listening to herself, Sexton writes in a letter to her friend Anne Clarke that "language" is "a new term for what I think I talk." While "it is hard to define," Sexton pinpoints its origins to her first stay in the psychiatric ward, making a direct connection between the mode of language in her therapy sessions and the "language talk" of her poetry: "When I was first sick I was thrilled (a language word translate, relieved) to get into the Nut House . . . I found this girl (very crazy of course) (like me I guess) who talked language . . . And then later . . . I found out Martin [Orne] talked language." Struggling to give Clarke a clearer definition, Sexton explains that "language is verbalizing the non-verbal" which is "better than saying 'I love you.'"[14] These moments of "language," which include nonverbal or paralinguistic sounds and actions—crying, coughing, laughing, holding hands, leaving abruptly—are evident in large measure on the tapes. The tapes also provide Sexton with ample opportunities for understanding poetic language as an attempt to express the slippage between audiation and expression. In a letter to Brother Dennis Farrell on August 2, 1963, she articulates this particularly frustrating disconnect: "Words bother me. I think that is why I am a poet. I keep trying to force myself to speak of the things that remain mute inside."[15]

Similarly, the apparatus is a boundary object for me that marks the slippery and disconnected divide between audiation and interpretation. I am drawn to Sexton's therapy text because it enacts resistances I likewise sense in her poetry: a material resistance to sociotechnical systems designed for presenting and analyzing verbal texts, Sexton's political resistance to gendered power relations, and language's resistance to categories such as the quotidian or the transcendent. I attune that the process of expressing oneself and reflecting on that expression is integral to better understanding how Sexton's therapy text relates to her poetry, but audiation is also what will make Sexton's therapy text (or any object of study) difficult to analyze with digital tools. If a scholar's role in living justly is to question who and what comes to matter, one opportunity for playing that role in DH is to articulate how and why reconciling an audiation of Sexton's therapy text with the digital analysis of its sound events is a bitch of a project.

Infrastructure Matters: Audio Analysis and Diffractive Measures

A consideration for playback intra-actions strikes at a core concern for proceeding responsibly with transdisciplinary methods, tools, and modes of work in DH that straddle objective and subjective methods of knowledge production.[16] Much like my exploration of the taping apparatus above, I can also use Barad's agential realist elaboration of the apparatus to account for the performative material and discursive practices of mattering that happen in the context of digital analysis.[17] With an agential realist perspective, I imagine using DH tools as a means of uncovering my or Sexton's mental models (what I am calling the practice of audiation) to better understand how material and discursive performativity happens and where (and how) agency occurs in the process of expression and analysis. Rather than understanding digital analysis as a means of producing "facts" or "data" about a cultural object, then, we understand the process of using DH tools productively as learning to recognize our own mental models, our own processes of audiation, as well as those baked into our tools, all of which co-create the possibility and the impossibility of meaning-making. If listening to Sexton's therapy text is cacophonous, digital tools can assist in audiation research practices by helping to articulate how its particular cacophonies, its material-discursiveness, resist analysis.

An agential realist approach to DH tools can include audiation as a concept that recognizes both the computable (the generalizable) and the meaningful (the positioned perspective). My mental model for what one (computer or human) could engage and therefore what perceivable results might come from using digital tools are based on (a) my experience listening to Sexton's therapy recordings: I had noticed that when Sexton did not want to respond to a question that Orne posed or when Sexton was having difficulty articulating a response, pauses were plentiful and, therefore, indicative of significant moments in their conversation; and (b) I knew that pauses were a feature that could be accurately measured by digital tools with which I was familiar, Audacity and Drift. Consequent to these experiences, I created a hypothesis that mattered in terms of both material and significance and could be measured. I hypothesized that participating in and listening to her own therapy sessions may have introduced the signifying potential of pauses into Sexton's poetry performances and therefore, if measured in comparison, there might be an increase or at least a difference in the patterns of her pauses before, during, and after the period of time, between 1961 and 1964, when Sexton was recording, listening to, and reflecting on listening to her therapy sessions.

Drift and Audacity

It is important to note that my hypothesis was based on my experience and scholarship in DH, which shows that in order to engage in meaningful analysis with computational tools, I must first determine features that are both significant (meaningful in context) and measurable (computable).[18] My scholarly interests in what is meaningful in Sexton's writings are outlined above, but knowing what was computable or measurable was predicated by several other factors. First, I had a knowledge of the field of sound analysis earned through my experience as primary investigator of the HiPSTAS (High Performance Sound Technologies for Access and Scholarship).[19] Second, I had ready access to certain tools—developed primarily in academia, in computer science, and funded by government agencies—and the means and knowledge to use them. Namely, I was part of a project called "Texts in Performance"[20] that was developing two tools: Gentle and Drift.[21] I chose to measure pauses because I knew Drift could measure silence in the context of analyzing archival poetry performances in humanities research.[22] I also used the more popular tool Audacity, because I could automatically mark silences and compare (and evaluate) the output with what Drift produced.[23]

In order to measure pauses, I chose a subset of recordings and used Drift and Audacity to analyze whether or not pauses might change in behavior over the course of Sexton's therapy and her career of performances. The measurable pause behaviors included the average pause length (per second, for pauses of at least 100, 250, and 500 milliseconds), the average pause rate (per second, for pauses of at least 100, 250, and 500 milliseconds), and the rhythmic complexity of pauses.[24] The first experiments I ran with Drift were to compare the behavior of pauses across Sexton's oeuvre over time and against the performances of other authors. Because the availability of recordings is often based on luck or happenstance, access to a perfect sample of recordings from similar or dissimilar poets was impossible. Instead, based on what was available to me, I compared recordings by white, female poets who also wrote and performed confessional poetry or simply performed in similar venues around the same time period as Sexton. The recordings I used included eight Sexton performances of different poems from 1959 compared against seven poems she performed in 1972, available from the Voice of the Poet compilation of her recordings. I also compared the pause behaviors across longer archival recordings including Sexton's 1964 poetry performance of multiple poems, two 1974 multipoem performances, and two of the therapy tape recordings. Finally, I compared the Voice of the Poet recording compilations of other female authors who performed more or less across similar spans of time as Sexton. Performances recorded of Sexton (born in 1928) were from 1959 to 1972 compared with Adrienne Rich (born 1929) performances from 1951 to 2000, Sylvia Plath (born 1932) performances until 1963, and Elizabeth Bishop (born 1911) performances until 1979. I visualized the results using Tableau.

At first, the results seemed meaningful. While figure 1.1 and figure 1.2 show that the average number of pauses (AP), the average pause length (APL), and the average pause rate (APR) were not remarkably different between 1964 and 1974 or across the poets, figure 1.3 seems to show that

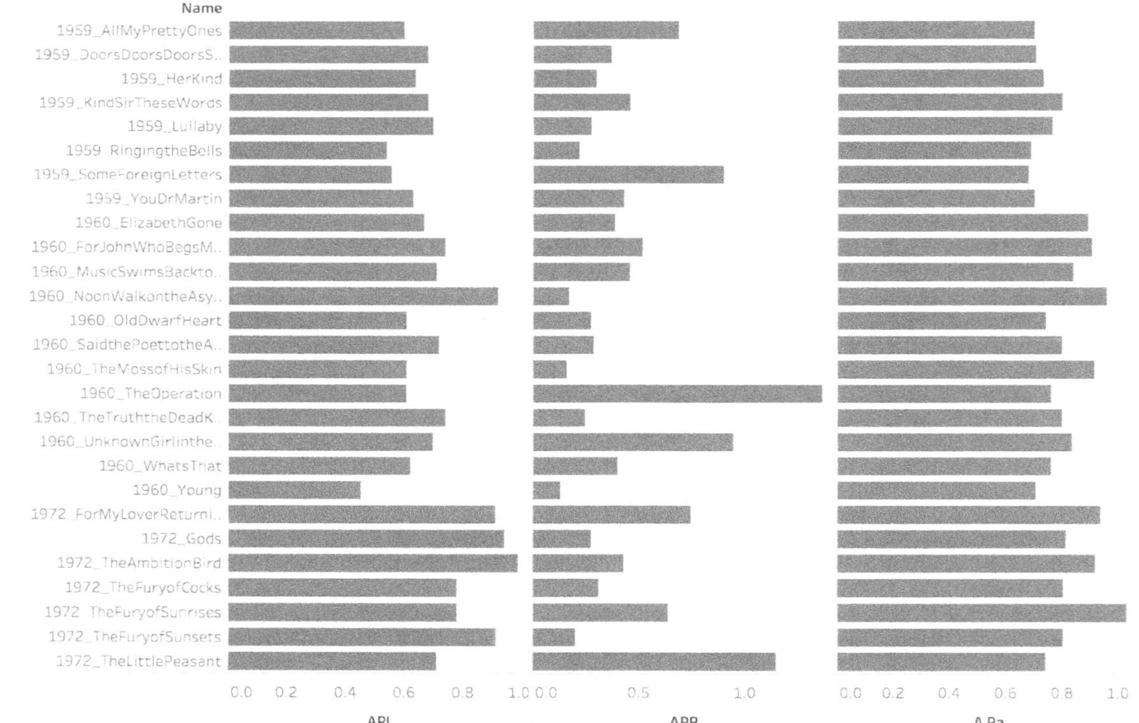

Figure 1.1. A histogram created in Tableau showing results from using Drift to analyze the average pause length (APL), the average pause rate (APR), and average number of pauses (AP) in twenty-seven recordings of Anne Sexton performing poems in 1959, 1960, and 1972 published in a Voice of the Poet (2000) compilation of recordings.

Figure 1.2. A scatter plot created in Tableau showing results from using Drift to compare the average number of pauses (AP), average pause length (AFL), the average pause rate (APR), pitch entropy (PE), pitch range (PR), rhythmic complexity of pauses (RCP), and words per minute (WPM) across Voice of the Poet compilations for Adrienne Rich (2002), Elizabeth Bishop (2000), Anne Sexton (2000), and Sylvia Plath (1999).

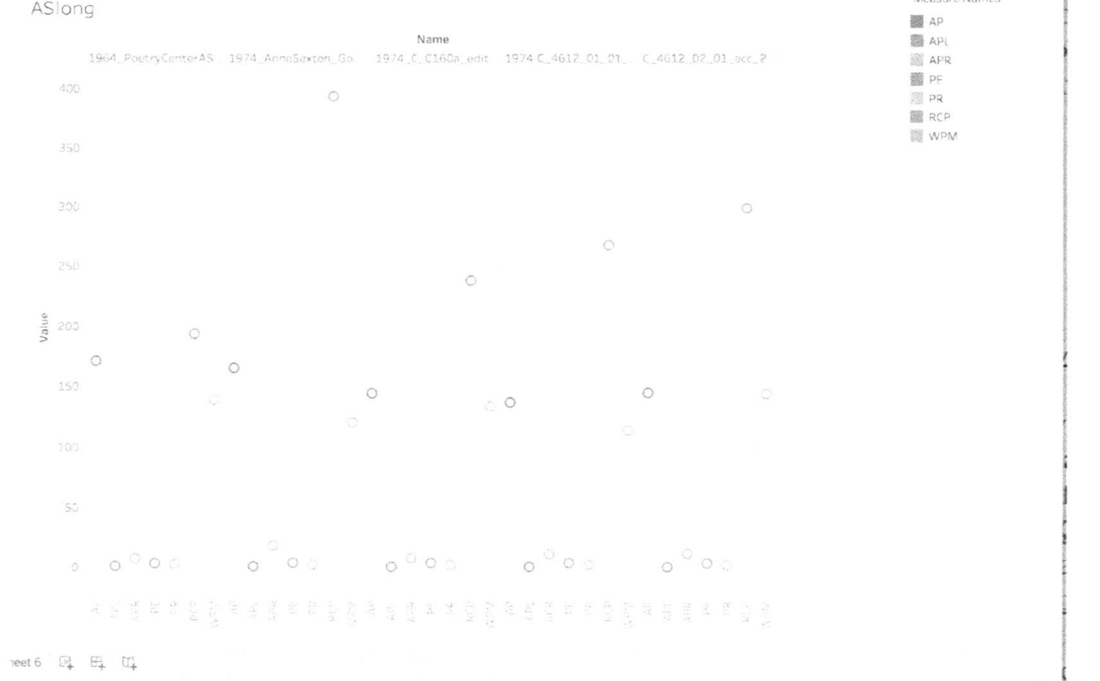

Figure 1.3. A scatter plot created in Tableau showing results from using Drift to compare the average number of pauses (AP), average pause length (APL), the average pause rate (APR), pitch entropy (PE), pitch range (PR), rhythmic complexity of pauses (RCP), and words per minute (WPM) across longer archival recordings including Sexton's 1964 poetry performance at the Poetry Center of the 92nd Street YM-YWHA and four recordings from the Harry Ransom Center: a 1974 performance at Goucher College, an unlabeled 1974 recording, and two therapy recordings.

the rhythmic complexity of pauses (RCP) is increasing from left to right across the 1964 and 1974 Sexton performances, and two of the therapy sessions. As I read these results, it seemed that Sexton's 1974 performances, much like the therapy sessions, were producing the most "complex" pause patterns, indicating a causal relationship between Sexton's listening to the therapy sessions and how she performed her poems.[25] The results were exciting because they seemed in tune with my audiation: my hypothesis was yielding something meaningful about changing patterns in Sexton's use of pauses.

Knowing through experience that my audiation of what I thought should happen might be influencing the results (including how I visualized the results I received from Drift), I visualized the data differently. Aggregating the data and visualizing long and short recordings across time from earliest to later recordings, I noted that the longer files were the files showing more pause complexity. This result seemed to indicate that, despite the Drift authors' declaration that "these measures are normalized for audio length," the version of Drift to which I had access was not normalizing measures based on the audio length.[26] It had a bug. That is, the recordings with the highest values for the rhythmic complexity of pauses are the longer recordings, and Drift was essentially reporting that longer recordings, which include more pauses in quantity due to the increased length of time also had more pause complexity. Consequently, I had a result from analyzing Sexton's recording that has very little to do with how the recording process may or may not have had an influence on how Sexton performed her poetry.[27] I hadn't learned anything I didn't already know.

While tools for text, audio, and image analysis are tools for generalizing how humans process information, a theory of audiation insists that tool developers articulate the conceptual model developed in the tool as a manipulable parameter. For instance, Audacity allows users to control parameters that change how silence—pauses—are measured. All recordings typically always have some background noise, which means pauses are not silence. They are low-range frequency noises. In the case of Sexton's recordings, what Audacity counted as silence was not the absence of sound, but whether or not the sound dropped below thirteen or twenty-six decibels. Figure 1.4 shows my analysis of silence using Audacity's measurements on an archival recording of Sexton reading at a poetry reading in 1974.[28] Below the audio wave, the lower frame shows two layers of analysis. The top layer (A) shows the results when silence has been defined as noise below thirteen decibels; the next layer (B), shows the results when silence has been defined as noise below twenty-six decibels. B seems more accurate based on my perception of what I hear. Tweaking this parameter in Audacity, where the

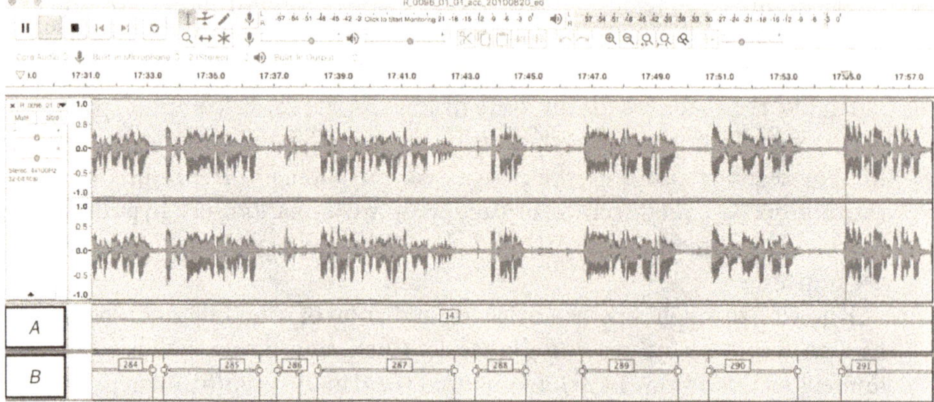

Figure 1.4. Two waveforms and two sets of numbered annotations created using Audacity on an archival recording of an untitled poetry reading by Anne Sexton, likely in 1973. The top layer set of annotations (A) on the waveform indicates moments of silence as defined as noise below thirteen decibels. The bottom set of annotations (B) more accurately depicts moments of silence as defined as noise below twenty-six decibels.

results changed so dramatically, led me to wonder how pauses were being counted or measured in Drift where, I discovered, I had no means to change that parameter based on my perceptions of the recording. Responding to disparities between what is generalizable, quotidian, and understood versus what is unique, transcendent, or provocative requires building the possibility for agency into digital tools and creating multiple possibilities for meaning-making. Tools have to allow for the flexible, iterative approaches that the practice of audiation requires.

Conclusion

Social and technical infrastructures pose difficulties when analyzing the Anne Sexton therapy text and the many other "texts" like and unlike it. A positionality to responsibly act for uncovering hidden histories, for better understanding inaccessible formats, and for enabling agency to influence what comes to matter means identifying opportunities for making matter and what matters differently.

In DH, we must be acutely mindful that what cut or intra-actions we choose to study are contingent on the tools we have at hand, our experiences, and our sense of what questions are worth asking such as those oriented in responsibility or justice. I am prioritizing the taping apparatus in Sexton's therapy text as a situated, sociotechnical phenomenon that is by nature entangled in human experience and material constraints and affordances. Diffractive measures that reposition the therapy text and Sexton's (and my own) sense of subjectivity show object and subject are not fixed. They are, instead, understood "through one another in ways that help illuminate differences as they emerge: how different differences get made, what gets excluded, and how those exclusions matter."[29] A sense of audiation helps to illustrate these differences. The sociotechnical entanglement of how matter and what matters signify in the Sexton therapy text depends on positionality (feminist inquiry), format and materiality (audio and the taping apparatus as sociotechnical phenomenon), and infrastructure development (as reflective of knowledge production and power).

Our role in constituting who and what matters may also be to point out what we cannot do. I'm choosing to focus on audio objects, how they are processed, accessed, stored, disseminated, and analyzed (all of which is what we do in DH), not only because this process may produce an increased understanding about Anne Sexton and her historical context, but also because these tapes provide a compelling use case for better understanding how and if working with difficult-to-use objects and subjects of study illuminates what and who has come to matter in literary production, in literary study, and in DH scholarship more generally. A concept of audiation requires agency in the process: if we are thinking in terms of audiation as an unavoidable variable present in the process of analysis no matter what tool we use, we must ask, what are we listening for and why? How do those concerns become part of infrastructure and tool development? We will never have the tools or devices that allow us to measure anything and all things, but we can learn to claim the agency it takes to realize that something different from what we expected is playing back and to ask why.

Notes

1. Bolter and Grusin, *Remediation*; Unsworth, "What Is Humanities Computing, and What Is Not?"; Samuels and McGann, "Deformance and Interpretation."

2. Barad, *Meeting the Universe Halfway*, 6.

3. In *The Sonic Color Line*, Jennifer Lynn Stoever demonstrates how listening practices are processes of "racial discernment, categorization, and resistance in the shadow of vision's alleged cultural dominance" (4). Stoever articulates the relationship between sound, race, and American life with two concepts that are to audiation: namely the sonic color line, which helps describe the process of racializing sound, and the listening ear, which is a consideration for how dominant listening practices accrue. Stoever disrupts the boundaries between "actual" and imagined sound in discourse communities.

4. Stoever, *The Sonic Color Line*, 35.

5. Barad, *Meeting the Universe Halfway*, x.

6. See Middlebrook, *Anne Sexton*; Grobe, "The Breath of the Poem"; Skorczewski and Sexton, *An Accident of Hope*; Golden, ed., *This Business of Words*.

7. In Clement, "Anne Sexton Listening to Anne Sexton," I introduce how Anne Sexton's practices of articulating the self in her poetry stem from listening to the tapes. My book *Dissonant Records: Listening to Literary Archives* (2024) discusses multiple cases in which audio recordings have influenced the work of literary authors.

8. Sexton's papers at the Arthur and Elizabeth Schlesinger Library on the History of Women in America at the Radcliffe Institute for Advanced Study include several hundred recordings of these therapy sessions. At the Harry Ransom Center at the University of Texas at Austin, there are four handwritten and typed journals in which Sexton wrote responses after or while listening to the taped sessions. While the journal PDFs are accessible to any registered visitors at the Ransom Center, the Schlesinger CDs are under strict rules for access: scholars must gain explicit permission from the literary executor, Sexton's daughter Linda Gray Sexton, before listening to the files, which are restricted to the reading room.

9. When Dr. Orne shared the tapes with Diane Middlebrook for her controversial biography (1992) and received a slew of *New York Times* editorials critiquing his actions, Dr. Orne notes that he tried to give the tapes back to Sexton in 1964, but she exhorted him to keep them to "help others." Orne writes in one 1991 response that "it was clear that she had a condition that traditionally was known as hysteria." Orne, "The Sexton Tapes."

10. Sexton, "Therapy Tape (January 31, 195?)."

11. Sexton, "The Freak Show," 40.

12. Barad, *Meeting the Universe Halfway*, 170.

13. Barad, *Meeting the Universe Halfway*, 361.

14. Sexton, Sexton, and Ames, *Anne Sexton*, 245.

15. Sexton, Sexton, and Ames, *Anne Sexton*, 171.

16. This concern is well-address in Da, "The Computational Case against Computational Literary Studies."

17. Barad, *Meeting the Universe Halfway*, 146. Citing Judith Butler's theories on performativity (1993) and Foucault's theories on discourse (1977 and 1978), Barad seeks to account for the relationship between discursive practices and material phenomena by exploring Niels Bohr's insights into the embodied nature of concepts (1958).

18. Hammond, "The Double Bind of Validation; Liu, "The Meaning of the Digital Humanities"; Rhody, "Topic Modelling and Figurative Language"; Witmore, "Latour, the Digital Humanities, and the Divided Kingdom of Knowledge."

19. I had participated in a previous project measuring the length of applause in poetry performances in the PennSound collection, which is published in Clement and McLaughlin, "Measured Applause."

20. Texts in Performance" was led by Marit MacArthur (a scholar of English and performance studies) and Neil Verma (a scholar of sound studies in radio/

television/film) and funded by the American Council of Learned Societies and the National Endowment for the Humanities.

21. Gentle, a collaboration between Robert Ochshorn (in computer science and design) and Max Hawkins (in computer science and art), was built on top of Kaldi, an open-source speech recognition toolkit written in C++ and developed at Johns Hopkins University, which uses neural network–based acoustic modeling and had been trained on thousands of hours of recorded telephone conversations (https://lowerquality.com/gentle).

The creators describe Drift, developed by Robert Ochshorn, as an "easy to use pitch trace exploration tool" that is based on Dan Ellis's algorithm for pitch tracing (making it "state-of-the-art . . . even on noisy recordings"). Ellis, once an electrical engineering professor at Columbia University, most recently is a research scientist developing AudioSet ("A large-scale dataset of manually annotated audio events") at Google Research.

22. MacArthur, Zellou, and Miller, "Beyond Poet Voice." MacArthur, Zellou, and Miller describe their use of TANDEM-STRAIGHT, a framework designed for tracking pitch and timing developed by Hideki Kawahara at Wakayama University in Japan, with the Advanced Telecommunications Research Institute and the Auditory Brain Project ("Beyond Poet Voice," 27).

23. Audacity is a free tool originally developed in 1999 by Dominic Mazzoni, a graduate student at Carnegie Mellon University under the direction of his advisor Roger Dannenberg, a professor of computer science, art, and music.

24. The "rhythmic complexity of pauses" is "calculated using the Lempel-Ziv algorithm to estimate Kolmogorov complexity" pause vs. speech of at least 100 milliseconds, measured across the recording. MacArthur, Zellou, and Miller, "Beyond Poet Voice," 30.

25. The complexity measure is calculated using the Lempel-Ziv algorithm (which is used in compression) to estimate Kolomogorov complexity, which reflects unique speech-pause patterns combined in order to reproduce "an observed speech-pause signal"; the complexity number indicates if the signal of repeated patterns is more or less predictable by the algorithm.

26. MacArthur, Zellou, and Miller, "Beyond Poet Voice," 30. It should be noted that I am not arguing against the veracity of the results published in "Beyond Poet Voice," which may not have been achieved using the same version of the tool to which I had access.

27. All of the algorithms that were used to create the rhythmic complexity of pauses measure are designed to simplify the complexities of the speech act in order to render it quantifiable and thus measurable. "TANDEM-STRAIGHT," which is the algorithm that underlies Drift, "applies signal processing algorithms based on human auditory processing to create a rich model of a recorded voice, which can then be analyzed and manipulated" (MacArthur, Zellou, and Miller, "Beyond Poet Voice," 27). If an audio files is not normalized for length, however, there will be more speech-pause patterns in the longer files and therefore TANDEM-STRAIGHT will be able to more easily predict that speech-pause patterns, yielding a higher RCP number simply because the recording is longer.

28. Sexton, "Therapy Tape, R 0096, January 4, 1975." This reading is only titled with an incorrect date and no location is noted. Anne Sexton died on October 4, 1974. The reading probably took place in 1973 since she mentions that her collection *The Death Notebooks* (1974) would be coming out in January.

29. Barad, *Meeting the Universe Halfway*, 30.

Works Cited

Arnold, Taylor, and Lauren Tilton. "Distant Viewing: Analyzing Large Visual Corpora." *Digital Scholarship in the Humanities* 34, no. Suppl. 1 (2019).

Audacity. https://www.audacityteam.org/.

AudiAnnotate. http://audiannotate.brumfieldlabs.com/.

"Audio, n." *OED Online.* Oxford University Press, December 2019. Accessed February 20, 2020. www.oed.com/view/Entry/13029.

Audioset. Google Research. https://research.google.com/audioset/.

Aviary. https://www.aviaryplatform.com/.

Barad, Karen Michelle. *Meeting the Universe Halfway: Quantum Physics and the Entanglement of Matter and Meaning.* Durham, NC: Duke University Press, 2007.

Bernstein, Charles. *Close Listening: Poetry and the Performed Word.* New York: Oxford University Press, 1998.

Bishop, Elizabeth, and J. D. McClatchy. *The Voice of the Poet Elizabeth Bishop.* New York: Random House Audio Publishing, Random House Audiobooks, 2000.

Bohr, Neils. *Atomic Physics and Human Knowledge.* New York: Wiley, 1958.

Bolter, J. David, and Richard A. Grusin. *Remediation: Understanding New Media.* Cambridge, MA: MIT Press, 1999.

Butler, Judith. *Bodies That Matter: On the Discursive Limits of "Sex."* New York: Routledge, 1993.

Clement, Tanya. "Anne Sexton Listening to Anne Sexton." *PMLA* 135, no. 2 (2020): 387–92. https://doi.org/10.1632/pmla.2020.135.2.387.

Clement, Tanya. "Towards a Rationale of Audio Text." *Digital Humanities Quarterly* 10, no. 3 (2016).

Clement, Tanya, and Stephen McLaughlin. "Measured Applause: Toward a Cultural Analysis of Audio Collections." *Journal of Cultural Analytics* 1, no. 1 (2016). https://doi.org/10.22148/16.002.

Council on Library and Information Resources and the Library of Congress. *The State of Recorded Sound Preservation in the United States: A National Legacy at Risk in the Digital Age.* Washington, DC: National Recording Preservation Board of the Library of Congress, 2010.

Da, Nan Z. "The Computational Case against Computational Literary Studies." *Critical Inquiry* 45, no. 3 (Spring 2019): 601–39.

Drift3. http://rmozone.com/drift/.

Foucault, Michel. *Discipline and Punish: The Birth of the Prison*. 1st American ed. New York: Pantheon Books, 1977.

Foucault, Michel. *The History of Sexuality*. Trans. Robert Hurley. New York: Pantheon Books, 1978.

Gill, Jo. "Textual Confessions: Narcissism in Anne Sexton's Early Poetry." *Twentieth Century Literature* 50, no. 1 (2004): 59–87.

Hammond, Adam. "The Double Bind of Validation: Distant Reading and the Digital Humanities' Trough of Disillusionment." *Literature Compass* 14, no. 8 (August 1, 2017).

GitHub. https://github.com/.

Golden, Amanda, ed. *This Business of Words: Reassessing Anne Sexton*. Gainesville: University Press of Florida, 2016.

Grobe, C. "The Breath of the Poem: Confessional Print/Performance circa 1959." *PMLA* 127, no. 2 (2012): 215–30.

Koopman, Colin, "Foucault's Historiographical Expansion: Adding Genealogy to Archaeology." *Journal of the Philosophy of History* 2, no. 3 (2008): 338–62.

Lingold, Mary Caton, Darren Mueller, and Whitney Trettien, eds. *Digital Sound Studies*. Durham, NC: Duke University Press, 2018.

Liu, Alan. "The Meaning of the Digital Humanities." *PMLA* 128, no. 2 (2013): 409–23.

MacArthur, Marit J., Georgia Zellou, and Lee M. Miller. "Beyond Poet Voice: Sampling the (Non-) Performance Styles of 100 American Poets." *Journal of Cultural Analytics*, (2018).

McCarty, Willard. "Modeling: A Study in Words and Meanings." In *Companion to Digital Humanities*, edited by Ray Siemens, John Unsworth, and Susan Schreibman. Oxford: Blackwell Publishing, 2004.

McGann, J. J. *Radiant Textuality: Literature after the World Wide Web*. New York: Palgrave, 2001.

McPherson, Tara. "Designing for Difference." *differences* 25, no. 2 (2014): 177–88.

Middlebrook, Diane Wood. *Anne Sexton: A Biography*. New York: Vintage Books, 1992.

Middleton, Peter. *Distant Reading: Performance, Readership, and Consumption in Contemporary Poetry*. Tuscaloosa: University of Alabama Press, 2005.

Minimal Computing. https://go-dh.github.io/mincomp/.

Monea, Alexander, and Jeremy Packer. "Media Genealogy: Technological and Historical Engagements of Power—Introduction." *International Journal of Communication* 10, no. 0 (June 2016): 19.

Oral History Metadata Synchronizer. https://www.oralhistoryonline.org/.

Orne, Martin. "The Sexton Tapes." *New York Times*, July 23, 1991.

Ostriker, Alicia. *Writing like a Woman*. Ann Arbor: University of Michigan Press, 1983.

Parikka, Jussi. *What Is Media Archaeology?* London: Polity Press, 2012.

Phelan, Peggy. *Unmarked: The Politics of Performance*. New York: Routledge, 1993.

Plath, Sylvia, and J. D. McClatchy. *The Voice of the Poet Sylvia Plath.* New York: Random House Audio Publishing, Random House Audiobooks, 1999.

Rhody, Lisa Marie. "Topic Modelling and Figurative Language." *Journal of Digital Humanities* 2, no. 1 (Winter 2012).

Rich, Adrienne, and J. D. McClatchy. *The Voice of the Poet Adrienne Rich.* New York: Random House Audio Publishing, Random House Audiobooks, 2002.

Samuels, Lisa, and Jerome J. McGann. "Deformance and Interpretation." *New Literary* History 30, no. 1 (1999): 25–56. https://doi.org/10.1353/nlh.1999.0010.

Sexton, Anne. *All My Pretty Ones.* Houghton Mifflin, 1962.

Sexton, Anne. Anne Sexton Papers, 1956–1988; March 7, 1961. MC 645, CD-3, reel 9. Schlesinger Library, Radcliffe Institute, Harvard University, Cambridge, MA. Accessed June 20, 2019. https://id.lib.harvard.edu/ead/sch00274/catalog.

Sexton, Anne. "Anne Sexton Reads at the Poetry Center." Internet Archive, April 29, 2016. archive.org/details/pacifica_radio_archives-BB3804.01.

Sexton, Anne. *The Complete Poems: Anne Sexton.* New York: Mariner Books, 1999.

Sexton, Anne. "The Freak Show." *American Poetry Review*, 2, no. 3 (1973): 38–40.

Sexton, Anne. "Journal, 1961." Anne Sexton Papers 1912–1996 (bulk 1953–1974), Box 44. Harry Ransom Center, University of Austin, TX.

Sexton, Anne. *Live or Die.* New York: Houghton Mifflin, 1966.

Sexton, Anne. "Therapy Tape (January 31, 195?)." Harry Ransom Center, University of Austin, TX.

Sexton, Anne. "Therapy Tape, R 0096, January 4, 1975." Harry Ransom Center, University of Austin, TX.

Sexton, Anne, and J. D. McClatchy, *The Voice of the Poet Anne Sexton.* New York: Random House Audio Publishing, Random House Audiobooks, 2000.

Sexton, Anne, Linda Gray Sexton, and Lois Ames. *Anne Sexton: A Self-Portrait in Letters.* New York: Houghton Mifflin, 1977.

Skorczewski, Dawn, and Anne Sexton. *An Accident of Hope: The Therapy Tapes of Anne Sexton.* New York: Routledge, 2012.

Sterne, J. "The MP3 as Cultural Artifact." *New Media & Society* 8, no. 5 (2006): 825–42.

Stoever, Jennifer Lynn. *The Sonic Color Line: Race and the Cultural Politics of Listening.* New York University Press, 2016. https://doi.org/10.18574/9781479899081.

Unsworth, J. "What Is Humanities Computing, and What Is Not?" In *Jahrbuch für Computerphilologie* 4, edited by Georg Braungart, Karl Eibl, and Fotis Jannidis. Paderborn: mentis Verlag, 2002. Accessed September 8, 2011. http://computerphilologie.uni-muenchen.de/jg02/unsworth.html.

The Versioning Machine. http://bleierr.github.io/v-machine/.

Wax. https://minicomp.github.io/wax/.

Witmore, Michael. "Latour, the Digital Humanities, and the Divided Kingdom of Knowledge." *New Literary History* 47, no. 2 (2016): 353–75.

2

Feminist DH:
A Historical Perspective

Excavating the Lives
of Women of the Past

MONIKA BARGET AND
SUSAN SCHREIBMAN

Introduction: Making the Invisible Visible

This chapter explores how the Irish history project Letters 1916–1923 adopted a feminist approach to surface marginalized women's voices in a heterogeneous historical collection of letters dominated by male voices. Begun in 2013, Letters 1916–1923 sought to revise the narrative of the revolutionary period in Irish history through a project of social relevance that breaks down barriers between the public and traditional academic research. It does this by creating a virtual collection of letters written between November 1915 and December 1923, a period of enormous social change, punctuated by conflict and political unrest. As such, it collects, transcribes, encodes, and publishes letters through a participatory process from almost eighty public and private sources in Ireland and abroad. Letters were chosen as expressions of the personal, of the everyday, and as significant documents in organizing and shaping lives.

As a history project, Letters 1916–1923 is a digital collection that presents life as it was experienced at the time and that serves a vehicle to broaden cultural understanding. As a technology project, it was designed for social inclusion, empowering nontraditional groups to participate in knowledge creation and to learn new technology skills.[1] As a memory project, it provides an intimate and personal view of the past, providing researchers and the public with unprecedented access to a range of primary sources, from official government communications to love letters.[2] It provides access to a society both very different and very like our own, helping the present generation to interpret the past more meaningfully as a way to understand our present.

The curation ethos of Letters 1916–1923 focuses on recovery in which the goal is to gather letters not only from canonical figures in Irish society, but from those whose voices would otherwise be lost to history. The very act of digitizing and building the collection in collaboration with different memory institutions and the public has brought hidden networks and alternative loci of power and influence to the fore.[3] Expanding methodologies to include both quantitative and qualitative methods, the case studies in this chapter recognize and reflect on the lives of women and encourage other researchers to trace women's lives even in places where they, at first, seem absent.

Despite the feminist ethos of collection building, the Letters 1916–1923 corpus remains dominated by men because of its historical context. At the time of writing, the gender ratio of letters in the collection is 80 percent male authors to 20 percent female (a ratio remarkably consistent throughout the project life cycle). While this percentage reflects the limited public capacity of women in the early twentieth century, it also betrays historical biases in private and public collecting as well as in commemoration. Extended digitization of materials beyond public archives is the first step to democratizing history—but a gender-conscious methodology is the second. The epistolary sources in the collection range from letters and postcards to telegraphs and simple notes. They cover every phase of the nascent Irish Republic from the Great War (1914–1918) and the Irish Easter Rising (1916) to the Irish War of Independence against Britain (1919–1921), and the post-independence tensions and the Civil War (1922–1923) fought over the Anglo-Irish treaty in which twenty-six Irish counties became part of an independent Ireland with six of the northern counties remaining part of the United Kingdom.

The mixed method approach adopted in this chapter, which we term middle-distance reading, provided both macro and micro views of this growing corpus[4] and helps us view male-dominated sources through a lens of inclusion.[5] The corpus of circa 4,500 letters used for full-text analysis is too small to be considered big data, but too large for a single scholar to meaningfully engage with its entirety via close reading. While the collection is continuously expanding and will never reach an ultimate point of conclusion (as it will be impossible to include all cataloged letters from our time period kept in archives, not to mention the many letters that are still hidden in private collections), it is still possible to research the letters for latent themes. Because of the open-ended nature of the corpus our approach is neither distant reading in which algorithms typically search through hundreds of thousands, even millions of texts, finding patterns that cannot be comprehended by a single individual;[6] nor is it close reading in which the researcher engages with a small number of closely analyzed texts. Rather, it is a balanced and cyclic combination of both.[7] A hallmark of middle-distance reading is the iterative integration of both algorithmic criticism and traditional source criticism.[8] This approach might also be described as involving patience, persistence, and innovation as it applies novel quantitative methods developed for other domains to humanities data.

Topic modeling, mapping, and network analysis proved useful for excavating the lives and contributions of women. In the first section of this chapter, we utilize topic modeling as a check on manually assigned content tagging. The second section is a case study centering on the overwhelmingly female network of the Irish War Hospital Supply Organisation (IWHSO) that supported the British war effort between 1915 and 1919. A mapping of the sites where women volunteered helps us understand the geographic and cultural scope of their networks and communication channels during the Great War. The case study in the third section situates a comparatively consistent family collection in the overall political and social framework of the Irish Civil War. Written between 1915 and 1923, the letters in this collection center on the life, family, and political affiliations of Charlie Daly, who opposed the Irish peace treaty with Britain and was executed in 1923. These case studies present different poles of women's engagement in the Irish revolutionary period (from the Third Home Rule Bill in 1914 to the post–Civil War period in 1923) that could only be sifted out from the traditionally male narratives of Irishmen fighting alongside or against the British through middle-distance analysis.

Using Statistical Analysis to Uncover Women's Agency in an Unbounded Text Corpus

Topic modeling was also used at various points in the project life cycle to check the viability of the metadata or category tagging applied by editors and contributors, and to surface topics that may have been overlooked. The manual tagging helped the project team keep track of changes in the content of the collection as it expanded from its early focus on events during 1916

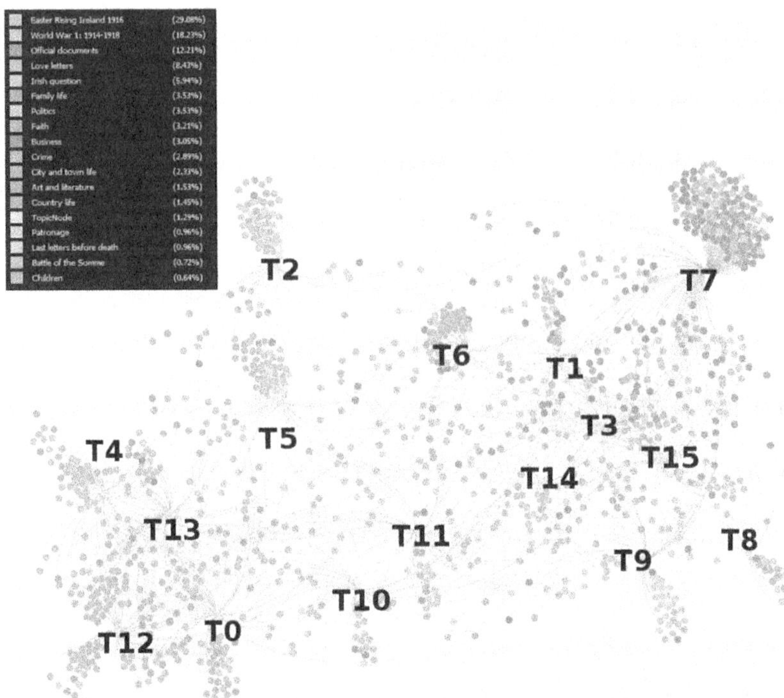

Figure 2.1. Affiliation of 1,344 categorized letters with fifteen machine-identified topics created by Bleier.

to the more expansive period of 1916–1923. In the first phase of the project, eighteen categories were used but later revised and limited to fourteen.[9] Some tags were renamed to broaden their meaning, others were combined. Counting the number of letters by men and women in each of these categories provided us with a preliminary insight into which themes each gender predominantly addressed, drawing our attention to potential misrepresentations in our data. To provide a check on our manually assigned metadata, we utilized topic model algorithms to identify relevant co-occurrences of words ("topics"). While Latent Semantic Analysis (LSA) and combinations of word distributional statistics and lexical definitions help cluster words with similar or identical meanings in large and complex corpora, our comparatively small corpus with many standardized expressions and limited overall vocabulary was better analyzed with Latent Dirichlet Allocation (LDA) and Non-Negative Matrix Factorization (NMF).

Roman Bleier created the first Letters 1916 topic model with a standard LDA algorithm in MALLET to analyze 1,344 letters covering the period from November 1915 to October 1916.[10] Figure 2.1 shows that the eighteen manually assigned tags except for "Easter Rising" strongly aligned with one or two algorithmically identified topics.[11]

Attaching the tags and topics to gender revealed that women were well represented in the "love letters" category,[12] including correspondence between two courting couples from the private Finn and Gorman collections; "family life" and "Irish question" categories; but especially in "World War I" (corresponding to T4 [topic 4] of the model). This distribution is explained by the fact that many women were likely to preserve the precious letters received from men at the front, and that they frequently sent wartime news and condolences to relatives and friends. By contrast, the category "official documents," which mainly consists of correspondence sent from and to the British administrative seat at Dublin Castle, was overwhelmingly populated by male correspondents. Although this snapshot was taken when the Letters 1916–1923 project was little more than a year old and the corpus relatively small, the fairly constrained role of women in the public sphere and their limited interaction with government officials were confirmed when the collection grew in number and extended to 1923. Exceptions were mainly due to class (upper-class women organizing charity work)[13] or related to highly politicized circles (suffragettes and Irish nationalists).[14]

In spring 2020, we performed another analysis of the by-then revised tags and used the Python package SciKit Learn, which permits combined LDA and NFM topic modeling.[15] The most readable results were achieved with Non-Negative Matrix Factorization as it attributes comparatively less weightage to the words with less coherence and produces smaller, more coherent topics compared to LDA. Another important decision was not to translate foreign languages to English first but treat foreign words as topics of their own. As phrases in French, German, and Irish were interspersed in the letters of specific communities (e.g., prisoners of war and Irish republicans), we wanted to capture these languages as distinct cultural or political statements. We used customized NLTK stop-word lists[16] to exclude technical terms such as "poststamp" or "street" in English as well as German, French, and Irish, but deliberately included Irish pronouns and auxiliary verbs.[17] Moreover, we included telling address information like "Dublin Castle" or "camp" to better disambiguate the meaning of very frequent words like "lord" or "poor" depending on context.

Table 2.1. Distribution of top eighteen NMF topics (dominant topics per letter) in a 2020 dataset of 3,049 transcribed letters

Top NMF topics in 2020 data	Number of letters in which topic dominates
T0 law	9
T1 personal	823
T2 politics	15
T3 Easter Rising	61
T4 WWI	60
T5 Irish	29
T6 home	282
T7 British administration	627
T8 French letters	15
T9 imprisonment	35
T10 economy	5
T11 people & places	91
T12 schedules	207
T13 education	10
T14 Irish question	284
T15 medicine	243
T16 peace keeping	45
T17 news & plans	208
No. of analyzed letters	3,049

The 2020 data set contained 4,515 letters of which 3,049 were fully transcribed and suitable for topic modeling. While the 2016 topic model retrieved an optimal number of fifteen topics, the 2020 analysis of the 3,049 fully transcribed letters showed that fifteen topics no longer sufficed. A first attempt to create fifteen updated topics showed that at least three topics (e.g., one relating to different aspects of law and business) could be differentiated further.[18] The newly generated eighteen topics mainly revolved around personal relations, administration, law, business, education, and politics but also betrayed a significant surge in the use of French and, above all, Irish, which was interspersed throughout republican correspondence (table 2.1).[19]

The 2020 topic model suggests that personal relations are by far the most frequent topic of letters overall, whereas different aspects of the contested British administration in Ireland rank second. These eighteen topics are more nuanced than the fourteen revised metadata categories introduced to enhance the user experience during the project redesign of 2018, but the thematic scope is nevertheless compatible, confirming the validity of our tagging choices and the gender ratio in the updated metadata categories. This analysis of manually assigned categories in the sub-corpus of transcribed women's letters (figure 2.2) showed that—in spite of a stable overall percentage of female writing overall (22 percent in 2015 and 20 percent

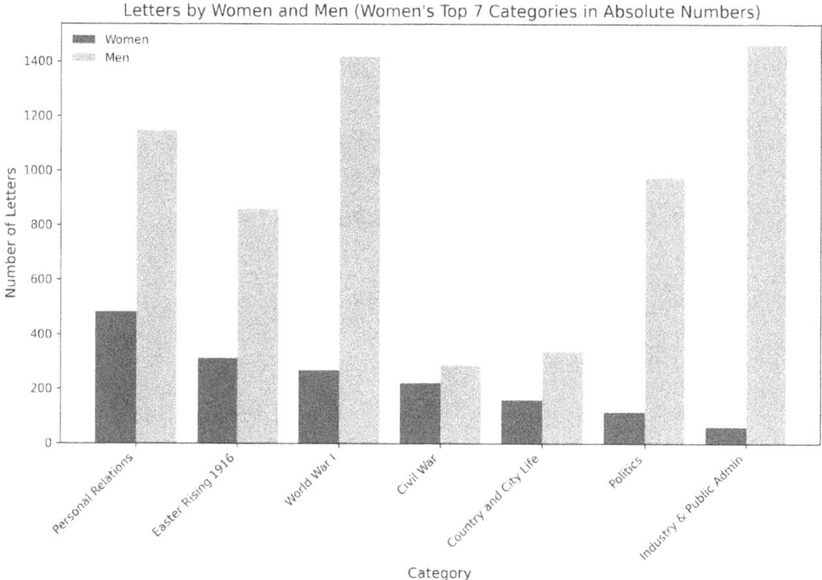

Figure 2.2. Top seven topics covered by women writers based on the gender ratio in the revised metadata tags. One hundred percent in each category represent letters by both men and women, excluding letters written by authors whose gender is unknown. As the analysis is not dependent on transcriptions, all 4,515 items in the 2020 dataset were included.

currently)—the proportion of women's letters in individual thematic areas shifted for various reasons.

"Personal relations" now appears as the most frequent category assigned to women's letters since we combined the tags "love letters," "children," and "family life" used in the first phase. Comparing the relative percentage of male and female letter-writers in each category (figure 2.3), 30 percent of letters on "personal relations" overall were written by women, placing this category above the 20 percent average female ratio across all tags. The most notable development within our collection, however, is that the fourth largest category in the women's letters now is the Irish Civil War (1922–1923) although we only started collecting such letters in the project's second phase. That "Civil War" has even become the category with the highest women-to-men ratio (43 percent to 57 percent respectively)[20] resulted from the large number of women authors in the Charlie Daly collection (now housed at the Kerry Library in Tralee) in which almost 50 percent of correspondents are female, as well as a considerable number of unionist letters by women from Northern Ireland.

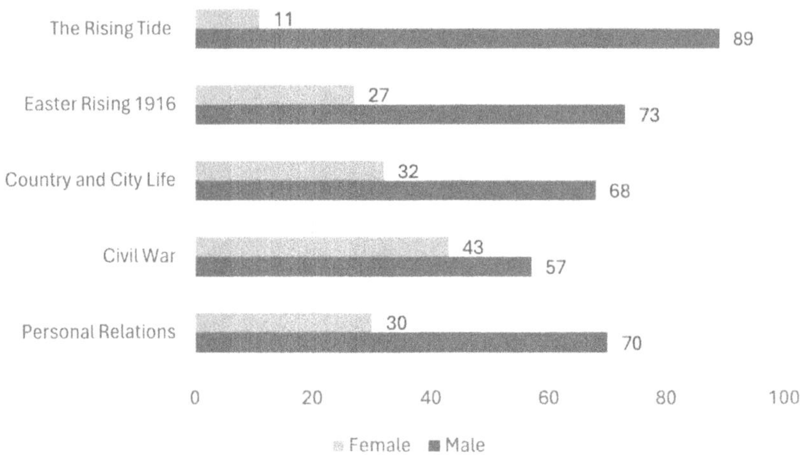

Figure 2.3. Direct comparison of gender distribution in top categories with female authors, based on the revised metadata categories in the 2020 dataset. The 4,515 letters analyzed belong to more than one category each. Letters of authors whose gender is unknown have been excluded.

That women's letters are rare in medicine (2 percent) and faith (1 percent), however, is the result of the project's own collection history. Women's letters on medicine and faith are underrepresented because the project includes large collections from the Royal College of Physicians, the Irish Jesuit and Capuchin archives, outweighing hitherto included letters from female religious, auxiliary nurses (VADs), and women physicians such as Kathleen Lynn.

Female Networks in the Irish War Hospital Supply Depot: An Example of Working with Fractured Datasets

In our attempt to balance biases in our data, we included non-epistolary sources from outside the Letters 1916–1923 project in our analysis. This led us from smaller, fractured sets of letters on the contribution of Irish women to the manufacturing and distribution of First World War hospital supplies to a multimodal analysis of the Irish War Hospital Supply Organisation (IWHSO), whose activities were recorded in reports, newspaper articles, and maps. In 1915, this organization was formed by female members of the upper classes (including Roman Catholics by and large loyal to the Crown) to coordinate and improve the production and shipping of bed-linen, bandages, stretchers, papier-mâché limbs, and other medical items to military hospitals at home and abroad.[21] The IWHSO was linked with the General Department of Voluntary Organisations in London and part of a larger imperial network.[22] Run and staffed predominantly by women, the Irish War Hospital Supply Organisation operated a central depot in Dublin as well as local branches that often specialized in gathering and drying sphagnum moss. This moss was valued for its inherent antiseptic qualities as well as its ability to absorb moisture and was fashioned into much-needed wound dressings when cotton was in short supply.[23]

Details of the women's activities in the IWHSO have come down to us through their own annual reports, which highlight the managerial skills of the women in charge. Each of the annual reports included a long list of the names of women supervising work parties on a county-by-county basis. While the lists detail the women's service times and productivity, additional sources (such as more general government publications on volunteering and newspaper articles) were needed to understand the spatial and interpersonal contours of this essential work at the home front.[24]

The Letters 1916–1923 team mapped all places associated with female IWHSO volunteers to trace the geographic distribution of the network over time, and to explore potential congruences between the physical proximity and family connections of the women involved. This mapping served as a form of distant reading that placed individual sources in the overall context of strategic considerations behind the supply infrastructure and showed the importance of existing travel routes and landmarks. Places of local depots are mentioned in the IWHSO annual reports, but also in existing online resources and contemporary maps.[25] In 2018, Pádraig MacCarron, Susan Schreibman, and Monika Barget began collecting all known places of activity and basic information on the women who lived or worked there in a CSV table that was filled semi-automatically. Information from historic Irish newspapers had to be added manually while the scanned reports could be read with OCR and data extracted via Python script. The initial results were published in an article for *History Ireland* and on the project website.[26] In 2019, Monika Barget continued the disambiguation of women's names using the 1911 census and genealogy databases, corrected misattributed place names, and geocoded the revised CSV table with the GOOGLE API.[27] We could then create an improved zoomable map of all identified IWHSO branch depots and work parties across Ireland, using QGIS and the QGIS2web extension.[28] In contrast to the initial map of 2018, the new map further differentiates local work parties by function, summarized in table 2.2.

Table 2.2. All identified IWHSO branch depots and work parties across Ireland

Types of depots and centers affiliated with the IWHSO	Description
IWHSO regional depots	Larger depots that took on important managerial tasks for a larger region and maintained correspondence with the government and British troops outside Ireland
General sub-depots (affiliated)	Sub-depots of the IWHSO taking care of a broad range of medical war supplies
Moss depots	Supply depots specialising in the sphagnum moss collection in Ireland
Moss collection centers	Local sphagnum moss collection centers (e.g., set up in parish halls and private homes)
Woodwork sub-depots (men)	Sub-depots staffed by male volunteers rather than women and focusing on woodwork
Function not specified	Centers/local work group whose function we could not identify

These functions were difficult to disambiguate as the official status of a work group within the IWHSO could change over time and descriptions such as "branch," "class," or "sub-depot" were not used consistently in the sources. It is especially hard to tell if a center was active in the production of all kinds of medical supplies or specialized in sphagnum moss collection. The data sheet accompanying our map provides further information on our sources and doubtful data.[29]

Nevertheless, the IWHSO mapping reveals a densely knit logistics networks of hospital supply producers even in rural areas. The centers that functioned as local sub-depots of the IWHSO were mainly situated on the Irish coast or on major transportation routes (e.g., the Royal Canal and railway lines). Larger towns often had several work parties. Four centers we have identified so far were woodwork sub-depots for men. Our mapping revealed that the Belfast area organized hospital supplies independently from Dublin from 1916. Dublin and Belfast were the most important harbors for the shipping of all war hospital supplies to the British army and affiliated organizations. The Belfast War Hospital Supply Committee reported directly to London, which is why work groups and depots in the northeast are not mentioned in any of the Dublin reports and the availability of data differs. Northern Irish newspapers are the best source for covering this development and have been used to refine our data.

The additional mapping of a selected sub-network of local work party managers in Connacht, a western province of Ireland, revealed that the

IWHSO network was by no means based on an a priori master plan drafted by the military administration but developed organically, driven by changing wartime demands, the regional availability of moss, and preexisting connections between women who could act as managers and multipliers.

The epicenter of IWHSO activities in Connacht was in County Galway, where sphagnum moss grew abundantly, and where Lady Clonbrock (Augusta Caroline Dillon), member of an aristocratic family with a large estate in Ahascragh, made use of her extensive personal contacts to support the war effort.[30] Lady Clonbrock's correspondence in the Letters 1916–1923 collection (photographed with permission of the National Library of Ireland) incited us to map the geographic distribution of the Connacht moss collection for more detailed insights into women's networking (see relevant links in Case Study 1 of our Github repository).[31] The web map of the Connacht efforts shows the places where individual women recruited by Lady Clonbrock or her acquaintances volunteered, highlighting the various periods of activity according to the official reports in different colors.[32]

The web map of women's activities in Connacht shows that recruitment took place in an area between Ballyturin/Gort in the south, Ballina/Béal an Átha in the north, Clifden on the west coast, and Ballinasloe toward the east. The names of the women active suggest that women co-volunteered with (older) relatives or were even recruited by them. The map has an interesting outlier for the second reporting period: A "Miss Jackson" is mentioned in the Connacht reports, but she was actually stationed in Malta, most likely supporting a British war hospital on site.

This geovisualization of data from the 1915/1916 and 1917/1918 reports illustrates that the first phase of Connacht moss collection started in Lady Clonbrock's home in Ahascragh and expanded to Clifden in the far west, covering areas where sphagnum moss was found in peat bogs. Lady Clonbrock and ten other women were no longer mentioned in the 1917/1918 report, having stopped working in moss collection for personal or war-related reasons. In most places, however, the women mentioned in 1915/1916 were succeeded by other women and new work groups were established in two places south of Galway. Mrs. Willcox in Recess was active in both periods but supported by a Miss K. Willcox in 1917/1918. Here the spatial mapping reveals an interesting generational phenomenon that may have been true for all of Ireland: older, married women ("Mrs.") introduced their daughters or nieces ("Miss") to the voluntary work, making the war effort a family matter in analogy to familial traditions of military service. Another interesting aspect highlighted by our research is that two centers affiliated with Galway were, for unknown personal or organizational reasons, situated in County Mayo and even Valletta in Malta. Miss Jackson in Valetta was most likely a member of the Galway upper class serving in a military hospital and organized moss deliveries from her home county.

Close reading of individual letters elucidated the genesis of regional women's networks through individual contacts, emphasizing the more organic, spontaneous side of the network and individual women's willingness to develop sustainability strategies. A letter dated April 20, 1916, from J. Eyre to Lady Clonbrock, for instance, gives detailed insight into how the country-wide network of sub-depots grew through the personal connections of (upper-class) women over time.[33] Other missing links are found in the Belgian Red Cross files, now kept at the Manchester Central Library.[34] Relating to the shipping of Irish medical supplies abroad, this regular and professional exchange between the IWHSO honorary secretaries and the male staff of other humanitarian organizations as well as British military highlights the intraregional connectedness of charitable wartime activities.[35] Close reading of women's correspondence, which may be incomplete and rare, and a more computationally driven distant reading of their networks inform each other: the role of individual women can only be fully appreciated if the collective contribution of women to historic events like the Great War is understood, as women often exerted influence through organic and unofficial networks separate from (yet intersecting with) the more formal and official male networks. Thus, the middle-distance approach links the *where* and *when* (distant reading) with the *how* (close reading) of the network's development. If the case study on the IWHSO had merely relied on close reading, the activities of the main supply and moss depots in Dublin would have been our only finding, disregarding the vast contribution of women in rural areas.

Female Agency and Interaction in the Irish Civil War— The Charlie Daly Collection

Even though the Letters 1916–1923 database contains four times as many letters by men as women at the time of writing, one collection added beginning in 2017 goes against these odds. This is the Charlie Daly correspondence between relations, friends, and acquaintances of the Irish republican commander and opponent of the Irish peace treaty with Britain, Charlie Daly. The correspondence dates from the years 1915 to 1923, ending with letters exchanged shortly after Daly's execution,[36] and consists of circa 500 items, 288 of which were added to the Letters 1916–1923 database by April 2020.[37] Although many sympathizers petitioned on Daly's behalf, he was ultimately executed by firing squad on March 14, 1923, only two months prior to the capitulation of the antitreaty forces in May that ended the Civil War.[38]

The Charlie Daly collection contains important political content, but with a view to feminist DH, its ratio of almost 50 percent female correspondents matters most. The 288 letters added to Letters 1916–1923 were written by 108 correspondents: 54 were men, 43 were women, and 11 were of unidentified gender.[39] This high number of women is even more impressive as the women were not only close relatives of Charlie Daly but also included extended family and friends from all walks of life. Katie Maria O'Sullivan was a teacher at a local school, Katherine Allman (later Sister Gertrude) decided to join a religious order, and Ellen Leonard corresponded with the Daly family in unison with her husband.

The network graph (Figure 2.4) we generated with Gephi from the metadata of the 288 Daly letters shows that the correspondence network partly predated the Civil War but grew to include men and women Charlie Daly met in the course of his paramilitary engagement and during his

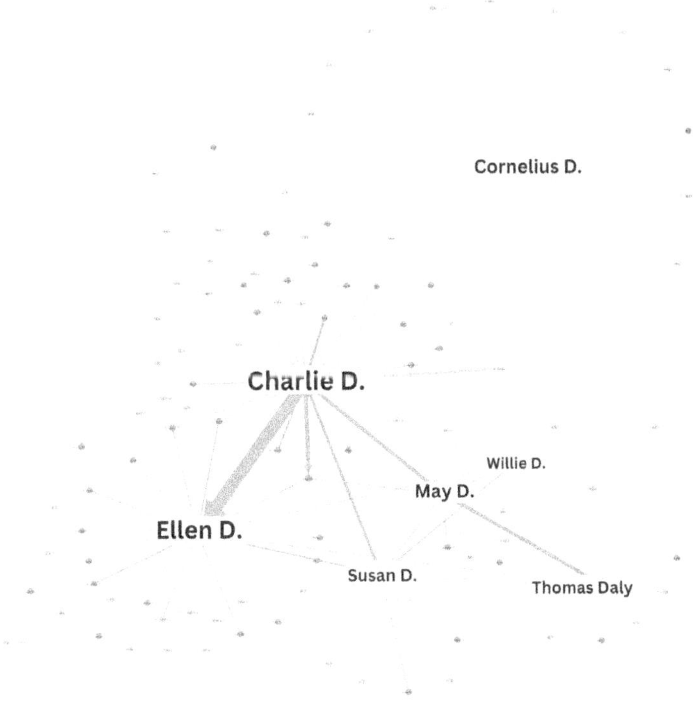

Figure 2.4. Network of correspondents in the Charlie Daly collection from County Kerry. The larger nodes in the network represent the main correspondents, and the thicker edges indicate a more frequent exchange of letters between two nodes

much-noted internment at Drumboe Castle in County Donegal between November 1922 and January 1923.[40] Charlie Daly (center) and his mother Ellen (bottom left) are the largest nodes, corresponding with both men and women. This is striking and differs from the earlier wartime collection period in which women and men (except for relatives) tended to correspond less with members of the opposite sex.

The graph also shows a large number of correspondents, of whom only a single letter is preserved, who expressed support for Charlie or offered their condolences to Ellen Daly after his death. Charlie's brother Cornelius (top right) is exclusively connected with men and one married couple. His letters in this network focus on his and Charlie's political activities and were exchanged with IRA members such as Con Lucy.[41] However, Charlie also discussed politics and paramilitarism in his letters to his mother.[42] Ellen Daly, for her part, shared information about the situation in Kerry while Charlie was imprisoned in Donegal. She told him about acquaintances who were likewise arrested for opposing the treaty. After Charlie's execution, Ellen Daly regularly wrote to her children, strengthening and supporting the family. The woman outside the Daly family who wrote and received the most letters is Katherine Allman, whom Charlie called his "best pal."[43] She entrusted her letters from the Daly family to Mary (May) Daly in the 1960s, laying the foundation for the present collection.

The close reading of the Civil War letters suggested an increased agency of female correspondents and a shared interest in education. Charlie Daly was a schoolteacher before the war, and his correspondents of both genders exchanged leaflets and books.[44] Women in his network openly voiced their own views of current events and Ireland's future.[45] To take but one example, Elizabeth "Lily" Whelan wrote to Charlie Daly in January 1923: "Let me know how you are getting along as soon as you have time. I have no Kerry news at all, only I suppose you have heard that the Ballybunion Station has been wrecked."[46]

Quantitative analysis confirmed that the style and content of the women's letters were very similar to men's. We used the available transcribed pages from 160 letters in the Daly collection for another topic model with SciKit Learn and customized NLTK stop-words. Iterative topic models retrieved five distinct topics (table 2.3).

Once again, the usage of the Irish language was accepted as a topic of its own as its prominence in republican circles of the 1920s marks a break with the earlier war period when the use of Irish had largely been confined to native speakers. In the Daly collection, Irish salutations, exclamations, or idiomatic expressions in an otherwise English letter clearly show the importance of the Irish language for a postcolonial Irish identity that was,

Table 2.3. Top six words in five topics generated from transcribed Daly letters with Python Scikit Learn

Topic no.	Interpretation	Word 1	Word 2	Word 3	Word 4	Word 5
Topic 0	exchanging news	get	got	know	write	letters
Topic 1	letters in Irish	sí	tá	sé	ó	na
Topic 2	remembering home, expecting visitors	last	home	went	week	time
Topic 3	hopes, fears, and plans for the future	great	hope	know	good	time
Topic 4	letters on Charlie's imprisonment and death	home	got	charlie	last	said

in the case of antitreaty activists, setting itself apart from British culture. Attributing the most frequent topics to gender, we find that the five letters written exclusively in Irish (Topic 1 with the first five words displayed) came from women although men frequently included Irish words in English letters.

Overall, the topic distribution across genders (figure 2.5) is very even, with a notable male peak in topic 0 ("news"). This was probably due to the fact that political prisoners, like Daly, were cut off from other communication channels and depended on letters to learn about recent events.

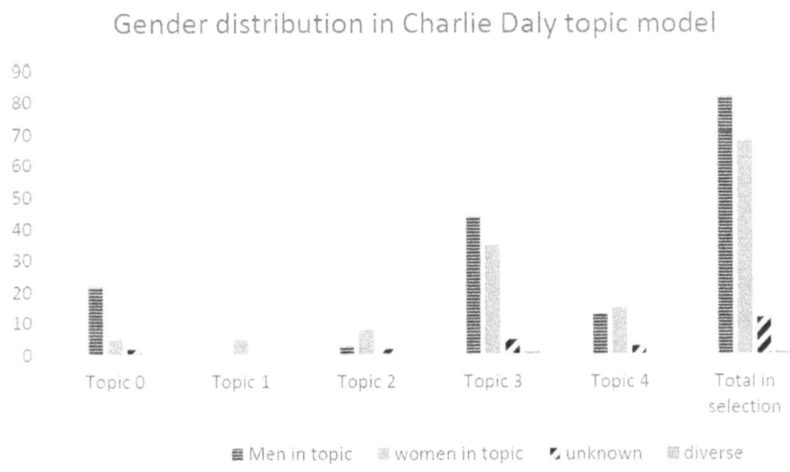

Figure 2.5. Gender distribution by topic in the Charlie Daly collection.

Family affairs, politics, religion, and the conditions of Charlie's imprisonment, however, were frequently discussed by men and women alike.[47]
These frequent overlaps of topics ranging from personal issues to national
politics and religion in a single letter were fostered because many letters
in the collection were written from or to prison and required a condensed
style and the evasion of censorship.[48]

The politicization of the women in the Daly family continued well after
Charlie's death when Ellen and other women exchanged condolences and
news from the north of Ireland. Mary (May) Daly, Charlie's oldest sister,
became active in the Irish Republican movement and ran as an election
candidate in North Kerry for Sinn Féin in the 1957 general election.[49]
Particularly after independence, many republican women who became
active in politics had lost a male loved one and continued his legacy.[50] But
the density of female political awareness in Charlie Daly's correspondence
network hints at a high level of female self-determination in Irish Republican circles more generally, reaching women of social strata that could not
have taken on public roles prior to Irish independence.

Conclusion: The Advantages of Middle-Distance Analysis and the Archaeology of the Invisible

In this chapter, mapping, topic modeling, and network analysis were used
symbiotically to reveal and contextualize close reading and to identify data
inconsistencies or informational gaps that needed further research. Close
reading was applied as a "zoom in" to check the plausibility of overarching
structures like the nationwide Irish war hospital supply network or the
correspondence network of Charlie Daly, his family, and friends. Middle-distance reading was an ideal solution for working with a plurality of
sources, data formats, and methods in which this iterative approach not
only revealed patterns, but also contextualized them.

Analyzing such pluralistic corpora at scale poses many technical and
methodological challenges. In both the case studies, the source data was
limited and incomplete, yet the iterative nature of the research process,
combining algorithmic criticism and traditional source criticism, provided
a methodology for drawing attention to what tends to be invisible when
reading closely, which, in turn, prompted close reading in a new light.

Feminist DH has a special obligation to explore and critically apply the
possibilities of both the traditional humanities and the digital transformation to preserve, interpret, and share often limited information on women's
lives. This means adopting a mindset of patience, persistence, and innovation resembling that of archaeologists who excavate relics of the past: You

might not find what you were initially looking for, but something else of value.[51] Sometimes it is even necessary to move the whole excavation site. In the case of the IWHSO volunteers, the intensity and internationality of the women's collaboration was not inherent in the letters from the Clonbrock collection that were first added to the Letters 1916–1923 database. Similarly, the different layers of male-female relationships in the Daly collection only stood out when close reading was combined with network visualization and topic modeling. Such unexpected but carefully traced discoveries make most of the digital work in feminist studies different from (big) "data mining" as extensive, well documented, and homogeneous collections (such as government archives of legal records) only serve as starting points for feminist historiography.

Feminist DH, as we define it, is not only about women but denotes an awareness of the unusual, hidden, and forgotten that can also foster the recognition of other minorities or marginalized agents. Feminist DH analyzes the development of social integration more broadly. This may necessitate a close collaboration of experts from different fields of the (digital) humanities, and information sciences as well as heritage institutions and representatives of the general public as inherent in the Letters 1916–1923 ethos. This multidisciplinary and participatory approach to history embraced by the Letters 1916–1923 project can serve as an inspiration to feminist studies more generally and encourage new explorations of limited or incomplete historical corpora with a not-so-obvious gender relevance.

Notes

The authors thank Brian Hughes, Sarah Lang, and Lisa Rhody for their careful reading of the chapter and for their many suggestions for improvement. Any remaining errors or misstatements belong to the authors.

1. This can be seen in a video of a transcriber journey available on Vimeo at https://vimeo.com/216643803.

2. Schreibman, Das Gupta, and Rooney, "Notes from the Transcription Desk."

3. D'Ignazio and Klein, "2. Collect, Analyze, Imagine, Teach."

4. Jockers, *Macroanalysis*, 24–25.

5. Tatlock et al., "Crossing Over," 1–2.

6. Moretti, *Distant Reading*; Boot, "Franco Moretti."

7. Jockers, *Macroanalysis*; Drouin, "Close- and Distant-Reading Modernism"; Jänicke et al., "On Close and Distant Reading in Digital Humanities."

8. Ramsay, *Reading Machines*.

9. Mapping of old and new categories available from https://github.com/MonikaBarget/FeministDH/blob/master/Letters1916-1923_categories.md.

10. Bleier, "Text Analysis of the 1916 Letters."

11. All images are available online in color and in an interactive format from https://monikabarget.github.io/FeministDH/.

12. Clarke and Letters 1916–1923 team, "Love Letters 1916–1923."

13. Cf. Marie Martin's letters to her family, Lady Clonbrock's correspondence with members of the Connacht Rangers and their female fund-raisers, and the letters of the Duffin family. See Letters 1916–1923 team, "Marie Martin"; Letters 1916–1923 team, "Augusta Caroline Dillon Clonbrock, Lady Clonbrock"; Duffin, "Letter from Olive Duffin to Her Mother, Maria Duffin, January 1916."

14. E.g., Kathleen Lynn and Hanna Sheehy Skeffington. See Lynn, "Letter from Dr Kathleen Lynn to the Deputy Adjutant General at Parkgate, 26 May 1916"; Letters 1916–1923 team, "Women's Suffrage in the Letters 1916–1923 Collection."

15. Bakharia, "Topic Modeling with Scikit Learn."

16. Barget, "Doing Digital History with Python III."

17. People and places (except the term "Ireland") were not dominating topics as the collection includes hundreds of letters from all over the world that are often not part of larger family collections. Where names recurred, they, too, were helpful for contextualization and topic interpretation, e.g., in the case of well-known Anglo-Irish government officials. See Barget, FeministDH (Github Repository).

18. Comparing all topic models of fifteen to twenty topics with twenty-five top words each, eighteen topics best reflected the scope of the collection. The comparison of topics was human-supervised, but a Python script was used to monitor the number of unique words and recurrences across topics as a possible indicator of topic diversity. Due to the genre specificities of early twentieth-century correspondence, all topic models created had more than fifty words that occurred in more than one topic, which is why automated calculation of topic coherence (e.g., with Jaccard index) seemed dispensable.

19. Cf. data table on GITHUB; see Barget, "Topic Model of Letters 1916–1923 Data Dump Exported in 2019."

20. See full data table in Barget, FeministDH (Github Repository).

21. Irish War Hospital Supply Organisation, *First Annual Report of the Sphagnum Department of the Irish War Hospital Supply Organisation*; Cullen, "War Work on the Home Front"; "Sphagnum Moss to the Rescue."

22. Department of the Director-General of Voluntary Organisations, *Army: Report on the National Scheme of Coordination of Voluntary Effort.*

23. Riegler, "Sphagnum Moss in World War I."

24. Newspaper clippings are found in the following collections: "Marconi Wireless Station"; Joint War Committee of the Order of the British Red Cross Society and the Order of Saint John of Jerusalem in England, "PP/AIR 2459"; Irish War Hospital Supply Organisation, *First Annual Report of the Sphagnum Department of the Irish War Hospital Supply Organisation*; Joint War Committee of the British Red Cross Society and the Order of St. John of Jerusalem in England, *Reports by the Joint War Committee and the Joint War Finance Committee.*

25. Light, "British Military Nurses"; Cullen, "War Work on the Home Front."

26. MacCarran, Schreibman, and Barget, "Map of Irish War Hospital Supply Depots and Sub-Depots."

27. Misattributions of place names occurred when villages or towns of the same name also existed outside Ireland or were inconsistently transliterated from Irish.

28. Barget and Schreibman, Zoomable Map of IWHSO Managers in Connacht."

29. Barget and Schreibman, "Case Study 1."

30. Crawford Wright, "Letter from Mabel C. Wright to Lady Clonbrock, 4 April 1916"; Dillon, "Letter from Lady Clonbrock to Mrs Budson, 19 April 1916." Also cf. the relevant blog post by the Letters 1916–1923 team, "Augusta Caroline Dillon Clonbrock."

31. Barget and Schreibman, "Case Study 1."

32. Cf. fully searchable spreadsheet with notes on family backgrounds and social status of the women: Barget and Schreibman, "Case Study 1."

33. Eyre, "Letter from J. Eyre to Lady Clonbrock on Collection of Moss for Surgical Dressings, 20 April 1916."

34. E.g. Maeterlinck, "Letter from M. Albert Maeterlinck, Belgian Red Cross, to John H. Billinge, Hon. Secretary of the Belgian Funds Committee, 24 September 1918"; Billinge, "Copy of a Letter from John H. Billinge to Eleanor Dallas Pratt, 26 April 1918."

35. Various correspondents, "PP/AIR 2464."

36. The collection history is partly described in the Kerry Library finding aids.

37. Barget and Schreibman, "Case Study 2," 2.

38. Joy, *The IRA in Kerry*; Horgan, *Dying for the Cause*.

39. Barget and Schreibman, "Case Study 2."

40. Barget and Schreibman, "Case Study 2," 2.

41. A detailed count of letters sent and received by each person is included in Barget and Schreibman, "Case Study 1."

42. Letters 1916–1923 team, "'A Mháthair Dhílis'—Ellen Daly's Correspondence with Her Children."

43. Daly, "Letter from Charlie Daly to Kate Allman, 30 October 1922," 6.

44. Barget, "Words in Gendered Topics."

45. Letters 1916–1923 team, "Marie Martin."

46. May refer to events at the Marconi Wireless Station in Ballybunion, see "Sphagnum Moss as a Surgical Dressing."

47. This similarity between men's and women's letters is evident in a comparison of the most common words used by both genders or by one gender only (Barget, "Words in Gendered Topics"). The words more distinctly associated with women's topics were verbs of movement or socializing ["coming," "going," "seeing (somebody)"]. Also, the words "love" and "sympathy" are mostly associated with women's letters as there are many letters of shared grief and consolation

exchanged after Charlie's death. Among the words specific to men's correspondence were "lads," "camp," "death," "thing"/"things," "want," "received," and "remember," which are indicative of the imprisonment during which many of Charlie's own letters were written.

48. Cf. Daly, "Letter from Charlie Daly to Kate Allman, 30 October 1922."

49. Letters 1916–1923 team, "Women in the Daly Collection."

50. There was a high level of "'patriarchal oppression of women' in the socially conservative Free State" which prompted many politically active women, especially those who had engaged in antitreaty circles, to emigrate to the United States. See Aiken, "'Sinn Féin Permits . . . in the Heels of Their Shoes,'" 116. Of the women who were politically influential within the young Irish Republic, a considerable number were related to men in politics. See White, "One Hundred Years of Dáil Éireann 1918–2018," 420–21.

51. Finding things of value by accident is a concept that goes back to English author Horace Walpole and is commonly termed "serendipity." See Quan-Haase, "Digital Humanities." Archaeology as metaphor in distant reading is inspired by the "archeology of knowledge" (*archéologie du savoir*) concept developed by Michel Foucault (Foucault and Rueff, "'Introduction' à *L'Archéologie du savoir*"; Erb, Ganahl, and Kilian, "Distant Reading and Discourse Analysis."

Works Cited

Aiken, Síobhra. "'Sinn Féin Permits . . . in the Heels of Their Shoes': Cumann Na MBan Emigrants and Transatlantic Revolutionary Exchange." *Irish Historical Studies* 44, no. 165 (May 2020): 106–30. https://doi.org/10.1017/ihs.2020.8.

Bakharia, Aneesha. "Topic Modeling with Scikit Learn." *Medium*, December 19, 2017. https://medium.com/mlreview/topic-modeling-with-scikit-learn-e80d33668730.

Barget, Monika. "Doing Digital History with Python III: Topic Modelling with Gensim, spaCy, NTLK, and SciKit Learn." *Digital Humanities Lab* (blog), January 15, 2021. https://dhlab.hypotheses.org/1693.

Barget, Monika. "Edges in the Charlie Daly Network." FeministDH (GitHub). 2020. https://github.com/MonikaBarget/FeministDH.

Barget, Monika. FeministDH (Github Repository). JavaScript; Python; 2020. https://github.com/MonikaBarget/FeministDH.

Barget, Monika. "Nodes in the Charlie Daly Network." FeministDH (GitHub). 2020. https://github.com/MonikaBarget/FeministDH. 2020.

Barget, Monika. "Topic Model of Letters 1916–1923 Data Dump Exported in 2019." FeministDH (Github). 2020. https://monikabarget.github.io/FeministDH/TopicModel2019.html.

Barget, Monika. "Words in Gendered Topics." FeministDH (GitHub). 2020. https://github.com/MonikaBarget/FeministDH. 2020d.

Barget, Monika, and Susan Schreibman. "Case Study 1: The Irish War Hospital Supply Organisation (IWHSO), 1915–1919." FeministDH (Github). 2020. https://monikabarget.github.io/FeministDH/casestudy1.html.

Barget, Monika, and Susan Schreibman. "Case Study 2: Female Correspondents in the Charlie Daly Collection from County Kerry, 1922–1923." FeministDH (Github). 2020. https://monikabarget.github.io/FeministDH/casestudy2 .html.

Barget, Monika, and Susan Schreibman. "Zoomable Map of IWHSO Managers in Connacht." FeministDH (Github). 2020. https://monikabarget.github.io/ FeministDH/IWHSOConnacht_interactive.html#5/45.821/2.247.

Billinge, John H. "Copy of a Letter from John H. Billinge to Eleanor Dallas Pratt, 26 April 1918." Explore Letters 1916–1923. http://letters1916.maynooth university.ie/item/5966.

Bleier, Roman. "Text Analysis of the 1916 Letters: Text Mining in Private Correspondence of Letters Related to the 1916 Easter Rising." 1916 Letter Analysis. January 2015. https://1916letteranalysis.wordpress.com.

Boot, Peter. "Franco Moretti: Distant Reading." *Textualscholarship*, no. 1 (January 9, 2014). https://www.textualscholarship.nl/?p=13965.

Clarke, Emma, and Letters 1916–1923 team. "Love Letters 1916–1923." Letters 1916–1923. 2018. http://letters1916.maynoothuniversity.ie/wp-post/love -letters-1916-1923.

Crawford Wright, Mabel. "Letter from Mabel C. Wright to Lady Clonbrock, 4 April 1916." Explore Letters of 1916. http://letters1916.maynoothuniversity .ie/explore/letters/70.

Cullen, Clara. "Sphagnum Moss to the Rescue." *UCD Library Cultural Heritage Collections* (blog). June 28, 2018. https://ucdculturalheritagecollections .com/2018/06/28/sphagnum-moss-to-the-rescue/.

Cullen, Clara. "War Work on the Home Front: The Central Sphagnum Depot for Ireland at the Royal College of Science for Ireland, 1915–1919." In *Medicine, Health and Irish Experiences of Conflict, 1914–45*, edited by David Durnin and Ian Miller, 155–70. Manchester: Manchester University Press, 2017.

Daly, Charlie. "Letter from Charlie Daly to Kate Allman, 30 October 1922." Letters 1916–1923. http://letters1916.maynoothuniversity.ie/item/5222.

Department of the Director-General of Voluntary Organisations. *Army: Report on the National Scheme of Coordination of Voluntary Effort Resulting from the Formation of the Department of the Director-General of Voluntary Organisations.* London: State Office, 1919.

D'Ignazio, Catherine, and Lauren Klein. "2. Collect, Analyze, Imagine, Teach." In *Data Feminism*, March 16, 2020. https://data-feminism.mitpress.mit.edu/ pub/ei7cogfn/release/2.

Dillon, Augusta (Lady Clonbrock). "Letter from Lady Clonbrock to Mrs Budson, 19 April 1916." Explore Letters of 1916. http://letters1916.maynoothuniversity .ie/explore/letters/79.

Drouin, Jeffrey. "Close- and Distant-Reading Modernism: Network Analysis, Text Mining, and Teaching the *Little Review*." *Journal of Modern Periodical Studies* 5, no. 1 (2014): 110–35. https://doi.org/10.5325/jmodeperistud.5.1.0110.

Duffin, Olive. "Letter from Olive Duffin to Her Mother, Maria Duffin, January 1916." Letters 1916–1923. http://letters1916.maynoothuniversity.ie/item/2632.

Erb, Maurice, Simon Ganahl, and Patrick Kilian. "Distant Reading and Discourse Analysis." *Le Foucaldien* 2, no. 1 (2016). https://foucaldien.net/collections/special/distant-reading-and-discourse-analysis/.

Eyre, J. "Letter from J. Eyre to Lady Clonbrock on Collection of Moss for Surgical Dressings, 20 April 1916." Explore Letters 1916–1923. http://letters1916.maynoothuniversity.ie/item/1412.

Foucault, Michel, and Martin Rueff. "'Introduction' à *L'Archéologie du savoir*." *Les Etudes philosophiques* 153, no. 3 (2015): 327–52.

Horgan, Tim. *Dying for the Cause: Kerry's Republican Dead*. Cork: Mercier Press, 2015.

Irish War Hospital Supply Organisation. *First Annual Report of the Sphagnum Department of the Irish War Hospital Supply Organisation (Royal College of Science Sub-Depot), Acting as the Central Sphagnum Depot for Ireland, Registered under the Director-General of Voluntary Organisations and Joint B.R.C.S. and St. John Stores Department, 83 Pall Mall, London*. Dublin: Alexander Thom, 1916.

Irish War Hospital Supply Organisation. *Third Annual Report of the Sphagnum Department of the Irish War Hospital Supply Organisation*. Dublin: Alexander Thom, 1919.

Jänicke, S., G. Franzini, M. F. Cheema, and G. Scheuermann. "On Close and Distant Reading in Digital Humanities: A Survey and Future Challenges." *Eurographics Conference on Visualization (EuroVis) State of the Art Report*, edited by R. Borgo, F. Ganovelli, and I. Viola (2015): 21.

Jockers, Matthew L. *Macroanalysis: Digital Methods and Literary History*. Urbana: University of Illinois Press, 2013.

Joint War Committee of the British Red Cross Society and the Order of St. John of Jerusalem in England. *Reports by the Joint War Committee and the Joint War Finance Committee of the British Red Cross Society and the Order of St. John of Jerusalem in England on Voluntary Aid Rendered to the Sick and Wounded at Home and Abroad and to British Prisoners of War, 1914–1919: With Appendices*. London: Published by His Majesty's Stationery Office, 1921.

Joint War Committee of the Order of the British Red Cross Society and the Order of Saint John of Jerusalem in England. "PP/AIR 2459: Certificates Awarded to Lily, Letitia, and Naomi Overend." Dublin, 1919. Overend Collection: F. Irish War Hospital Supply Depot. OPW-Maynooth University Archive and Research Centre at Castletown.

Joy, Sinéad. *The IRA in Kerry, 1916–1921*. London: Collins, 2005.

Letters 1916–1923 team. "Augusta Caroline Dillon Clonbrock, Lady Clonbrock." Letters 1916–1923. 2018. http://letters1916.maynoothuniversity.ie/wp-post/augusta-caroline-dillon-clonbrock-lady-clonbrock.

Letters 1916–1923 team. "Marie Martin." Letters 1916–1923. 2018. http://letters1916.maynoothuniversity.ie/wp-post/marie-martin.

Letters 1916–1923 team. "'A Mháthair Dhílis'—Ellen Daly's Correspondence with Her Children." Explore Letters 1916–1923. September 27, 2018. http://

letters1916.maynoothuniversity.ie/wp-post/a-mhathair-dhilis-ellen-dalys
-correspondence-with-her-children.

Letters 1916–1923 team. "Women in the Daly Collection." Explore Letters 1916–
1923. October 25, 2018. http://letters1916.maynoothuniversity.ie/wp-post/
women-daly.

Letters 1916–1923 team. "Women's Suffrage in the Letters 1916–1923 Collection."
Explore Letters 1916–1923. September 27, 2018. http://letters1916.maynooth
university.ie/wp-post/womens-suffrage.

Light, Sue. "British Military Nurses." Scarletfinders. 2013. http://www.scarlet
finders.co.uk/.

Lynn, Kathleen. "Letter from Dr Kathleen Lynn to the Deputy Adjutant General
at Parkgate, 26 May 1916." Letters 1916–1923. http://letters1916.maynooth
university.ie/item/836.

MacCarran, Pádraig, Susan Schreibman, and Monika Barget. "Map of Irish War
Hospital Supply Depots and Sub-Depots." Letters 1916–1923. November 2018.
http://letters1916.maynoothuniversity.ie/learn/wp-content/uploads/2018/11/
supply_depots.html.

Maeterlinck, Albert. "Letter from M. Albert Maeterlinck, Belgian Red Cross,
to John H. Billinge, Hon. Secretary of the Belgian Funds Committee, 24
September 1918." Explore Letters 1916–1923. http://letters1916.maynooth
university.ie/item/5979.

"Marconi Wireless Station." Ballybunion, County, Kerry Ireland. 1916. https://
www.ballybunion.ie/history-and-folklore/marconi-wireless-station-2.html.

Moretti, Franco. *Distant Reading*. London: Verso, 2013.

Quan-Haase, Anabel. "Digital Humanities: The Continuing Role of Serendipity in Historical Research." *ResearchGate* (February 2012). https://doi.org/
10.1145/2132176.2132246.

Ramsay, Stephen. *Reading Machines: Toward an Algorithmic Criticism*. Topics in
the Digital Humanities. Urbana: University of Illinois Press, 2011.

Riegler, Natalie N. "Sphagnum Moss in World War I: The Making of Surgical
Dressings by Volunteers in Toronto, Canada, 1917–1918." *Canadian Bulletin
of Medical History* 6, no. 1 (Spring 1989): 27–43. https://doi.org/10.3138/
cbmh.6.1.27.

Schreibman, Susan, Vinayak Das Gupta, and Neale Rooney. "Notes from the
Transcription Desk: Visualising Public Engagement." *English Studies* 98, no.
5 (2017): 506–25. https://doi.org/10.1080/0013838X.2017.1333754.

"Sphagnum Moss as a Surgical Dressing." *British Medical Journal* 1, no. 2895
(June 24, 1916): 893.

Tatlock, Lynne, Matt Erlin, Douglas Knox, and Stephen Pentecost. "Crossing Over: Gendered Reading Formations at the Muncie Public Library,
1891–1902." *Journal of Cultural Analytics* 1, no. 1 (2018): 31. https://doi.org/
10.22148/16.021.

Various correspondents. "PP/AIR 2464: Bound Volume of Letters Received
by the Irish War Hospital Supply Depot, 40 Merrion Square, Dublin,

from Hospitals in Britain, France and Belgium and the French Red Cross,
in Response to Emergency Supplies Sent by the Depot." Airfield Estate,
Dundrum. Overend Collection: F. Irish War Hospital Supply Depot. OPW-
Maynooth University Archive and Research Centre at Castletown, 1920.
White, Anthony. "One Hundred Years of Dáil Éireann 1918–2018: Elections,
Personalities, and Issues." *Studies: An Irish Quarterly Review* 107, no. 428
(2018): 419–26.

3

Textiles and Technology

Needlework as Data Storage and Feminist Process

JAIME LEE KIRTZ

After the 2016 election, numerous media sources reported that environmental scientists, fearing that the incoming Trump administration would restrict or erase key data, engaged in acts of "guerrilla archiving" in order to preserve US federal climate change data.[1] These potential threats also troubled a group of friends in Washington State, who subsequently formed the Tempestry Project, a collaborative fiber arts project whose members create knitted and crocheted tapestries using climate change datasets. Combining textile arts, data science, and environmental activism, the tapestries visually represent changing temperatures while simultaneously archiving climate change data in material form.[2] These climate tapestries combine the (assumed) feminine gendered space of fiber arts with the tools and methods employed to interpret and store data, considered part of a "masculine culture of technology" and science.[3] Although textile arts and data science may seem an unlikely pair, they share a history of practices and collaborations. In this chapter, I argue that data practices and textile arts are entwined through their shared histories and gendered performances and that understanding their relationship reframes a digital humanities' approach to data, and its own disciplinary history, in a fundamentally feminist way.

Recently, feminist interventions and critiques of data science have received increased attention, and many of these works continue earlier feminist digital humanities projects that involved digitization and storage.[4] Many of these recent works are grounded in the notion that data is never truly "raw" and is instead always framed by its selection and naming as data itself.[5] Sociopolitical and historical inequalities are also present in the traditional classification hierarchies used in the production and evaluation of data, which in turn reinscribes problematic power structures. Consequently, machine learning programs and algorithmic media that use data for training and operational purposes become embedded with inequalities and reproduce biases. There have been numerous calls for scholarship that combats the continuation of social inequalities in digital culture, and I draw from many of the responding works that incorporate feminist approaches emphasizing how the "material, embodied, affective, labor-intensive, and situated character of engagements with computation can operate experientially for users in shared spaces."[6] In particular, I focus on the notion of materiality in discussing data, as "the materiality of technology affords or inhibits the doing of particular gender power relations."[7] Much of the current research into data materiality and feminist praxis has focused on data visualizations, such as Kim Brilliante Knight's "Danger, Jane Roe!" project that uses wearable technology, fashioned into representations of female sex organs, to communicate Twitter (now X) data relating to anti-abortion movements. Bringing together technology and textiles, the project illustrates how "artistic data visualization does not employ clarity or transmissibility as a mode but rather provokes a visceral or emotive response from the viewer, foregrounding subjectivity in contrast to the aims of science."[8] Knight points out and challenges both the ascribed masculinity of science with the normative feminization of sewing and embroidery by referencing "traditional notions of feminine domesticity, while also invoking DIY subversion, messiness, and imperfection."[9] In this chapter, I argue for a similar shift in thinking about data storage through textile arts that expose the gendered inequalities and associations in technologies and their histories while also considering how those same practices can be employed for subversive and alternative means of data storage.

To do so I perform a sociohistorical, technical exploration of data technologies; specifically, I look at the architectural design, the material production processes, and the foundational logic of data storage components like hard drives and circuit boards. I focus on intersections between textile arts and needlework to reveal the ways data-centric media artifacts and technologies evolved out of tools and techniques associated with domestic spheres typically gendered feminine, and those are often produced and assembled by women and people of color. I argue that the obfuscation of these practices often extends and even amplifies social inequalities and oppressive forces through the exclusion of women's work in digital humanities and data science. As such, this chapter takes textile arts, its histories, contexts, and methods, and brings them into conversation with digital humanities by tracing shared histories and parallel practices within often overlooked and (largely) femme and feminized spaces. Thus, I turn to the textiles themselves and consider what textiles, specifically their materiality and situatedness, can add to the conversation about future data storage initiatives through notions of embodiment.

Data and Technological Design

Textiles have long served as a metaphor for computing: Ada Lovelace remarked that "the Analytical Engine weaves algebraical patterns just as the Jacquard-loom weaves flowers and leaves."[10] Woven tapestries share architectural traits and design characteristics with circuit boards: both rely on geometric shapes to form outer boundaries, patterns, and images. Woven textiles use an interlocking grid system that alternates the elevation of the longitudinal yarn (the warp) and the transverse yarn that goes over-and-under the warp (the weft). Similarly, a gridlike pattern of through-holes and signal traces following parallel trajectories form along invisible geometric pathways and matrices of circuit boards.

Material connections between computing and textile arts extend beyond the circuit board to many other forms of data storage media like memory hardware. For example, the Apollo spacecrafts used "core rope memory," which is a form of "information storage that uses wires running through or around magnetic ferrite cores to create binary 'zeros' or 'ones.'"[11] Magnetic-core memory, developed at the same time, consists of a memory plane that uses a series of "tiny donuts made of magnetic material strung on wires into an array" that can be magnetized in binary patterns of zeroes and ones.[12] Both core rope memory and magnetic-core memory employ grid structures of uniformly sized wires that are evenly spaced and intersect perpendicularly, making them nearly identical to even weave fabrics that are used in embroidery.[13] Just as information in the form of cores are woven around wires, thread is woven around the intersections between threads in cross-stitching.[14]

Relying on the architectural and visual similarities, the substitution of textiles for computing in the aforementioned metaphor is also one of the ways in which computing connects to issues of gender. Throughout Western history, textile arts, specifically sewing and needlework, have been intricately connected to and understood through notions of femininity, domesticity, and gender norms.[15] Sewing and other forms of needlework like embroidery have been described as an "essential womanly accomplishment" that acts as "an instrument in the formation of female character."[16] Numerous feminist historians have illustrated how the naturalization of sewing as feminine emerges out its localization in the domestic, its connection to the feminine tasks of childrearing and housework, and its associations with feminine characteristics of love and care. As Rozsika Parker argues, textile arts not only reinscribe feminine norms but also contribute to the construction of gender identity. Gender and technology are co-constitutive: "gender relations can be thought of as materialised in technology, and masculinity and femininity in turn acquire their meaning and character through their enrolment and embeddedness in working machines."[17]

Data and Production Processes

The metaphor of textile arts as computing is important as it has been cited by employers when hiring women workers for technology assembly. One of the most salient examples of how this metaphor is used for gender-based hiring practices is through the employment of Navajo women in semiconductor assembly in the 1960s and 1970s. In 1965 Fairchild Semiconductor Corporation built an assembly plant on a Navajo reservation in Shiprock, New Mexico, that employed hundreds of Navajo women.[18] The various Fairchild corporate materials, such as company's brochures, internal articles, and press releases, often reference the geometric aesthetic and design similarities between circuit boards and Navajo blankets, implying a natural connection between textile arts and computing technologies based on architectural similarities.[19] One brochure even uses photographs of Navajo women weaving directly juxtaposed with images of these women working at the assembly plant on the semiconductors.[20] Visual juxtaposition between photographs of women weaving tapestry and manufacturing technology implies that the architectural structures and the labor practices are analogous.

The Fairchild semiconductor plant is just one example of how technologies like data storage media and data-driven devices can serve as a starting point to uncover hidden labor histories: we know "there is always hidden labor—often performed by women and people of color."[21] Following Sarah Ahmed's critique of screening techniques and Catherine D'Ignazio and Lauren F. Klein's emphasis on making labor visible, I turn to examples like the Fairchild plant brochure to examine the ways gendered and gendering dimensions are not only byproducts of the conflation of electronics assembly and textile arts, but also central motivations for it. Fairchild emphasizes women's bodies in the promotion material, through framing the women as "culture workers who produced circuits as part of the 'reproductive' labor of expressing Navajo culture."[22] The use of female reproductive abilities to describe manufacturing work is a concealment technique that configures structures of oppression as a natural order, drawing from problematic discourses on gender and textile arts and conflating skill, labor, and women's bodies. By naturalizing the connection between gendered bodies and traits that the gendered body is and "has always been not simply material (i.e., natural) but rather a hybrid construction of materiality and discourse."[23] By conflating gendered labor with production, companies like Fairchild have been able to exploit their workers financially, compensating women less than men. As the production of textile arts correlates to electronics assembly, so too the gendered and gendering dimensions of textile arts correlates to manufacturing.

Furthermore, drawing attention to the gender of workers shifts discussion away from the technical knowledge and skills needed to produce complex goods, instead framing women workers' abilities as natural traits rather than learned skills. This is particularly prevalent in contemporary electronics manufacturing, wherein corporations argue that young women are ideal candidates for assembly positions because they possess "desirable attributes as dexterity and docility" as well as "nimble fingers, small hands, [and] proclivity for working on the small scale."[24] Traits, such as dexterity and nimbleness, are in fact social constructions arising from numerous factors such as gender performativities and sociohistorical narratives around textile arts; yet, these traits are perceived as innate and bodily, that is, as natural traits of women. By naturalizing traits of dexterity, specifically natural to gendered bodies, the women's bodies become the "real" skill and material. Because textile arts like embroidery and weaving were perceived as domestic activities, the associated textile art skills are similarly associated with housework. In other words, domestic skills are "transformed into a natural attribute of . . . female physique and personality . . . rather than being recognized as work."[25]

This is also seen in Father Roberto Busa's characterization of punch card as female. As Julianne Nyhan and Melissa Terras point out, DH scholarship has uncovered the contributions of early punch card operators "who transcribed the (pre-edited) texts of Thomas Aquinas and related authors into machine-actionable data using punched card technology."[26] These operators were often women who were either pupils at Busa's keypunch school or operators working at Busa's Literary Data Processing Centre and were hired due to Busa's belief that women were naturally inclined toward punch card operation.[27]

Assumptions of domestic skill as an extension of natural feminine abilities is also rooted in gendered divisions between skilled and unskilled labor formed during the Industrial Revolution, when male laborers leveraged a monopoly over technical skills by excluding women from unions and trades in general.[28] The discursive construct of natural, gendered abilities translated into skills extends "the assumption of women's essential proclivity for delicate busywork" and, consequentially to labeling women's labor as "unskilled."[29]

Characterizing women's work as unskilled has contributed to the erasure and exclusion of women from larger historical narratives in computing, specifically those around data storage and archives. Women were instrumental to the development and assembly of memory planes in the mid-twentieth century at NASA; however, until recently, women have been largely absent from historical computing narratives. These memory types, called LOL memory, were used in the Apollo missions and were essential to the development of modern data storage. NASA engineers named this type of memory as "Little Old Ladies (LOL) memory" due to the assembly workers being predominately women, and this technology is still often referred to as LOL memory today.[30] However, finding information about women's role in LOL development and production proves difficult, and the lack of wider recognition is endemic to digital culture. Recognizing the similarities between textile arts and computing exposes the context in which contemporary data practices emerge, which is to say out of historically problematic inequalities, assumptions, and erasures.

Data Processing and Interpretation Logic

As well as sharing material architectures, gendered labor practices, and invisibility of women workers, the tools for reading or processing data has roots in textile arts history. This is particularly evident in the development of punch cards and their adoption by computing culture. Punch cards—paper tape with a series of punched holes that are read by a machine—were originally developed as a means to program intricate weaving patterns and were employed by Jacques Marie Jacquard in his invention of the first automated weaving machine, the Jacquard loom.[31] The Jacquard loom coordinates a configuration of levers and rods attached to threads and weaves by using the rods to hook and pull specific threads through the warp according to a pattern fed through the machine via a series of punched cards. The configuration of holes punched on each card creates a series of instructions that produce a patterned textile. In other words, the set of punched cards "program" the loom.[32] In this way, weaving with a Jacquard loom bears similarities to computing, as both rely on data input to govern operations.[33] In fact, the Jacquard loom and its use of punch cards served as inspiration for later computing technology—not just for instructional purposes but as a means of data storage and processing because it provided a material solution to the automatic storage and execution of calculations that confronted Charles Babbage when creating his Difference Engine. Babbage realized the potential of the Jacquard machine to store calculations and "initiate new operations during the process, with the results of ongoing calculations feeding back into the machine," which led to the creation of the Analytical Engine, generally thought of as the first general-purpose computer design.[34]

Despite the impact of the Jacquard loom on the development of Babbage's Analytical Engine, histories of modern computational methods often erased the technical genealogy. In the late 1800s inventor Herman Hollerith developed a punch card system for data processing partially based on Babbage's design: each card recorded series of holes positioned to represent data (i.e., a code). Once punched, cards were fed into a machine that combined and tabulated results.[35] While Hollerith neglected to cite Jacquard loom technology in his patent, historians speculate that Hollerith was likely inspired by the use of punch cards in the Jacquard loom as well as by Babbage's design.[36] Hollerith's punch card data processing patent extends the technology into new areas. For example, in 1890, Hollerith's punch card data processing system is used to tabulate census data. Other early use cases include tracking inventories and medical records during World War I, locating railroad cargo, tracking library books, and accounting in payroll departments.[37] Hollerith's punch card system continued to be developed by engineers at his company (IBM), and punch cards quickly became a "symbol of information machines" and up until the mid-1970s many computer programmers used punch cards as the main technology for storing code.[38] However, this history often excludes women's role in the development and employment of punch cards for information processing, similar to the erasure of women in Father Busa's *Index Thomisticus* project.[39]

Data Storage and Material Meaning

Whereas the feminine tradition of making found in textile arts is expressly material, the masculinization of technology and technical skills depends on metaphors of immateriality. In sewing, patterns operationalize process in paper form; fabric stores supply raw materials; individuals work on and make clothing by turning raw materials into tangible objects following a prescribed pattern. In contrast, the cloud is marketed as a virtual storage facility that presents its metaphorical meaning as reality and in doing so "renders the physical, infrastructural realities of remote data storage into a palatable abstraction for those who are using it, consciously or not."[40] The metaphor relies on similarities between natural clouds and cloud databases, namely that cloud databases are offsite, opaque, and of vast capabilities, and that clouds are ephemeral entities, without fully solidified shapes, and open to many interpretations or meanings. However, the cloud actually consists of a network of various technologies, cables, and protocols and involves massive server farms and data storage devices.[41] These devices invoke materiality not just at the level of the technological artifact but at the level of data itself. For example, common computer storage occurs on hard drive disks (HDD), wherein data is written onto and read from spinning magnetic disks much like CDs and records. HDDs write by aligning the field charge of the disks' magnets and each alignment or "state" represents a unit of information, for example, data.[42] Solid state drives (SSD) are increasingly popular form of computer storage that do not write data through changing magnetic fields as HDDs do, but instead affect the charge of individual cells within series of logic gates, and thus at a subatomic level create material changes by moving electrons to create either positive or negatively charged cells. Thus, data is both metaphorical and materially written onto and within storage technologies and this reveals the deeply material and physical nature of data storage.

Feminist projects like the Tempestry Project challenge perceptions of data as immaterial through storage technologies by making the material aspects of data visible. Tempestry Project participants produce tactile objects that translate and store data in visible and interactive ways, drawing attention to the agency of material itself. Tapestries consist of a series of colored line, with each line of the textiles represents "a year's temperature range in one location through 365 knitted, crocheted, or woven rows of yarn, each color-coded to a standard spectrum of 32 yarn colors, each color representing a 5-degree temperature range, from a cold black to a hot red."[43] The tempestries store and visualize data and provide a technological artifact and representational system, and the textiles provide an example of data storage media that "combines modern scientific record-keeping and various cultures' historic storytelling through needlework textiles."[44] The tapestries function similarly to HDDs and SSDs by representing information through the arrangement and alignment of yarn. However, they differ in what is made visible and accessible to users and audiences.

A textile can be seen both at the level of a whole, where an image or pattern emerges, and at the level of discrete units, that is, individual stitches. It is through these knots, loops, and holes in the fabric or textile, which are visible to the human eye, that stitches—whether knitted, purled, or embroidered—reveal their own creation process. For example, the distance between individual knit stitches indicates the amount of tension and the knitter's casting methods. Thus, each stitch encodes information about how it is made and the work that goes into making it. The multilevelness of textiles is important as it is what allows us to understand the who, what, and how of its creation process, becoming "answerable for what we learn how to see."[45] Examining the different levels of the textile places the data in situational context and provides a means to see important production aspects.

Representations of climate change and temperature are often communicated to the public through graphs or digital data visualizations, which can feel abstract or too scientific. Tempestries are tactile objects that are designed to be interpreted by physical touch as well as sight, which personalizes and embodies the abstract representation of climate numbers and therefore draws on affect and emotion to convey urgency. Recently, the Tempestry Project collaborated with the US National Parks to produce a series of tempestries that compared a national park's temperature range from the year 2016 to the same park's temperature range a hundred years earlier in 1916 (or the earliest available data).[46] These tempestries were then placed throughout the corresponding parks for visitors to touch and photograph.[47] The physical interaction with the tempestries in the locations that they represent challenges the stereotypical black boxing of data and the divorcing of data from context. The tempestries have been deliberately placed and made hypervisible, thus breaking typical conduct for nonnatural objects in national parks and bring the climate change data into contact with its subject matter and material.

The 2005 Knitting Map is another example of a project that is environmental-centric and combines knitting and data practices; it also provides an example of feminist objectivity and situated knowledge in practice. The project took place over the course of a year with thousands of older, working-class Irish women collaborating to create one large textile based on city-specific data.[48] Two types of data were given to the women to be interpreted through the knitting process in real time: weather data from a local Cork station determined yarn color while traffic busyness captured on CCTV cameras located around the city of Cork determined the complexity and type of knitting stitches used.[49] Thus, as data came in, the knitters reacted and changed their knitting practices in response to the concurrent data. The processes of interpreting the data through stitch type and color means that the knitters "reworked the actual digital information about busyness being sent up to them from the city, and they did so by integrating this data with their hands (their digits) in processes of communal hand-knitting."[50] In this sense, the female knitters came to determine what and how data, and by extension knowledge about the city, was communicated through their interpretation and the material data storage object, that is, the knitted textile.

As both uniquely feminine representations of data and compostable, onsite storage technologies, the examples of the knitting map textile and the tempestries call "into question the very notion of an objective and efficient transmission of information" and subvert traditional channels of scientific information distribution and storage.[51] In both of these examples, the knitter is placed in the position of determining what counts as data or information, how it is interpreted and stored, and what possible meanings or knowledge are produced by data. As such, the knitters engage in a type of feminist objectivity, making knowledge claims from their own situated positionality and connected to others through the conjoining of individual contributions. Furthermore, the actual material object—the finished textile—offers information about the process of knowledge production through the concurrently visibility of the whole textile and the discrete stitches. Through the combination of this material duality and what it reveals about the knowledge making/knitting process with the knitters' role in selecting, interpreting, and materializing data, the Knitting Map and the Tempestry Project exemplify approaches to data that are contextually located, community-oriented, and connected to the people involved, the materials used, and even the physical spaces in which these projects occur.

Feminist Data Futures

From the Jacquard loom and its role in early data processing to employment of female workers in semiconductor plants and NASA, there is a tradition of feminist data practice that has a physical genealogy in computational culture. We can learn from those histories and draw on them to remake digital tools in the service of new forms of knowledge production and data practices—ones that draw on embodiment, affect, and community to remake new modes of production, processing, and storage of information. To do so, we need to build on feminist practices of interrogating complicated histories and gendered erasures and to ground data in the personal and embodied. Examining historical feminist data practices reveals the shared narratives, objects, and labor of knitting and data technologies and together, textiles and data technologies provide a link between the past, present, and future, bringing histories, current data tools, and speculative practices into conversation with one another.

What the relationship between data technologies and textile arts shows is that data embodiment involves both making data physical and tactile *and* situating data historically, culturally, and communally. Through making data tactile and engaging with multiple senses, audiences or viewers respond and interpret the data on a visceral, personal level. The Tempestry

Project transforms abstract climate change data into "into matters of care is a way of relating to them, of inevitably becoming affected by them, and of modifying their potential to affect others."[52] Furthermore, co-participant creation can create meaningful engagement with data visualizations and the storage itself, as seen in the Tempestry Project, wherein knitters select temperature data on dates meaningful to them. It is this element of meaningful participant interaction with data visualization, processing, and storage technologies through materiality that has the potential to shape future data practices and to affect people's connection to data and consequently topics that the data represents.

The affective and emotional potentials of data go beyond the physical aspect of materiality. Alison Adam argues that artificial intelligence robots may be physically situated, but are not situated culturally; therefore, "their type of embodiment leaves out feminine forms of embodiment such as looking after and caring for other bodies."[53] Knitting for practical purposes and as a means of "care" has often been connected to women-centric communities, from mid-century knitting "stitch and bitch" clubs to "feminist knitting as a tool for community-building and ally-dentification" in recent political protests, such as the Pussyhat Project.[54] The connections among textile arts, care, and community has a long history; for example during the Renaissance, a division between art and craft resulted in a hierarchy emerged that attributed value to art, which was created predominantly by men "in the public sphere, for money," whereas craft, for example, needlework and textile arts, was produced in the domestic sphere for "love" or care-based functionality.[55]

Despite the devaluation of care in labor histories, doing care is a key intervention in feminist science and technology studies and technofeminism. Feminist scholars often describe care as involving the repair and maintenance of technologies, the everyday labors, the consideration of other things including nonhumans, and the attention to marginalization, erasure, and forms of power in technology and science.[56] Many of these dimensions resonate with the historical and contemporary feminist data practices discussed in this chapter and support the notion that caring is critical to embodiment. For example, in the Knitting Map project, the physicality of knitting contributes to embodiment, but it is the cultural situatedness and the feminine modes—the aspects of care, emotional connection, maternal histories, localization, and collective activity—involved in knitting that make it an embodied practice. Because of the project's embodiment of knitting, the body cannot be discursively erased in the same way it is in modern electronics assembly and data storage technologies. As such the visibility of bodies and embodiment of the project sought to "make such a gesture using feminine and female labour aspired to rework the relationship between femininity and power" in a specific sociocultural context.[57]

In this chapter, I turn to historical illustrations of gendered data technologies and their deep connection to textile arts because these examples provide important context for contemporary data tools. These historical case studies also orient my own research, helping to direct me to current DH projects that incorporate data and needlework. Understanding the role of textile arts and gender in the history of computing and data technologies provides key information about how different technologies and data practices were developed, what is excluded or erased from continuous and current technologies, and ultimately how power works through these technologies. Furthermore, the historical and contemporary case studies vitally bring attention to both the materiality of data storage and processing technologies and situated cultural practices, thereby articulating embodiment through traditions of feminist data practices. Focusing on embodiment challenges the immaterial conceptions of data storage, brings attention to the historical and contemporary gendered dimensions of technology, and creates opportunities for audiences and creators to experience data in tactile and affective ways. It is these specific qualities and attributes of embodiment that reflect a kind of feminist DH praxis by speaking to feminist values of care, community, and affect. The relationship between textiles and data technologies points to ways in which we can develop future data technologies and methods that remake data as embodied and contribute to the feminist DH project.

Notes

1. Mortillaro, "U of T Heads 'Guerrilla Archiving Event' to Preserve Climate Data Ahead of Trump Presidency."

2. Onion, "The Quilters and Knitters Who Are Mapping Climate Change."

3. Wajcman, *Feminism Confronts Technology*, 21.

4. For examples of earlier work see: Martha Nell Smith ("Dickinson Electronic Archives," MONK), Susan Brown, Patricia Clements, and Isobel Grundy (the Orlando Project), Alison Booth ("Collective Biographies of Women"), Lorraine Janzen Kooistra ("Yellow Nineties 2.0"). For recent work see also: Catherine D'Ignazio and Lauren F. Klein (*Data Feminism*), Jacqueline Wernimont and Elizabeth Losh (*Bodies of Information: Feminist Debates in Digital Humanities*), Tara McPherson (*Feminist in a Software Lab*), Wendy Hui Kyong Chun (*Discriminating Data*), Safiya Noble (*Algorithms of Oppression*), Ruha Benjamin (*Race after Technology*), Simone Browne (*Dark Matters: On the Surveillance of Blackness*), Virginia Eubanks (*Automating Inequalities*), Jennifer Gabrys (*Program Earth*), Kate Crawford (*Atlas of AI*), Miriam Posner, Rena Bivens.

5. Gitelman, *"Raw Data" Is an Oxymoron.*

6. Wernimont and Losh, "Wear and Care," 98.

7. Wajcman, "Feminist Theories of Technology," 150.

8. Knight, "'Danger, Jane Roe!'" 7.

9. Knight, "'Danger, Jane Roe!'" 9.

10. Wong, Westfahl, and Chan, eds., *World Weavers*, 219.

11. Rosner et al., "Making Core Memory."

12. "Magnetic Core Memory."

13. Even weave refer to fabrics where the warp (vertical) and weft (horizontal) threads are the same size, i.e., even, and thus create a square grid surface upon which embroidery threads are then stitched ("Even Weave").

14. Cross-stitch is a technique which consists of "two slanting stitches that cross each other in the center" (Leslie, *Needlework through History*, 54). The stitch stretches diagonally across the +-shaped intersections of the warp and weft, thereby forming an X shape.

15. There are instances throughout history where textiles have been associated with masculine-coded jobs, such as sailors, tailors, and religious leaders ("men of the cloth"). However, I refer here to the way it has been connected to the concept of gender itself.

16. Scanlon, *Inarticulate Longings*; Mitchell, "A Stitch in Time?" 186.

17. Wajcman, "Feminist Theories of Technology," 149.

18. Nakamura, "Indigenous Circuits."

19. Shiprock Dedication Commemorative Brochure.

20. Shiprock Dedication Commemorative Brochure.

21. D'Ignazio and Klein, *Data Feminism*, 185.

22. Nakamura, "Indigenous Circuits," 921. Working in the Shiprock assembly plants exposed workers to highly toxic materials. Scientists found correlations between birth defects and female assembly workers, thus effecting the workers' ability to reproduce (Precarity Lab, *Technoprecarious*).

23. Balsamo, *Technologies of the Gendered Body*, 12.

24. Chan, Selden, and Ngai, Dying for an iPhone; Vágnerová, "'Nimble Fingers' in Electronic Music," 251.

25. Federici, *Revolution at Point Zero*, 16.

26. Nyhan and Terras, "Uncovering 'Hidden' Contributions to the History of Digital Humanities," 3.

27. Nyhan and Terras, ""Uncovering 'Hidden' Contributions to the History of Digital Humanities."

28. Wajcman, *Feminism Confronts Technology*.

29. Vágnerová, 'Nimble Fingers' in Electronic Music," 254.

30. Rosner et al., "Making Core Memory."

31. Kuchera, "The Weavers and Their Information Webs."

32. Monteiro, *The Fabric of Interface*.

33. Wong, Westfahl, and Chan, eds., *World Weavers*, 219.

34. Monteiro, *The Fabric of Interface,* 28.

35. Pugh, *Building IBM*.

36. Lubar, "'Do Not Fold, Spindle or Mutilate'"; Pugh, *Building IBM*.

37. Lubar, "'Do Not Fold, Spindle or Mutilate.'"

38. Lubar, "'Do Not Fold, Spindle or Mutilate,'" 46.

39. Nyhan and Terras, "Uncovering 'Hidden' Contributions to the History of Digital Humanities," 313.

40. Holt and Vonderau, "Where the Internet Lives," 172.

41. Hu, *A Prehistory of the Cloud*.

42. Kirschenbaum, *Mechanisms*.

43. Wajda, "Weather Wisdom."

44. Wajda, "Weather Wisdom."

45. Haraway, "Situated Knowledges," 583.

46. Zambello, "Crafters Work to Create the National Park Tempestry Project"; "National Parks Tempestry Project."

47. Holson, "Knitters Chronicle Climate Change One Stitch at a Time."

48. Gilson and Moffat, eds., *Textiles, Community, and Controversy*.

49. Gilson and Moffat, eds., *Textiles, Community, and Controversy*; Gilson, "Navigation, Nuance, and Half/Angel's Knitting Map"; Turney, "Stitched Up?"

50. Gilson, "Navigation, Nuance, and Half/Angel's Knitting Map, "5.

51. Knight, "'Danger, Jane Roe!'" 7.

52. De La Bellacasa, "Matters of Care in Technoscience," 99.

53. Adam, *Artificial Knowing*; Suchman, "Feminist STS and the Sciences of the Artificial."

54. Kuchera, "The Weavers and Their Information Webs."

55. Parker, *The Subversive Stitch*, 5.

56. De La Bellacasa, "Matters of Care in Technoscience"; Haraway, *Simians, Cyborgs, and Women*; Fisher and Tronto, "Toward a Feminist Theory of Caring."

57. Gilson, "Navigation, Nuance, and Half/Angel's Knitting Map," 5.

Works Cited

Adam, Alison. *Artificial Knowing: Gender and the Thinking Machine*. London: Routledge, 1998. https://doi.org/10.4324/9780203005057.

Balsamo, Anne Marie. *Technologies of the Gendered Body: Reading Cyborg Women*. Durham, NC: Duke University Press, 1996.

Chan, Jenny, Mark Selden, and Pun Ngai. *Dying for an iPhone: Apple, Foxconn, and the Lives of China's Workers*. Chicago: Haymarket Books, 2020.

De La Bellacasa, Maria Puig. "Matters of Care in Technoscience: Assembling Neglected Things." *Social Studies of Science* 41, no. 1 (February 2011): 85–106. https://doi.org/10.1177/0306312710380301.

D'Ignazio, Catherine, and Lauren F. Klein. *Data Feminism*. Cambridge, MA: MIT Press, 2020.

"Even Weave." Textile Research Centre. April 24, 2017. https://trc-leiden.nl/trc-needles/materials/woven-and-interlocking-materials/even-weave.

Federici, Silvia. *Revolution at Point Zero: Housework, Reproduction, and Feminist Struggle*. Oakland, CA: PM Press; Brooklyn, NY: Common Notions; Brooklyn, NY: Autonomedia, 2012.

Fisher, Bernice, and Joan Tronto. "Toward a Feminist Theory of Caring." In *Circles of Care: Work and Identity in Women's Lives*, edited by Emily K. Abel and Margaret K. Nelson, 29–42. SUNY Series on Women and Work. Albany: State University of New York Press, 1990.

Gilson, Jools. "Navigation, Nuance, and Half/Angel's Knitting Map: A Series of Navigational Directions." *Textiles, Community and Controversy: The Knitting Map*, edited by Jools Gilson and Nicola Moffat. London: Bloomsbury Publishing, 2019.

Gilson, Jools, and Nicola Moffat, eds. *Textiles, Community, and Controversy: The Knitting Map*. Ebook. Bloomsbury Publishing, 2019.

Gitelman, Lisa. *"Raw Data" Is an Oxymoron*. Cambridge, MA: MIT Press, 2013.

Haraway, Donna. *Simians, Cyborgs, and Women: The Reinvention of Nature*. New York: Routledge, 1991.

Haraway, Donna. "Situated Knowledges: The Science Question in Feminism and the Privilege of Partial Perspective." *Feminist Studies* 14, no. 3 (1988): 575–99.

Holson, Laura. "Knitters Chronicle Climate Change One Stitch at a Time." *New York Times*, February 22, 2020. advance-lexis-com.proxy.lib.sfu.ca/api/document?collection=news&id=urn:contentItem:5Y8C-9GT1-DXY4-X0JM-00000-00&context=1516831.

Holt, Jennifer, and Patrick Vonderau. "Where the Internet Lives: Data Centers as Cloud Infrastructure." In *Signal Traffic: Critical Studies of Media Infrastructures*, edited by Lisa Parks and Nicole Starosielski, 71–92. Urbana: University of Illinois Press, 2015.

Hu, Tung-Hui. *A Prehistory of the Cloud*. Cambridge, MA: MIT Press, 2015.

"The IBM Punched Card." IBM Corporation, March 7, 2012. http://www-03.ibm.com/ibm/history/ibm100/us/en/icons/punchcard/.

Jennings, Stephanie C. "The Horrors of Transcendent Knowledge: A Feminist-Epistemological Approach to Video Games." In *Woke Gaming: Digital Challenges to Oppression and Social Injustice*, edited by Kishonna L. Gray and David J. Leonard, 155–71. Seattle: University of Washington Press, 2018.

Kirschenbaum, Matthew G. *Mechanisms: New Media and the Forensic Imagination*. Cambridge, MA: MIT Press, 2008.

Knight, Kim Brillante. "'Danger, Jane Roe!': Material Data Visualization as Feminist Praxis." In *Bodies of Information: Intersectional Feminism and Digital Humanities*, edited by Elizabeth M. Losh and Jacqueline Wernimont, 3–24. Minneapolis: University of Minnesota Press, 2018.

Kuchera, Susan. "The Weavers and Their Information Webs: Steganography in the Textile Arts." *Ada: A Journal of Gender, New Media, and Technology*, no. 13 (May 2018). https://doi.org/10.5399/uo/ada.

Leslie, Catherine Amoroso. *Needlework through History: An Encyclopedia*. Westport, CT: Greenwood Press, 2007.

Losh, Elizabeth M., and Jacqueline Wernimont, eds. *Bodies of Information: Intersectional Feminism and Digital Humanities.* Minneapolis: University of Minnesota Press, 2018.

Lubar, Steven. "'Do Not Fold, Spindle or Mutilate': A Cultural History of the Punch Card." *Journal of American Culture* 15, no. 4 (December 1992): 43–55. https://doi.org/10.1111/j.1542-734X.1992.1504_43.x.

"Magnetic Core Memory." Computer History Museum, 2011. https://www.computerhistory.org/revolution/memory-storage/8/253.

Mitchell, Rosemary. "A Stitch in Time?: Women, Needlework, and the Making of History in Victorian Britain." *Journal of Victorian Culture* 1, no. 2 (March 1996): 185–202. https://doi.org/10.1080/13555509609505923.

Monteiro, Stephen. *The Fabric of Interface: Mobile Media, Design, and Gender.* Cambridge, MA: MIT Press, 2017.

Mortillaro, Nicole. "U of T Heads 'Guerrilla Archiving Event' to Preserve Climate Data Ahead of Trump Presidency." CBC, December 14, 2016. https://www.cbc.ca/news/technology/university-toronto-guerrilla-archiving-event-trump-climate-change-1.3896167.

Nakamura, Lisa. "Indigenous Circuits: Navajo Women and the Racialization of Early Electronic Manufacture." *American Quarterly* 66, no. 4 (2014): 919–41.

"National Parks Tempestry Project." https://spark.adobe.com/page/SynDUSs9izWdc/.

Nyhan, Julianne, and Melissa Terras. "Uncovering 'Hidden' Contributions to the History of Digital Humanities: The Index Thomisticus' Female Keypunch Operators." *Digital Humanities* 2017 (2017): 313–15.

Onion, Rebecca. "The Quilters and Knitters Who Are Mapping Climate Change." *Slate Magazine*, February 8, 2020. https://slate.com/technology/2020/02/quilts-knitting-cross-stitch-climate-change.html.

Parker, Rozsika. *The Subversive Stitch: Embroidery and the Making of the Feminine.* New ed. London: I. B. Tauris, 2010.

Plant, Sadie. "The Future Looms: Weaving Women and Cybernetics." *Body & Society* 1, no. 3–4 (November 1995): 45–64. https://doi.org/10.1177/1357034X95001003003.

Precarity Lab. *Technoprecarious.* London: Goldsmiths Press, 2020.

Pugh, Emerson W. *Building IBM: Shaping an Industry and Its Technology.* Cambridge, MA: MIT Press, 1995. http://www.vlebooks.com/vleweb/product/openreader?id=none&isbn=9780262281942.

Rosner, Daniela K., Samantha Shorey, Brock R. Craft, and Helen Remick. "Making Core Memory: Design Inquiry into Gendered Legacies of Engineering and Craftwork." *Proceedings of the 2018 CHI Conference on Human Factors in Computing Systems* (April 2018): 1–13. https://doi.org/10.1145/3173574.3174105.

Scanlon, Jennifer. *Inarticulate Longings: The Ladies' Home Journal, Gender, and the Promises of Consumer Culture.* New York: Routledge, 1995.

Shiprock Dedication Commemorative Brochure. Fairchild Semiconductor, September 6, 1969. Computer History Museum, X7847.2017, 102770254. https://

archive.computerhistory.org/resources/access/text/2017/01/102770254-05-01
-acc.pdf.

Suchman, Lucy. "Feminist STS and the Sciences of the Artificial." In *The Handbook of Science and Technology Studies*, edited by Edward J. Hackett, Olga Amsterdamska, Michael Lynch, and Judy Wajcman, 3rd ed., 139–64. Cambridge, MA: MIT Press, 2008.

Turney, Joanne. "Stitched Up?: The Knitting Map in Context." In *Textiles, Community, and Controversy: The Knitting Map*, edited by Jools Gilson and Nicola Moffat. Ebook. Bloomsbury Publishing, 2019.

Vágnerová, Lucie. "'Nimble Fingers' in Electronic Music: Rethinking Sound through Neo-Colonial Labour." *Organised Sound* 22, no. 2 (August 2017): 250–58. https://doi.org/10.1017/S1355771817000152.

Wajcman, Judy. *Feminism Confronts Technology*. College Park: Pennsylvania State University Press, 1991.

Wajcman, Judy. "Feminist Theories of Technology." *Cambridge Journal of Economics* 34, no. 1 (January 2010): 143–52. https://doi.org/10.1093/cje/ben057.

Wajda, Shirley. "Weather Wisdom: Some Thoughts on the Tempestry Project and Kit Craftivism." *Medium*, February 17, 2020. https://medium.com/@shirley wajda/weather-wisdom-some-thoughts-on-the-tempestry-project-and-kit -craftivism-261a78301f35.

Wernimont, Jacqueline, and Elizabeth Losh. "Wear and Care: Feminisms at a Long Maker Table." In *The Routledge Companion to Media Studies and Digital Humanities*, edited by Jentery Sayers, 97–107. New York: Routledge, 2018. https://doi.org/10.4324/9781315730479.

Wong, Kin-yuen, Gary Westfahl, and Amy Kit-sze Chan, eds. *World Weavers: Globalization, Science Fiction, and the Cybernetic Revolution*. Hong Kong: Hong Kong University Press, 2005.

Zambello, Emily. "Crafters Work to Create the National Park Tempestry Project." *National Parks Traveler*, April 3, 2019. https://www.nationalparkstraveler .org/2019/04/crafters-work-create-national-park-tempestry-project.

II

Infrastructures

4

Feminist Infrastructure Building

SUSAN BROWN AND LAURA MANDELL

Our lot is cast with technoscience,
where nothing is so sacred that it cannot
be reengineered and transformed so
as to widen our aperture of freedom,
extending to gender and the human.
—Laboria Cuboniks, "Xenofeminism"

A feminist digital-humanities infrastructure is an infrastructure that resists in some way, shape, or form the bifurcation of humanity into m/f. Catherine D'Ignazio and Lauren Klein offer this task of feminist design—and it applies to everything from designing interfaces and visualizations to designing infrastructures—as the first and most important: "Rethink binaries."[1] First outlining the challenges to thought or critique posed by the tendency of infrastructure toward the naturalization or transparency of infrastructure, this chapter moves from the less to the more visible in pulling out common threads from feminist engagements with infrastructure. Such efforts can be viewed as contributions to "advancing scholarship related to diversity" through what Alan Liu calls a "diversity stack"[2] although we position them as forming a feminist infrastructural ecosystem that helps resist binary or reductive thinking.

But What Is an Infrastructure?

Infrastructure can be characterized as happening invisibly, behind the scenes, for instance to make water flow from a faucet when turned on. As we use them, infrastructures pull our behavior into rivulets of common practice; insofar as cognition is embodied, our bodies absorb knowledge and affect as we turn the dials, which is to say, strike the keys. Infrastructures define affordances, interpellate subjects, make arguments, foster relations and intimacies; and they are themselves in many respects defined both by the subjects who engage with them and their local, institutional, and global conditions of possibility. As Liu notes, infrastructures create "the social-cum-technological milieu that at once enables the fulfillment of human experience and enforces constraints on that experience."[3] But when infrastructures are emerging, as are digital infrastructures, they aren't *yet* infrastructures because they are not operating so smoothly as to fade into the background. Their "smoothness" comes not only from the material technology of the infrastructure, but also from adaptations made by the users of the infrastructures: what once required intellectual effort becomes an unconscious raising of the hand to turn on the faucet, made conscious as a gesture only if the faucet is broken or the water too hot.[4]

Although public infrastructures are large, well organized, and relatively slow-moving, digital infrastructures proliferate quickly around any demand for digital communication and information delivery, which is to say they encompass back-end and front-end information technologies.[5] In the digital context, multiple contenders for the status of infrastructure arise; some become established through institutions or habits, and others die out or transform into something else. Academic infrastructure may be enveloped in feminized notions of service and embodiment, troubling fundamental category work and distinctions that otherwise go uncontested.[6] In an ideal process, users and developers work together through give-and-take to develop an infrastructure that isn't too hard to use habitually—and for which becoming acclimated has enough incentives to make using it worthwhile, anything from gathering status as a super user to accessing a movie or an ebook.

Digital infrastructures have to be worth it to use—worth it partly thanks to their design, but also partly because the incentives were right and the adaptations relatively easy. Marketing as well as other social forces shape user desire. For example, compare the limited incentives to adopt email in the 1980s to those now: some digital forms cannot be submitted without an email address. If a piece of software isn't worth it, if users can get what they want more easily another way or stop desiring it because it's too difficult to access, the digital infrastructure will fall out of use. Infrastructures are nothing apart from use, that is, nothing apart from people.

Although infrastructures are both visible and tangible, their use is predicated on their becoming naturalized and incorporated into actions, diminishing users' ability to discern their influence. Susan Leigh Star points out that infrastructures become "transparent,"[7] not in the sense that they fully disclose themselves, but rather in the sense that a window is transparent for viewing the world. They are transparent because people do not have to think about them when they use them. No one has to know how to lay asphalt in order to drive on a highway, but a person could learn a lot about how to lay asphalt if stuck in traffic for road repair.

What it takes to build and sustain infrastructure, as well as how it works, becomes visible when it breaks.[8] This fact sets up a double-bind for those who want to build equity and/or advocacy into their own systems.[9] An infrastructure embeds point of view, argument, and values in the way it organizes information and the relationships between its parts, in the kinds of knowledge it both presumes and valorizes, and the affordances it offers to users, whether through the back end or through a graphical user interface (GUI). Infrastructure builders make choices that define the agency of their users. Such choices are always a product of technological affordances and constraints, social relationships, historical context, communities of practice, and paradigms.

Digital infrastructures channel their specialized worlds. Ideologically laden, their operations become part of habitus, of everyday life,[10] and, as Liu implies, interwoven with ideology in the fabric of lives. Infrastructures mediate conscious thought formulation about tasks into gestures that are unthought, automatic. An early site design book carried the title *Don't Make Me Think*.[11] Infrastructures replace thinking with the shorthand of an embodied gesture or the familiarity of an established workflow; enabling a filter on a dating or real estate site replaces with one click the need to reaffirm, repeatedly, certain choices.

The goal of media critique is to break such processes open in order to bring to light the premises and assumptions, the norms and values, built into an infrastructure, and then, via that knowledge, to disturb its functioning. Builders of infrastructure concerned with equity benefit from critique insofar as it promotes understanding what kinds of things infrastructures naturalize. But here we find the paradox, the double bind: The power of infrastructures lies not only in *what* they naturalize, but *that* they naturalize. If we were to practice "critical making" by building an infrastructure that refused to replace conscious thought with filters, that refused to obscure the decision-making process in each one of a series of repetitive gestures, people would stop using it. They might even say it was broken. If "Don't Make Me Think" is the mantra of existing infrastructures, how can we offer alternatives that are desirable while thought-provoking?

To think about feminist infrastructure building, we begin with less visible considerations of labor and standards, followed by hardware and software, and finish with interfaces, the most visible aspect of digital infrastructures. In what follows we track research and practice that address features such as obfuscation and simplification in different layers of what is increasingly called the "stack." Feminist infrastructure initiatives, better understood as contributing to an ecosystem rather than a stack, resist or rethink the sexism imbricated in systems.

Critiquing the Stack

Given that infrastructure "has much of the same scale, complexity, and general cultural impact as the idea of 'culture' itself,"[12] we are in the midst of a more general turn toward understanding infrastructure as a broadly constitutive force. Benjamin Bratton's densely theorized and seductive description of a planetary megastructure that overwrites traditional understandings of geopolitical sovereignty employs the metaphor of "The Stack." His complex and evocative model attempts to move beyond binaries[13] and has been adapted by Liu to articulate the powerful notion of a "diversity stack" for Digital Humanities (DH).[14] Yet, although Bratton's notion of geodesign "draws from (and into) its specific planetary situatedness," and he positions "Earth" as the Stack's "schematic foundation. . . . the driving force and form of its logic,"[15] *The Stack* emphasizes the rigidity and stability of the "technological totality."[16] DH may be considered a small component of such a "stack" and as such to reflect its characteristics, for instance in the four layers of the open-source LAMP stack—the Linux operating system, Apache server, MySQL database, and PHP, Perl, and Python code often employed to build websites.[17] The feminist engagements with infrastructure we explore here offer an alternative emphasis on feminist infrastructural contributions as constituting not a stack but an ecosystem situated not only within academia but also in particular contexts, with an accompanying interest in the forms of relationality, resistance, and dynamism that are occluded by Bratton's stress on governance.

Feminisms offer a wide range of generative and critical engagements with infrastructure building for "tracing circuits of power, norms, and agency that are realized in particular modes of relations."[18] Without falling into facile charges of DH as neoliberal, we recognize with Miriam Posner that the technologies we use entail impediments to creating infrastructure that embodies radical critique. Infrastructures impart normative values, "values and ethical principles [that are] inscribe[d] in the inner depths of the built information environment"[19] but, despite their universalizing drive, infrastructures are always already operating within and shaped by particular social, institutional, and national contexts. Infrastructure building on feminist principles thus offers a powerful form of critique while grappling with myriad constraints and determinants.

Labor

Historians of infrastructures such as the railroad and the telegraph point to the pain and duress inflicted upon the laborers forced to build them.[20] For academic institutions currently confronting new technologies, labor causes duress in the absence of supportive institutional infrastructures for DH work; precarious labor is a matter of serious concern in these efforts.[21] We focus here on the labor of building specifically digital infrastructures, which is caught up in this larger concern since such infrastructures, particularly feminist ones that are funded from grants, are often built and maintained by teams partially or fully staffed with precarious labor. As the technological background, infrastructure is "a system of substrates"[22] that is invisible unless it breaks, planting it firmly in the (re)productive economies of housework and carework.[23] Its functioning model is therefore gendered as feminine, along with all the pitfalls that entails: the invisibility of labor and the failure to credit this work as both an intellectual and laborious endeavor. Debates over infrastructure often elide the essential human agents without which no infrastructure can run. The elision of human contributions sustains the illusion of infrastructures as neutral and equally accessible, making the importance of labor-centric initiatives such as the FemTechNet or HASTAC networks hard to perceive as infrastructure.

The gendered association of infrastructure with service[24] has inflected the rise of concerns around care and repair.[25] Infrastructure work is not associated with individual credit; it is unsexy intellectually to the extent that it creates the pipes that other people send stuff along or sustains the conditions for intellectual labor. Like reproductive and domestic work, the invisible repetitive labor of creating and sustaining academic infrastructure falls outside of dominant models of productivity, typically located beyond the funding structures that sustain research. For example, in Europe, major DH infrastructure initiatives like CLARIN and DARIAH have been funded separately from research, whereas infrastructure created by smaller research projects often has great difficulty sustaining itself. This can create challenges when there is a close relationship between infrastructure building and feminist critique. This is not to say that such models cannot contribute to feminist infrastructure efforts. The Humanities Networked Infrastructure (HuNI) was funded as part of a large infrastructure funding campaign in Australia,[26] as is the Linked Infrastructure for Networked Cultural Scholarship (LINCS). Funding models that divorce research from infrastructure, however, work against critical infrastructure development. A refusal to fund research time per se in connection with infrastructure projects reinforces the view that research software is neutral. This in turn perpetuates the status quo, since substantial research is needed to create systems that reflect critique, such as "revising conventional approaches to knowledge systems" in the case of HuNI, or using Linked Open Data to represent cultural complexity, including notions of gender beyond m/f.[27] The invisibility of the intellectual labor invested in infrastructural initiatives, and particularly critical ones, does damage. It artificially separates building from thinking. It perpetuates the myth that technologies are neutral and their construction trivial and makes producing critical infrastructure harder. It also exacerbates the challenge of sustainability by forcing much infrastructure work, perhaps particularly feminist infrastructure that may not align easily with institutions, to rely on temporary and contingent positions, and to be hampered by the continual scramble to find operational funding. These challenges are one facet of the broader problems facing digital networks of care that impact scholars living at the intersections of race, gender, sexuality, and class.[28]

Standards

As is especially observable in digital infrastructures, standards subtend infrastructure insofar as they require widespread implementation. In so doing, they homogenize. Advocates of global DH and critical race theorists advocate resisting such homogenization as oppressive. For example, there is the movement for minimal computing as advocated by many in the Global South or GO::DH, or the "poor theory" of Ackbar Abbas and David Theo Goldberg, whose "commitment to open source input and incessant reformulation entails that it values heterogeneity over homogenization, intensely interactive pluriculture over monoculture, crowdsourcing over hermeticism, with constant recalibration in the face of error, failure, and loss."[29] Yet alternative innovations are often reliant on the heavily male-dominated open-source movement, which is trying to do better via initiatives such as the Open Source Diversity project or Feminist Principles of the Internet.[30] The many efforts to make space for women within tech culture are in a sense engaged in revising the pernicious notion that "man" is the neutral norm of humanity, a ubiquitous example of a false standard long critiqued by feminist theorists including Simone de Beauvoir in *The Second Sex*. As Beauvoir's title indicates, this standard involves subordination that leads to both bias and violence,[31] which must in turn be addressed in a myriad of ways. For instance, Pollicy, a Uganda-based civic technology organization, has initiatives ranging from internet safety guides to an antitrafficking platform, and FemTechNet's Centre for Solutions to Online Violence offers a host of resources. These infrastructural efforts are akin to various forms of women's centers established by second-wave feminists.

A commitment to the critical use of technology within DH can be seen in feminist initiatives to establish, apply, and maintain standards. The Text Encoding Initiative (TEI) has grown through a symbiotic relationship with the "encoded bodies" of the Women Writers Project;[32] the metadata format of the Advanced Research Consortium, inherited from NINES.org, adopted the Resource Description Framework to promote contextualizing, remixing, finding things through terms in current scholarly use, and sharing through a community folksonomy;[33] and the ontology of the Canadian Writing Research Collaboratory represents the intersectionality and contingency of social identities.[34] Data models and standards are infrastructural resources that have pervasive impacts across a wide range of systems and contexts. For instance, Tara McPherson found that data models supported by relational database technologies were crucial in enabling designers and researchers collaboratively to "create scholarship that could not exist in print" through the journal *Vectors*.[35] Likewise, the TEI implementation of the Extensible Markup Language (XML) standard provides a digital model or "theory of the text" that has been applied to the creation of "digital editions, teaching anthologies, research corpora, full-text thematic research collections, digital archives," as well as derivative datasets and presentation modes such as graphs, maps, and network visualizations.[36]

Hardware

Still most opaque in some ways is the most fundamental level of infrastructure, the material layer of hardware that many would equate with infrastructure. There are so many layers of abstraction between the movement of electrons through circuit boards and the operations of a computer that their implications are hard to grasp, but many feminist theorists have resisted facile mappings of either gender or mind/body distinctions onto binary code.[37] Hence, in Donna Haraway's figure of the cyborg, technology is incorporated in the body as infrastructure.[38] Historicizing our relationship to the materiality of computing is key. Lori Emerson promotes "infrastructural thinking" through undertaking media archaeology work from a situated and embodied perspective.[39] Both by working with original machines and looking at industry debates over interfaces, she traces how we have arrived in a time when "users have little or no comprehension of the digital computer as a medium."[40]

Networks are both a powerful metaphor and realities that transmit information or knowledge in the form of power. They enable, but also provide government and corporate entities with the means of surveillance and extraction, as well as of controlling access. Feminist infrastructure, such as the artivism of micha cárdenas discussed below, may require autonomy from or subversion of global networks, and inequality of network access may mean infrastructure must be accessible offline or adaptable to sporadic connectivity, as highlighted by the minimal computing movement. Rather than viewing the net as a hegemonic totality, Emerson argues that understanding the implications of networks on which much DH infrastructure runs means unpacking the messy, collaborative, processual, and contingent histories obscured by "Great Man Stories."[41]

Feminist critical making involving wearable computing elucidates and intervenes in our embodied relationships to digital devices.[42] Kim Brilliante Knight highlights the intersection of accessibility and transparency in the LilyPad Arduino designed for wearable apps: "Leah Buechley, the creator of the LilyPad, describes it as having a soft, colorful, beautiful aesthetic that she hopes will affect the world of engineering applications. As a result, both the LilyPad controller and the stitches used to connect it to other components are often consciously made visible as part of wearable projects."[43] Because LilyPad projects are often fabric- or fashion-based projects, they trouble the boundaries between the gendered arenas of "high" tech as opposed to lowlier "craft" activities oriented toward aesthetics and play; they shift the materiality of computing infrastructure from industrial to domestic contexts.

Nevertheless, computational hardware is a profound factor in infrastructure. Whereas Bratton argues that the stack is not deterministic, McPherson has argued that the very basis of contemporary computer operating systems is founded on a "lenticular" logic in the way that certain things are partitioned off from others as computers store code separately from data.[44] Accordingly, despite her ground-breaking work on the open-access Scalar platform, McPherson says "I know that Scalar is not a deep challenge to the workings of corporate and computational capital."[45] The admission acknowledges the major impediments to imbuing infrastructure with the critical values to which one adheres. The technologies that undergird publishing platforms or virtual research environments impose real constraints on how systems can be built, particularly if they are to meet accessibility requirements, work modularly, and adopt standards—accepted data formats and established technologies.

Software

Much explicitly feminist infrastructural work has involved software in one way or another, perhaps because it is more amenable to intervention than hardware. The set of programs, procedures, and routines that tell a computer what to do, software is most visible to users in playing digital games. Digital artist Mary Flanagan teaches critical game design from a feminist perspective. Not only is she a great maker, as can be seen in her 2009 book *Critical*

Play: Radical Game Design, but she is also critically adept at unearthing the values imparted by digital games.[46] Jane McGonigal, another game designer, melded self-help discourse to gamification in *Superbetter*, an app designed to counter her own struggles with post-concussion syndrome.[47] Zoë Quinn used the Twine platform to create the deceptively simple game *Depression Quest* (2013), which became the target of GamerGate, as an educational tool. Such gaming projects understand software not as an escape, but as an intervention in the material world.

Infrastructure does not emerge in isolation, Lucy Suchman argues. Its profound imbrication with lives and subjectivities, bodies and built worlds, therefore situates it as a prime location for critical intervention along with other forms of knowledge organization. McPherson, a self-described "feminist in a software lab," designed *Vectors* and *Scalar* for difference, to create an intersectional, collaborative space within which scholars and users could "rethink their relationship to the computational and to enter into a complex assemblage of aesthetics, technology, pedagogy, creativity, and new publics."[48] Anne Balsamo draws on the work of Karen Barad to stress the extent to which iterative design and development constitute a situated form of inquiry into the complex and shifting "intra-actions" among subjects and their environments, an inescapably relational process in which the diversity of participants matters.[49] For instance, the software created for an "interactive memorial," digital experiences constructed around the AIDS quilt, includes: (1) an open-source mobile web application called AIDS QUILT TOUCH; (2) a tangible tabletop interactive that enables viewers to SEARCH the database of Quilt images to find a specific image and to BROWSE the archive of Quilt panel images; and (3) a community sourcing application that engages people in analyzing and archiving information about the Quilt.[50]

Collectively, this software counters the official historical narrative about interactions between AIDS "patients" or "victims" and the "hero scientist"[51] with a less homophobic history of intra-actions, debunking the notion "that there are separate individual agencies," in this case, human actors, and replacing it with the idea that the causal agents mitigating the AIDS epidemic "emerge[d] through" relations among all the materialities, power dynamics, individuals, and groups involved.[52] This perspective resists an understanding of software as a stable thing "run" by a separate person, and instead sees agency as more complexly dispersed across a range of human and nonhuman interrelationships: "the digital application was never a singular thing with set boundaries or well-defined edges. It was always, and still is, an unfolding set of possibilities, animated in the intra-actions that include human fingers striking keys, middleware reading machine code, machine code acting on lines of zeros and ones, materials conducting energy in the form of heat, and so on."[53]

Relations and Intimacies

Deb Verhoeven points out that attending to the "acts and technologies of 'connection'" will "move us beyond thinking of connectivity as binary or thinking of infrastructure as a form of mediation" to "address the social or relational aspects of infrastructure." For her, "the restless, transformative, and connective work of infrastructure can be understood as a form of inventiveness and interpretive resourcefulness,"[54] manifested in the HuNI infrastructure that enables people to create networks by defining links between objects across different cultural collections rather than working from a fixed taxonomy or ontology.

In contrast, the Advanced Research Consortium (ARC), led by Laura Mandell and built on information architecture developed by Bethany Nowviskie,[55] *does* require participants to adhere to multiple intersecting taxonomies. However, ARC metadata categories have been created from the ground up as it grew from NINES.org to 18thConnect.org to mesa-medieval.org to modnets.org and studiesinradicalism.org and beyond.[56] Each new organization's digital projects need new metadata categories for discoverability, which are then debated and decided on by all directors of the ARC communities.[57] ARC metadata thus evolves to meet the needs of the larger scholarly community, and its "agile metadata development"[58]—agile like the tortoise—enables changes when exclusions are identified. Although they take apparently contradictory approaches to metadata development, both HuNI and ARC are grounded in the principle that taxonomic infrastructures must emerge from and be responsive to the communities they serve.

Such relations engender intimacies. As Ara Wilson puts it, "Infrastructure is a systematic assemblage of objects, codes, and procedures that, whether it fails or succeeds, is often an embedding environment for intimate life."[59] As lived components of daily lives, infrastructures "mix human and nonhuman agencies" and "are entwined with social relations."[60] Jacqueline Wernimont therefore calls attention to interface as relationship: "[D]igital archives are [not only thresholds to things but] also thresholds between actions. That 'thingness' and those actions are as much an experience of the user as they are of the encoder, programmer, and editor. Finding ways to enable user engagement in production would . . . embody a more radical feminist approach to our understanding of technology as entailing 'interplay between designing and use, or between designer and user' [Rosser 2005, 11]."[61]

The logical extension would be dynamic interfaces in which users could partner more deeply and radically than in the past not only in the contribution of content, which is the main concern in Wernimont's piece, but also in the ongoing reshaping of the infrastructures that in turn shape them.

Interface and Access

Reflecting the profound regard for relationality that runs through intersectional feminist theory, Milena Radzikowska and collaborators articulate six principles for feminist interface design:

1. Challenge existing methods, beliefs, systems, and processes;
2. Focus on an actionable ideal future;
3. Look for what has been made invisible or underrepresented;
4. Consider the micro, meso, and macro;
5. Privilege transparency and accountability; and
6. Expect and welcome being subjected to rigorous critique.[62]

These principles notably stress intention and analysis rather than full instantiation of them, since limitations ranging from resistance in the technological materials[63] to funding constraints work against the full embodiment of such goals within a production-quality interface. In addition, developing new interface languages and affordances based on such critique requires iteration and community participation, from published reviews of digital work to more effective user-designer feedback loops, requires time and attention. However, the recent flowering of feminist design thinking, such as that proposed by Catherine D'Ignazio and Lauren Klein,[64] bodes well for future initiatives.

Although not necessarily engaging directly with the rhetoric of interfaces, much feminist infrastructure work focuses on access to digital content and spaces. One area of broad activity is in content creation that enables access to otherwise unavailable material or perspectives. As cultural analytics become more influential, the provision of well curated and structured datasets becomes increasingly pressing. As many have pointed out, our research is only as good as our data, and much of our data is woefully impoverished, either because it is mute on the subject of gender and other identity categories, or because it is biased by the processes of collection, often of the libraries or archives on which it is based, so as to underrepresent women, racialized, 2SLGBTQIA+, and other marginalized authors or content.[65] By analogy with the library as the so-called "lab" or fundamental infrastructure of the humanities, the production and open dissemination of digital content, no matter how modest, that enables feminist analysis and reuse becomes a component of an ecosystem of feminist infrastructure. As experiments in the conditions of possibility for feminist work in DH, multitudinous projects have been structured to facilitate inquiry into gender and other intersecting social categories. These projects now comprise a vital component of our research infrastructure. But binaries threaten to solidify into essential or biological categories in the field of text-mining, or "cultural analytics."[66]

Making content accessible in ways that offer alternatives to binaries and promote reuse itself requires infrastructure, of course. Many librarians have embraced open-access publication as a form of social justice. The Canadian Writing Research Collaboratory (CWRC) emerged from the Orlando Project as a space in which other projects could create, publish, and share content.[67] CWRC's online tools also aim to eliminate often gendered barriers to participating in DH by reducing up-front costs and the level of technical expertise required. Marii Nyröp's Wax software for producing static exhibition websites[68] emerges from the minimal computing movement, which recognizes that many are disadvantaged because of global inequalities by uneven access to expertise, hardware, and bandwidth. Wax meshes beautifully with a feminist concern for the gendered dynamics of care and repair. Such infrastructures allow disadvantaged groups to mobilize content and simultaneously promote standards and interoperability for reuse and preservation, so that open-access content can have a future.

Open access can in certain contexts pose as much of a problem as copyright, however.[69] Privileging openness can run against the need of some communities for control or privacy, given how their cultural knowledge has been expropriated in the past. Leveraging "Indigenous models of information management," Kimberly Christen says, the Mukurtu content management system "was built from the ground up with Indigenous communities in mind."[70] A central feature of Mukurtu is the ability to restrict access to members of particular communities, and to apply Traditional Knowledge Labels to indicate terms of local access and use, which may for instance be seasonal or gendered. Some libraries are now beginning to incorporate Traditional Knowledge licenses in their cataloging.[71]

The "open" web and many social media platforms in fact provide a virtual playground on which people, mostly men, engage in very real harassment of and violence against women, people of color, queer and trans people, Indigenous people, and other marginalized groups with the effect of making digital spaces less accessible, as in the case of GamerGate.[72] Hence the importance of private spaces within which groups can engage in networking, education, and research. FemTechNet, for instance, has operated both as an open and as a closed (but still welcoming) group using a range of social media platforms and tools,[73] illustrating the extent to which feminist infrastructure can in some cases be defined by a group's relational intentionality and community practices rather than specific technologies.

Physical spaces are also crucial. Many DH centers led by women, along with the emergent feminist maker-space movement,[74] are all about making technological spaces safe, accessible, and welcoming to women. Wernimont and Losh invoke the exemplary "Local Autonomy Networks (Autonets)"— off the corporate internet grid, communicating among members via wearable garments—designed by artist micha cárdenas.[75] cárdenas sought to create these networks of communication as "abolitionist infrastructures for community-based safety"[76] to be used to resist violence against women, 2SLGBTQIA+ people, people of color, and other targeted groups. Although technological limitations led to a shift in focus toward embodied gesture and performance, the project underscores the extent to which technological affordances emerge within or are refused by particular spaces. All of these projects evince an ethics of care like that enacted in the summer of 2020, when the COVID-19 pandemic made it impossible to hold the international Digital Humanities conference as planned in Ottawa. Pivoting to an online conference for more than nine hundred registrants was facilitated by the open, inclusive, and collaboratively produced infrastructure of the Humanities Commons WordPress customization, directed by Kathleen Fitzpatrick and an instance of the infrastructural conditions in which the "generous thinking" Fitzpatrick advocates becomes real.[77]

A Feminist Infrastructural Ecosystem

Verhoeven renames feminist infrastructure "infrapuncture," gesturing toward acupuncture or relieving stresses. She invites us to "think about what a better version of infrastructure could be that could intervene at critical locations." She reminds us that infrastructures are "circuits of action and reaction" that "do not begin and end with technology," and that building an infrastructure requires "a theory of world making, if we are to matter."[78]

Feminist DH infrastructure work is best framed theoretically, we have argued, not as a stack, but as an ecosystem in which actors and activities interrelate and intra-act, impacting each other in the context of local environments that themselves differ remarkably. It encompasses the provision of training initiatives, spaces, and networking opportunities enabled by conference organization and digital humanities centers, as well as the installation and running of hardware or the creation of software designed in some way to recognize, mobilize, or embody the difference that gender analysis makes. It also includes content-provision projects that might not seem, on their face, to constitute infrastructure. A feminist DH infrastructure aims to redistribute power in order to achieve equity and empowerment.[79] It consequently embraces pluralism: identity, inclusivity, and diversity. It respects all participants as agents, giving credit where it is due and making labor visible.

Suchman describes the kind of responsibility involved in infrastructure:

> Agencies—and associated accountabilities—reside neither in us nor in our artifacts but in our intra-actions. The question, following Barad, is how to configure assemblages in such a way that we can intra-act

responsibly and generatively with and through them. [. . .] [The] perspective suggested here takes persons and machines as contingently stabilized through particular, more and less durable, arrangements whose reiteration and/or reconfiguration is the cultural and political project of design in which we are all continuously implicated. Responsibility on this view is met neither through control nor abdication but in ongoing practical, critical, and generative acts of engagement.[80]

The "ongoing practical, critical, and generative acts of engagement" that constitute contributions to feminist DH infrastructure, broadly conceived, involve rethinking binaries, making labor visible, embracing pluralism, acknowledging affective and rhetorical effects, and redistributing power. An infrastructure becomes "feminist" by making apparent in some way through its own inclusiveness the unstated exclusions endemic to digital infrastructures. Although infrastructure building fueled by a concern to address gender and other forms of inequity encompasses a broad range of activities and scales from the local to the transnational, from the minimal to the platform, these threads are woven, variously in response to local situations or particular concerns, through them all.

Infrastructures are necessarily constrained both by their situatedness and by the double-bind of instigating change within contexts in which most users expect habituation rather than disruption, seamlessness rather than resistance. But Barad's generative interpretation of constraints as "dynamics of possibility"[81] invites us to engage in feminist infrastructure work that is animated by critique and care, theory and generosity, and thus advance the project, in the words of Cuboniks invoked at the outset, to "widen our aperture of freedom."

Notes

Many thanks to Liz Losh, Ravynn Stringfield, and the editors for suggestions that made this a better piece.

1. D'Ignazio and Klein, "Feminist Data Visualization," §3.1.
2. Liu, "Toward a Diversity Stack," 130.
3. Liu, "Drafts for Against the Cultural Singularity (book in progress)." For a discussion of definitions of infrastructure from the beginning of the term's origin, see A. Wilson, "The Infrastructure of Intimacy" (264–65).
4. Bowker and Star, "How to Infrastructure," 231–33.
5. S. Brown, "Delivery Service," 2019.
6. S. Brown, "Delivery Service," 2019.
7. Star and Ruhleder, "Steps toward an Ecology of Infrastructure"; Star, "An Ethnography of Infrastructure," 381; Bowker and Star, "How to Infrastructure," 231.

8. Losh, "The Rhetoric of Infrastructure," 22; Liu and Gold, "Session Description—Critical Infrastructure Studies"; Chun, "What We Talk about When We Talk about DH."

9. The field of value-sensitive design argues that values are embedded in computer systems of all kinds and proposes consciously incorporating values rather than taking them as they come. See Hoven, "ICT and Value Sensitive Design"; Friedman, Kahn, and Borning, "Value-Sensitive Design and Information Systems."

10. Chun, *Updating to Remain the Same.*

11. Krug, *Don't Make Me Think.*

12. Liu, "Drafts for *Against the Cultural Singularity.*"

13. Bratton, *The Stack*, 355.

14. Liu, "Toward a Diversity Stack," 135.

15. Bratton, *The Stack*, 107, 355.

16. Bratton, *The Stack*, xviii.

17. "LAMP (software bundle)."

18. A. Wilson, "The Infrastructure of Intimacy," 253.

19. Star, "An Ethnography of Infrastructure," 379.

20. Losh, "The Rhetoric of Infrastructure," 2019.

21. Berens, "DH Adjuncts."

22. Star, "An Ethnography of Infrastructure," 380.

23. For a discussion of carework, particularly within a Black feminist graduate student context, see Stringfield's chapter in this volume.

24. Brown, "Delivery Service."

25. Klein, "The Carework and Codework of the Digital Humanities." See also "Forum: Ethics, Theories, and Practices of Care," 423–51.

26. Verhoeven, "As Luck Would Have It."

27. Verhoeven, "As Luck Would Have It," 21. Linked Open Data is machine legible through published ontologies and vocabularies: LINCS datasets can specify gender differently than m/f/other: https://vocab.lincsproject.ca/. The project's data structures and vocabularies work together to represent gender and sexuality from an intersectional feminist perspective. See also *Homosaurus.*

28. See Stringfield's chapter in this volume.

29. Goldberg, "The Afterlife of the Humanities." See also Thorat's chapter in this volume.

30. Beneschott, "Is Open Source Open to Women?"; Reagle, "Free as in Sexist?"; "Open Source."

31. Wajcman, *Feminism Confronts Technology*; Hill, Corbett, and St. Rose, *Why So Few?*; Perez, *Invisible Women.*

32. Flanders, "The Body Encoded."

33. Nowviskie, "Collex," 1.

34. Brown et al., "Cultural (Re-)formations."

35. McPherson, *Feminist in a Software Lab*, 118, 128.

36. Flanders, Bauman, and Connell, "Text Encoding," 105–6.

37. E.g., Halberstam, "Automating Gender"; Wajcman, *Feminism Confronts Technology.*

38. Haraway, "A Manifesto for Cyborgs."

39. Emerson, "The Media Archaeology Lab as Platform for Undoing and Reimagining Media History," 175.

40. Emerson, *Reading Writing Interfaces*, xviii–xix.

41. Emerson, "Writing Telematics//Other Networks in Canada."

42. Wernimont and Losh, "Wear and Care Feminisms at a Long Maker Table."

43. Knight, "Making Space," 2017.

44. McPherson, "Why Are the Digital Humanities So White?," 144.

45. McPherson, *Feminist in a Software Lab*, 241.

46. Flanagan and Nissenbaum, *Values at Play in Visual Games*.

47. McGonigal, *Reality Is Broken*, 2011.

48. McPherson, *Feminist in a Software Lab*, 243.

49. Balsamo, *Designing Culture*, 35–36.

50. Balsamo, "The AIDS Memorial Quilt."

51. Wilson, "AIDS Memorial Quilt Digital Experiences Project."

52. Barad, *Meeting the Universe Halfway*, 33. In concrete terms, those who style Dr. Anthony Fauci as the hero scientist combatting the AIDS virus forget, as he acknowledges, that he was dragged kicking and screaming into the research arena by AIDS activists: neither alone created effective treatments; the "hero" of this story are the agencies comprised of their "mutual entanglement."

53. Balsamo, *Designing Culture*, 47.

54. Verhoeven, "As Luck Would Have It," 9, 11.

55. COLLEX—the COLLection and EXhibit builder—was created for NINES.org (Networked Infrastructure for Nineteenth-Century Scholarship) by Dr. Nowviskie working with programmer Erik Hatcher, among others; Elizabeth Sadler later worked with Erik Hatcher to create Blacklight, an evolution of COLLEX (Nowviskie, Sadler, and Hatcher, "Adapting an Open-Source Scholarly Web 2.0 System for Findability in Library Collections"; see also Nowviskie, "COLLEX").

56. ARC metadata categories are specified here: http://wiki.collex.org/index.php/Submitting_RDF. For more information about ARC as a community, see ARC.

57. Mandell, "Principles for Metadata Reform."

58. Mandell, "Revitalizing the ARC Infrastructure through Linked Open Data."

59. A. Wilson, "The Infrastructure of Intimacy," 274.

60. A. Wilson, "The Infrastructure of Intimacy," 261–62.

61. Wernimont, "Whence Feminism?," para. 23.

62. Radzikowska et al., "A Speculative Feminist Approach to Design Project Management," 101.

63. Nowviskie, "Resistance in the Materials."

64. D'Ignazio and Klein, "Feminist Data Visualization."

65. S. Brown, "Categorically Provisional"; Mandell, "Gendering Digital Literary History."

66. Mandell, "Gender and Cultural Analytics."

67. S. Brown, "Scaling Up Collaboration Online."

68. Nyröp and Gil, "Credits."

69. It is beyond the purview of this chapter to discuss the open access movement in general, but access to digital archives requires that a number of different infrastructures be in place, legal as well as technological.

70. Christen, "Tribal Archives, Traditional Knowledge, and Local Contexts," 5.

71. "Traditional Knowledge (TK) Labels."

72. Mortensen, "Anger, Fear, and Games."

73. Wernimont and Losh, "Wear and Care Feminisms at a Long Maker Table."

74. Toupin, "Feminist Hackerspaces"; Martin, "Centering Gender."

75. Wernimont and Losh, "Wear and Care Feminisms at a Long Maker Table," 104. See also the chapter by Wernimont and Stevens in this collection.

76. cárdenas, *Poetic Operations*, 49.

77. Fitzpatrick, *Generous Thinking*, 232–35.

78. Verhoeven, "Identifying the Point of It All."

79. Bardzell, "Feminist HCI," 1301; Fiesler, Morrison, and Bruckman. "An Archive of Their Own," 2; D'Ignazio and Klein, "Feminist Data Visualization," 2–3.

80. Suchman, *Human-Machine Reconfigurations*, 285–86.

81. Barad, *Meeting the Universe Halfway*, 177.

Works Cited

Abbate, Janet. *Recoding Gender: Women's Changing Participation in Computing.* Cambridge, MA: MIT Press, 2012.

ARC (the Advanced Research Consortium). https://ar-c.org.

Balsamo, Anne. "The AIDS Memorial Quilt and the Design of Digital Memorial Experiences." Association for Death Education and Counseling Conference. April 28, 2018. https://www.management-hq.com/wp-content/uploads/2018/05/Conference-Program-1.pdf

Balsamo, Anne. *Designing Culture: The Technological Imagination at Work.* Durham, NC: Duke University Press, 2011.

Barad, Karen. *Meeting the Universe Halfway.* Durham, NC: Duke University Press, 2007.

Bardzell, Shaowen. "Feminist HCI: Taking Stock and Outlining an Agenda for Design." In *Proceedings of the SIGCHI Conference on Human Factors in Computing Systems* (April 2010): 1301–10. 2010. http://doi.org/10.1145/1753326.1753521.

Beneschott, Breanden. "Is Open Source Open to Women?" *Toptal.* https://www.toptal.com/open-source/is-open-source-open-to-women.

Berens, Kathi Inman. "DH Adjuncts: Social Justice and Care." In *Debates in the Digital Humanities 2019*, edited by Gold and Klein, 437–41.

Bowker, Geoffrey C. "Information Mythology and Infrastructure." In *Information Acumen: The Understanding and Use of Knowledge in Modern Business*, edited by L. Bud-Frierman, 231–247. London: Routledge, 1994.

Bowker, Geoffrey C., and Susan Leigh Star. "How to Infrastructure." In *Handbook of New Media: Social Shaping and Social Consequences*. London: Sage, 2010.

Bowker, Geoffrey C., and Susan Leigh Star. *Sorting Things Out: Classification and Its Consequences*. Cambridge, MA: MIT Press, 2000.

Bratton, Benjamin H. *The Stack: On Software and Sovereignty*. Cambridge, MA: MIT Press, 2016.

Brown, John Seely, and Paul Duguid. *The Social Life of Information*. Cambridge, MA: Harvard Business Review Press, 2017.

Brown, Susan. "Categorically Provisional." *PMLA* 135, no. 1 (2020): 165–74.

Brown, Susan. "Delivery Service: Gender and the Political Unconscious of Digital Humanities." In *Bodies of Information: Intersectional Feminism and Digital Humanities*, edited by Elizabeth Losh and Jacque Wernimont. Minneapolis: University of Minnesota Press, 2019.

Brown, Susan. "Scaling Up Collaboration Online: Toward a Collaboratory for Research on Canadian Writing." *International Journal of Canadian Studies* 48 (2014): 233–51.

Brown, Susan. "Why LINCS?" *LINCS: Linked Infrastructure for Networked Cultural Scholarship*, August 11, 2020.

Brown, Susan, Colin Faulkner, Abigel Lemak, Kimberley Martin, Alliyya Mohammed, Jade Penancier, and Robert Warren. "Cultural (Re-)formations: Structuring a Linked Data Ontology for Intersectional Identities." *Digital Humanities 2017 Conference Abstracts*. https://dh2017.adho.org/abstracts/580/580.pdf.

cárdenas, micha. *Poetic Operations: Trans of Color Art in Digital Media*. Durham, NC: Duke University Press, 2022.

cárdenas, micha. "Trans of Color Poetics: Stitching Bodies, Concepts, and Algorithms." *The Scholar and the Feminist Online* 13, no. 3–14, no. 1 (2016). https://sfonline.barnard.edu/micha-cardenas-trans-of-color-poetics-stitching-bodies-concepts-and-algorithms/.

Center for Solutions to Online Violence. FemTechNet. http://femtechnet.org/csov/.

Christen, Kimberly. "Tribal Archives, Traditional Knowledge, and Local Contexts: Why the 's' Matters." *Journal of Western Archives* 6, no. 1 (2015): article 3.

Chun, Wendy Hui Kyong. *Updating to Remain the Same: Habitual New Media*. Cambridge, MA: MIT Press, 2016.

Chun, Wendy Hui Kyong. Roundtable discussion, "What We Talk about When We Talk about DH: Interdisciplinary Vocabularies." Sponsored by the Association for Computers and the Humanities, Annual Meeting of the Modern Language Association, 2016.

Clement, Tanya, Lori Emerson, Elizabeth Losh, and Thomas Padilla. "Reimagining the Humanities Lab." DH2018 Conference, Mexico City, June 26–29, 2018. https://dh2018.adho.org/en/reimagining-the-humanities-lab/.

Cuboniks, Laboria [pseud.] "Xenofeminism: a Politics for Alienation." n.d. Accessed February 6, 2019. http://www.laboriacuboniks.net/#adjust/1.

CWRC (Canadian Writing Research Collaboratory). https://cwrc.ca/.

Davis, Leslie, Zachary Griffith, and Jacob Neely. "Traditional Knowledge and Digital Archives: An Interview with Kim Christen." *disClosure: A Journal of Social Theory* 27, no. 1 (2018): 5.

D'Ignazio, Catherine, and Lauren F. Klein. "Feminist Data Visualization." Workshop on Visualization for the Digital Humanities, IEEE VIS 2016, Baltimore, MD, 2016. http://www.kanarinka.com/wp-content/uploads/2015/07/IEEE_Feminist_Data_Visualization.pdf.

Emerson, Lori. *Reading Writing Interfaces*. Minneapolis: University of Minnesota Press, 2014.

Emerson, Lori. "Writing Telematics//Other Networks in Canada." Digital Textualities/Canadian Contexts Conference, University of Alberta, September 21, 2016.

Emerson, Lori. "The Media Archaeology Lab as Platform for Undoing and Reimagining Media History." In *Hands on Media History: A New Methodology in the Humanities and Social Sciences*. New York: Routledge: 2020. 175–86.

Fiesler, Casey, Shannon Morrison, and Amy S. Bruckman. "An Archive of Their Own: A Case Study of Feminist HCI and Values in Design." *Proceedings of the SIGCHI Conference on Human Factors in Computing Systems*, San Jose, CA, May 7–12, 2016.

Fitzpatrick, Kathleen. *Generous Thinking: A Radical Approach to Saving the University*. Baltimore: Johns Hopkins University Press, 2019.

Flanagan, Mary. *Critical Play: Radical Game Design*. Cambridge, MA: MIT Press, 2009.

Flanagan, Mary, and Helen Nissenbaum. *Values at Play in Digital Games*. Cambridge, MA: MIT Press, 2014.

Flanders, Julia. "The Body Encoded: Questions of Gender and the Electronic Text." *Electronic Text: Investigations in Method and Theory* (1997): 127–44.

Flanders, Julia, Syd Bauman, and Sarah Connell. "Text Encoding." In *Doing Digital Humanities*, edited by Constance Crompton, Richard J. Lane, and Ray Siemens, 104–23. London: Routledge, 2016.

"Forum: Ethics, Theories, and Practices of Care." In *Debates in the Digital Humanities 2019*, edited by Gold and Klein, 423–51.

Friedman, Batya, Peter H. Kahn, and Alan Borning. "Value-Sensitive Design and Information Systems." In *Human-Computer Interaction in Management Information Systems: Foundations*, edited by P. Zhang and D. Galletta. New York: M. E. Sharpe, 2006.

Gold, Matthew K., and Lauren F. Klein, eds. *Debates in the Digital Humanities*. Minneapolis: University of Minnesota Press, 2012, 2016, 2019. https://dhdebates.gc.cuny.edu/.

Goldberg, David Theo. "The Afterlife of the Humanities." Irvine: University of California Humanities Research Institute, 2014. https://web.archive.org/web/20150215101429/http://humafterlife.uchri.org/.

Halberstam, J. "Automating Gender: Postmodern Feminism in the Age of the Intelligent Machine." *Feminist Studies* 17, no. 3 (1991): 439–60.

Haraway, Donna. "A Manifesto for Cyborgs: Science, Technology, and Socialist Feminism in the 1980s." In *The Postmodern Turn: New Perspectives on Social*

Theory, edited by Steven Seidman, 82–115. Cambridge: Cambridge University Press, 1994.

Hicks, Marie. *Programmed Inequality: How Britain Discarded Women Technologists and Lost its Edge in Computing*. Cambridge, MA: MIT Press, 2017.

Hill, Catherine, Christianne Corbett, and Andresse St. Rose. *Why So Few? Women in Science, Technology, Engineering, and Mathematics*. American Association of University Women, 2010. https://eric.ed.gov/?id=ED509653

Homosaurus: An International LGBTQ+ Linked Data Vocabulary. Digital Transgender Archive. https://homosaurus.org/.

Hoven, Jeroen van den. "ICT and Value Sensitive Design." In *The Information Society: Innovations, Legitimacy, Ethics, and Democracy*, edited by P. Goujon, Sylvain Lavelle, Penny Duquenoy, Kai Kimppa, and Veronique Laurent, 67–72. Boston: Springer, 2007.

HuNI (Humanities Networked Infrastructure). https://huni.net.au.

Klein, Lauren. "The Carework and Codework of the Digital Humanities." Talk given at the American Antiquarian Society, May 2015. Accessed December 9, 2018. http://lklein.com/2015/06/the-carework-and-codework -of-the-digital-humanities/.

Knight, Kim Brilliante. "Making Space: Feminist DH and a Room of One's Own." Paper presented to the Annual Meeting of the Modern Language Association, January 2017. Rpt. *Minimal Computing*, February 17, 2018. Accessed September 22, 2019. https://go-dh.github.io/mincomp/thoughts/2017/02/18/ knight-makingspace/.

Krug, Steve. *Don't Make Me Think*. N.p.: New Riders, 2006.

"LAMP (software bundle)." *Wikipedia*. https://en.wikipedia.org/wiki/ LAMP_(software_bundle).

Lampland, Martha, and Susan Leigh Star, eds. *Standards and Their Stories: How Quantifying, Classifying, and Formalizing Practices Shape Everyday Life*. Ithaca, NY: Cornell University Press, 2008.

LINCS (Linked Infrastructure for Networked Cultural Scholarship). https:// lincsproject.ca.

Liu, Alan. "Drafts for *Against the Cultural Singularity* (book in progress)." May 2, 2016. http://liu.english.ucsb.edu/drafts-for-against-the-cultural-singularity. See also https://hcommons.org/deposits/item/mla:699/.

Liu, Alan. "Toward a Diversity Stack: Digital Humanities and Diversity as a Technical Problem." *PMLA* 135, no. 1 (2020): 130–51.

Liu, Alan, and Matthew K. Gold. "Session Description—Critical Infrastructure Studies." Paper presented to the Annual Meeting of the Modern Language Association, January 6, 2018. Accessed August 23, 2020. https://criticalin- frastructure.hcommons.org/session-description/.

Losh, Elizabeth. "The Rhetoric of Infrastructure: American Colonialism and the Military Telegraph." In *Rhet Ops: Rhetoric and Information Warfare*, edited by Jim Ridolfo and William Hart-Davidson, 19–32. Pittsburgh: University of Pittsburgh Press, 2019.

Mandell, Laura. "Gender and Cultural Analytics: Finding or Making Stereotypes?" In *Debates in the Digital Humanities 2019*, edited by Gold and Klein, 3–26.

Mandell, Laura. "Gendering Digital Literary History: What Counts for Digital Humanities," In *A New Companion to Digital Humanities*, edited by Susan Schreibman, John Unsworth, and Ray Siemens, 2nd rev. ed., 511–24. Malden, MA: Wiley-Blackwell, 2016. https://doi.org/10.1002/9781118680605.ch35.

Mandell, Laura. "Principles for Metadata Reform [for ARC]." n.d. Accessed August 23, 2020. https://wiki.collex.org/index.php/Principles_for_Metadata_Reform.

Mandell, Laura. "Revitalizing the ARC Infrastructure through Linked Open Data." "Infrastructural Interventions," Online Workshop, June 21–22, 2021, King's Digital Lab, King's College Department of Digital Humanities, and Critical Infrastructures Studies Initiative [cistudies.org]. https://cistudies. org/events/digital-humanities-critical-infrastructure-studies-workshop-series/ infrastructural-interventions/#mandell)

Martin, Kimberly. "Centering Gender: A Feminist Analysis of Makerspaces and Digital Humanities Centers." Scholarly Paper. Indiana University, November 28, 2017. http://hdl.handle.net/2022/21827.

McGonigal, Jane. *Reality Is Broken: Why Games Make Us Better, and How They Can Change the World.* New York: Penguin, 2011.

McPherson, Tara. *Feminist in a Software Lab: Difference + Design.* Cambridge, MA: Harvard University Press, 2018.

McPherson, Tara. "Why Are the Digital Humanities So White?" In *Debates in the Digital Humanities 2012*, edited by Gold and Klein, 139–60.

Mortensen, Torill Elvira. "Anger, Fear, and Games: The Long Event of #GamerGate." *Games and Culture* 13, no. 8 (2018). https://doi. org/10.1177/1555412016640408.

Nowviskie, Bethany. "Collex: Facets, Folksonomy, and Fashioning the Remixable Web." Paper presented to the 19th Joint International Conference of the Association for Computers and Humanities, and the Association for Literary and Linguistic Computing, University of Illinois–Urbana-Champaign, 2007. https://pdfs.semanticscholar.org/381e/b4e9616b1bdd111882d9cd0cd324039 8331a.pdf.

Nowviskie, Bethany. "COLLEX: Semantic Collections & Exhibits for the Remixable Web." *Electronic Book Review* (2007). http://www.electronicbookreview .com/thread/enfolded/remixable.

Nowviskie, Bethany. "Digital Humanities in the Anthropocene." *Digital Scholarship in the Humanities* 30, suppl_1 (2015). i4–i15.

Nowviskie, Bethany. "Resistance in the Materials." Paper presented to the Annual Meeting of the Modern Language Association, 2013. http://nowviskie .org/2013/resistance-in-the-materials/.

Nowviskie, Bethany, and Dot Porter. "The Graceful Degradation Survey: Managing Digital Humanities Projects through Times of Transition and Decline." *Digital Humanities* (2010): 7–10.

Nowviskie, Bethany, Elizabeth Sadler, and Erik Hatcher. "Adapting an Open-Source Scholarly Web 2.0 System for Findability in Library Collections (or: 'Frankly, Vendors, We Don't Give a Damn')." In *Library 2.0: Initiatives in Academic Libraries*, edited by Laura B. Cohen, 58–72. Chicago: Association of College and Research Libraries, 2007.

Nyröp, Maril, and Alex Gil. "Credits." *Wax.* https://minicomp.github.io/wax/credits.

"Open Source." Feminist Principles of the Internet. https://feministinternet.org/en/principle/open-source.

Open Source Diversity. https://opensourcediversity.org/.

Ostrom, Elinor. *Understanding Institutional Diversity.* Princeton, NJ: Princeton University Press, 2005.

Perez, Caroline Criado. *Invisible Women: Data Bias in a World Designed for Men.* New York: Abrams Press, 2019.

Posner, Miriam. "What's Next: The Radical Unrealised Potential of Digital Humanities." In *Debates in the Digital Humanities 2016*, edited by Gold and Klein, 32–41. http://dhdebates.gc.cuny.edu/debates/text/54.

Radzikowska, M., J. Roberts-Smith, X. Zhou, and S. Ruecker. "A Speculative Feminist Approach to Design Project Management." *Strategic Design Research Journal* 12, no. 1 (2019): 94–113.

Ratto, Matt. "Ethics of Seamless Infrastructures: Resources and Future Directions." *International Review of Information Ethics* 8, no. 8 (2007): 20–27.

Reagle, Joseph. "Free as in Sexist?: Free Culture and the Gender Gap." *First Monday* 18, no. 1 (2013). https://firstmonday.org/ojs/index.php/fm/article/view/4291.

Rosser, Sue. "Through the Lenses of Feminist Theory: Focus on Women and Information Technology." *Frontiers: A Journal of Women Studies* 26, no. 1 (2005): 1–23.

Rowan, Rory. "Extinction as Usual?: Geo-Social Futures and Left Optimism." *e-flux journal 56th Venice Biennale*, Supercommunity: Apocalypsis, July 31, 2015. http://supercommunity.e-flux.com/texts/extinction-as-usual-geo-social-futures-and-left-optimism/.

Schreibman, Susan. "About." *The Versioning Machine.* 2016. http://v-machine.org/about/.

Star, Susan Leigh. "An Ethnography of Infrastructure." *American Behavioral Scientist* 43, no. 3 (1999): 377–91.

Star, Susan Leigh, and K. Ruhleder. "Steps toward an Ecology of Infrastructure: Design and Access for Large Information Spaces." *Information Systems Research* 7, no. 1 (1996): 111–34.

Suchman, Lucy A. *Human-Machine Reconfigurations: Plans and Situated Actions.* 2nd ed. New York: Cambridge University Press, 2007.

Suchman, Lucy. "Interview with Ann Balsamo." *Feminism, Technology, and Systems 2: Infrastructure* (video). New York: School of Media Studies, The New School, 2013. https://vimeo.com/79740274.

Thrift, Nigel. "The Insubstantial Pageant: Producing an Untoward Land." *Cultural Geographies* 19, no. 2 (2012): 141–68.

Toupin, Sophie. "Feminist Hackerspaces: The Synthesis of Feminist and Hacker Cultures." *Journal of Peer Production* 5 (2014): 1–9.

"Traditional Knowledge (TK) Labels." *Local Contexts*. http://localcontexts.org/tk-labels/.

Verhoeven, Deb. "As Luck Would Have It: Serendipity and Solace in Digital Research Infrastructure." *Feminist Media Histories* 2, no. 1 (2016): 7–28.

Verhoeven, Deb. "Identifying the Point of It All: Towards a Model of 'Digital Infrapuncture.'" Mp3. Opening Keynote for Digital Humanities at Oxford Summer School 2016. Accessed July 19, 2024. https://podcasts.ox.ac.uk/opening-keynote-identifying-point-it-all-towards-model-digital-infrapuncture.

Wajcman, Judy. *Feminism Confronts Technology*. Philadelphia: University of Pennsylvania Press, 1991.

Wernimont, Jacqueline. "Whence Feminism? Assessing Feminist Interventions in Digital Literary Archives." *Digital Humanities Quarterly* 7, no. 1 (2013). Accessed September 22, 2019. http://digitalhumanities.org:8081/dhq/vol/7/1/000156/000156.html.

Wernimont, Jacqueline, and Elizabeth Losh. "Wear and Care Feminisms at a Long Maker Table." In *The Routledge Companion to Media Studies and Digital Humanities*, edited by Jentery Sayers, 97–107. New York: Routledge, 2019.

Wilson, Ara. "The Infrastructure of Intimacy." *Signs: Journal of Women in Culture and Society* 41, no. 2 (2016): 247–80.

Wilson, David. "AIDS Memorial Quilt Digital Experiences Project." Public Interactives Research Lab, University of Texas at Dallas, July 23, 2015. Accessed August 22, 2020. https://labs.utdallas.edu/public-interactives/aids-memorial-quilt-digital-experiences-project-2012/.

5

From Lab to Cooperative

A Feminist Infrastructural Reimagining

JACQUELINE WERNIMONT
AND NIKKO L. STEVENS

> How are we to become hosts
> of this new world?
> —Laboria Cuboniks, "Xenofeminism:
> A Politics for Alienation"

> In order to survive institutions, we need to
> transform them, but we still need to survive
> the institutions we are trying to transform.
> —Sarah Ahmed, Twitter (now X),
> April 16, 2019

Susan Leigh Star observes that infrastructure is designed to be invisible and appear natural, becoming visible only upon rupture or interruption.[1] Space is a central feature of infrastructural politics, whether understood in terms of the spaces to work, dream, or play.[2] As academics, we ask for room to explore and rooms in which to be together with our collaborators, students, materials, and tools. Physical spaces offer us not only room to exist (together or alone) but also opportunities to transform the world around us. As the xenofeminist collective Laboria Cuboniks suggests, "spatial transformation" is "an integral component in any process of feminist futurity."[3] Deb Verhoeven has coined the term "infrapuncture" to think about impermanence and spatial and political transformations that are aimed at relieving stress or pressure from within the structures of which we are already a part.[4] Together the xenofeminist manifesto and Verhoeven's theorization suggest that there are models of academic and political feminist infrastructure through which we can imagine powerful small-scale interventions (ruptures?) in large-scale structures, including "a transformation of deliberate construction, seeking to submerge the white-supremacist capitalist patriarchy in a sea of procedures that soften its shell and dismantle its defenses, so as to build a new world from the scraps."[5] In this chapter we present and contextualize the Nexus Digital Co-op as one such small-scale intervention that differs from the laboratory model increasingly seen in humanities research. Even as a short-lived experiment, we believe Nexus can give us insight into the cooperative movement as an alternative infrastructure for academic research and production. Please note as you read that our colleague Elizabeth Grumbach was central to this work but was not able to join us in writing due to other commitments.

Understanding Labs across Domains

In the last twenty years, discussions of digital humanities (DH) labs have proliferated to such a degree that *Digital Humanities Quarterly* published a special issue on the topic in 2020. Editors of that special issue, Mila Oiva and Urszula Pawlicka-Deger, offer a thorough review of the state of scholarship on DH labs and the "mutual relations between situatedness, infrastructure, and digital/humanities practices."[6] Less than a year later *The Lab Book* (2021) by Darren Wershler, Lori Emerson, and Jussi Parikka, came out and offered the "extended lab" heuristic to help grapple with the reality that "labs are everywhere," including in spaces as seemingly far from the scientific bench lab as the fashion industry, bars, and humanities and arts divisions.[7]

Many DH labs, like their counterparts in other disciplines, are spaces wherein professionalization is an important function that extends the practices of the lab into the future real-world practices of its personnel. Steven Jones notes that "the results of such lab work are layered systems, built and rebuilt by maker-scholars as starting places" from which both new knowledge and new knowledge-makers are launched.[8] Rebecca Frost Davis and Brian Alexander suggest that not only are labs an infrastructure for professionalization, they also can "lighten the load" of the humanities faculty researchers by creating a pipeline for both people and projects wherein newer students work "under supervision by faculty and older students until they are ready for independent research."[9] DH labs have been imagined as sites of student education and professionalization, as well as a kind of labor distribution largely absent from humanities research prior to the mid-twentieth century.[10]

As Wershler, Emerson, and Parikka note, the model of a laboratory familiar in the sciences has been the subject of extended scholarly attention, particularly within Foucauldian and Latourian traditions of science studies (examples include work by Donna Haraway, Karin Knorr Cetina, Stephen Shapin, Ian Hacking, Lorraine Daston, and Peter Gallison).[11] Both the Foucauldian and Latourian traditions read the research lab as a space that produces new knowledge and modes of scholarly practice. One of the great strengths of the lab as an infrastructure is its ability to disrupt boundaries between the research institution and the outside world. Joseph Rouse observes that laboratory knowledge *requires* extending the materials and practices of disclosure and tracking beyond the lab walls.[12] Wershler, Emerson, and Parikka similarly note that labs "can and do extend [their] influence out into the world," including "the performance of particular kinds of techniques."[13] These techniques are often highly disciplinary, both in the sense of disciplines of knowledge and in the sense that bodies are trained to perform particular tasks in highly circumscribed ways. Those who don't become properly disciplined are disruptive in a traditional lab.

Even as they transform the world within and beyond, labs can act as microcosms of the institutions in which they are housed, reproducing external inequalities. Principal investigators (PIs) can be focused on maintaining control—of the space, the process, and the products being produced. "Control is the heart of science" and PIs who lose control over their labs risk losing control over their science.[14] However, maintaining control over a lab also means controlling technicians, students, and others who might work in the lab. Paradoxically, given the power dynamics, technicians are frequently workers who have the deepest contextual and tacit knowledge of lab operations despite the reality that their positions may be undervalued.[15]

The reproduction of rigid hierarchies and pervasive inequality in the lab highlights that not all boundaries are subject to the boundary-breaking magic of labs. Barriers for women are pronounced in the bench sciences,[16] and the work of technicians in science labs is also highly gendered.[17] Further, traditional laboratory work has tended to maintain boundaries between various ranks of scholar-researchers, technicians and researchers, and gender minorities, women, and men. The same is true in the "hybrid labs" foregrounded in *The Lab Book*, where the authors note that "labs operate to train and refine their denizens into different kinds of subjects that are all part of the hybrid assemblage, but with varying degrees of power and agency."[18]

None of this agrees particularly well with a feminist and liberatory approach to education—one in which hierarchies are disrupted and learning is an active process that does not require people to exist as "beings for others."[19] More liberatory approaches to education have been theorized and modeled at least since Paulo Friere's *Pedagogy of the Oppressed* was published in English translation in 1970.[20] If institutions can shape in harmful directions, we would like to hope that we can expect educational paradigm shifts to similarly manifest within academic labs and research sites.

Indeed, we see some evidence of this in labs that tend to be explicitly feminist. Such labs vary in form but tend to explicitly use alternative structures to enable everyone to grapple with the intersecting operations of power through vectors like race, class, sexuality, and ability. The Civic

Laboratory for Environmental Action Research (CLEAR) is a standout example. A "feminist, anti-colonial, marine science laboratory," directed by Max Liboiron at Memorial University of Newfoundland, CLEAR conducts research on environmental plastics. Using an equity framework, the CLEAR team is guided by an extensive lab book that details the ethical orientations and mechanical processes of the lab.[21] Their process, which includes fostering consensus, valuing carework, and acknowledging social location, challenges normative modes of scientific publishing.[22] The CLEAR lab notebook makes awareness of and intervention in structures of white supremacy and colonial epistemologies foundational to researching marine plastics. Liboiron and the CLEAR lab's practice is a powerful example of valuing the social and ethical operations of the lab as integral to the research work and outcomes. It is also an ongoing example of infrapuncture: as Liboiron observes, "lab work is often 'compromised,' meaning we reproduce some of the systems we are trying to change even as we change them. This isn't a failure but the condition of doing feminist science in science."[23]

This condition of simultaneously enacting feminist, anticolonial, antiracist knowledge creation while also being a part of fundamentally violent and appropriative systems features across a number of DH labs. These have included but are not limited to the work of the Immersive Reality Lab for the Humanities; the Alliance for Networking Visual Culture (ANVC) and related publishing platforms Scalar and Vectors, which Tara McPherson writes about in her *Feminist in a Software Lab*; the Media Archeology Lab, founded by Lori Emerson; Jessica Marie Johnson's Sex and Slavery Lab; and Elizabeth Losh's Equality Lab.[24] Each of these humanities labs enacts alternative models differently, but they share a focus on building and sustaining communities that traditional corporate and academic structures tend to ignore or suppress. For many, this includes emphasizing "the importance of working with communities as sites of the co-construction of knowledge to build trust, acknowledge expectations of reciprocity, and give appropriate credit for contributions."[25] It also often entails "creating a space—both physical and virtual—for sustained practice" that recognizes that theory and practice are neither separate nor separable.[26]

As the foregoing list suggests, humanities labs can be led or founded by a single scholar, leaving them somewhat precarious. Scholars have and continue to experiment with other models as well, including collectives like Colored Conventions Project, FemTechNet, SCRAM, Chicana por mi Raza, and collaboratories like HASTAC. We also see a range of other collaborative groups like Recovering the U.S. Hispanic Literary Heritage, Group for Experimental Methods in Humanistic Research, and Caribbean Digital.[27] Each of these has featured the kind of relationship building that Kim Tallbear, Moya Bailey, and Shawn Wilson have described in their theorizations of relationality in research.[28] The emphasis on relations, relational epistemologies, and relational research can be an important part of research collectives. Insofar as the foregoing examples have been able to enact more progressive modalities of being, working, and producing knowledge together, we agree with the sense that DH and humanities labs can foster a unique kind of scholarly community—enacting relationality in ways that are designed to disrupt, and perhaps puncture, traditional disciplinary boundaries and entrenched power relations.

At the same time, we are wary of the utopian rhetoric about spaces in which "diverse individuals, with different skillsets," converge in "lab environments where librarians, computer scientists, and historians or literary critics come together to theorize problems and meet technological challenges together."[29] A similar sort of narrative appears in digital social sciences as well, as in the Sciences Po MediaLab's reflection on its work in an "interdisciplinary laboratory associating social scientists, code developers, and information designers."[30] Retrospectives such as these suggest not only that the boundaries of expertise and department are dissolved in doing laboratory work, but also that digital technologies and methods will "eventually dissolve(s) the classic distinctions of our discipline: qualitative/quantitative in data, situation/aggregation in methods, and micro/macro in theory."[31] Noteworthy, however, is the way in which boundaries between different kinds of academic expertise remain relatively intact in the above, perhaps even reproducing the hierarchies of the science lab director and technician. We wonder if the bringing together of people in a lab construct makes it easier to categorize them—as humanists, programmers, historians—and thereby instrumentalize people into their contributory roles. What's more, we worry that articulating humanities labs as magical, boundary-busting infrastructures ignores the ways in which they can fail to support diversity in terms of race, class, gender, sexuality, and/or ability.[32] Could a cooperative be a viable alternative model?

The Cooperative Model and the Nexus Co-op

In order to be liberatory, knowledge must
be a "field in which we all labor."
—bell hooks, *Teaching to Transgress*

Cooperatives depend not simply on interpersonal relationships in terms of affect or sociality but also in terms of economics and transparency.[33] As a shared venture, cooperative members address the scarcity and inequality of corporate and institutional practices with a set of relational structures that manifest both trust and hopefulness. Members must believe that the resources that they invest into the co-op will benefit them; the shape and functioning of the co-op is contingent on this hopeful investment by its members. Formal cooperative structures date back to nineteenth-century European efforts to "contest the meaning of modernity" and its attendant injustices.[34] The cooperative was seen as a revolutionary structure—a labor-focused form of resistance to social, cultural, and economic changes that accompanied the agricultural and industrial revolutions, including new or deepening hierarchies.[35] Cooperatives can be organized around production, acquisition, or distribution—common economic objectives—but with a commitment to sharing benefits equally with those involved. As an economic and social organizing model, co-ops generally have a flatter organizational structure and require members to "buy" into the co-op with capital (money, resources, labor). We were particularly interested to understand how a cooperative might push against the fiscal and social changes of conventional academic lab practices.

In this spirit, Elizabeth Grumbach and Jacque Wernimont designed Nexus Digital Co-op as a feminist, antiracist infrastructure, which drew on the long tradition of cooperatives as alternative administrative and labor structures designed to help individuals meet common needs. As both a physical space and a set of communal resources, Nexus operated as an opt-in association of researchers located within the Institute for Humanities Research (IHR) at Arizona State University (ASU). The co-op intentionally remained fairly agnostic about what could "count" as digital research, creating room for both digital methods and analog work on the digital. An important part of the Nexus ethos was our assumption that all researchers had valuable expertise, whether historical, social, methodological, or technical. Grumbach and Wernimont established this as a founding principle in order to push back against the perception that DH is only for those with advanced technical skills and as a way of recognizing that analog skills are critical to successful collaboration. It was also a way to challenge a student-faculty-staff dynamic that assumes that education flows in a single direction based on seniority in a recognized field.

The co-op benefited from brick-and-mortar infrastructures at ASU and required administrative support that needed to be centralized and managed by an authority. Grumbach acted as that authority, serving as project manager of both the co-op itself and the projects within. Grumbach also designed and managed the Nexus website with design contributions by Christin Quissell and Susan Anderson. Stephanie Silva, a business manager at ASU, managed the Nexus budget. The co-op was launched with a small one-year budget line within the larger budget of the IHR. Most of the funding for supplies and events within Nexus came from research budgets secured for particular projects by Wernimont and our colleague in the History Department, Matthew Delmont. In the following we discuss valuable features of the Nexus Co-op: creating opportunities, sharing, and flattening hierarchies.

Creating Opportunities

Primary research and publication opportunities for humanities students and community members are relatively unusual within higher education. Where they do exist, they tend to be "on" a more senior scholar's project and it is rare to see faculty do mundane work on behalf of a student-scholar, staff colleague, or even for one another. Our goal was to have labor distributed among all co-op members and to have real publication opportunities for emerging scholars. Our projects were completed by teams of researchers at all levels, working in shared space. Perhaps the best example of academic work produced in the co-op was the Park Central Mall project. Introduced by co-op member Matthew Delmont, the Park Central Mall project was a multimedia, archival effort built as a Scalar site.[36] In a lab model, Delmont would have set up his own historical research lab and then produced the work in which he became the expert. In a more service-oriented center or production lab, Delmont would have been able to drop archival materials off at the lab and return when work was complete—both a delegation of tasks and an erasure of the labor required to bring the project to fruition. However, as part of Nexus, Delmont brought not only the archival materials and some funding, but also his time and labor. A significant portion of this particular project was the collection and production of a series of oral histories from people who had either worked or shopped (or both) at the Park Central Mall during its heyday in the 1960s. This work, which eventually produced seventy-five first-person stories, was led by Kristine Navarro-McElhaney, an oral historian and a research staff member of the School of Historical, Philosophical, and Religious Studies at ASU. Navarro-McElhaney was assisted in both the collection of the oral histories and their production and storage by Daniel Milowski, Jonathan England, Samantha Notick, and Daniel Samlaska. This facet of the work culminated in two exhibits that were held in the Park Central building in downtown Phoenix and designed by Navarro-McElhaney and a set of student collaborators.

Operating in parallel was the production of a small digital collection that could serve as an online portal to the Park Central Mall history. This entailed selecting and photographing several media assets related to the mall, as well as contextual and historical research on various events that took place there. An ASU graduate student, Jennifer Byron, was hired to do this work over the course of a single semester (we collectively felt financial renumeration was important for a graduate student). As a member of the co-op, Delmont was then able to set up a dedicated workspace within Nexus where Byron and Navarro-McElhaney's students could work and where the archival materials could be safely stored. Additionally, he was able to depend on the project management oversight of Grumbach as the work continued. Importantly, Delmont's contributions as the faculty member who brought in the project were not limited to just "his" project; as a cooperative member, he was a valuable part of our general working collective and contributed effort elsewhere as well. Reflecting our concern with equitable credit for scholarship, Byron is listed as first author on the digital site, with Grumbach second, and faculty members Wernimont and Delmont third and fourth. This made it possible for Byron and Grumbach to include the project vitas as a major scholarly effort in a way that is likely to be legible to others and reflect time spent on the project. All students involved across the project are listed on the project credits.

While the Park Central Mall project progressed, Wernimont also started the WoundPerson project. WoundPerson began as a visualization designed to provoke curiosity into the amount of data produced by wearable technology, and resulted in an IEEE publication,[37] as well as a set of installation-ready pieces. Like the Park Central Mall project, WoundPerson was an interdisciplinary project facilitated by the structure of the co-op that leveraged Wernimont's early modern knowledge and Stevens's technical experience as co-equal contributions. The physical and administrative space created by Nexus enabled Wernimont (faculty) and Stevens (student) to collaborate visibly, encouraging other co-op members to feel welcome contributing. Elements of the larger project, which was to include visualizations for the quantified baby/child and quantified pet were not finished, but involved the work of Wernimont and Stevens, along with faculty members Soren Hammerschmidt and Sarah Florini, and staff members Leah Newsom and Elizabeth Grumbach. Across these two projects undergraduate and graduate students were able to direct areas of inquiry and develop scholarly pieces that were published and exhibited. Staff members were engaged in the research and creative work and received credit for both their infrastructural work and their intellectual contributions. Faculty were able to see projects come to fruition, but also worked on behalf of products that benefited students and staff colleagues.

Sharing

Projects like the Park Central Mall project and WoundPerson were made possible by the focus on collective resources. When Wernimont and Grumbach envisioned Nexus, they hoped that one of its key benefits was as an umbrella for sharing aspects of academic life that we are trained to treat as scarce. Nexus facilitated the sharing of space, opportunity, resources, and labor against an academic culture that fosters competition. While a cooperative is generally formed by the membership, Grumbach and Wernimont knew this was an unfamiliar infrastructure within an academic research setting. Rather than begin with the members, Wernimont and Grumbach began with the idea and sought to enroll members. Faculty, staff, and students were invited to bring research projects and ideas to the Nexus Co-op for development, advancement, testing, or completion. Members had access to the equipment and expertise of Nexus, including computing resources, imaging technology, wearable and desktop fabrication tools, design resources, e-textiles, and more. The physical space was open to member researchers across all ranks and explicitly opened to people in the local Tempe-area community. While this element likely needed more time to develop, we were pleased that people unaffiliated with the university participated in multiple events, from lunch conversations to project discussions and demos. Having a community-based oral history project in the Park Central Mall project was helpful in developing these relationships beyond the institution.

Members were empowered to house their own equipment within the co-op space as well. This feature of resource sharing was central to our sense of what the co-op could offer that other research models might not. We had heard from faculty who had machines, books, and raw materials sitting in individual offices and we encouraged members to think of these as shared resources and as the Nexus space and project manager as the best way to manage that sharing. In this way, we were able to foster a space where we were actually resource-rich, despite being everywhere surrounded by the language of budget cuts, technical lack, and resource-scarcity.

In their initial planning Grumbach and Wernimont decided that the research and creative work done within Nexus would depend on the interests/capabilities of co-op members. While we did not have enough cycles of operation to ensure that we fully tested the idea of a democratic selection of projects, the impetus was again to draw on and highlight the strengths of the group as constituted rather than feel lack because of certain kinds of skills being absent in our community. Additionally, this feature allowed for us to create structures to support the transparency that is so central to the success of many co-ops. Co-ops have both a mutual benefit and education function; co-ops must be seen not just benefitting their members but educating their members about the nuances about the sector of the economy in which the co-op exists.[38] This doubling of education and creation is particularly well suited to educational research settings. As with labs, participation in co-ops exposes students to the work of senior/graduate students, staff, and faculty. Unlike most labs, however, co-op members work as peers *toward a mutually agreed-upon project.*

Flattening Hierarchies

The value of collective decision making about research agendas should not be underestimated, and we think this is a distinctive feature of the Nexus co-op and one way that we worked to realize a less hierarchical space. While the co-op itself did not have a strictly flat structure (Wernimont was director, Grumbach project manager), researchers (students, staff, and faculty) worked as peers on project teams. Flattening the hierarchies of the co-op promoted the agency of those involved, creating an infrastructure for knowledge work in which "we all labor" as suggested by the bell hooks epigraph above (it is also analogous to the teacher-student/student-teacher structure promoted by Friere).[39] Co-ops are not inherently feminist or egalitarian; Sally Hacker notes in her study of Mondragón, an old and large worker cooperative in Spain, that gender-based workplace inequality is as prevalent within the cooperative model as it has been in others.[40] More recently we have seen that corporations experimenting with flat hierarchies can also experience well-known problems with the "tyranny of structurelessness" and the choice to not name ongoing power dynamics.[41] From the outset it was clear that Nexus would need structures that would enable people to productively engage in research; we could not simply trust that a flat hierarchy concept would lead to productivity and equality in practice.

Some of this structure came from the space itself and our narrative descriptions of the way the collective would work. Co-op members collectively committed to enlivening the space together—we were intentionally sharing space, which led to new opportunities for people across ranks to work together. Higher education is often imagined as a place where faculty, staff, and students encounter each other in work. More often the case is that spaces are structurally demarcated for each group to work independently. For Stevens, a grad student during this time, sharing space with faculty while they worked demystified the process of producing "good research." Working as a member of Nexus gave students the opportunity to sit with faculty and watch them work and think, both on their own projects and on shared work. The (more) public and intergenerational nature of the work done in Nexus was a powerful example of the ways that even experienced researchers travel a messy, inconsistent, and challenging path to producing knowledge. Because faculty were acting as peer researchers and they agreed to treat student researcher experience as valid and valuable, the process of producing work in Nexus was a joyful communal reshaping of the unknown into the known. It was a manifestation of the insight that "knowledge emerges only through invention and re-invention, through the restless, impatient, continuing, hopeful inquiry human beings pursue in the world, with the world, and with each other."[42]

Hierarchies often manifest in the degree of cost and benefit that different actors in a project/production contribute and receive. In academic spaces this tends to be realized as much in academic credit as in pay grades. We had no power to alter people's pay, so we did what we could with academic credit and labor. Nexus was a producer's co-op, one where people leveraged shared resources in the making of research outputs. Conventionally, members of a production cooperative will "buy" into the co-op and the pooled funds will be used to support collective operations. While we did aim to have some cost-sharing down the line, we initially asked only that people contribute intellectual or material labor (this was the only way to ensure that people from all ranks at the university and beyond could participate). What "counted" as work was flexible, though members agreed to commit thirty-six hours per academic year. This could include but was not limited to grant and project scoping, coauthoring funding requests, writing up research outcomes, creating methods, artwork, or tools, conducting primary or secondary research, contributing area expertise, or offering editorial work. While cost-sharing was a goal, we always wanted to ensure that people were literally working together. Project leads were not exempt.

This was an area where we found ourselves doing a great deal of educating our faculty colleagues. Wernimont met with several faculty who were far more interested in simply sending their projects, their students, or both over to Nexus so that we could train the students and/or implement projects. In one instance a faculty colleague was extremely exasperated at the idea that they would need to also work as a member of the cooperative (they did not join). Others, however, shared the vision and began to write grant applications and project narratives that would include work within the cooperative.

Producer co-ops conventionally share the proceeds of their work, and in this academic setting it was guaranteed that members who contributed substantial work to a single project are included in all bylines and publication credits for that work. Wernimont, as faculty director, agreed to write letters on behalf of members for job, tenure, and other review processes. For the WoundPerson publication, Wernimont and Stevens agreed that Stevens would have first author because the value of that first-author position for a graduate student was greater than for a newly tenured faculty member. When it came time to include portions of that project on our vitas, including the "Anatomies for the 21st Century" installation pieces, we changed the author order for balance and with the recognition that the creative pieces were less likely to be counted as significant scholarly contributions. This is an area where we think we could have done more. In particular, we could have deployed Liboiron's process in order to discuss author order with one another, making sure that it was perceived as fair to those involved. As Liboiron notes, "women and junior researchers [. . .] consistently receive less credit for equal work" (as do trans and gender-nonconforming scholars) and while we were mindful of this in the development of the cooperative, we could have done more to ensure fully equitable distribution of contribution credit, particularly in the case of the Park Central Mall project, which received media attention that was realized along more familiar faculty-as-author lines.[43]

Concluding Thoughts: Sustainability versus Infrapuncture

Given the amount of work that went into creating the cooperative and educating people about how it might work, we were disappointed to find that when Wernimont left ASU for Dartmouth College, the co-op dissolved. On the one hand, just a semester of operation makes the kind of institutional buy-in that would have allowed Nexus to persist very unlikely, even though Grumbach remained a part of the Humanities Center staff. On the other, the institution could well have chosen to support the innovative structure we had created by continuing it forward. That said, Verhoeven's notion of infrapuncture as small-scale and ephemeral action offers us a way to think differently about the value of the year of thinking and talking that went into making that semester possible. While the cooperative did not exist long enough to grapple with some of the most familiar struggles endemic to this kind of infrastructure (like internal member conflict), we did experience another familiar challenge: lack of participation by benefit-seeking members.[44] We had more than twenty members who signed up for the co-op, but we really had just a core of five or six who committed to being present and working in the space and on Nexus projects. We expected this and made the decision to not repeatedly exhort people to come in and contribute.

In addition to the structural insights Wernimont gained while working to envision and enact the cooperative with Grumbach and the other colleagues, we were encouraged by the vibrancy of the community that began to develop. We had people who stopped by to see our progress or to simply engage with the primary materials in both projects. We had free-flowing conversations and co-working sessions that did, in our view, productively punch holes in the boundaries between faculty, staff, and students. We were able to both co-work quietly and to share in fun and sometimes loud group think sessions. A community of shared work and expertise did evolve, and it was delightful to be a part of that community. As Sarah Ahmed's epigraph for this piece suggests, we need to both transform our institutions and survive as we do that work. This temporary, small-scale infrapuncture was very much a survival tool. It shielded us, and we hope others, from a general sense of malaise about the status of higher education funding and publicly engaged scholarship. It also transformed the discourse around us from one of scarcity and competition to a reality of copiousness and collaboration.

In the calculus of feminist interventions, it is likely that one is not enough—whether in higher education or elsewhere. Our experience with Nexus does not mean we all need co-ops instead of labs. Rather, while reading and writing for this chapter, we have come to understand that all infrastructures can function as levers, as refuges or undercommons, and as future engines. The lab remains a powerful imaginary that is legible to university administrators. We suspect that rather than thinking of any one structure as best, we would do well to value a range of possible research structures, including labs and cooperatives, as well as collectives, prides, packs, kitchen tables, beauty shops, and more.[45] We have named many such efforts over the course of this chapter in part as a way of pointing to the fact that this proliferation is already at work. This is something we take as both hopeful and diagnostic; such proliferation speaks to the unease with which feminist infrastructures and knowledge production, especially those originating or engaging with Black, Latinx, and Indigenous theorizing and practice, sits within traditional academic structures. But it is also a signal— sometimes quiet, other times louder—of the joys we find in working with another to survive, transform, and thrive.

Notes

This chapter has benefited not only from the collaborative environment of the Nexus cooperative itself, but also from discussion during the 2016 Creating Feminist Infrastructure in the Digital Humanities panel at DH 2016 and the 2019 Feminist Labs event at the University of Colorado, Boulder. We also wish to thank our editors and anonymous reviewers for their feedback, which have greatly improved this work.

1. Star, "The Ethnography of Infrastructure."

2. As Stefano Harney and Fred Moten remind us, "space" in universities is often afforded to those in positions of race, class, and gender power. See Harney and Moten, *The Undercommons.*

3. Cuboniks, "Xenofeminism."

4. Verhoeven, "Identifying the Point of It All."

5. Cuboniks, "Xenofeminism."

6. Oiva and Pawlicka-Deger, "Lab and Slack," 21.

7. Wershler, Emerson, and Parikka, *The Lab Book*, 1.

8. Jones, *The Emergence of the Digital Humanities*, 174.

9. Alexander and Frost Davis, "Should Liberal Arts Campuses Do Digital Humanities?"

10. While the student labor model may not have been robust in humanities disciplines in earlier periods, the acknowledgments in many scholarly monographs point to the largely invisible assistive labor performed by wives, sisters, and assistants to male academics.

11. Haraway, *Simians, Cyborgs, and Women*; Latour, Woolgar, and Salk, *Laboratory Life*; Daston and Galison, *Objectivity*; Shapin, "Cordelia's Love"; Hacking, *The Social Construction of What?*; Cetina, *Epistemic Cultures*.

12. Rouse, "Foucault and the Natural Sciences," 143.

13. Wershler, Emerson, and Parikka, *The Lab Book*, 13.

14. Hackett, "Essential Tensions."

15. Barley and Bechky, "In the Backrooms of Science."

16. Monroe et al., "Gender Equality in Academia."

17. Garforth and Kerr, "Let's Get Organised."

18. Wershler, Emerson, and Parikka, *The Lab Book*, 18.

19. Friere, *Pedagogy of the Oppressed*, 74.

20. Friere, *Pedagogy of the Oppressed*.

21. See *Civic Laboratory for Environmental Action Research (CLEAR) Lab Book*.

22. Liboiron et al., "Equity in Author Order."

23. Liboiron, "How to Titrate like a Feminist."

24. Learn more about these labs at their websites: Immersive Reality Lab for the Humanities; the Alliance for Networking Visual Culture (ANVC); the Media Archeology Lab; Sex and Slavery Lab; Equality Lab.

25. Clement, Emerson, and Losh, "Reimagining the Humanities Lab—DH2018."

26. McPherson, *Feminist in a Software Lab*.

27. See also Svensson's roundup of centers and labs: "The Landscape of Digital Humanities." Learn more at the websites for Chicana por mi Raza; Recovering the U.S. Hispanic Literary Heritage; Caribbean Digital V.

28. Bailey, "#transform(ing)DH Writing and Research"; TallBear, "Caretaking Relations, Not American Dreaming"; Wilson, *Research Is Ceremony*.

29. Senchyne, "Between Knowledge and Metaknowledge."

30. Venturini et al., "An Unexpected Journey."

31. Venturini et al., "An Unexpected Journey."

32. For more on the inequalities of scientific labs see Carter, Razo Dueñas, and Mendoza, "Critical Examination of the Role of STEM in Propagating and Maintaining Race and Gender Disparities"; Johnson et al., "Authoring Identity

amidst the Treacherous Terrain of Science"; and Clancy et al., "Survey of Academic Field Experiences (SAFE)."

33. Fairbairn, *Three Strategic Concepts for the Guidance of Co-operatives.*

34. Fairbairn, "History of Cooperatives," 24, 27.

35. Zeuli and Cropp, *Cooperatives.*

36. "Historic Park Central Mall."

37. Stevens and Wernimont, "Seeing 21st Century Data Bleed through the 15th Century Wound Man."

38. Fairbairn, *Three Strategic Concepts for the Guidance of Co-operatives*, 15.

39. Freire, *Pedagogy of the Oppressed.*

40. Hacker, *Pleasure, Power and Technology.*

41. "Why GitHub Finally Abandoned Its Bossless Workplace"; and Freeman, "The Tyranny of Structurelessness."

42. Freire, *Pedagogy of the Oppressed*, 72.

43. Liboiron et al., "Equity in Author Order," 1.

44. Egerstrom, "Obstacles to Cooperation."

45. On kitchen tables as sites of critical research, see Kohl and McCutcheon, "Kitchen Table Reflexivity." On beauty shops as theory see Steele's "The Virtual Beauty Shop."

Works Cited

Alexander, Bryan, and Rebecca Frost Davis. "Should Liberal Arts Campuses Do Digital Humanities? Process and Products in the Small College World." In *Debates in the Digital Humanities* (2012). http://dhdebates.gc.cuny.edu/debates/text/25.

Alliance for Networking Visual Culture (ANVC). "About the Alliance." https://scalar.me/anvc/about/.

Bailey, Moya. "#transform(ing)DH Writing and Research: An Autoethnography of Digital Humanities and Feminist Ethics." *Digital Humanities Quarterly* 12, no. 4 (2015). http://digitalhumanities.org/dhq/vol/9/2/000209/000209.html.

Barley, S., and B. A. Bechky. "In the Backrooms of Science: The Work of Technicians in Science Labs." *Work and Occupations* 21, no. 1 (1994): 85–126. https://doi.org/10.1177/0730888494021001004.

Brown, Susan, Patricia Clements, Isobel Grundy, Stan Ruecker, Jeffery Antoniuk, and Sharon Balazs. "Published Yet Never Done: The Tension between Projection and Completion in Digital Humanities Research." *Digital Humanities Quarterly* 3, no. 2 (2009). http://www.digitalhumanities.org/dhq/vol/3/2/000040/000040.html.

Caribbean Digital V. "The Team." http://caribbeandigitalnyc.net/2018/team/.

Carter, Deborah Faye, Juanita E. Razo Dueñas, and Rocío Mendoza. "Critical Examination of the Role of STEM in Propagating and Maintaining Race and Gender Disparities." In *Higher Education: Handbook of Theory and Research,* edited by M. B. Paulsen and L. W. Perna, 39–97. Berlin: Springer, 2019. https://doi.org/10.1007/978–3–030–03457–3_2.

Cetina, Karin Knorr. *Epistemic Cultures: How the Sciences Make Knowledge*. Cambridge, MA: Harvard University Press, 2009.

Chicana por mi Raza. https://chicanapormiraza.org/.

Civic Laboratory for Environmental Action Research (CLEAR) Lab Book. https://civiclaboratory.files.wordpress.com/2017/12/clear-lab-book.pdf.

Clancy, Kathryn B. H., Robin G. Nelson, Julienne N. Rutherford, and Katie Hinde. "Survey of Academic Field Experiences (SAFE): Trainees Report Harassment and Assault." *PLoS ONE* 9, no. 7 (2014): e102172.

Clement, Tanya, Lori Emerson, and Elizabeth Losh. "Reimagining the Humanities Lab—DH2018." Paper presented at the DH2018, Mexico City, Mexico, June 26, 2018. https://dh2018.adho.org/en/reimagining-the-humanities-lab/.

Cuboniks, Laboria. "Laboria Cuboniks | Xenofeminism." Accessed July 3, 2019. https://www.laboriacuboniks.net/.

Daston, Lorraine, and Peter Galison. *Objectivity*. Cambridge, MA: MIT Press, 2010.

Egerstrom, Lee. "Obstacles to Cooperation." In *Cooperatives and Local Development: Theory and Applications for the 21st Century*, edited by C. D. Merrett and Norman Walzer, 70–91. Armonk, NY: M. E. Sharpe, 2004.

Emerson, Lori. "Media Archaeology Lab." https://loriemerson.net/media-archaeology-lab/.ee

Fairbairn, Brett. "History of Cooperatives." In *Cooperatives and Local Development: Theory and Applications for the 21st Century*, edited by C. D. Merrett and Norman Walzer, 23–51. Armonk, NY: M. E. Sharpe, 2004.

Fairbairn, Brett. *Three Strategic Concepts for the Guidance of Co-operatives: Linkage, Transparency, and Cognition*. Saskatoon: Centre for the Study of Co-operatives, University of Saskatchewan, 2003.

Freeman, Jo. "The Tyranny of Structurelessness." *Berkeley Journal of Sociology* 17 (1972). 151–64.

Freire, Paolo. *Pedagogy of the Oppressed*. 30th Anniversary ed. New York: Bloomsbury, 1970.

Garforth, L., and A. Kerr. "Let's Get Organised: Practicing and Valuing Scientific Work Inside and Outside the Laboratory." *Sociological Research Online* 15, no. 2 (2010): 1–15. https://doi.org/10.5153/sro.2146.

The Group for Experimental Methods. http://xpmethod.plaintext.in/about.html.

Hacker, Sally. *Pleasure, Power, and Technology: Some Tales of Gender, Engineering, and the Cooperative Workplace*. London: Routledge, 2017. https://doi.org/10.4324/9781315276298.

Hackett, Edward J. "Essential Tensions: Identity, Control, and Risk in Research." *Social Studies of Science* 35, no. 5 (2005): 787–826. https://doi.org/10.1177/0306312705056045.

Hacking, Ian. *The Social Construction of What?* Rev. ed. Cambridge, MA: Harvard University Press, 2000.

Haraway, Donna J. *Simians, Cyborgs, and Women.* New York: Free Association Books, 1996.

Harding, Sandra G. *The Science Question in Feminism.* Ithaca, NY: Cornell University Press, 1986.

Harney, Stefano, and Fred Moten. *The Undercommons: Fugitive Planning and Black Study.* Wivenhoe, UK: Minor Compositions, 2013.

"Historic Park Central Mall." 1986. Accessed July 5, 2019. http://scalar.usc.edu/works/historic-park-central-mall/index.

hooks, bell. *Teaching to Transgress.* New York: Routledge, 2014. https://doi.org/10.4324/9780203700280.

Immersive Reality Lab for the Humanities. http://irlhumanities.org/.

Johnson, Angela, Jaweer Brown, Heidi Carlone, and Azita K. Cuevas. "Authoring Identity amidst the Treacherous Terrain of Science: A Multiracial Feminist Examination of the Journeys of Three Women of Color in Science." *Journal of Research in Science Teaching* 48, no. 4 (2011): 339–66.

Jones, Steven E. *The Emergence of the Digital Humanities.* New York: Routledge, 2013. https://books.google.com/books?id=yWBtAAAAQBAJ.

Kember, Sarah, and Joanna Zylinska, *Life after New Media.* Cambridge, MA: MIT Press, 2012.

Kohl, Ellen, and Priscilla McCutcheon. "Kitchen Table Reflexivity: Negotiating Positionality through Everyday Talk." *Gender, Place & Culture* 22, no. 6 (2015): 747–63. https://doi.org/10.1080/0966369X.2014.958063.

Latour, Bruno, Steve Woolgar, and Jonas Salk. *Laboratory Life: The Construction of Scientific Facts.* 2nd ed. Princeton, NJ: Princeton University Press, 1986.

Liboiron, Max. "How to Titrate like a Feminist." CLEAR, May 26, 2019. Accessed July 9, 2019. https://civiclaboratory.nl/2019/05/26/how-to-titrate-like-a-feminist/.

Liboiron, Max, J. Ammendolia, K. Winsor, A. Zahara, H. Bradshaw, J. Melvin, . . . G. Liboiron. "Equity in Author Order: A Feminist Laboratory's Approach." *Catalyst: Feminism, Theory, Technoscience; Toronto* 3, no. 2 (2017). http://dx.doi.org/10.28968/cftt.v3i2.28850.

Liu, Alan Y. "The Meaning of the Digital Humanities." *PMLA* 128, no. 2 (2013): 409–23. https://doi.org/10.1632/pmla.2013.128.2.409.

Liu, Alan. "What Are the Humanities?" *4Humanities* 12, no. 21 (2014). https://4humanities.org/2014/12/what-are-the-humanities/.

Livio, Maya, and Lori Emerson. "Towards Feminist Labs: Provocations for Collective Knowledge-Making." November 21, 2019. https://loriemerson.net/2019/11/21/towards-feminist-labs-provocations-for-collective-knowledge-making.

McPherson, Tara. *Feminist in a Software Lab: Difference + Design.* Cambridge, MA: Harvard University Press, 2018.

Media Archeology Lab. https://mediaarchaeologylab.com/about/who/.

Monroe, Kristen, Saba Ozyurt, Ted Wrigley, and Amy Alexander. "Gender Equality in Academia: Bad News from the Trenches, and Some Possible Solutions." *Perspectives on Politics* 6, no. 2 (2008): 215–33. https://doi.org/10.1017/S1537592708080572.

Nowviskie, Bethany. "Digital Humanities in the Anthropocene." *Digital Scholarship in the Humanities* 30 (suppl_1), (2015): i4–i15. https://doi.org/10.1093/llc/fqv015.

Oiva, Mila, and Ursula Pawlicka-Deger. "Lab and Slack: Situated Research Practices in Digital Humanities—Introduction to the DHQ Special Issue." *Digital Humanities Quarterly* 14, no. 3 (2020). http://www.digitalhumanities.org/dhq/vol/14/3/000485/000485.html.

ParhaHyphen-Labs. http://www.hyphen-labs.com/.

Recovering the U.S. Hispanic Literary Heritage. Group for Experimental Methods in Humanistic Research. http://xpmethod.plaintext.in/.

Rouse, Joseph. "Foucault and the Natural Sciences." In *Foucault and the Critique of Institutions*, edited by J. Caputo and M. Yount, 137–62. State College: Pennsylvania State University Press, 1993.

Sayers, Jentry. "Prototyping the Past." *Visible Language* 49, no. 3 (2015). http://visiblelanguagejournal.com/issue/172/article/1232.

Sayers, Jentery, and Tiffany Chan. "Prototyping the Past: The Maker Lab in the Humanities at the University of Victoria." *The Maker Lab in the Humanities (MLab)*, May 10, 2016. https://whatisamedialab.com/2016/05/10/prototyping-the-past-the-maker-lab-in-the-humanities-at-the-university-of-victoria/.

Senchyne, Jonathan. "Between Knowledge and Metaknowledge." In *Debates in the Digital Humanities 2016*, edited by Michael K. Gold and Lauren F. Klein, 368–76. Minneapolis: University of Minnesota Press, 2016. http://www.jstor.org/stable/10.5749/j.cttlcn6thb.33.

Sex and Slavery Lab. http://ssl.adphd.org/.

Shapin, Steven. "Cordelia's Love: Credibility and the Social Studies of Science." *Perspectives in Science* 3, no. 3 (1995).

Spiro, Lisa. "This Is Why We Fight: Defining the Values of the Digital Humanities." In *Debates in the Digital Humanities*, edited by Michael K. Gold, 16–35. Minneapolis: University of Minnesota Press, 2012.

Star, Susan Leigh. "The Ethnography of Infrastructure." *American Behavioral Scientist* 43, no. 3 (1999): 377–91. https://doi.org/10.1177/00027649921955326.

Steele, Catherine Knight. "The Virtual Beauty Shop: Crafting a Digital Black Feminism in the Blogosphere." Paper presented at the Digital Blackness Conference, Rutgers University, New Brunswick, NJ, April 22, 2016. https://www.youtube.com/watch?v=afExzX-wtxY.

Stevens, Nikki (Nikko), and Jacqueline Wernimont. "Seeing 21st Century Data Bleed through the 15th Century Wound Man." *IEEE Technology and Society Magazine* 37, no. 4 (2018): 46–54. https://doi.org/10.1109/MTS.2018.2876214.

Svensson, Patrik. *Big Digital Humanities: Imagining a Meeting Place for the Humanities and the Digital*. Ann Arbor: University of Michigan Press, 2016. https://doi.org/10.3998/dh.13607060.0001.001.

Svensson, Patrik. "The Landscape of Digital Humanities." *Digital Humanities Quarterly* 4, no. 1 (2010). http://digitalhumanities.org/dhq/vol/4/1/000080/000080.html.

TallBear, Kim. "Caretaking Relations, Not American Dreaming." *Kalfou* 6, no. 1 (2019). https://tupjournals.temple.edu/index.php/kalfou/article/view/228.

Tracy, Marc, and Tiffany Hsu, "Director of M.I.T.'s Media Lab Resigns after Taking Money from Jeffrey Epstein." *New York Times*, September 7, 2019. https://www.nytimes.com/2019/09/07/business/mit-media-lab-jeffrey-epstein-joichi-ito.html.

Underwood, Ted. "Why Digital Humanities Isn't Actually the Next Big Thing in Literary Studies." December 27, 2011. https://tedunderwood.com/2011/12/27/why-we-dont-actually-want-to-be-the-next-thing-in-literary-studies/.

Unstable Design Lab. http://unstable.design/.

Venturini, Tommaso, Mathieu Jacomy, Axel Meunier, and Bruno Latour. "An Unexpected Journey: A Few Lessons from Sciences Po Médialab's Experience." *Big Data & Society* 4, no. 2 (2017). https://doi.org/10.1177/2053951717720949.

Verhoeven, Deb. "Identifying the Point of It All: Towards a Model of Infrapuncture." Paper presented at the Oxford DH Summer School, Oxford University, July 4, 2016.

Wershler, Darren, Lori Emerson, and Jussi Parikka. *The Lab Book: Situated Practices in Media Studies.* Minneapolis: University of Minnesota Press, 2022.

"Why GitHub Finally Abandoned Its Bossless Workplace," Bloomberg, September 6, 2016. https://www.bloomberg.com/news/articles/2016-09-06/why-github-finally-abandoned-its-bossless-workplace.

Wilson, Shawn. *Research Is Ceremony: Indigenous Research Methods.* Black Point, NS: Fernwood Publishing, 2009.

Zeuli, Kimberly A., and Richard Cropp. *Cooperatives: Principles and Practices in the 21st Century.* Madison: University of Wisconsin Extension Service, 2004. https://staging.community-wealth.org/sites/clone.community-wealth.org/files/downloads/report-zeuli.pdf.

Zylinksa, Joanna. *Minimal Ethics for the Anthropocene.* Ann Arbor, MI: Open Humanities Press, 2014.

6

Infrastructures for Diversity

Feminist and Queer Interventions in Nordic Digital Humanities

JENNY BERGENMAR,
CECILIA LINDHÉ,
AND ASTRID VON ROSEN

In the last ten years, digital humanities (DH) centers and labs have been established throughout the Nordic countries. In 2016, the first annual conference of the DH in the Nordic Countries (DHN, now DHNB, Digital Humanities in the Nordic and Baltic Countries; an associate organization of the European Association of Digital Humanities) was held. There have also been calls from research councils to support the emergence of DH research, such as Digitization and Accessibility of Cultural Heritage (DIGARV) in Sweden, and collaborations within the European infrastructure consortiums Common Language Resources and Technology Infrastructure (CLARIN) and Digital Research Infrastructure for the Arts and Humanities (DARIAH).[1] This chapter explores how DH infrastructures in institutional frameworks can make space for feminist, queer, and activist perspectives, methods, and collaborations. Exploring the feminist and queer approaches of two different projects, Expansion and Diversity and Queerlit, this chapter suggests that the digital humanities benefit from creating new partnerships and research contexts, outside of established institutional environments. What these two projects have in common is that they challenge the institutionalized power structures within academic infrastructures. In the case of Expansion and Diversity this means a recovery of marginalized spaces, agents, and materials in performing arts history; in Queerlit, modifying a national bibliographic database to make LGBTQI literary heritage visible, relying on community expertise. "What would digital scholarship and the humanities disciplines be like if they centered around processes and possibilities of social and cultural transformation as well as institutional preservation?" Alexis Lothian and Amanda Philips asked in their article "Can Digital Humanities Mean Transformative Critique?"[2] This chapter asks the same question, but with direct reference to DH infrastructures: How can DH infrastructures support "cultural transformation as well as institutional preservation" in the context of Nordic digital humanities? By the term "infrastructure," we refer to facilities that enable research into specific areas. In DH, such infrastructure often relates to available digital materials, methods, and tools.

The ethos of "cultural transformation" is an important part of the definition of feminism this chapter takes as its starting point: Feminism is transformative and must be able to accommodate non-academic initiatives and collaborations. Thus, digital humanities feminism must embrace diversity and allow DH to be "heterogeneous and complex,"[3] thereby including an intersectional perspective.[4] Since discussions about the boundaries of digital humanities as an academic field tend to be gendered, an inclusive definition of DH is employed herein, encompassing not only data-intensive and tech-heavy approaches, but also work that is more invested in supporting community and participatory initiatives and bridging the gap between activists and researchers. Gabrielle Griffin has pointed out that the debates within DH are similar to those within the field of women's and gender studies during its formation and academic consolidation in the 1970s and 1980s.[5] However, DH brings together the conventionally female-dominated humanities with male-dominated technology domains.[6] Perhaps this is a clue to the enduring debates about the boundaries of DH, as the field is often construed as having to do only with technology or "building."[7]

This particular understanding of DH seems to be present in Nordic DH, based on contributions to the DHN conferences. The conference abstracts reveal that gender was the topic of six contributions in the 2016 DHN conference.[8] A full text search for the words "feminist" and "queer" gave no result for any conference during the period 2016–2019. The 2017 conference had seven contributions concerning gender, either having gender as a keyword, or including gender as a focus in the abstract. The 2018 conference had three gender-related contributions, and the DHN 2019 *Book of Abstracts* shows that three contributions concern gender issues.[9] Counting contributions in this way might be a bit simplistic, since there is a possibility that the presenters discussed gender issues in their presentations even when such issues did not manifest in the abstracts. The opposite might also be true; mentions of gender research or gender perspectives in the abstracts do not necessarily mean that such lines of inquiry were developed in the presentations. Some cases might also be examples of "the conflation of gender with sex and the naturalization of a culturally constructed binary opposition" often present in cultural analytics.[10] However, a conclusion can still be drawn from this cursory quantitative analysis: In Nordic DH, critical perspectives such as gender, queer, or feminist perspectives are marginal. This finding is in line with the analysis of topics in the Alliance of Digital Humanities Organizations' (ADHO) annual conference made by Nickoal Eichmann-Kalwara, Jeana Jorgensen, and Scott B. Weingart.[11] It has also been pointed out, in an analysis of the DHN 2018, that in the DHN conferences, "data modelling and natural language processing both feature more often than in the international DH conference."[12]

This chapter does not focus on analyzing the background of why critical perspectives on gender and sexuality are so absent from the conferences; however, it is clear that, within the DHN infrastructure, the use of technology is more highly valued or is deemed to be more pertinent than critical perspectives on power and intersectional identities. It has been discussed whether data-intensive approaches such as these in themselves operate to dissuade female researchers or feminist inquiry.[13] Although computational analysis does not per se preclude feminist perspectives, feminist digital humanists have pointed out that its ethos of positivist empiricism is at odds with feminist practices.[14] Building digital infrastructures, on the other hand, serves as a productive way to make issues of difference and marginalization present. In this discussion, we will provide examples of two "interventions" into digital infrastructure that explicitly seek to apply feminist and queer methodologies. The first is Expansion and Diversity: Digitally Mapping and Exploring Independent Performing Arts in Gothenburg 1965–2000, a project seeking to build an inclusive infrastructure for the history of performing arts in Sweden.[15] The second is Queerlit Database Metadata Development and Searchability for LGBTQI Literary Heritage, an intervention into literary history that recovers a tradition of queer literature.[16]

This chapter has three parts: the first two investigate how feminist and queer perspectives can be implemented in digital infrastructures, and the concluding part employs the concepts of "waste" and "recovery" to discuss diversity in digital infrastructures.

Expansion and Diversity: An Infrastructure for and with Performing Arts

Digital humanities has stimulated the humanities to use computational, interpretative tools and to develop new infrastructures for intersectional work. A key question is how such infrastructures can be understood and negotiated, and how they can be more driven by human, cultural, humanistic, and even feminist values.[17] Recently, DH has begun to analyze and critique the usage of such digital approaches, as well as how computational tools and methodologies might challenge power systems.[18] To underline the importance of infrastructure on a critical level, Alan Liu has reflected on the hypothesis that DH and new media studies could combine in a new field called "critical infrastructure studies."[19] In general, proposed models for hosting cultural heritage data frequently refer to infrastructure as providing access to data and resources. For example, the Swedish Research Council's report *Orientation Proposal for the Organization of Swedish E-Infrastructure for Research* (2020) mentions the humanities as an area where advanced digital infrastructure will be decisive for the future.[20] The main focus of the report, however, is on storage and calculation capacity. Infrastructure is largely framed as such—as equipment, databases, data, and tools. Humanistic research questions are rarely addressed or embedded critically.[21] Yet, digital software, code, calculation systems, information visualizations, and so forth are neither transparent nor value-neutral, but contain assumptions and values from fields of science other than the humanities. For example, Johanna Drucker argues that current examples of data visualizations lack the interpretive framework required for humanities-oriented methodologies.[22] Therefore, it is crucial not to assume digital infrastructures and computational categories as value-neutral carriers of information; rather, they should be conceptualized as driving agents in research and processes of representation.[23] Infrastructure in this sense refers not just to databases, applications, and interfaces, but also to the cultural, social, and epistemic embeddedness and critical potential of such structures.

One aim of the Expansion and Diversity project is to be informed by epistemological and critical interrogations, such as how scholarly arguments made through the research platform are negotiated and shaped by its infrastructural properties. Another aim of the project is to account for diversity in a local context and to create an inclusive and transparent history of late twentieth-century performing arts in the city of Gothenburg, Sweden.[24] During the 1960s, traditional theater institutions were challenged by the rise of new movements of performing arts in Sweden. In several articles and entries in the collective Expansion and Diversity project's open-access database, von Rosen and other project members have shown how this movement challenged hierarchies by both moving beyond conventional genre formats and performing in unique and unusual locations, such as on the city streets, in gyms, and in parks. This new repertoire was also quite eclectic, ranging from experimental dance via physical theater to migrants' performances and puppetry.[25] The project attempts to collect sites and persons who worked in both the city center and the surrounding area in order to create an online resource that challenges the mainstream narratives of Swedish theater history. While traditional theater historiography has highlighted a few select genres, this project seeks to embrace diversity both by emphasizing the local arena of the city of Gothenburg and by synthesizing multiple perspectives and media materialities, with priority given to local and more experiential ways of knowing. One example, by and large excluded in Swedish and international historiography, is the artistic, pedagogical, and social work conducted in the local context by Black dance artist Claude Marchant, from his arrival in the city in 1967 until the years around 1990 when he retired.[26] Looking into experiential, bodily knowledge, Marchant not only taught jazz dance and other dance techniques to everybody interested, but also engaged in youth dance education, allowing children and their families to learn how to make costumes, set design, and props for dance events in both established and new, at times outdoor settings. By doing so, Marchant made it possible for a new generation of dancers to build careers outside the elitist ballet school, which only admits very few students to develop their talents. For the Expansion project's researchers, it was only by a history from below that it became possible to access and analyze Marchant's undeniable importance for independent dance in Gothenburg. During the exploration, scholars found that in particular a group of white, pioneering female performers witnessed to Marchant's way of passionately celebrating their dedication to dance. To those belonging to the first generation of independent dancers, Marchant was a creative and fearless role model, who taught them to fulfil their own artistic dreams.

In *Data Feminism,* Catherine D'Ignazio and Lauren Klein list *embrace pluralism* ("synthesizing multiple perspectives") and *consider context* ("data are not neutral or objective") as two out of seven core principles for data feminism.[27] They also note the danger of committing what Gayatri Spivak has termed "epistemic violence,"[28] which is the risk of making incorrect assumptions when researchers work with large datasets, particularly when they are several steps removed from the dataset's context. To keep this risk to a minimum, a crucial aspect of Expansion and Diversity was to collaborate with local practitioners and the public and to create and host an open-access and transparent database. The project has had an ongoing dialogue (e.g., through interviews and exchange of archival materials) with practitioners mentioned in the datasets; thus, the work can be described as a participatory process.[29] The infrastructures (i.e., the open-access database and interface) make it possible to increase public and scholarly engagement and accessibility. The project intervenes in the traditional database format that simply records groups, people, locations, and dates statically in different ways: through researcher driven tagging growing out of the collaborative process, and by creating dynamic visualizations of relations between places and people, thereby recovering the forgotten persons, networks, genres, and locations of performing arts.

The Expansion and Diversity project's research platform currently allows the creation and editing of research data and will support spatiotemporal and network analyses. The database consists of short, comprehensible research articles signed by the person writing them (by openly acknowledging researcher involvement, previous anonymous text practices are changed), comments on independent performing arts groups and venues, interviews with key individuals, and personal texts written by the practitioners themselves. By focusing on local practices, a unique landscape of the performing arts arises: one in which we encounter bodies, stories, expressions, and driving forces that previously had no, very little, or misleading places in history. The analyzed research material consists of digitized newspaper materials, such as preperformance articles, reviews, interviews with performers, and political debate. It also includes explorations of often-undervalued source materials such as adverts, information, and calendars in combination with materials often found in performing arts archives such as programs and performance photographs. For instance, the project's explorations into puppetry art through newspaper materials (in particular interviews) revealed a complex and highly qualified puppetry art context for the years around 1970 in Gothenburg. Thus, lost, forgotten, or downplayed histories were recovered and shared with the broader public. Data on performances and places for rehearsals further substantiated the role of local puppetry art performers and pedagogues, and also their international connections. Traces of these kinds of performing arts practices are frequently scattered through different kinds of source materials and different media formats, such as images, text, video, and audio.

By elevating, for example, the importance of contexts such as space, embodiment, and emotion, as well as the multi-sensuous aspects of the research data, the project aims to further the value of multiple forms of knowledge and thereby rethink binaries and hierarchies and challenge unequal power structures. In fact, some of the research outcomes and publications point toward a shift from a predominately quantitative into a performative research paradigm,[30] where the collaborative, history-from-below approach underpinning the data collection for the Expansion database bridges the qualitative and the quantitative. Social network analyses, visualizations, and statistical methods are used to map and analyze the material, providing quantitative and qualitative perspectives that highlight the multisource nature and diversity of the network. However, in the case of data visualization, emotion and affect are often excluded, as are embodiment and expression. Drucker argues for the need for and importance of digital interfaces that incorporate humanistic principles in their organization, and calls for "humanist computer languages, interpretative interfaces, and information systems that can tolerate inconsistency among types of knowledge representation, classification, fluid ontologies, and navigation."[31]

It would be possible to extend this further by "elevating emotion and embodiment," which is the third principle of data feminism,[32] resonating with the emerging performative research paradigm.[33] This is particularly crucial in the case of performing arts, where it is essential to critically assess the spatial and performative dimensions of the various expressions of the performing arts, such as sound, visual input, body movements, emotion, and related experiences.[34] Regarding visualizations, D'Ignazio and Klein write that "[E]motion and affect, embodiment and expression, embellishment and decoration are the aspects of human experience associated with women, and thus devalued by the logic of our master stereotype."[35] The authors conclude, in tandem with the Black feminist sociologist Patricia Hill Collins, that the "ideal knowledge situation [is] one in which 'neither ethics nor emotions are subordinated to reason'"; in practice, this means "honoring context, architecting attention, and taking action to defy stereotypes and reimagine the world."[36]

Moreover, Drucker points out that ways of handling spatial information often "do not involve any affective or experiential features and DH seldom surfaces the physical character of a place or event."[37] Therefore, the research platform will develop functions that allow qualitative research questions by establishing spatiotemporal connections among a place, the documentation of events at that place, and the bodily experience of being in that place. The employment of critical DH perspectives and practices on database modeling, spatial mapping, and network analysis, will hopefully demonstrate how a multimodal platform can create more just, accessible, and diverse histories of performance. Another approach is a *mis-en-place* methodology, mobilizing the affective researcher body in activations of archival remains and data in the database to open up for multisensory knowledge processes, always in becoming.[38]

Queering the Bibliographic Database

Disenfranchised groups often leave few historical sources behind, especially narrations told from their perspective.[39] In the Nordic countries, there are a few initiatives collecting and documenting LGBTQI cultural heritage;

examples include the Archives and Library of the Queer Movement (QRAB) and the Unstraight Museum in Sweden, and Skeivt Arkiv—the National Norwegian Archive for Queer History in Norway.[40] Their organization and level of institutional support differ. QRAB and the Unstraight Museum are nongovernmental, nonprofit organizations, run by volunteers. Skeivt Arkiv functions as a part of the Department of Special Collections at the University Library in Bergen and, unlike the other two archives, has paid staff. Thus, the archives' conditions differ, and their digital accessibility varies. The Unstraight Museum is more of a digital platform than a physical collection, while QRAB and Skeivt Arkiv are the opposite. All the archives are concerned with history-making: collecting publications, artifacts, and oral histories. They primarily include subjective experiences—counterstories to the ones supported by canonical methods with their traces of exclusionary practices. However, the archives also share what Mathias Danbolt has called "a queer paradoxology of archives":[41] on the one hand, there is a need for definitions and categorizations, as in any archive; on the other hand, doing so conflicts with the very concept of queer, which allows for fluidity. Furthermore, as pointed out by Ann Cvetkovitch, among others, the practices of a queer archive must differ from those of public archives and must depart from other conceptions of what constitutes source material. Cvetkovitch's "archive of feelings" provides room for ephemeral memories and feelings, making the archive a place not only for collections, but also for collectives that may experience and act together.[42]

In this context, prose literature, poetry, and drama emerge as an interesting source for LGBTQI heritage. The documentation of queerness in literary fiction lacks the truth claim of actual historical materials, and might instead be construed as an important part in the creation of queer cultural memory.[43] Literature can in itself be regarded as archives of cultural memory; it is a useful source for understanding LGBTQI experiences and the forms of prejudice, oppression, and violence (symbolic and actual) that have affected this group.[44] There is a long tradition in the LGBTQI community of collecting, cataloging, and sharing literature related to the subjective experiences of sexual and gender minorities. Identifying and capturing LGBTQI themes through indexing is important for both research and the public, as such literature reflects societal values and can reflect individual experiences of sexuality and gender identity. Cait McKinney has described this development as taking place long before any digital infrastructures: "Indexers armed with paper cards and a facility for sorting, filing, and describing lesbian materials stepped in to address these access problems by building community-based subject guides."[45]

This community-based action is an ongoing effort, but now uses digital tools. Today, this issue is also dealt with in libraries, where demand and need for access to relevant fiction are shown to be important both bibliographically, as seen in attempts to highlight this literature in collections and catalogs, and through displays such as rainbow shelves. The Queerlit project engages in the question of canon by recovering a history of LGBTQI literature through the creation of a bibliographical database of queer fiction "intervening" in an already established infrastructure: namely, the National Union Catalog (Libris), which is the joint catalog of the Swedish public and research libraries. In this way, Queerlit helps bridge the gaps between DH scholars and library infrastructures, academic work, and community work. When using the National Union Catalog, it used to be impossible to identify a corpus of, for example, young adult literature from the 2000s with a specific LGBTQI theme or motif, as for example "coming out" or "transgender." Even though there are some LGBTQI terms included in the Swedish Subject Heading System that is used in the National Union Catalog, these are in many cases not included in the biographical record in Libris, due to the low level of indexing of fictional literature. The terms included are also too broad and general to be used for discovering literature with specific LGBTQI motifs or characters.[46] One example is the young adult novel *Pojkarna* (translated to English as *Girls Lost* in 2020),[47] written by Jessica Schiefauer. It won critical acclaim and one of Sweden's most renowned literary prizes, the August Prize, in 2011. It is a story about a group of teenage girls who choose to become boys by way of magic as a protest against the restricting gender roles affecting girls. Thus, the transformation from girl to boy is the main theme of the novel, and one of the girls makes the final decision to remain a boy. For this character, the transformation is not just a way of escaping sexism, but of finally feeling at home in one's body. Even so, the record in Libris does not list any terms describing this trans theme more than the wide and abstract "transformations." It also lists "gender roles," "identity," "sexual harassment," and "coming-of-age." These words do describe the book to some extent but does not make the title accessible to the user interested in fictional stories about transgender. In fact, Swedish Subject Headings used in Libris only includes the general term "transgendered people," while more specific ones such as "trans men," "trans women," or "transitioning" are absent. A consequence of the invisibility of LGBTQI in the terms applied to this bibliographic record is also that *Pojkarna* and similar works are not searchable or made visible as part of young adult literature with an LGBTQI theme, or as a part of a longer tradition of literature representing transgender. The intervention by Queerlit into the National Union Catalog is precisely to make such connections possible.

It is an acknowledged problem within library and information studies that classification and indexing can never be neutral. The "tools purporting to provide 'universal' access, such as the Dewey Decimal Classification, Library of Congress Classification, and Library of Congress Subject Headings, provide inadequate access to marginalized groups," according to Grant D. Campbell.[48] Bonnie Ruberg, Jason Boyd, and James Howe identify subject indexing as a productive place to make queer interventions in the DH and ask how controlled vocabularies, such as those in the Library of Congress Subject Headings, may allow for "queer messiness."[49] However, there is an inherent epistemological tension between the endeavor to apply fixed terms to texts and queer theory's critique of universalizing terms. Scholars in gay and lesbian studies were early to point out the bias of classification systems and subject headings, and engaged in a project of correcting terms and expanding vocabularies in order to better represent actual experiences.[50] This could be described as a modernist approach, using rational and scientific methods to create knowledge and correct misconceptions. Queer theory, on the other hand, starts from a postmodern understanding that emphasizes the impossibility of arriving at adequate and fixed terms, especially if those terms are to describe something as fluid as identity. "'Queer' as a descriptor occupies an unstable position," as Ruberg, Boyd, and Howe write.[51] But even if indexing terms always will be preliminary and approximate ways of describing complex experiences in literary form, they are nevertheless valuable as guides for readers to experience recognition in fictional characters, and for scholars to explore how norm-breaking sexuality and gender identities have been imagined through history.

If indexing LGBTQI materials is in itself a challenge, yet another issue is that literary texts are difficult to index. How do you determine the subject content of a novel? As Campbell has pointed out, we find ourselves in need of "some theoretical framework for distinguishing data from interpretation" to help us to differentiate stable content from variable meanings.[52] But literary theory does not provide any solutions to this problem; instead, it underlines the subjectivity in any reading. Furthermore, when it comes to the concept of queer reading, distinguishing stable meaning from a text is perhaps even more problematic. Queer readings can be of different kinds: symptomatic reading, which uncovers what is hidden in the text; or different kinds of surface readings, which focus on what is clearly visible in texts, such as tropes, motifs, and relations.[53] For subject indexing, the latter is evidently easier to handle than the former. To some extent, the distinction between symptomatic readings and surface readings corresponds to the distinction

Campbell makes between "meaning" and "aboutness," where the former signifies subjective interpretation and the latter refers to an "intrinsic element of a document's intellectual content."[54] Queer surface reading might also seem to be compatible with computational analysis, since it does not focus on uncovering what is silenced or unconscious in a text—complexities that a computer cannot easily detect. Literary tropes signaling queerness might still require a level of expertise to be understood as queer, even if they are present on the surface of the text. Campbell's conclusion is that complexity and ambiguity are inevitable, consensus is unattainable, and all classifications will be vulnerable to critique. Even so, the distinction between "meaning" and "aboutness" is an important one, since it allows us to make visible explicit depictions of non-normative sexualities or gender practices. For example, it might be debatable which exact terms should be used to describe the homophobic and misogynistic fantasies about lesbianism in a classic such as August Strindberg's *The Defense of a Madman* (written in French 1887–1888); however, it is indeed helpful for the scholar interested either lesbianism or homophobia in literary history if it is made searchable by terms indicating this content. Before the intervention of Queerlit, the only provision Libris made for this title was the terms "Fiction" and "Swedish fiction." Recognizing instable, queer meanings and readings does not, after all, preclude subject indexing; it does, however, urge one to consider these descriptors as necessarily subject to revision and reevaluation, and to scrutinize one's indexing practices.

Indexing terms and subject-heading systems are infrastructures in themselves, functioning as maps to navigate a vast terrain of texts. Efforts to create better metadata are often connected to the construction of physical collections, as in the case of QRAB. In addition to crowdsourcing queer life narratives, QRAB has salvaged material from the closed library of the Swedish Federation for Lesbian, Gay, Bisexual, Transgender, Queer and Intersex Rights (RFSL), collected more LGBTQI material through donations, and initiated a translation into Swedish of the *Homosaurus*, a subject-specific online linked data vocabulary.[55] As an infrastructure, Queerlit combines the construction of a subject-specific bibliographic database containing literary texts with the development of a Swedish thesaurus, built on the basis of *Homosaurus*, in order to create better access to these materials. The Queerlit database is integrated as a sub-database in Libris, the National Union Catalog in Sweden. Embedding the metadata from Queerlit into Libris enables the inclusion of queer materials in a bibliographic infrastructure that extends beyond LGBTQI materials. This integration into the larger Libris infrastructure not only ensures more long-term sustainability, but also allows increased access for a broader audience than a separate, subject-specific database could offer.

However, there might be risks in utilizing an already existing infrastructure for a project such as this. Libris normally indexes material with Swedish Subject Headings (SAO), an indexation system that presently contains 34,265 terms. SAO is topically broad and can at best be used to find LGBTQI literature, but not to find specific motifs of interest for research, as the examples of *Girls Lost* and *The Defense of a Madman* have shown. Recently, the LGBTQI network within the Swedish Library Association suggested that the terms "Nonbinary persons" and Nonbinary gender identity" be included in SAO. This illustrates that more specific terms are still lacking.

So, to transform Libris and SAO into a more LGBTQI-inclusive infrastructures, collecting relevant materials in a sub-database is insufficient; access through terms corresponding to queer experiences and subjectivities must also be added. "Indexes to materials marginalized from the historical record or from institutions such as public libraries break paths for users, wearing lines in the grass where no one has walked before," writes McKinney, underlining the value of indexing as an infrastructure in a very concrete way.[56] But how, then, to determine which paths are important enough to tread? One queer methodology might be to combine authorized terms with folksonomies. While controlled vocabularies are usually aimed toward uniformity and universality, folksonomies—that is, user-generated, collaborative categorization—tend to support multiplicity and diversity. Melissa Adler provides a comparative study of controlled terms in Library of Congress Subject Headings and user-generated tags in LibraryThing for transgender books, showing a discrepancy between the authorized Library of Congress terms and the language actually used by the people who read the books in question.[57] In Queerlit, folksonomies like the one described by Adler has been used to assess which terms are currently lacking in the SAO. Social tagging may not replace controlled vocabularies, however; as K. J. Rawson, director of the Digital Transgender Archive, writes, tagging "can produce a different discourse, a different mode of archival speech, than the highly predetermined model of standardized descriptive categories."[58] To make room for this different mode of archival speech, Queerlit has employed collaborative methods, inviting librarians and the public to contribute to the bibliography and to the description of the titles included. We also build on previous work in the LGBTQI community, collecting and describing literature in grassroots digitization projects, or in printed bibliographies. We have also constructed a separate interface, to complement the more standardized Libris web search interface, in this way to rethinking interface as a site for interaction and relationality, rather than accepting that an interface must always be defined by control and restrictions, permitting only limited input.[59]

Conclusion: Waste and Recovery in Digital Humanities Infrastructures

Through the Expansion and Diversity and Queerlit projects, we have seen that databases can be constructed to make space for diversity and complexity, and that digital infrastructures can become more heterogeneous and intersectional. To conclude, we return to the question of Nordic digital humanities infrastructures through the concepts of "waste" and "recovery." By "waste," we want to capture that which does not fit into existing digital infrastructures or is rejected because it is not identifiable as "proper" digital humanities research. The concept of recovery is used in line with Amy Earhart: as pointing to feminist attempts toward broader canon revision and to "digital recovery projects," that is, "archives and editions that used digitization to expand what such scholars saw as an outmoded new critical literary canon that excluded work by women, people of color, queers, and others."[60]

An important aspect of both projects is to create collaborations with activists and others, who have collected materials, performed volunteer work, and at times also created metadata for it. An example is Claude Marchant's hugely important private collection, forming a part of the Expansion project, in the future to be included in the National Collections of Music, Theatre and Dance. Another example is QRAB's work to collect and catalog queer materials, thus acquiring important skills in dealing with the complex questions involved in handling queer heritage. Private archival collections aimed at preserving the legacy of performers, or previous digital recovery projects carried out by activists and individual scholars such as blogs or personal websites documenting queer literature, should not be disqualified for being outside of the boundaries of memory institutions or academia. Instead of letting these DIY initiatives go to waste, they can be transformed into digital datasets and recycled into larger digital infrastructures and in that way become more accessible. For instance, the decision to integrate the Queerlit database into Libris is a strategy to recover the queer experiences in literary history, without separating them from literature in general.

To function as transformative, the developers of digital infrastructures must pay attention to what has not been given space or has been cleared away. In their contribution to *Debates in the Digital Humanities 2019*, Katie Rawson and Trevor Muños suggest that indexing is a more appropriate term for what is usually referred to as "data cleaning": "an array of other terms that people use alongside 'cleaning' (wrangling, munging, normalizing, casting) name other important parts of working with data, but indexing best captures the crucial interplay of scalability and diversity."[61] What is cleaned out of datasets, of course, becomes waste. The possibility of including data on any performing arts place in the world in the Expansion project's database, and the reliance on collective, activist work in Queerlit resonates with Rawson and Muños's aim to develop ways of working that "validate local experiences of data without removing them from a more global network of information exchange."[62] Moreover, in Expansion and Diversity, ephemeral materials are recovered and reintegrated into historical contexts. Other stories, contexts, places, agents, and experiences emerge when varied sources, materials, and formats are included in the infrastructure. Both projects also involve a transformative shift from academia and memory institutions as privileged places for knowledge production, to collective and inclusive knowledge creations, where pluralism is embraced and the labor made by others, inside and outside of academia, is made visible.[63] In this way, infrastructure may not only function as recovery, but also as a reparative work, "intervening in, and mending, existing [. . .] infrastructures."[64]

This chapter started with a reflection on how DH in the Nordic countries has expanded and consolidated itself, aided by institutional infrastructures such as centers, labs, and conferences. It is clear that a kind of waste is produced by gatekeeping in scholarly research infrastructures, like the DHN/DHNB conferences. The question is, what best qualifies as DH research in the Nordic context? What kind of studies are discarded in the peer review process? As mentioned in the introduction, gender and queer perspectives are largely absent from the DHN books of abstracts 2016–2019; at the same time, studies employing data mining and natural language processing to investigate larger corpora are common. To return to our original question, it is clear that although digital humanities infrastructures can support "cultural transformation as well as institutional preservation,"[65] the digital humanities in the Nordic and Baltic countries, as an infrastructure, mainly supports the latter. It is still an open question if digital projects invested in feminist and queer research will feel at home in a digital humanities environment favoring tech-heavy and data-intensive research that sometimes come with a commitment to "objective," rather than "performative" knowledge production. The two subjects discussed in this chapter concern databases and digital infrastructures—subjects likely to fit well into a traditional digital humanities context. At the same time, they are involved in an active creation of new data, and critical interventions into infrastructures serving to recover, as well as to create, other experiences and visualize marginalized actors. As we have shown in our research examples, data collection and database development may include practitioner involvement, knowledge exchange, and building of legitimacies across academic and other borders.

To support cultural transformation, digital infrastructures need to build upon a theoretical understanding of power relations, and a constructive and critical exchange with people and communities with interest in the data, and analysis, that are produced. This is not just a way of securing pluralism, but also a question of quality when it comes to the contextualization, interpretation, and dissemination of the data. Mobilizing ideas from the performative research paradigm, we propose that digital infrastructures can be considered active agents in processes of transformative knowledge production, always in becoming.

Notes

1. Golub et al., "Digital Humanities in Sweden and Its Infrastructure," 4.

2. Lothian and Philips, "Can Digital Humanities Mean Transformative Critique?"

3. Verhoeven, "Be More than Binary."

4. Risam, "Beyond the Margins."

5. Griffin, "Intersectionalized Professional Identities and Gender in the Digital Humanities in the Nordic Countries," 968.

6. Griffin, "Intersectionalized Professional Identities and Gender in the Digital Humanities in the Nordic Countries," 966.

7. Koh, "Niceness, Building, and Opening the Genealogy of Digital Humanities."

8. The book of abstracts from the DHN2016 conference is no longer available online. Starting with DHN2018, conference proceedings have been published in the CEUR workshop proceeding series, https://ceur-ws.org. There is a Zotero bibliography available, https://www.zotero.org/groups/2503578/dhnb-bibliography, compiled by Annika Rockenberger. See also Rockenberger, "Digital Humanities in the Nordic and Baltic Countries—A Living Bibliography."

9. The numbers derive from a full text search of the books of abstracts 2016–2018, since not all of the books of abstracts include keywords. The 2019 book of abstracts is not available as a single file that can be searched. In this case, the abstracts were manually reviewed. DHN 2020 (since 2020 called DHNB, Digital Humanities in the Nordic and Baltic Countries) has not been included here, since the conference was postponed, and the book of abstracts delayed due to COVID-19.

The contributions to the conferences that are counted in the above section are the following:

2016: Anne Birgitte Rønning, "Dagny Juel Przybyzsewska i Samtiden"; Paige Morgan, "A Wealth of Choices"; Jenny Bergenmar, "Reception History across Languages"; Steven Coates, "Nordic Englishes on Twitter"; Viola Parente-Čapková, "Travelling TexTs"; and Lisbeth Larsson, Maria Sjöberg, and Lars Borin, "Swedish Women Online from the Middle Ages to the Present."

2017: Steven Coats, "Multilingual Clusters and Gender in Nordic Twitter"; Lars Bagøien Johnsen and Siv Frøydis Berg, "Body Parts in Norwegian Books"; Katherine Faull, Trausti Dagsson, and Michael McGuire, "Reading Moravian Lives"; Johanna Ilmakunnas, "Senses and Emotion of Early-Modern and Modern Handicrafts"; Åsa Olovsson, "Young People's Historical Thinking in the Face of Digitized Sources"; Kim Tallerås, Tonje Vold, and David Massey, "Places and Journeys of the Contemporary Norwegian Novel: A Pilot Study"; and Jon Svensson, Roger Mähler, Mats Deutschmann, Anders Steinvall, and Satish Patel, "Use of Digital Methods to Switch Identity-related Properties."

2018: Heidi Karlsen, "Interdisciplinary Advancement through the Unexpected"; Ellen Rees, "A Computational Assessment of Norwegian Literary 'National Romanticism'"; and Roger Mähler, Anders Steinvall, Jon Svensson, Mattias Lindvall-Östling, and Mats Deutschmann, "'See Me, Not My Gender or Social Class.'"

2019: Jens Morten Hansen, "Sex-Mining the Digital Bookshelf"; Mats Dahllöf and Karl Berglund, "Topic Modeling and Gendered Themes in Two Corpora of Swedish Prose Fiction"; and Heidi Karlsen, "Women's Place in Norwegian Society 1830–1880."

10. Mandell, "Gender and Cultural Analytics."

11. Eichmann-Kalwara, Jorgensen, and Weingart, "Representation at Digital Humanities Conferences (2000–2015)," 84–86.

12. Mäkelä and Tolonen, "DHN2018—an Analysis of a Digital Humanities Conference," 2.

13. Nowviskie, "What Do Girls Dig?"; Mandell, "Gender and Cultural Analytics."

14. Rhody, "Beyond Darwinian Distance."

15. von Rosen et al., *Expansion and Diversity*.

16. Matsson et al., *Queerlit* database.

17. D'Ignazio and Klein, *Data Feminism*.

18. E.g., Liu, "Toward Critical infrastructure Studies"; Berry and Fagerjord, Digital Humanities"; Dobson, *Critical Digital Humanities*; Marino, *Critical Code Studies*; D'Ignazio and Klein, *Data Feminism*.

19. Liu, "Toward Critical infrastructure Studies."

20. Swedish Research Council, Orientation proposal for the organization of Swedish e-infrastructure for research.

21. Lindhé et al., "Curating Mary Digitally"; Svensson, *Humanistisk Infrastruktur*.

22. Drucker, *Visualization and Interpretation*.

23. D'Ignazio and Klein, *Data Feminism*; Berry and Fagerjord, *Digital Humanities*; Drucker, *Visualization and Interpretation*.

24. Publications by Astrid von Rosen, with Fia Adler Sandblad, Cecilia Lindhé, Helena Holgersson, Mikael Strömberg, Jonathan Westin, Ida Storm, Johan Åhlfeldt, and Victor Wåhlstrand Skärström in the Expansion and Diversity research database are accessible at https://expansion.dh.gu.se/.

25. von Rosen et al., *Expansion and Diversity*.

26. von Rosen, "Om Claude Marchant."

27. The seven core principles listed in *Data Feminism* are: examine power, challenge power, elevate emotion and embodiment, rethink binaries and hierarchies, embrace pluralism, consider context, and make labor visible. See D'Ignazio and Klein, *Data Feminism*, 27.

28. D'Ignazio and Klein, *Data Feminism*, 148.

29. von Rosen, "'Dream No Small Dreams!'"; von Rosen, "Om Claude Marchant"; von Rosen, "Digital Caregiving."

30. von Rosen, "Digital Caregiving."

31. Drucker, *Graphesis*, 178.

32. D'Ignazio and Klein, *Data Feminism*, 101.

33. Östern et al., "A Performative Paradigm for Post-qualitative Inquiry."

34. For an in-depth study on the performative aspects in researching audio files from Anne Sexton's archive, see Clement's chapter in this volume.

35. D'Ignazio and Klein, *Data Feminism*, 101.

36. D'Ignazio and Klein, *Data Feminism*, 101.

37. Drucker, *Visualization and Interpretation*, 12.

38. von Rosen, "Costume in the Dance Archive."

39. García, *Literature as History*.

40. Archives and Library of the Queer Movement, Queerrörelsens Arkiv och Bibliotek—QRAB; The Unstraight Museum; Skeivt arkiv.

41. Danbolt, *Touching History*, 114–15.

42. Cvetkovitch, *An Archive of Feelings*.

43. Doan, "Queer History/Queer Memory," 155.

44. Holmqvist, *Transformationer*, 34.

45. McKinney, *Information Activism*, 105.

46. Golub, Bergenmar, and Humlesjö, "Searching for Swedish LGBTQI Literature," 467.

47. Schiefauer, *Pojkarna*.

48. Campbell, "Queer Theory and the Creation of Contextual Subject Access Tools for Gay and Lesbian Communities," 290.

49. Ruberg, Boyd, and Howe, "Toward a Queer Digital Humanities," 120.

50. Drabinski, "Queering the Catalog."

51. Ruberg, Boyd, and Howe, "Toward a Queer Digital Humanities," 119.

52. Campbell, "Queer Theory and the Creation of Contextual Subject Access Tools for Gay and Lesbian Communities," 293–94.

53. Björklund and Lönngren, "Now You See It, Now You Don't."

54. Campbell, "Queer Theory and the Creation of Contextual Subject Access Tools for Gay and Lesbian Communities," 295.

55. *Homosaurus*.

56. McKinney, *Information Activism*, 114.

57. Adler, "Transcending Library Catalogs."

58. Rawson, "Accessing Transgender/Desiring Queer(er?)," 552.

59. Bartnett et al., "QueerOS."

60. Earhart, *Traces of the Old, Uses of the New*, 63.

61. Rawson and Muños, "Against Cleaning."

62. Rawson and Muños, "Against Cleaning."

63. D'Ignazio and Klein, *Data Feminism*, 27.

64. See the chapter by Thylstrup, Agosthino, Dirckinck-Holmfeld, and Veel in this volume.

65. Lothian and Philips, "Can Digital Humanities Mean Transformative Critique?"

Works Cited

Adler, Melissa. "Transcending Library Catalogs: A Comparative Study of Controlled Terms in Library of Congress Subject Headings and User-Generated in LibraryThing for Transgender Books." *Journal of Web Librarianship*, no. 3 (2009): 309–33.

Archives and Library of the Queer Movement, Queerrörelsens Arkiv och Bibliotek—QRAB. Regional State Archives in Gothenburg. http://www.qrab.org/index.php?&lang=en.

Bartnett, Fiona, Zach Blas, Micha Cárdenas, Jacob Gaboury, Jessica Marie Johnson, and Margaret Rhee. "QueerOS: A User's Manual." In *Debates in the Digital Humanities 2016*, edited by Matthew K. Gold and Lauren F. Klein. Minneapolis: University of Minnesota Press, 2016. https://dhdebates.gc.cuny.edu/read/untitled/section/e246e073-9e27-4bb2-88b2-af1676cb4a94.

Berry, David M., and Anders Fagerjord. *Digital Humanities. Knowledge and Critique in a Digital Age.* Cambridge: Polity, 2017.

Björklund, Jenny, and Ann-Sofie Lönngren. "Now You See It, Now You Don't: Queer Reading Strategies, Swedish Literature, and Historical (In)visibility." *Scandinavian Studies* 92, no. 2 (2020): 196–228.

Campbell, Grant D. "Queer Theory and the Creation of Contextual Subject Access Tools for Gay and Lesbian Communities." In *Feminist and Queer Information Studies Reader*, edited by Patrick Keilty and Rebecka Dean, 290–308. Sacramento, CA: Litwin Press, 2013.

Cvetkovich, Ann. *An Archive of Feelings: Trauma, Sexuality, and Lesbian Public Cultures.* Durham, NC: Duke University Press, 2003.

Danbolt, Mathias. *Touching History. Art, Performance, and Politics in Queer Times.* Bergen: University of Bergen Press, 2013.

D'Ignazio, Catherine, and Lauren F. Klein. *Data Feminism.* Cambridge, MA: MIT Press, 2020.

Digital Humanities in the Nordic Countries Annual Conference (DHN). *Book of Abstracts 2016.*

Digital Humanities in the Nordic Countries Annual Conference (DHN). *Book of Abstracts 2017.* https://gupea.ub.gu.se/handle/2077/52239.

Digital Humanities in the Nordic Countries Annual Conference (DHN). *Book of Abstracts 2019.* https://cst.dk/DHN2019Pro/DHN2019BookofAbstracts.pdf.

Digital Humanities in the Nordic Countries Annual Conference (DHN). *Proceedings of the Digital Humanities in the Nordic Countries 3rd Conference,* edited by Eetu Mäkelä, Mikkp Tolonen, and Jouni Touminen, Helsinki, Finland, 2018. *CEUR Workshop Proceedings*, vol. 2084. https://ceur-ws.org/Vol-2084/,urn:nbn:de:0074-2084-4.

Doan, Laura. "Queer History/Queer Memory: The Case of Alan Turing." *GLQ* 23, no. 1 (2017): 113–36.

Dobson, James. *Critical Digital Humanities: The Search for a Methodology*. Urbana: University of Illinois Press, 2019.

Drabinski, Emily. "Queering the Catalog: Queer Theory and the Politics of Correction." *Library Quarterly* 83, no. 2 (2013): 94–111.

Drucker, Joanna. 2014. *Graphesis: Visual Forms of Knowledge Production*. meta-Labprojects series. Cambridge, MA: Harvard University Press.

Drucker, Johanna. *Visualization and Interpretation: Humanistic Approaches to Display*. Cambridge, MA: MIT Press, 2020.

Earhart, Amy. *Traces of the Old, Uses of the New: The Emergence of Digital Literary Studies*. Ann Arbor: University of Michigan Press, 2015.

Eichmann-Kalwara, Nickoal, Jeana Jorgensen, and Scott B. Weingart. "Representation at Digital Humanities Conferences (2000–2015)." In *Bodies of Information: Intersectional Feminism and the Digital Humanities*, edited by Elizabeth Losh and Jacqueline Wernimont, 72–92. Minneapolis: University of Minnesota Press, 2018. https://doi.org/10.5749/j.ctv9hj9r9.9.

Expansion and Diversity. https://expansion.dh.gu.se/.

García, Mario T. *Literature as History: Autobiography, Testimonio, and the Novel in the Chicano and Latino Experience*. Tucson: University of Arizona Press, 2018.

Golub, Koraljka, Jenny Bergenmar, and Siska Humlesjö. "Searching for Swedish LGBTQI Fiction: Challenges and Solutions." *Journal of Documentation* 78, no. 7 (2022): 464–84.

Golub, Koraljka, Elisabet Göransson, Anna Foka, and Isto Huvila. "Digital Humanities in Sweden and Its Infrastructure: Status Quo and the Sine Qua Non." *Digital Scholarship in the Humanities*, no. 14 (2019): 1–10.

Griffin, Gabriele. "Intersectionalized Professional Identities and Gender in the Digital Humanities in the Nordic Countries." *Work, Employment, and Society* 33, no. 6 (2019): 966–82.

Holmqvist, Sam. *Transformationer: 1800-talets Svenska translitteratur genom Lasse-Maja, C.J.L Almqvist och Aurora Ljungstedt*. Göteborg and Stockholm: Makadam förlag, 2017.

Homosaurus: An International LGBTQ+ Linked Data Vocabulary. https://homosaurus.org.

Koh, Adeline. "Niceness, Building, and Opening the Genealogy of Digital Humanities: Beyond the Social Contract of Humanities Computing." *Differences* 25, no. 1 (2014): 93–106.

Lindhé, Cecilia, Ann-Catrine Eriksson, Jim Robertsson, and Mattis Lindmark. "Curating Mary Digitally: Digital Methodologies and Representations of Medieval Material Culture." In *Research Methods for Creating and Curating*

Data in the Digital Humanities, edited by Matt Heyler and Gabriele Griffi, 140–57. Edinburgh: Edinburgh University Press, 2016.

Liu, Alan. "Toward Critical infrastructure Studies: Digital Humanities, New Media Studies, and the Culture of Infrastructure." University of Connecticut, Storrs. February 23, 2017. https://liu.english.ucsb.edu/toward-critical-infrastructure-studies-u-connecticut/.

Lothian, Alexis, and Amanda Philips. "Can Digital Humanities Mean Transformative Critique?" *Journal of e-Media Studies* 3, no. 1 (2013). http://journals.dartmouth.edu/cgi-bin/WebObjects/Journals.woa/1/xmlpage/4/article/425.

Mäkelä, Eetu, and Mikko Tolonen. "DHN2018—an Analysis of a Digital Humanities Conference." *Proceedings of the Digital Humanities in the Nordic Countries 3rd Conference*, Helsinki, Finland, March 7–9, 2018, CEUR Workshop Proceedings, 1–9. http://ceur-ws.org/Vol-2084/preface.pdf.

Mandell, Laura. "Gender and Cultural Analytics: Finding or Making Stereotypes." In *Debates in the Digital Humanities 2019*, edited by Matthew K. Gold and Lauren F. Klein. Minneapolis: University of Minnesota Press, 2019. https://dhdebates.gc.cuny.edu/read/untitled-f2acf72c-a469-49d8-be35-67f9ac1e3a60/section/5d9c1b63-7b60-42dd-8cda-bde837f638f4.

Marino, Mark. *Critical Code Studies.* Cambridge, MA: MIT Press, 2020.

Matsson, Arild, et al. *Queerlit*, version 1.5. Gothenburg Research Infrastructure in Digital Humanities at University of Gothenburg, 2023. https://queerlit.dh.gu.se.

McKinney, Cait. *Information Activism: A Queer History of Lesbian Media Technologies.* Durham, NC: Duke University Press, 2020.

Nowviskie, Bethany. "What Do Girls Dig?" In *Debates in the Digital Humanities*, edited by Matthew K. Gold. Minneapolis: University of Minnesota Press, 2012. https://dhdebates.gc.cuny.edu/read/untitled-88c11800-9446-469b-a3be-3fdb36bfbd1e/section/76729465-02aa-4abb-8f14-90af33e5c340#p3b2.

Østern, Tone Pernille, with Sofia Jusslin, Kristian Nødtvedt Knudsen, Pauliina Maapalo, and Ingrid Bjørkøy, "A Performative Paradigm for Postqualitative Inquiry." *Qualitative Research*, July 7, 2021, 1–18. https://doi.org/10.1177/14687941211027444.

Rawson, K. J. "Accessing Transgender/Desiring Queer(er?). Archival Logics." In *Feminist and Queer Information Studies Reader,* edited by Patrick Keilty and Rebecca Dean, 542–60. Sacramento, CA: Litwin Press, 2013.

Rawson, Katie, and Trevor Muños. "Against Cleaning." In *Debates in the Digital Humanities 2019*, edited by Michael K. Gold and Lauren F. Klein. Minneapolis: University of Minnesota Press, 2019. https://dhdebates.gc.cuny.edu/read/untitled-f2acf72c-a469-49d8-be35-67f9ac1e3a60/section/07154de9–4903-428e-9c61-7a92a6f22e51#ch23.

Rhody, Lisa. "Beyond Darwinian Distance: Situation Distant Reading in a Feminist *Ut Pictura Poesis* Tradition." *PMLA* 132, no. 3 (2017): 659–67.

Risam, Roopika. "Beyond the Margins: Intersectionality and the Digital Humanities." *Digital Humanities Quarterly* 9, no. 2 (2015). http://www.digitalhumanities .org/dhq/vol/9/2/000208/000208.html.

Rockenberger, Annika. "Digital Humanities in the Nordic and Baltic Countries—A Living Bibliography." In *Proceedings of the 6th Annual Conference of Digital Humanities in the Nordic and Baltic Countries—DHNB2022*, edited by Karl Berglund, Matti La Mela, and Inge Zwart. *CEUR Workshop Proceedings*, vol. 3232. Uppsala: University of Uppsala 2022. https://ceur-ws.org/ Vol-3232/, urn:nbn:de:0074-3232-0.

von Rosen, Astrid. "Om Claude Marchant: Ett historiografiskt bidrag till svart danshistoria i Sverige." *Nordic Journal of Dance—Practice, Education and Research* 12, no. 1 (2021): 4–21. https://www.nordicjournalofdance.com/Nordic Jounal%2012(1)DOI.pdf.

von Rosen, Astrid. "Costume in the Dance Archive: Towards a Records-centred Ethics of Care." *Studies in Costume and Performance* 5, no. 1 (2020): 33–52. https://doi.org/10.1386/scp_00012_1.

von Rosen, Astrid. "Affect and Digital Caregiving: Challenging the Performing Arts Canon with a 'Dig Where You Stand' Database." *Archives and Records* 43, no. 2 (2022): 128–42. (forthcoming 2023).

von Rosen, Astrid. "'Dream No Small Dreams!': Impossible Archival Imaginaries in Dance Community Archiving in a Digital Age." In *Rethinking Dance History*, edited by Geraldine Morris and Larraine Nicholas, 148–59. London: Routledge, 2017.

von Rosen, Astrid, Fia Adler Sandblad, Cecilia Lindhé, Helena Holgersson, Mikael Strömberg, Jonathan Westin, Ida Storm, Johan Åhlfeldt, and Victor Wåhlstrand Skärström. *Expansion and Diversity: Digital Mapping and Analysis of Independent Performance in Gothenburg 1965–2000 (Swedish Research Council 2019–2021) Research Database*. https://expansion.dh.gu.se/.

Ruberg, Bonnie, Jason Boyd, and James Howe. "Toward a Queer Digital Humanities." In *Bodies of Information: Intersectional Feminism and the Digital Humanities*, edited by Elizabeth Losh and Jacqueline Wernimont, 108–28. Minneapolis: University of Minnesota Press, 2018. https://doi.org/10.5749/j .ctv9hj9r9.11.

Schiefauer, Jessica. *Pojkarna*. Stockholm: Bonnier Carlsen, 2011. Translated into English by Saskia Vogel as *Girls Lost*. Dallas: Deep Vellum Publishing, 2020.

Skeivt arkiv. https://skeivtarkiv.no.

Strindberg, August. *En dåres försvarstal. Samlade Skrifter*, no. 26. Translation into Swedish by John Landquist. Stockholm: Albert Bonniers förlag, 1914. Originally written in French with the title *Le Plaidoyer d'un fou* (1887–1888).

Svensson, Patrik. *Humanistisk Infrastruktur*. Riksbankens Jubileumsfond Rapport (2019), 1. http://www.rj.se/globalassets/rapporter/rj_wrapport_2019 -1_190508.pdf?fbclid=IwAR13oAoTaVVPxpPqcWYj6rXyvll6NSQb1n Z55m_bXr8H8A6IVKclGdFaM4Q.

Swedish Research Council, and the Association of Swedish Higher Education Institutions. *Inriktningsförslag för organisering av svensk e-infrastruk-
tur för forskning* [Orientation proposal for the organization of Swedish
e-infrastructure for research], 2020. https://www.vr.se/analys/rapporter/
vara-rapporter/2020-03-12-inriktningsforslag-for-organisering-av-svensk
-e-infrastruktur-for-forskning.html.
Unstraight Museum. https://www.unstraight.org.
Verhoeven, Deb. "Be More than Binary." In *Bodies of Information: Intersectional
Feminism and the Digital Humanities*, edited by Elizabeth Losh and Jacqueline
Wernimont, 71. Minneapolis: University of Minnesota Press, 2018. https://
doi.org/10.5749/j.ctv9hj9r9.8.

7

Exploring Constellations of Care and Professionalization in Black Feminist Digital Humanities

A Black Woman Graduate Student's Reflection

RAVYNN K. STRINGFIELD

This chapter is a testimony to Black graduate students' self-empowerment through building skills in the digital sphere, outside of the formal classroom, as well as a form of bearing witness to the limitations of academic training. The pages that follow detail how networked possibilities provide the appropriate foundation and infrastructure for Black graduate students in the digital humanities to survive the academy when physical campus support is lacking or fails them—fails us. Because of the situated nature of this argument in my lived and embodied experiences as a Black woman graduate student undertaking a digital humanities training on my own, many of these claims are supported by personal narrative. First theorized by Carol Hanish, the phrase "the personal is political" is further theorized by bell hooks in *Talking Back: Thinking Feminist, Thinking Black*, and legitimizes the use of autoethnographic research critical to foundational scholars in Black digital humanities theory and praxis. It also emulates the guiding frameworks of critical race theory, the core tenets of which involve storytelling.

Considering the variety of situated and embodied labor practices performed by Black scholars in the digital humanities better facilitates answering a core question: what do *you* believe constitutes digital humanities work? This kind of fundamental and difficult self-inquiry about possible motivations for including and excluding the digital projects of colleagues is more challenging to undertake than simply cataloging what "counts" as DH.

Yet we must investigate the parameters constructed around the field despite the discomfort, as this chapter invites critical and necessary self-reflection, unpacking the crucial role additional digital networks play in the current success of Black graduate students who continue to feel marginalized by academic vetting practices.

As Moya Z. Bailey has argued in "All the Digital Humanists Are White, All the Nerds Are Men, but Some of Us Are Brave," *who* counts as a digital humanist often excludes those who may be most active on social networks of care and repair, particularly if the area of concern seems to involve communities outside the academy, as in the case of action research that focuses on Black girl studies. Bailey poignantly asks: "What counts as a digital humanities project?" Such a question zeroes in one of the main issues at stake: why is the work that Black girls are doing online not seen as scholarly?[1] These are questions that I have grappled with as I cultivate a scholarly identity. Despite doing care work for my community, amplifying marginalized voices, and promoting transparency about how one moves through spaces like the academy in the digital, I was hesitant to label my work as digital humanities. But this is no new phenomenon: Bailey discusses the work of Carla Stokes, whose dissertation centered Black girls' self-making in the digital. Jessica Marie Johnson, too, describes the process of *becoming* in the digital: "I went online to try to speak myself into existence by speaking to myself. I started my first blog . . . as a way to survive."[2] My hesitancy to self-identify as a digital humanist, I realized, had less to do with my personal relationship to digital technologies, and more to do with the ways I could enter the field as it currently is constructed and reconcile it with my full sense of self and belonging.

My coming-of-age story is digital: as a preteen and teenager, writing in online spaces, from carefully crafted away messages on AOL Instant Messenger (AIM) to long LiveJournal articles and eventually Tumblr posts, was the most obvious way to make myself legible and heard in situations that otherwise often rendered me invisible and voiceless. After years of self-making online, it seemed the natural move to document my journey into the academy by crafting a digital space for myself, and eventually others. In August 2016, I began a weekly blogging practice devoted to publicly documenting and untangling as much of my graduate school journey as possible on a site I called *Black Girl Does Grad School* (*BGDGS*).[3] I quickly realized how little I knew or understood about the academy and I chose to combat the opacity of doctoral training by being as transparent as possible, for myself and others who might follow. *BGDGS* became about resistance and retreat, offering me space to debrief and decompress after a long week of navigating the new-to-me intricacies of academic infrastructure, but it was also about rendering Black girls visible. It is about the messy and chaotic quest to find a spot where one belongs in the academy. It is about discovering and being open to where it leads—how I stumbled into the digital humanities and made a home for myself. It is about being insistent about one's inherent right to take up space, especially when it seems to be the business of technology, and the oft hidden gatekeeping tendencies of the academy, to keep Black girls out.[4]

How we avoid replicating what digital humanist and education scholar Roopika Risam has characterized as the "violence" of the digital archive in the process of cultural translation is intrinsically tied with the way graduate students are trained. Graduate students trained in the digital humanities, particularly the Black digital humanities, often have deep-rooted relationships with their Black mentors in the field. While this can be true of many types of mentor relationships, affective labor is particularly expected of Black femme scholars toward their graduate students. This intimate labor enables junior scholars to learn, grow, and practice their craft. Notably Jessica Marie Johnson has described her own intimate labor as a "digital black femme love practice" in "4DH + 1 Black Code/Black Femme Forms of Knowledge and Practice."[5] She also observes that there are four types of digital work, but that the work of "witnessing and mourning"[6] is an intellectual practice, even if it is often not recognized as such.

Honoring Johnson's meditations on bearing witness as intellectual labor and framing them in the context of carework that is integral to graduate student training, this chapter contends with four facets of digital humanities scholarship, training, and engagement. When combined with a Black feminist ethics, these facets have made the academy a survivable place for me: (1) connecting with colleagues and mentors via social media, (2) engaging with peers in specialized conferences and physical spaces, (3) developing and assembling recovery-oriented digital humanities projects, and (4) learning new skills in classroom and workshop settings. This is not to say that other human and institutional infrastructures do not exist, but that these four subsects of digital humanities training have been directly influential in the development of my identity as a scholar, writer, and thinker.

Social Media and Digital Publication Platforms

Emerging scholars use Twitter (now X) to connect with one another in person during breaks in digital humanities conferences, engage in conversation about ideas proposed in panels, and communicate and network with senior scholars in their fields. Although not often described as "DH" infrastructural work, activities of blogging and tweeting have been integral to shaping the human infrastructure of care in the Black digital humanities. For me, social media relationships, which often supplement relationships forged in ephemeral space such as conferences, have been integral to my success as a graduate student at a Predominantly White Institution (PWI). In her more recent work on the virtual beauty shop, digital communications scholar and author of *Digital Black Feminism* Catherine Knight Steele examines how Black digital spaces also foster the transfer of technical expertise, much as the algorithms of complex hair braiding patterns have been shared among communities of co-learners in physical establishments. Steele uses this metaphor to challenge a White-centric narrative of innovation that excludes entrepreneurial figures like Madame C. J. Walker and erases their patents from histories of technology. Working with Jennifer Korn, Steele has argued that social media helps those who are failed by the conventional "guru" model of mentoring, which does little to support scholars of color. This paradigm reinforces "rigid, defined roles in which assistance flows from the mentor to the mentee in the specific context of career development, separate from other life areas."[7] According to Korn and Steele, social media allows Black academics to find mentors and peers outside of their own institutions and to develop relationships that may be more open to different power conurations. My own tweeting practice has opened up opportunities to visit classrooms to present research, chair panels at conferences, obtain early access to new works in my field relevant to my dissertation work, and secure invitations to review books when my name is passed along by a Twitter mutual who sees potential in my work.[8] The opportunities sometimes occur instantaneously; often community members forward opportunities at the forefront of their minds I would not otherwise see via direct message or in the replies to a tweet.

While tweeting can provide an in-the-moment connection with conference participants, long-form blogging has also been useful for synthesizing and circulating main ideas from conferences, while also providing an opportunity to facilitate a longer dialogue about questions raised in these otherwise transitory face-to-face meetings. The desire to render blogs as a medium nearing obsolescence, or even dormant, does not represent the reality of how Black digital humanists still use this function. Blogs, like my own *Black Girl Does Grad School,* provide important opportunities for Black digital communion and collegiality. Away from such conferences, emergent digital humanists of color have taken to WordPress, Medium, and other platforms for online composing to support each other. Graduate students of color not only encourage each other during their conference presentations by actively engaging, quoting, and questioning their peers, but also strive to create community in the more isolating situation of lone scholarly composition by supporting each other in their writing practices as they prepare for comprehensive examinations, submit articles for peer review, complete dissertation chapters, or explore writing opportunities outside of the academy.

Blogging provides an arena for training in carework, but it also offers an important check on carework. A valuable aspect of sites such as *Black Girl Does Grad School* is its ability to perform a "digital black femme love practice" by providing spaces wherein Black women are encouraged to be transparent and honest about their experiences in the academy.[9] This work offers spaces of both retreat and refusal: a safe haven, though digital and not physical, to recede into, where a Black woman's digital humanist perspectives are heard, valued, and amplified by those with similar experiences—and also a place to engage critically with constraints of the academy on Black women.[10] While it is an act of carework, the blog as a collective entity with many guest authors and commentators is also an act of refusing to care for anyone but themselves at that moment. Prioritizing one's self in a system that encourages putting oneself last is a valiant act of resistance aided by the platform blogging provides.

When considering spaces such as Twitter, blogging, and other digital publication platforms, like magazines and open access journals, one of the primary benefits of being a part of those spaces is the ability to think through one's work in a different way. Twitter necessitates concision, blogging necessitates identifying one small piece of a larger problem to investigate for one piece that may be part of a larger series, and magazine writing necessitates the ability to clearly articulate your findings to an audience who may be interested, but unfamiliar, with the particulars of your area of expertise. Writing in these various digital publics sharpens different aspects of one's ability to engage with a problem and communicate your findings effectively. Furthermore, an engagement with public audiences through digital publications is often an additional way to find and connect with those who are thinking about the questions you raise, but in a different way. Sharing personal essays and articles in venues such as *ZORA, Catapult,* and *Shondaland* have brought me in conversation with other thinkers in different facets of the academy and outside of it all together: librarians, literary magazine editors, theater artists, visual artists, and more.[11] The ability to craft communities outside of the academy has proved important to how I develop my own scholarship, especially when one considers the goal of my work is to investigate Black girls' creative and imaginative practices. Those practices come from every possible hidden crevice and to only engage with what has been written about in the academy is to overlook a treasure trove of possibilities. Thus, engaging in these digital publics and conversations becomes a necessity for thoughtful analysis and work.

Conferences and Physical Spaces

Steele put her digital Black feminist theory into practice in her role as organizer of the ground-breaking "Intentionally Digital, Intentionally Black" conference, held at the University of Maryland in 2018. In an October 2018 entry in *Black Girl Does Grad School*, I wrote that this "temporary space . . . was constructed in such a way that everyone could feel included and cared for. From the pronouns on our badges and gender-neutral bathrooms at the Riggs Center, to the lactation and quiet rooms, participants were cared for in a way which should be standard. . . . These touches (which were by no means 'small') helped effectively translate the communities of safety we have been building online into a physical space."[12] At the conference, Steele undertook a challenging task in trying to constitute interactions in the built environment of the university that might aspire to mirror the conditions of online care networks, since often what seem to be performances of generosity or hospitality come with their own microaggressions in the academy if conditions of fundamental precarity are ignored.[13]

Not only did the stream of contemporaneous commentary at these conferences validate the ideas of speakers and audience members, but it also performed affective labor that was understood as reparative in an academic environment that was often hostile to minority scholars assigned to the "third shift" of academic carework around diversity. FemTechNet defines the duties of this shift as "the hidden labor of informal mentoring and supporting of all students," "the often unacknowledged role of diversity representative," and "the inadequacy or absence of our own professional mentors."[14] Sara Ahmed similarly describes the high cost of working for organizations that do not share a commitment to feminist principles and the exhausting work of bridging "a gap between a symbolic commitment and a lived reality."[15] For those already performing the service labor of maintaining digital humanities platforms and managing infrastructural responsibilities, this burden of diversity work is likely to be perceived as even more weighty, particularly if an institution bears direct responsibility for past injustices and is attempting reparation through a digital humanities project. Social media may perform critically needed affective labor to sustain digital information infrastructures, particularly among emerging scholars, who are beginning to learn that they might have been delegated this "third shift" of diversity work and have consequently decided to invest their energies more productively in caring for each other.

Symposia such as William & Mary's "Race, Memory, and the Digital Humanities and My Mother Was a Computer," which focused on bringing explicitly feminist digital humanities scholars invested in questions of race and sexuality into a physical space, introduced me into a world of digital humanities populated by women and women of color. I was able to meet several scholars influential to my work in person and then sustain conversation and community with them subsequently through Twitter. These scholars and their work, both digital and analog, provide me with models of scholarship to aspire to, as well as mentorship not always readily available at my institution.

Recognizing students' need for an affirming and supportive environment for experimentation and self-fashioning, William & Mary's Equality Lab combines a commitment to the ethic of care through collectivity in order create a safe space for experimentation, growth, and self-discovery. The Equality Lab, currently facilitated by digital rhetorician Elizabeth Losh, "provides an environment to foster collaborative and interdisciplinary research by using digital tools to answer fundamental questions about the nature of equality across many different domains."[16] In practice, it provides a space for researchers at various stages—primarily faculty, graduate students, and undergraduates—to gather and work together. The researchers of the Equality Lab share projects with one another, have become each other's first readers and viewers, and offer feedback and critique to make their work stronger. Like many of the other spaces I have inhabited and discussed throughout this piece, the Equality Lab also provides networks of care. Graduate digital researchers use the space not only for scholarship and academic support, but also for game nights, Valentine's Day events, and relaxing in community. In some ways, it functions as what media scholar S. Craig Watkins terms "innovation labs of tomorrow,"[17] but in the academy—a space where young, up-and-coming scholars can tinker and create using tech to achieve their goals. The only difference between the innovators Watkins describes and the researchers of the Equality Lab is that many of them do this work as their livelihood, and not a side passion project. The Equality Lab is a space at W&M to create and collaborate at all levels. Part of the appeal is that you can know nothing at all about DH but are nevertheless welcome to come and to learn with us. In our ongoing efforts, the Equality Lab continues to work toward becoming a safe space for all.

DH Projects

The work the William & Mary "Lemon Project: A Journey of Reconciliation" does with digital projects is an example of how digital humanities tools and platforms can be used to engage with students and community members, while centering questions of carework, space and place, and invisible labor. "The Lemon Project" is a multifaceted approach to rectifying wrongs perpetrated by William & Mary against African Americans and a public history project rooted in research on slavery and Jim Crow segregation that engages with community outreach and student involvement as part of its core praxis. The "Lemon Project" is explicitly committed to caring for students and community members affected by legacies of slavery and segregation. It offers histories that complicate the dominant narrative about the place of institutional power and majoritarian memory and forgetting. This ability to rethink historical figures offers William & Mary students the chance to grapple with the less savory parts of our institution's history; it was likely a shock for many of them to learn that the first residential African American students at the college were still alive and were about the age of many of their grandparents," emphasizing that segregation was less than a lifetime ago for some. The "Lemon Project" helps to recuperate the people and labor whose lives and contributions have been a part of this campus since its inception, but who were erased in the institution's official histories.

As a graduate assistant for the "Lemon Project" in 2017–2019, I was able to use my work as a space for both DH learning and teaching outside of formal credentialing mechanisms, bringing together digital tools and the corrective historical work of the "Lemon Project" as a facilitator for the annual Branch Out Alternative Break trip.[18] William & Mary's undergraduate community service trip organization, Branch Out Alternative Break, has had a longstanding partnership with the "Lemon Project" to produce an annual on-campus, public history–oriented trip over the three-day Martin Luther King Jr. Day weekend. Former graduate assistant Ari Weinberg introduced digital work as a core tenant of the trip in 2015 and in the years that followed, including during my tenure as a graduate assistant, undergraduate students researched and curated digital projects using platforms like Omeka or WordPress to investigate some aspect of race in relation to the college. These digital humanities skills would prove useful on the job market and as I developed future research projects of my own.

Past Branch Out projects have included "Time Will And Should Tell All: A Century of the William & Mary Flat Hat" by the 2017 Branch Out Alternative Break students, an investigation of how dialogues about race evolved in the university's student-run newspaper *The Flat Hat,* and "Building a Legacy: A Sense of Place for the First Residential African Americans at William & Mary" by the 2018 iteration of the trip, which enabled the students to think critically about what is it to give spaces, particularly those they inhabit every day, layers of meaning.[19]

"Building a Legacy" provides an interesting case study for how students come to engage with the history of their institution. In this project, the students were able to interview the first three African American residential students who matriculated in 1967 about how spaces at William & Mary came to be important to them. Kim Gallon has eloquently argued for deploying a "technology of recovery" in the Black digital humanities, which is "characterized by efforts to bring forth the full humanity of marginalized peoples through the use of digital platforms and tools."[20] She points out that "recovery rests at the heart of Black studies as a scholarly tradition that seeks to restore the humanity of black people lost and stolen through systemic global racialization."[21] It is important to note that an additional meaning of "recovery" is also important for Black digital scholars, because they must also create spaces for affective recuperation and resilience in order to survive and thrive in academia. As Amy Earhart has pointed out, too often the work of recovery is devalued in the digital humanities—despite its prehistory in that recovery work—in favor of invention myths around tools. This practice in digital recovery work in one's own institutional archives helps new scholars develop necessary practical skills while providing space for them to decide how they will process, document, and share this history of which they are now a part.

Classroom and Workshop Pedagogy

As Safiya Noble argues in *Algorithms of Oppression*, algorithmic biases erase Black girls' identities in the social world, so if digital humanities efforts adopt tools uncritically, they likely reencode racist norms. Noble's work in particular shows how racist norms get reencoded, demonstrating how simple search queries enact racist and sexist stereotyping of Black girls and encodes their bodies all the while through a lens of assumed objectivity—unless we make an active effort to interrogate our digital practices and create more ethical projects. This is the intersectional work that digital humanists such as Angel David Nieves and Dorothy Kim are engaged in at their own institutions—and which they bring to international venues such as the Digital Humanities Summer Institute (DHSI). I was afforded the opportunity to learn in community with these scholars in a course they cotaught entitled, "Race, Social Justice, and Digital Humanities: Applied Theories and Methods." Such institutes and courses are integral to graduate training as students begin to adopt labels and titles that make their work legible to others, particularly as they begin to develop identities as digital humanists. Kim and Nieves offered a supportive, low-stakes environment to explore digital humanities as a field of interest, while centering the work of more marginalized digital humanists. It introduced entry points to the field, such as artificial intelligence, ethics, and social media that workshop participants explored according to their interests during and after DHSI. Such career-development and field training experiences should be offered regularly to Black graduate students, preferably with institutional, financial support.[22]

The Race and Social Justice class developed a final presentation for the week-long course, which could be used as a guide for the class and for others in the process of creating an ethical digital humanities project. The presentation was comprised of four parts: an inquiry into the infrastructure of DHSI, guidelines for designing and producing digital humanities projects, future questions to consider, and a bibliography of texts meant to encourage dialogue about race and social justice among individuals and teams creating these projects.

The following questions to consider were meant to provoke self-reflection about the nature of one's digital project:

1. What is the history of the DH tool you're using?
2. When you think of the journey to creating your DH project, how do you weigh the importance of process and product?
3. What silences are present in your DH project? Does your project give back to the communities it draws from?
4. How does your project harm and not harm? How is your DH project weaponized and/or how could it be weaponized in the future?
5. When do you find yourself thinking critically about your DH project? Who inspires you to think critically about race and social justice in your DH project? Do outside agencies or events cause you to think critically about your DH project?
6. What readings would you use to start discussing social justice and race in your DH project and research?

What we do with those answers, and choose to do with that self-knowledge, helps guide digital humanities toward more just and community-oriented projects.

For example, newly established digital collectives like Yomaira C. Figueroa and Jessica Marie Johnson's *Electric Marronage* project offer collaborative and supportive hubs around which graduate students of color can work and organize. The project foregrounds fugitivity in four parts ("escaping," "stealing," "feeling," and "whatever"), and brings in scholars at all levels to engage with these themes from their own vantage points. This includes curation of interviews, blog posts, photography, and other pieces of visual arts; it spans the website, Twitter, and Instagram; and offers workshop opportunities. The nature of 2020, given the COVID-19 pandemic, has required many of us to become more engaged and active users of digital tools. The migration of events, conferences, and workshops online as opposed to being confined to physical spaces has enabled anyone with access to the internet to enter into new spaces, and by extension new conversations and communities. *Electric Marronage* was able to offer a virtual two-day Twine workshop led by digital humanities scholar Marisa Parham, whose long form interactive essay ".break .dance" challenges all assumptions about what scholarship is and can be. Her workshop gave participants the ability to stretch our minds and consider how to think *with* the structure of a particular digital humanities tool, in this case Twine—a tool for interactive storytelling, which requires no coding. However, the way that Parham taught the software encouraged us to see the intermingling of coding language with our own in order to blend it to something new. The continued production of online workshops and curricula like these for graduate students who cannot travel or lack institutional and financial support are arguably very useful for career development and training.

As I write here, Black graduate students' access to other Black scholars can be limited depending on your institution and geographic location, among other factors. These smaller workshop opportunities in which we can engage with digital humanities scholars who keep Black feminist ethics at the core of their work and who perhaps would not be able to interactive with otherwise, give us models to emulate and potential connections to mentors. So for an emerging scholar, these types of academic situations that prioritize ethical training and carework for scholars of color, particularly Black scholars, are critical to the success of the students and candidates. What something like Race, Social Justice, and Digital Humanities offers is a set of transferable skills, which will be useful in a variety of situations. Much of successful digital humanities work is contingent on the ability to critically question a project, develop foresight about how one's project might be used (or weaponized), and build and sustain teams.

Conclusion

The growing and evolving field of Black digital humanities offers many possibilities for Black graduate students. In spite of the few institutionalized and established Black digital humanities programs as part of Black Studies departments, many Black graduate students find a haven and home in this work as it exists in online spaces. Through social media, which we may use to find mentors and peers, collaborative digital labs and projects, and work-shopping opportunities, Black graduate students find both communities of care as well as opportunities to develop training that aids in our professionalization as scholars. It is my hope that institutions strengthen their investment in the Black digital humanities, as well as the small pockets we have created on our own without institutional support—that we continue to see Mellon grants awarded to Black digital collaborative projects, more job listings in the subfield, and more opportunities for graduate students to learn from each other and sharpen their skills, whether it be in conferences or workshop spaces. The good news is that many of these already exist; I ask for more readily accessible and well-funded opportunities for Black graduate students to investigate our digital lives as worthy and valuable, simply because they are.

Notes

1. Bailey, "All the Digital Humanists Are White, All the Nerds Are Men, but Some of Us Are Brave."

2. Johnson, "Alter Egos and Infinite Literacies, Part III," 52. Matthew Delmont works at this issue from the point of view of an assistant professor and considers the way in which we may reconsider the professionalization of graduate students: "I hope that tenure does not remain the only horizon for what it means for digital projects to count. I am tired of offering graduate students and untenured faculty the same advice I would have received a decade ago: 'Finish the book and get tenure before doing a digital project.' I would rather encourage them to create the kinds of scholarship they want to see in the profession and in the world." See Delmont, "'Does It Count?'"

3. Stringfield, *Black Girl Does Grad School* (blog).

4. André Brock Jr. argues in *Distributed Blackness* that one of the foremost untruths of our time is that Black people are fundamentally technophobic. Brock argues that Black people actually love the playfulness available to us in the digital. See also Parham, "Sample | Signal | Strobe." For more on the difficulties women of color face in academia, see Muhs et al., eds., *Presumed Incompetent*.

5. Johnson, "4DH + 1 Black Code," 667.

6. Johnson, "4DH + 1 Black Code," 666.

7. Korn and Steele, "Mentors and Sister-Friends," 167.

8. To date, I have presented virtually in classrooms and for graduate student organizations at Simmons College, Stanford University, University of Massachusetts Amherst, University of Texas at Austin; chaired a digital humanities panel at the 2021 Northeastern Historical Association conference; and had a review of *Distributed Blackness: African American Cybercultures* published in *Media Industries*, all of which I can directly contribute to personal relationships with other academics around the country on Twitter. In particular, because my program

at William & Mary does not have an emphasis in digital humanities, only the specific work of one scholar, Elizabeth Losh, these supplementary experiences have been critical to building my expertise in a subfield in which I would not have gotten much additional institutional support.

9. Johnson, "Markup Bodies."

10. More on this in "my "#BlackScholarJoy."

11. For example, I was able to interview Dr. Eve L. Ewing for *Catapult Magazine* in May 2021. Dr. Ewing is career sociologist at the University of Chicago, but is also a poet, comics writer for Marvel comics, and active and fervent participant in her community in Chicago. While I was primarily investigating her relationship to the Black girl superhero, Riri Williams (a.k.a. Ironheart) in the interview, Ewing had a number of critical insights to what it means to invest in a community and the role art can play in that collective upbringing. The conversation pushed me to consider the futures that are possible in my own writing at every turn—and it now shows in my dissertation work. See Stringfield, "How Eve L. Ewing Makes Her Stories Fly."

12. Stringfield, "Making the Digital Physical."

13. Losh, "Against Mentoring."

14. FemTechNet Collective, "FemTechNet."

15. Ahmed, *Living a Feminist Life*, 90.

16. The Equality Lab's mission statement can be found on the William & Mary Equality Lab home page: https://www.wm.edu/as/equality-lab/.

17. Watkins, *Don't Knock the Hustle*, 18.

18. I worked as the graduate assistant for the "Lemon Project: A Journey of Reconciliation" from 2017 to 2019, contributing a mix of social media curation, creating and executing engaging projects and events for students to get more involved in the history of race and racism at William & Mary, and archival research.

19. "Time Will and Should Tell All"; "Building on a Legacy."

20. Gallon, "Making a Case for the Black Digital Humanities."

21. Gallon, "Making a Case for Black Digital Humanities."

22. I was able to attend the 2019 DHSI with institutional support from the William & Mary Library, which provided tuition assistance for a handful of faculty and graduate students interested in attending.

Works Cited

Ahmed, Sara. *Living a Feminist Life*. Durham, NC: Duke University Press, 2017.

Bailey, Moya Z. "All the Digital Humanists Are White, All the Nerds Are Men, but Some of Us Are Brave." *Journal of Digital Humanities*, March 9, 2012. http://journalofdigitalhumanities.org/1-1/all-the-digital-humanists-are-white-all-the-nerds-are-men-but-some-of-us-are-brave-by-moya-z-bailey/.

Bailey, Moya Z. "#transform(ing)DH Writing and Research: An Autoethnography of Digital Humanities and Feminist Ethics." *Digital Humanities*

Quarterly 9, no. 2 (2015). http://www.digitalhumanities.org//dhq/vol/9/2/000209/000209.html.

Block, Sharon. "Erasure, Misrepresentation and Confusion: Investigating JSTOR Topics on Women's and Race Histories." *Digital Humanities Quarterly* 14, no. 1 (2020).

Brock, André Jr. *Distributed Blackness: African American Cybercultures*. New York: NYU Press, 2019.

Brown, Susan. "Delivery Service: Gender and the Political Unconscious of the Digital Humanities." In *Bodies of Information: Intersectional Feminism and the Digital Humanities*, edited by Jacqueline Wernimont and Elizabeth M. Losh, 261–85. Debates in the Digital Humanities. Minneapolis: University of Minnesota Press, 2018. https://muse.jhu.edu/book/63071/.

"Building on the Legacy." Lemon Lab. 2018. https://lemonlab.wm.edu/exhibits/show/building-a-legacy. (No longer available.)

Cole, Danielle, Izetta Autumn Mobley, Jacqueline Wernimont, Moya Bailey, T. L. Cowan, and Veronica Paredes. "Accounting and Accountability: Feminist Grant Administration and Coalitional Fair Finance." In *Bodies of Information: Intersectional Feminism and the Digital Humanities*, edited by Elizabeth Losh and Jacqueline Wernimont, 57–68. Minneapolis: University of Minnesota Press, 2019.

Colored Conventions Project (digital project). http://coloredconventions.org/.

Delmont, Matthew. "'Does It Count?' Scholarly Communication and African American Digital History | Perspectives on History | AHA." *Historians.Org*, November 1, 2016. https://www.historians.org/publications-and-directories/perspectives-on-history/november-2016/does-it-count-scholarly-communication-and-african-american-digital-history.

"DHSI_2019_Race_And_SJ_Final_Presentation_050719." Race, Social Justice, and DH: Applied Theories and Methods Course, Digital Humanities Summer Institute, June 2019. Google Slides presentation.

Electric Marronage (digital project). https://www.electricmarronage.com/.

FemTechNet Collective. "FemTechNet: A Collective Statement on Teaching and Learning Race, Feminism, and Technology." *Frontiers: A Journal of Women Studies* 39, no. 1 (April 19, 2018): 24–41. https://muse.jhu.edu/article/690808.

Ferguson, Roderick A. *We Demand: The University and Student Protests*. Berkeley: University of California Press, 2017.

Foreman, P. Gabriele, et al. "Writing about 'Slavery'? This Might Help." Accessed June 16, 2019. https://docs.google.com/document/d/1A4TEdDgYslX-hlKezLodMIM71My3KTN0zxRv0IQTOQs/mobilebasic.

Gallon, Kim. "Making a Case for the Black Digital Humanities." In *Debates in the Digital Humanities*, edited by Matthew Gold, 2012. Accessed June 9, 2019. http://dhdebates.gc.cuny.edu/debates/text/55.

Johnson, Jessica Marie. "4DH + 1 Black Code / Black Femme Forms of Knowledge and Practice." *American Quarterly* 70, no. 3 (September 2018): 665–70. https://doi.org/10.1353/aq.2018.0050.

Johnson, Jessica Marie. "Alter Egos and Infinite Literacies, Part III: How to Build a Real Gyrl in 3 Easy Steps." *Black Scholar* 45, no. 4 (October 19, 2015): 47–61. https://doi.org/10.1080/00064246.2015.1080921.

Johnson, Jessica Marie. "Markup Bodies: Black [Life] Studies and Slavery [Death] Studies at the Digital Crossroads." *Social Text* 36, no. 4 (137) (December 1, 2018): 57–79. https://doi.org/10.1215/01642472-7145658.

Korn, Jenny Ungbha, and Catherine Knight Steele. "Mentors and Sister-Friends: The Intersection of Race, Multiplicity, and Holism with Online Social Media." In *Women of Color Navigating Mentoring Relationships: Critical Examinations*, edited by Keisha Edwards Tassie and Sonja M. Brown Givens, 165–78. Lanham, MD: Lexington Books, 2018.

Losh, Elizabeth. "Against Mentoring." *American Quarterly* 70, no. 3 (September 29, 2018): 685–91. https://doi.org/10.1353/aq.2018.0053.

Liu, Alan. "Where Is Cultural Criticism in the Digital Humanities?" In *Debates in the Digital Humanities*, edited by Matthew Gold, 2012. http://dhdebates.gc.cuny.edu/debates/text/20.

Manovich, Lev. "Database as Symbolic Form." *Convergence* 5, no. 2 (June 1, 1999): 80–99. https://doi.org/10.1177/135485659900500206.

McPherson, Tara. "Why Are the Digital Humanities So White? Or Thinking the Histories of Race and Computation." In *Debates in the Digital Humanities*, edited by Matthew Gold, 2012. http://dhdebates.gc.cuny.edu/debates/part/4.

Muhs, Gabriella Gutierrez, Yolanda Flores Niemann, Carmen G. Gonzalez and Angela P. Harris. *Presumed Incompetent: The Intersections of Race and Class for Women in Academia*. Boulder: University Press of Colorado Press, 2012. https://doi.org/10.2307/j.ctt4cgr3k.

Noble, Safiya Umoja. *Algorithms of Oppression: How Search Engines Reinforce Racism*. New York: New York University Press, 2018.

Parham, Marisa. ".break .dance." *Small Axe archipelegos* 3, no. 3 (2020). http://smallaxe.net/sxarchipelagos/issue03/parham/parham.html.

Parham, Marisa. "Sample | Signal | Strobe: Haunting, Social Media, and Black Digitality." In *Debates in the Digital Humanities 2019*, edited by Michael K. Gold and Lauren F. Klein. Minneapolis: University of Minnesota Press, 2019.

Risam, Roopika. *New Digital Worlds Postcolonial Digital Humanities in Theory, Praxis, and Pedagogy*. Evanston, IL: Northwestern University Press, 2019.

Steele, Catherine Knight. "The Digital Barbershop: Blogs and Online Oral Culture within the African American Community." *Social Media + Society* 2, no. 4 (October 1, 2016). https://doi.org/10.1177/2056305116683205.

Steele, Catherine Knight. "The Virtual Beauty Shop: Crafting a Digital Black Feminism in the Blogosphere." Accessed June 9, 2019. https://www.academia.edu/24777350/The_Virtual_Beauty_Shop_Crafting_a_Digital_Black_Feminism_in_the_Blogosphere.

Stringfield, Ravynn K. *Black Girl Does Grad School* (blog). https://blackgirldoesgradschool.com.

Stringfield, Ravynn K. "#BlackScholarJoy: The Labor, Resistance, and Joy Practices of Black Women Graduate Students." *Digital Humanities Quarterly* 16, no. 3 (2022).

Stringfield, Ravynn K. "How Eve L. Ewing Makes Her Stories Fly." *Catapult*, May 19, 2021. https://catapult.co/dont-write-alone/stories/interview-with-dr-eve-ewing-by-ravynn-stringfield.

Stringfield, Ravynn K. "Making the Digital Physical: AADHum's 'Intentionally Digital, Intentionally Black' Conference." *Black Girl Does Grad School* (blog), October 21, 2018. https://blackgirldoesgradschool.com/2018/10/21/intentionallydigitalintentionallyblack/.

Taylor, Toniesha. "DH Speaker Series: Toniesha Taylor on Afrofuturism as DH." *Scholars' Lab*. https://scholarslab.lib.virginia.edu/events/dh-speaker-series-toniesha-taylor/.

"Time Will and Should Tell All." Lemon Lab. 2017. https://lemonlab.wm.edu/exhibits/show/timewillandshouldtellall.

Watkins, S. Craig. *Don't Knock the Hustle: Young Creatives, Tech Ingenuity, and the Making of a New Innovation Economy.* Boston: Beacon Press, 2019.

William & Mary Equality Lab. https://www.wm.edu/as/equality-lab/.

8

Infrapolitics, Archival Infrastructures, and Digital Reparative Practices

NANNA BONDE THYLSTRUP,
DANIELA AGOSTINHO,
KATRINE DIRCKINCK-HOLMFELD,
AND KRISTIN VEEL

> Somewhere in the interstitial spaces
> of digital infrastructure, we might
> find another way of living.
> —Deb Verhoeven,
> "As Luck Would Have It"

Archival Imaginaries and Infrastructures

The ongoing accumulation, storage, and management of information in today's algorithmic societies raise important questions that have long been at the heart of cultural theories of the archive. Contemporary information infrastructures evoke a familiar problematic in postcolonial and feminist archive theories: the ambivalence of archives as both beset by knowledge gaps and traces of violence, and providing opportunities to confront such biases through methods that complement the absences of the archives with materials and narratives that center the experiences of documented communities.[1] In this chapter, we draw on the work of the Uncertain Archives research group[2] to reflect upon how information infrastructures manifest such archival problematics and to reflect on methods for intervening in and reimagining them. We begin from the premise that the digital infrastructures into which information is now gathered display continuities with political and epistemological questions that have previously been addressed within the "archival turn" in the humanities (questions about access, selection, exclusion, omissions, harmful exposure, and reductive classification).[3]

But digital infrastuctures also bear witness to shifts—in materiality and scale—that require critical attention.[4] While digital infrastructures often appear as new modes of information management that render older forms of archival orders obsolete, digital infrastructures in fact often repeat—with a difference—the imaginaries, epistemologies, injustices, and anxieties exemplified by previous archival orders.[5] Combining cultural theories and feminist infrastructure studies, this chapter suggests that while digital infrastructures have significant and often oppressive implications for their archival subjects, they also open up spaces for infrastructural negotiation, disobedience, and contestation.

We begin the chapter by foregrounding the political potential of infrastructures through the notion of infrapolitics. Conceived as the unobtrusive realm of political struggle, the concept of infrapolitics is mobilized here in relation to infrastructures to discuss the complex negotiations between conformity and dissent that play out through infrastructures. We then zoom in on two infrastructural interventions that raise questions about the shortcomings and possibilities of infrastructures and infrastructure-building: interventions in open-source knowledge infrastructures and in digital colonial archives. Through these selected examples, drawn from our practice and experiences, we show how infrapolitics operates through conformity to infrastructural standards as well as infrastructural repurposing and reinvention. We end with reflections on scale and communal practices of care and foreground the role of "reparative practices" for growing small worlds of sustenance that allow for the cultivation of different presents and futures.

Digital Infrapolitics

To conceptualize the politics of digital infrastructure, the following pages extend the concept of *digital infrapolitics*. The concept of infrapolitics has a long trajectory, conceptualizing hidden dissent or contestation. In his work *Domination and the Arts of Resistance*, James C. Scott argues that paying close attention to political acts that are disguised or take place offstage helps us to discern a realm of possible dissent, including the social and normative basis of practical forms of resistance (such as shirking, theft, and flight), as well as the values that might, if conditions permit, sustain more visible forms of rebellion. Scott advances the term "infrapolitics" to center these hidden terrains, which he refers to as the "unobtrusive realm of political struggle."[6] Paying attention to infrapolitics implies shifting one's gaze away from the transparent and open politics of liberal democracies and the loud politics of protests, demonstrations, and rebellions, to focus instead on "the circumspect struggle waged daily by subordinate groups [,which] is, like infrared rays, beyond the visible end of the spectrum."[7] Scott's concept gives another name to dissenting and freedom practices by minority and marginalized cultures that fly under the radar of power and dominant conceptions of politics through quieter and inconspicuous life forms. With important distinctions between them, Tina Campt calls them "quotidian practices of refusal,"[8] Stefano Harney and Fred Moten call them "the undercommons,"[9] and Saidiya Hartman refers to them as "revolutions in a minor key."[10] These thinkers prompt us to shift our collective attention from the high visibility of unequal public spheres to instead attune to the "lower frequencies"[11] of political intervention and how such lower frequencies, as Rianka Singh puts it, can afford new possibilities for survival.[12] Acknowledging and drawing on these different conceptions, we mobilize Scott's term here to foreground how dissent may link to questions of infrastructure.

While Scott himself wrote little directly on infrastructure, his points resonate with infrastructure studies' attention to the political and invisible dimension of infrastructures.[13] This is in line with feminist infrastructure studies and their emphasis on the invisible but essential reproductive labor that sustains and enables the visible realm of social life. Central to this thinking is Susan Leigh Star's notion of infrastructure as "an embedded strangeness, a second-order one, that of the forgotten, the background, the frozen in place."[14] In her landmark article "The Ethnography of Infrastructure," Star put forward a definition of infrastructure that remains influential to this day: when infrastructure works as it should, it becomes invisible and unnoticed.[15] Star's definition allows us to perceive the ways in which digital humanities and digital archival infrastructures mediate, combine, connect, and converge upon different institutions, social networks, and devices through interoperable platforms and channels. The infrapolitics of digital archives is thus geared toward both standardization (code, platform, cultural algorithms) and variation (creative interventions, contestations, and subversions). It is exactly these features that make the politics of digital infrastructures occur at a low frequency; if they are noticed at all, they often appear as boring "lists of numbers and technical specifications."[16] And their construction and maintenance often occur "behind the scenes" so that their effects become naturalized and often taken for granted.

If the optimal functioning of infrastructures is equated with invisibility, as Star suggests, then infrastructures are similarly associated with the social reproductive labor historically ascribed to women, people of color, migrants, and low-status workers.[17] In "The Infrastructure of Intimacy," Ara Wilson points out that infrastructures "obscure the labor and politics involved in [their] functioning."[18] As other contributions in this volume testify to,[19] the feminization and erasure of labor becomes particularly relevant in digital humanities projects and programs, which are heavily dependent on reproductive labor (especially by women of color) that remains largely unacknowledged and devalued. With the notion of digital infrapolitics, we wish to expose such areas of obscured labor and politics in the archives and to recognize digital infrastructures as a structuring force that offers control and creativity. Bringing out the infrapolitics of digital infrastructures, as is the aim of this chapter, allows us to recognize labors of infrastructural maintenance, care, and repair—which usually remain illegible by dominant political lexicons—as key modes of political action. In the following sections, we examine infrastructural interventions in open-source knowledge infrastructures and in digital colonial archives and demonstrate how infrapolitics plays. This notion of infrapolitics is crucial, we argue, to understand and intervene in the sociotechnical systems that subtend information infrastructures.

Editing: Feminist Engagements with Contested Knowledge Infrastructures

As this book testifies to, the past decade has seen an increase in feminist, intersectional, and anticolonial interventions that aspire to add, change, and challenge open-source knowledge production through off- and online communal events.

Wikipedia has in particular become a crucial site of feminist and decolonial interventions, where scholars and practitioners engage with the open-source infrastructures to counter its male, white, Western bias through edit-a-thons that seek to amplify the presence of women, people of color, and the narratives and perspectives from the Global South. To paraphrase Diane Nelson's work on mathematics and numeracy, such interventions risk reifying the problematic idea that if women and communities and narratives made marginal could "code more" (become computer literate) and hence write more, they would also "count more." But feminist and postcolonial critical digital humanities work also open up new spaces for contesting such premises by bridging critical analyses with material activities.

Inspired by the latter strands of scholarship and practice, the Uncertain Archives research group in 2015 co-organized such a feminist Wikipedia edit-a-thon in Copenhagen, together with the feminist-activist group Renegade Runners. In conjunction with this, we organized a symposium to offer space not only for production, but also reflection on the politics inherent in the logic of crowdsourcing, data literacy, and open-source knowledge infrastructures.[20] The event allowed participants to complicate the infrapolitics of quantification and openness in Wikipedia.[21] Specifically, the symposium interrogated how Wikipedia's performative openness produces new opacities and how these new opacities conceal patterns of abuse and discrimination. In addition, we also attended to the interstitial openings in Wikipedia, to explore how they could be reconfigured into new forms of feminist collaboration and knowledge production that could in turn create new and more equitable social worlds.

Like many other feminist edit-a-thons, ours was thus concerned with creating content and building a reflective community of care. Our efforts were inspired by the community-building efforts of Art+Feminism, a group informed by critical pedagogy and intersectional feminist organizing principles that trains and supports communities through creation and editing Wikipedia articles and media. Art+Feminism strives toward improved representation of cis and trans women, nonbinary people, people of color, and Indigenous communities in the writing and editing of Wikipedia. Moreover, Art+Feminism follows a Safe/Brave Space Policy to develop strategies and tools that help communities deal with, prevent, and document online harassment or misbehavior that may occur during edit-a-thons. The collective responds to a "desperate need for information activism in the realm of gender politics on the web"[22] by online and offline organizing, creating situated and social infrastructures, and ensuring that they are inclusive. Inclusivity also means tending to hands-on needs, including accessibility, childcare, and food. Only then, the group argues, can the actual infrastructural intervention begin, with the sharing and learning of skills through face-to-face tutorials. This skill-sharing crucially includes support for the affective labor that most such interventions entail.

As Michael Mandiberg points out, much of the labor around Wikipedia (and the reason many women and other minoritized groups opt out) requires people not only to create knowledge, but also to sustain that knowledge. Edits are often deleted by Wikipedia editors on the grounds that they do not abide by the platform's exhaustive standards and rules for edition; and sometimes these contestations take on a nature of harassment in so-called "edit-wars," where information is removed even if the edits are accurate, informative, and grounded in peer-reviewed knowledge.[23] Dariusz Jemielniak, for instance, describes his attempts to edit the Wikipedia entry on "glass ceiling" and how he got caught up in an edit-war after an editor annulled his amendments to the concept. He explains how, in the end, he was able to get his edits approved, not by proving that his definition of "glass ceiling" was more accurate, but by conforming rigorously to the platform's protocols for editing.[24] Other times, editorial contestations take a much more abusive and personal turn. The GamerGate controversy is a famous example of this problem.[25] The problems are structural as Pax Ahimsa Gethen, a queer agender trans male Wikipedian, explains in a blog post: "The thing is, if all trans people are driven away from editing Wikipedia by trans-antagonism—which comes from established editors and administrators as well as anonymous users—then only cisgender people will decide how we should be represented in the encyclopedia. That, to me, is unacceptable. But as much as I want to be included, I don't feel that I should have to volunteer my time to be abused. I face enough ridicule and discrimination in my daily life as it is."[26]

Editorial abuse and contestation manifest in Wikipedia's "talk pages," effectively relegating editorial infrapolitics out of view from everyday users. As critical classification studies scholar Melissa Adler notes, "for the most part these kinds of conversations are unnoticed and hidden beneath the entries that appear to have achieved consensus. The erased minority points of view are hidden in layers of a palimpsest. This is true of the content of the entries, but also of the categories used to designate what those entries are about."[27] Concealing editorial negotiations becomes more problematic when they turn abusive, effectively making invisible the sometimes violent exchanges that underlie the text that surfaces.

Feminist and postcolonial interventions emphasize that Wikipedia is haunted by many of the structural inequalities, colonial and patriarchal focal points that also skew most other encyclopedias in terms of topics, profiles, and framings. The collaborative modality of most feminist and anticolonial Wikipedia edit-a-thons offers technical and social means and opportunities to counter, renegotiate, and invent new ways of existing in and with the digital and its infrastructures by practicing an infrapolitics that mobilizes resistance in and through standards and protocols. Moreover, it provides a social context through which to stand together, off- and online, rather than alone.

Such interventions are not only inspiring examples of how technologies can be wielded to create better feminist and anticolonial infrastructures, but they also raise questions about the shortcomings and affordances of the modular nature of open-source knowledge infrastructures and editing practices that feminist software, archive, and infrastructure theories can help us to unpack. Notably, in her discussion of modularity, computational systems, and race, Tara McPherson points out that the epistemology and practice of modularity promotes a worldview in which a troublesome part might be discarded without disrupting the troublesome whole.[28] Today's information infrastructures have furthered this type of modularity at the expense of contextuality, obscuring the blind spots for gender and race that are historically embedded in archival infrastructures.

McPherson's analysis raises important questions for digital humanities infrastructures and the infrapolitics of information. How can we grapple with the fact that while we change small bits of information to create more equity, these small bits of information remain lodged in racist and misogynist infrastructures? This question echoes puzzles that have long haunted feminist and postcolonial archival thought: is it possible, through infrastructural interventions, to radically overturn the structural inequalities that still form the base root of archival infrastructures? Is it possible, for instance, to radically transform Wikipedia as a feminist site for knowledge production even if it is rooted in a culture of misogyny and capitalism? After all, Wikipedia was founded by Jimmy Wales, a self-professed adherent of Ayn Rand, and whose career before Wikipedia involved the establishment of Bomis, which Wales himself has described as a "guy-oriented search engine"[29] aimed at a similar market to *Maxim* magazine, complete with a section of photos called "Bomis Babes."[30]

The question, then, is whether these misogynist origins will continue to haunt archival infrastructures in both physical and digital form, or whether it is possible to unsettle such patriarchal infrastructures and give rise to new ones. One might advocate forgetting Wikipedia altogether and focus one's energy instead on building new archival infrastructures. As Françoise Vergès asked rhetorically at a seminar organized by Daniela Agostinho on archives and social justice: "How much time do we want to spend decolonizing the colonial archive instead of building new archives? Because it keeps going back into its old forms in its very founding."[31]

This critical reflection on the infrapolitics of Wikipedia does not undermine feminist digital humanities projects engaging with its contested infrastructures. It does, however, provide us with an opportunity to reflect not only on the contexts we create, but also on the infrapolitics of the conditions under which we create them. How to ensure that information lodged in a spreadsheet does not become de- and recontextualized, perhaps even weaponized? How to protect archives that matter? And how to counter colonial economies of information transmission?

Archives That Matter: Colonial Archives, Aesthetic Infrastructures, and Rerouting Practices

Another site of intervention revolves around the urgent need for critical engagements with colonial archives' digitization processes. The recent digitization of the archives of Danish colonialism in the former Danish West Indies (today the US Virgin Islands) is a case in point. This digitization project carried out by Danish cultural heritage institutions was presented as a promise of greater access to historical records, particularly for Virgin Islanders, from whom these archives were removed more than a century ago, after Denmark sold the islands to the United States in 1917.[32] In 2018, following the open-accessing of these records, Uncertain Archives organized the symposium and workshop "Archives That Matter," inviting artists and scholars from the Virgin Islands, Ghana, Europe, and the United States to explore crucial questions about infrapolitics, while making new interventions in the archives.[33] Extending Tina Campt's insights, "Archives That Matter" foregrounded possibilities to reimagine both the content of digitized collections as well as the conditions in which we encounter them.[34]

At the event a series of issues and concerns were raised, first and foremost the question of what counts as access, given that the documents "shared" via digitization and open-access infrastructures are still archived and kept outside the frame of reference of Virgin Islanders, so that their important perspectives and context are still missing from the records. This results in what Mette Kia Krabbe Meyer and Temi Odumosu have called the "one-eyed archive," an archive that represents the Danish colonial worldview even if it entangles Afro-Caribbean and Indigenous subjectivities, experiences, and modes of knowledge production.[35] In addition, the records were digitized but never handed over to Virgin Islanders, while transcription and translation are still lacking, especially given that many records are handwritten in Danish, making it difficult to read even for trained historians. Further issues include the scarcity of and incorrections in the metadata, and the search system being almost impossible to navigate if one is not familiar with the sociotechnical system or already knows what terms and materials to look for. In addition, at the time the materials were released to the institutional platforms, access to internet in the Virgin Islands was limited due to the two hurricanes that hit the region, resulting in unequal terms of digital access to the archives.

These concerns testify to how digital infrastructures are not neutral; they organize attention, distribute visibility, and structure how we enter a relationship with knowledge and people.[36] For these reasons, digital infrastructures can amplify some of the epistemic problems besetting colonial archives. As Amalia S. Levi and Tara A. Inniss put it, digitization cannot save what was never accounted for, what was never described properly, and what has not been documented.[37] Digital infrastructures for colonial archives are thus a complex terrain for infrapolitics, as they structure our encounters with these records in ways that can magnify colonial economies of seeing and possessing.

Such colonial economies are not only embedded in the archival records; they are embedded in the digital infrastructures themselves, and in the digital environments where such infrastructures come to exist. As Tonia Sutherland forcefully argues, the digital sphere is structured by race in ways that render Black and brown bodies as records for consumption, all too often with retraumatizing effects.[38] Scholars in the digital humanities have pointed out that the notion of datafication itself is deeply embedded in colonial histories of quantification.[39] If left unattended, Jessica Marie Johnson cautions, the violence of these processes can "reproduce themselves in digital architecture."[40] Moreover, as Jeffrey Moro notes, "while informatic forms such as the database or spreadsheet allow us structured access to information, they impoverish our affective and experiential understanding of fundamentally unknowable events."[41] This means that, ultimately, "by imagining the Middle Passage as data, as fungible, manipulable, discrete, countable—we are not necessarily doing something new to it. We are participating in a deep time of datafication." How then to adequately acknowledge those accounted and unaccounted for by these archives? How to "suspend damage"[42] in a digital archival encounter?

Infrastructural interventions in these contexts often take place at the level of description—for instance, through interventions that replace racist and misogynist descriptions in archives with metadata that is communally produced and premised on local knowledge and values. While these are unquestionably important interventions, the same question we posed above about Wikipedia necessarily surfaces: how can we grapple with the fact that while we change small bits of information to create more adequate descriptions, these small bits of information remain lodged in colonial infrastructures?

Here we recall the vital work of Black digital humanists that draw attention to the power of repurposing existing technologies to foster alternative practices and counterpublics.[43] Such repurposing can be seen as a form of infrapolitics that operates in and through the circuits of dominant technologies to tread new ground and trace new lines of flight. These rerouting practices, we suggest, emphasize the aesthetic nature of infrastructures. Here we understand infrastructures as fundamentally aesthetic in the sense that they condition what becomes visible, sayable, and knowable in the world.[44] Recognizing the powerful aesthetic force of infrastructures also allows us to see how infrastructures can be transformed through aesthetic praxis to foster more creative and sensitive encounters with colonial archives. An aesthetic understanding of infrastructures points to the need to intervene not only in existing metadata, but also in the gaps and missing datasets, as artist Mimi Onuoha suggests in her project *The Library of Missing Datasets* (2016). At the same time, such an aesthetic understanding prompts us to imagine alternative infrastructures that foreground the material, affective, sensorial, and embodied knowledge that the colonial archives alone cannot account for.[45] To further explore this we will highlight two moments of interventions in the archives that emerged out of or in conjunction with "Archives That Matter."

The work of the Virgin Islands Studies Collective (VISCO) has been groundbreaking in centering the context in which infrastructures are situated, since contexts shape what becomes knowable and sayable. The Black feminist collective VISCO was founded in the Virgin Islands in 2017 by the visual artist La Vaughn Belle, anthropologist Tami Navarro, philosopher Hadiya Sewer, and novelist, poet, and professor Tiphanie Yanique, with the intention to center not only the archives, but also archival access and the nuances of archival interpretation and intervention.[46] For the special issue of *Archives That Matter* the collective engaged the digitized Danish prison records of the Fireburn Queens, a group of four women who led the Fireburn labor revolt in 1878 against the Danish planters on St. Croix.[47] Each member of VISCO responded to one of the prison records of the four women. Their reflections combine speculation, fabulation, fiction, Black feminist theory, and critique to respond to the gaps and silences in the archive. VISCO's intervention highlights that in the aftermath of the mass digitization of Denmark's colonial archives, there is an urgent need to explore not only the contents of the archive, but also to expand the context within which these archives are situated, experienced, and interpreted. As Navarro asks about visual archives, "how different it would be if such images were not just digitized by Danish institutions and *shared* with those in the Virgin Islands, but housed—and, importantly, situated there?"[48] She contends that the way in which these documents are currently archived and "shared" via digitization is outside the frame of reference for Virgin Islanders, and that vital context that they could provide is currently missing. Not just, for instance, names and social locations of photographed subjects, but more broadly in centering Black life in the interpretation of the historical records.[49] One of their central planned interventions is therefore the creation of a virtual museum, where archival material that is held in Danish archives and has recently been digitized can be rehoused in a radically different context, in which Black life is fully centered.

These questions prompt us to imagine what it would be like if colonial archives could find a new life outside standardized digital infrastructures. What possibilities for knowledge, reckoning, and recognition would such an infrastructure open up? In collaboration with David Berg, an artist and photographer from St. Croix, and CHANT (Crucian Heritage and Nature

Tourism) in St. Croix, Katrine Dirckinck-Holmfeld ran an experiment for rerouting the archival infrastructure. In 2018, as part of the event "Connecting with the Archives: Reclaiming Memory" in Frederiksted, St. Croix, organized by Frandelle Gerard, director of CHANT, Dirckinck-Holmfeld printed more than two hundred photographs from the archives, focusing primarily on Black life from Frederiksted. Selected together with David Berg and Mette Kia Meyer, research librarian at the Royal Danish Library, the photographs were printed into a seven-by-two-meters-long paper roll and transported from Copenhagen to St. Croix, where Dirckinck-Holmfeld handed them over to CHANT. Participants of the event were then able to engage with these photographs within the physical, material, and affective context from which they were removed, reconnecting the archive through an infrastructure in which the community constitutes the frame of reference.[50]

This quasi-literal smuggling experiment can be seen in light of Irit Rogoff's conceptualization of smuggling as an "operating methodology," a "potent model through which to track the flights of knowledge, of materials, of visibility and of partiality all of whose dynamic movements are essential for the conceptualisation of new cultural practices."[51] This act of rerouting, as a form of infrapolitical intervention, interrupts the circulation of digital files under the colonial regimes enlarged by digitization, to instead redistribute them toward an alternative infrastructure for archival engagement.

From this perspective infrastructures can become a means of transformation and inventiveness.[52] As Deborah Cowen notes, "alternative worlds require alternative infrastructures, systems that allow for sustenance and reproduction."[53] Cowen suggests that perhaps the greatest railroad ever built was the Underground Railroad, an infrastructure built not from railway connections but from safe houses, passageways, and people who made escape from bondage imaginable for fugitive enslaved people. The Underground Railroad, Cowen remarks, "is a breathtaking reminder of the power of oppressed peoples to build infrastructures that work to make another world possible."[54] These considerations about infrastructures and our work with archives that matter point to the need to imagine alternative infrastructures to engage and resituate colonial archives beyond the digital infrastructures where they are currently made accessible. They also compel us to enrich the meaning of infrastructures to take into consideration the material, affective, sensorial, and embodied infrastructures necessary to center the knowledge and frames of reference of documented communities and those most impacted by Danish colonialism and its ongoing afterlives.

On Care, Scale, and Reparative Practices

Attending to the infrapolitics of editing and rerouting offers examples of how digital infrastructures can work as structuring realms of social life, where not only control, but also negotiation, creativity, and alternatives can flourish. They also point to how engagement with standards[55] and quiet and "quotidian practices"[56] such as building context, relationships, communities, and intimacies can bring about sustained change. These cases speak in different ways to our proposition and method for a feminist, antiracist digital humanities, guided by what we term "reparative critical practices" in the cultural archive of coloniality/power of digital infrastructures.

The notion of "reparative critical practice" that we invoke here is informed by Eve Sedgwick's influential call for a "reparative reading." Rather than a temporal closure or a finite gesture that calls an end to something, repair is a continuous process that emphasizes the need to continue to repair damage that is ongoing. This means that the notion of repair, rather than the reconstitution of something to its previous whole (which would run the risk of the modular approach that McPherson calls out), is tied to a poetic dimension, to the possibility of imagining a future different from the present. With Sedgwick we thus situate repair as a "reparative practice" to emphasize the processual, transformative, and quotidian labor of repairing the past into something new. "What we can best learn from such [reparative] practices," Sedgwick wrote, are "the many ways in which selves and communities succeed in extracting sustenance from the objects of a culture—even of a culture whose avowed desire has often been not to sustain them."[57] Drawing on Sedgwick, the reparative practice we propose is about learning how to grow worlds of sustenance from infrastructures not always meant to sustain us, in order to cultivate and live out a different future.

Paying attention to reparative practices allows us to reflect on one crucial question that we would like to consider as a final reflection: as digital collections and infrastructures grow and become ever more present and entangled with each other, how to correlate scale and care? Is it possible to enact reparative work at scale?

As Anna Tsing shows, scale is not a neutral frame for viewing the world.[58] While Tsing's references come from software systems, she locates their logics in the colonial plantation economy. As she notes, one important model of scalability design was European sugarcane plantations in colonized places. "These plantations," she writes, "developed the standardized and segregated nonsocial landscape elements" that "showed how scalability might work to produce profit (and progress)."[59] "Plantations," then, "gave us the equivalent of pixels for the land,"[60] which also embeds digital infrastructures within colonial epistemologies. Like McPherson's work on modularity, Tsing's historical account of scalability gives us cause to reflect on the ways in which infrastructural interventions conceptualize and make the world we desire, including the naturalization of expansion as a way to create more just environments. Expansion here refers not only to "gigantism" in information architectures,[61] but also to data collections, that are often framed as "the bigger, the better." With Tsing we might ask, then: What is it that we want to grow? Who profits from this growth, and who suffers or is left out? As we have shown with our work with archives that matter, the scale of mass digitization raises a series of unresolved issues that the size of the collection alone cannot resolve. Ultimately, it is not only about digitizing more than 1.5 km of shelf material, but also about creating more equitable forms of sharing and making those records available to the scrutiny and interpretation of impacted communities through their own terms of reference. This entails creating the context and conditions for a "critical digital catalogue"[62] to emerge, supported by infrastructural practices that facilitate critical interpretation and reimagination of the collections.

What we have termed rerouting practices are an example of "digital reparative practices" that intervene at the level of scale. Rerouting practices interrupt the circulation of digital files under the colonial regimes enlarged by digitization, to instead redistribute them toward an alternative infrastructure for archival engagement. To come back to our aesthetic understanding of infrastructures, this means that infrastructures can be reimagined by creating new configurations and forms toward greater sovereignty. In this we are inspired by St. Croix–based visual artist La Vaughn Belle and her proposition to redraw the boundaries of Empire. In her video work *Between the Dusk and Dawn (how to navigate an unsettled empire)* (2023), Belle positions herself between Point Udall in St. Croix and Point Udall in Guam, the eastern and westernmost point of the American Empire. Filming the sunrise in St. Croix and the sunset in Guam, Belle describes herself as drawing new maps with her body. Belle's reimagining of the lines of American Empire to draw new maps allows us to think about envisioning new routes that recenter Black, Indigenous, and feminist experiences unaccounted for in the archives. The existing digital infrastructures, unilaterally rolled out from Denmark, can be the starting point for a new and multilateral "data-geography"[63] that links communities from the Virgin Islands, Ghana, Kalaallit Nunaat (Greenland), and India, communities differently impacted by the scalability of Danish colonialism and whose archives and critical interventions can be reconnected through their own frames of reference.

Coming back to the question of what it is that we want to grow, we suggest that feminist digital humanities can intervene in digital infrastructures in various modalities simultaneously, bringing them into solidarity in "reparative critical practices": on the one hand, in intervening in and mending existing colonial, racist, and gendered infrastructures to reduce the damage they have caused and continue to cause; on the other hand, in upending the sociotechnical systems that subtend those infrastructures and giving rise to new, inventive, and more equitable infrastructures. Rather than interventions that offer finite gestures or closure, such reparative practices should give continuous cause for reflection on the changing ethics of infrastructure, and on how we might continuously grow other ways of living with, through, and beyond these technologies.

Notes

The authors would like to thank Marianne Ping-Huang for her support and infrastructure-building efforts, which have been crucial to sustaining this project. This work has been supported by the European Research Council, grant number 123563.

1. Risam, *New Digital Worlds*, 47.

2. The Uncertain Archives research group originated at the Department of Arts and Cultural Studies, University of Copenhagen, funded by a grant by the Danish Research Council. The group has since then extended its scope and can today be regarded as a collective that brings together scholars and artists based at different institutions in Denmark and abroad, dedicated to thinking critically about the unknowns, errors, and vulnerabilities of archives in an age of datafication.

3. Stoler, *Carnal Knowledge and Imperial Power*.

4. Chun and Friedland, "Habits of Leaking"; Nakamura, "'I WILL DO EVERYthing That Am Asked'"; Noble, *Algorithms of Oppression*; Sutherland, "Making a Killing."

5. Agostinho, Dirckinck-Holmfeld, and Søilen, "Archives That Matter."

6. Scott, *Domination and the Arts of Resistance*, 183.

7. Scott, *Domination and the Arts of Resistance*, 183.

8. Campt, *Listening to Images*.

9. Harney and Moten, *The Undercommons*.

10. Hartman, *Wayward Lives, Beautiful Experiments*.

11. Campt, *Listening to Images*.

12. Singh, "Resistance in a Minor Key."

13. Easterling, *Extrastatecraft*; Mitropoulos, *Contract and Contagion*.

14. Star, "The Ethnography of Infrastructure," 379.

15. This definition has been challenged by postcolonial infrastructure studies that point to the fact that infrastructures, especially those outside the wealthy North, are not necessarily invisible and seamless, and that breakdown and leaky circuits are not an interruption of infrastructural functionality but an essential

part of the vital materiality of an infrastructure. This brings the labor and politics that goes into their maintenance into sharper focus. See Anand, "Accretion."

16. Star, "The Ethnography of Infrastructure."

17. The invisibilization of infrastructures is in many ways endemic to contemporary capitalism, and its reliance on, and further development of, new technologies for control and management, modularization and transportation. It is thus often co-opted by neoliberal forces, for instance in the form of free trade zones (Easterling, *Extrastatecraft*) and new forms of exploitative digital labor, for instance Amazon's Mechanical Turk (Irani, "The Cultural Work of Microwork") and the globalized content moderation industry (Roberts, *Behind the Screen*), which all rely on the harmonization, homogenization, and replication of digital infrastructures, and of projecting an imaginary existence beyond sovereign control.

18. Wilson, "The Infrastructure of Intimacy," 270.

19. See chapters by Brown and Mandell; Stringfield; and Wernimont and Stevens, in this volume.

20. See Borgen, Thylstrup, and Veel, "Introduction."

21. Ping-Huang, "Archival Biases and Cross-Sharing."

22. Evans, Mabey, and Mandiberg, "Editing for Equality."

23. Mandiberg, "The Affective Labor of Wikipedia."

24. Jemielniak, "Breaking the Glass Ceiling on Wikipedia."

25. Salor, "Neutrality in the Face of Reckless Hate."

26. Gethen, "Ten Years a Wikipedian."

27. Adler, "Wikipedia and the Myth of Universality," 36.

28. McPherson, "U.S. Operating Systems at Mid-Century."

29. Mangu-Ward, "Wikipedia and Beyond."

30. Hansen, Wikipedia Founder Edits Own Bio."

31. Vergès, "Memories of Struggles and Visual/Sonic Archives."

32. While a large portion of the archives was moved to Denmark after the sale of the islands, archivist and archival scholar Jeannette Bastian has noted that there were several shipments of records to Copenhagen before the sale, namely around earlier attempts to sell the islands. Bastian, *Owning Memory*. See also Agostinho, "Archival Encounters."

33. The event was realized with support from the University of Copenhagen and the Digital Research Infrastructure for the Arts and Humanities (DARIAH-EU).

34. Here we echo Tina Campt's listening as "a method that requires us to interrogate both the archival encounter, as well as the content of archival collections, in multiple tenses and temporalities in ways that attend to both their stakes and possibilities." Campt, *Listening to Images*, 8.

35. Krabbe Meyer and Odumosu, "One-Eyed Archive," 40.

36. Verhoeven, "As Luck Would Have It."

37. Levi and Inniss, "Decolonizing the Archival Record about the Enslaved."

38. Sutherland, "Making a Killing," 37.

39. Johnson, "Markup Bodies"; Moro, "Want of Water, Want of Data"; Wernimont, *Numbered Lives*.

40. Johnson, "Markup Bodies," 58.

41. Moro, "Want of Water, Want of Data."

42. Tuck, "Suspending Damage."

43. Gallon, "Making a Case for the Black Digital Humanities"; Lu and Steele, "'Joy Is Resistance'"; Brock, *Distributed Blackness*; Johnson, "Xroads Praxis"; see also Stringfield, this volume.

44. Larkin, "The Politics and Poetics of Infrastructure."

45. Agostinho, Dirckinck-Holmfeld, and Soilen, "Archives That Matter."

46. Virgin Islands Studies Collective (VISCO), "Ancestral Queendom," 19.

47. The records were transcribed and translated within the context of the Fireburn Files Project, coordinated by Dr. Helle Stenum, with support from Dr. Heidi Bojsen, who provided English translations of the prison records from the original Danish.

48. Virgin Islands Studies Collective (VISCO), "Ancestral Queendom," 24.

49. See also Flewellen, "African Diasporic Choices."

50. See Agostinho, Dirckinck-Holmfeld, and Søilen, "Archives That Matter." See also Krabbe Meyer and Odumosu, "One-Eyed Archive."

51. Rogoff, "Smuggling—An Embodied Criticality," 3.

52. Verhoeven, "As Luck Would Have It."

53. Cowen, "Infrastructures of Empire and Resistance."

54. Cowen, "Infrastructures of Empire and Resistance."

55. Star, "The Ethnography of Infrastructure."

56. Campt, *Listening to Images*.

57. Sedgwick, "Paranoid Reading and Reparative Reading," 35.

58. Tsing, "On Nonscalability."

59. Tsing, "On Nonscalability," 510.

60. Tsing, "On Nonscalability," 510.

61. Steiner and Veel, *Tower to Tower*.

62. Meyer and Odumosu, "One-Eyed Archive," 58.

63. Here we draw on Kodwo Eshun and Ros Gray's notion of ciné-geography, which describes "situated cinecultural practices in an expanded sense, and the connections—individual, institutional, aesthetic and political—that link them transnationally to other situations of urgent struggle." Eshun and Gray, "The Militant Image."

Works Cited

Adler, Melissa. "Wikipedia and the Myth of Universality." *Nordisk Tidsskrift for Informationsvidenskab Og Kulturformidling* 5, no. 1 (2016): 37–41.

Agostinho, Daniela. "Archival Encounters: Rethinking Access and Care in Digital Colonial Archives." *Archival Science* 19, no. 2 (2019): 141–65.

Agostinho, Daniela, Katrine Dirckinck-Holmfeld, and Karen Louise Grova Søilen. "Archives That Matter: Infrastructures for Sharing Unshared Histories:

An Introduction." *Nordisk Tidsskrift for Informationsvidenskab Og Kulturformidling* 8, no. 2 (2019): 1–18.

Anand, Nikhil. "Accretion." Theorizing the Contemporary. *Fieldsights*, September 24, 2015. https://culanth.org/fieldsights/accretion.

Appel, Hannah, Nikhil Anand, and Akhil Gupta. "Introduction: Temporality, Politics, and the Promise of Infrastructure." In *Promise of Infrastructure*, edited by Nikhil Anand, Hannah Appel, and Akhil Gupta, 1–40. Durham, NC: Duke University Press, 2018.

Bastian, J. *Owning Memory: How a Caribbean Community Lost Its Archives and Found Its History*. Westport, CT: Libraries Unlimited, 2003.

Bergfeld, Mark, and Sarah Farris. "The COVID-19 Crisis and the End of the "Low-skilled" Worker." *Spectre Journal*, May 10, 2020. https://spectrejournal.com/the-covid-19-crisis-and-the-end-of-the-low-skilled-worker/.

Borgen, Maibritt, Nanna Bonde Thylstrup, and Kristin Veel. "Introduction." *Nordisk Tidsskrift for Informationsvidenskab Og Kulturformidling* 5, no. 1 (2016): 3–8.

Boulos, Maged N Kamel, et al. "Wikis, Blogs, and Podcasts: A New Generation of Web-based Tools for Virtual Collaborative Clinical Practice and Education." *BMC Medical Education* 6, no. 41 (2006). https://doi.org/10.1186/1472-6920-6-41.

Brock, André Jr. *Distributed Blackness: African American Cybercultures*. New York: NYU Press, 2020.

Campt, Tina. *Listening to Images*. Durham, NC: Duke University Press, 2017.

Christen, Kim. "On Not Looking: Economies of Visuality in Digital Museums." *The International Handbooks of Museum Studies:* Vol. 4, *Museum Transformations*, edited by Annie E. Coombes and Ruth B. Phillips, 365–86. Hoboken, NJ: Wiley-Blackwell, 2015.

Chun, Wendy Hui Kyong, and Sarah Friedland. "Habits of Leaking: Of Sluts and Network Cards." *differences* 26, no. 2 (2015): 1–28.

Cowen, D. "Infrastructures of Empire and Resistance." Blog. 2017. https://www.versobooks.com/blogs/3067-infrastructures-of-empire-and-resistance.

Dirckinck-Holmfeld, Katrine. "(Para)paranoia: Affect as Critical Inquiry," *Diffractions*, no. 1, 2nd series (2019). https://doi.org/10.34632/diffractions.2019.1475.

Easterling, Keller. *Extrastatecraft: The Power of Infrastructure Space*. London: Verso, 2016.

Eshun, Kodwo, and Ros Gray. "The Militant Image: A Ciné-Geography." *Third Text* 25, no. 1 (2011): 1–12. https://doi.org/10.1080/09528822.2011.545606.

Evans, S., J. Mabey, and M. Mandiberg. "Editing for Equality: The Outcomes of the Art+Feminism Wikipedia Edit-a-thons," *Art Documentation: Journal of the Art Libraries Society of North America* 34, no. 2 (2015): 194–203.

Flewellen, Ayana Omilade. "African Diasporic Choices: Locating the Lived Experiences of Afro-Crucians in the Archival and Archaeological Record." *Nordisk Tidsskrift for Informationsvidenskab Og Kulturformidling* 8, no. 2 (2019): 54–74.

Gallon, Kim. "Making a Case for the Black Digital Humanities." In *Debates in the Digital Humanities*, edited by Matthew Gold and Lauren F. Klein. Minnesota: University of Minneapolis Press, 2016. http://dhdebates.gc.cuny.edu/debates/text/55.

Gethen, Pax Ahimsa. "Ten Years a Wikipedian." *Medium*, August 29, 2018. https://medium.com/@funcrunch/ten-years-a-wikipedian-fd0a7c574d2a.

Graziano, Valeria, Marcell Mars, and Tomislav Medak. "Pirate Care." *ArtForum*, May 11, 2020. https://www.artforum.com/slant/valeria-graziano-marcell-mars-and-tomlsav-medak-on-the-care-crisis-83037.

Hansen, Evan. "Wikipedia Founder Edits Own Bio." *Wired*, December 19, 2005.

Harney, Stefano, and Fred Moten. *The Undercommons: Fugitive Planning and Black Study*. Wivenhoe, UK: Minor Compositions, 2013.

Hartman, Saidiya. *Wayward Lives, Beautiful Experiments: Intimate Histories of Social Upheaval*. New York: W. W. Norton, 2019.

Irani, Lilly. "The Cultural Work of Microwork." *New Media & Society* 17, no. 5 (2015): 720–39.

Jemielniak, D. "Breaking the Glass Ceiling on Wikipedia." *Feminist Review* 113, no. 1 (2016): 103–8. https://doi.org/10.1057/fr.2016.9.

Johnson, J. M. "Markup Bodies: Black [Life] Studies and Slavery [Death] Studies at the Digital Crossroads." *Social Text* 36, no. 4 (2018): 57–79.

Johnson, J. M. "Xroads Praxis: Black Diasporic Technologies for Remaking the New World." *small axe archipelagos* 3 (2019). http://smallaxe.net/sxarchipelagos/issue03/johnson.html.

Koh, Adeline, and Roopika Risam. "THE REWRITING WIKIPEDIA PROJECT." *Postcolonial Digital Humanities* (n.d.). https://dhpoco.org/rewriting-wikipedia/.

Krabbe Meyer, Mette Kia, and Odumosu, Temi. "One-Eyed Archive: Metadata Reflections on the USVI Photographic Collections at the Royal Danish Library." *Digital Culture & Society* 6, no. 2 (2020): 35–62. https://doi.org/10.14361/dcs-2020-0204.

Lamb, Brian. "Wide Open Spaces: Wikis Ready or Not." *Educause Review* 39, no. 5 (2004): 36–48.

Larkin, Brian. "The Politics and Poetics of Infrastructure." *Annual Revue of Anthropology* 42 (2013): 327–43.

Levi, Amalia S., and Tara A. Inniss. "Decolonizing the Archival Record about the Enslaved: Digitizing the *Barbados Mercury Gazette*," *Archipelagos—a Journal of Caribbean Digital Praxis* 4 (2020). http://archipelagosjournal.org/issue04/levi-inniss-decolonizing.html.

Lu, Jessica H., and Catherine Knight Steele. "'Joy Is Resistance': Cross-platform Resilience and (Re)invention of Black Oral Culture Online." *Information, Communication & Society* 22, no. 6 (2019): 823–37. https://doi.org/10.1080/1369118X.2019.1575449.

Mandiberg, M. "The Affective Labor of Wikipedia: GamerGate, Harassment, and Peer Production." *Social Text* (2015). http://socialtext-journal.org/affective-labor-of-wikipedia-gamergate/.

Mangu-Ward, K. "Wikipedia and Beyond: Jimmy Wale's Sprawling Vision." *Reason Magazine*, June 2007, 2010.

McPherson, Tara. "U.S. Operating Systems at Mid-Century." In *Race after the Internet*, edited by Lisa Nakamura and Peter Chow-White. New York: Routledge, 2012.

Mitropoulos, Angela. *Contract and Contagion: From Biopolitics to Oikonomia*. Brooklyn, NY: Minor Compositions, 2013.

Moro, J. "Want of Water, Want of Data: The Trans-Atlantic Slave Trade Database and Oceanic Computing." Paper presented at the SIGCIS conference Stored in Memory, St. Louis, MO, 2018.

Nakamura, Lisa. "'I WILL DO EVERYthing That Am Asked': Scambaiting, Digital Show-Space, and the Racial Violence of Social Media." *Journal of Visual Culture* 13, no. 3 (2004): 257–74.

Noble, Safiya Umoja. *Algorithms of Oppression: How Search Engines Reinforce Racism*. New York: NYU Press, 2018.

Ping-Huang, Marianne. "Archival Biases and Cross-Sharing." *Nordisk Tidsskrift for Informationsvidenskab og Kulturformidling* 5, no. 1 (2016): 53–62.

Risam, Roopika. *New Digital Worlds: Postcolonial Digital Humanities in Theory, Praxis, and Pedagogy*. Evanston, IL: Northwestern University Press, 2018.

Roberts, Sarah T. *Behind the Screen: Content Moderation in the Shadows of Social Media*. New Haven, CT: Yale University Press, 2019.

Rogoff, Irit. "Smuggling—An Embodied Criticality." European Institute for Progressive Cultural Policies, 2006. http://transform.eipcp.net.

Salor, Enrinc. "Neutrality in the Face of Reckless Hate: Wikipedia and Gamergate." *Nordisk Tidsskrift for Informationsvidenskab Og Kulturformidling* 5, no. 1 (2016): 23–29.

Scott, James C. *Domination and the Arts of Resistance: Hidden Transcripts*. New Haven, CT: Yale University Press, 1990.

Sedgwick, Eve Kosofsky. "Paranoid Reading and Reparative Reading; or, You're So Paranoid, You Probably Think This Introduction Is About You." In *Novel Gazing: Queer Readings in Fiction*, edited by Eve Kosofsky Sedgwick, 1–37. Durham, NC: Duke University Press, 1997.

Singh, Rianka. "Resistance in a Minor Key: Care, Survival, and Convening on the Margins." *First Monday* 25, no. 4–5 (2020). https://firstmonday.org/ojs/index.php/fm/article/view/10631.

Star, S. L. "The Ethnography of Infrastructure." *American Behavioral Scientist* 43, no. 3 (1999): 377–91. https://doi.org/10.1177/00027649921955326.

Steiner, Henriette, and Kristin Veel. *Tower to Tower: Gigantism in Architecture and Digital Culture*. Cambridge, MA: MIT Press, 2020.

Stoler, Ann Laura. *Carnal Knowledge and Imperial Power: Race and the Intimate in Colonial Rule.* Berkeley: University of California Press, 2002.

Sutherland, Tonia. "Making a Killing: On Race, Ritual, and (Re)membering in Digital Culture." *Preservation, Digital Technology & Culture* 46, no. 1 (2017): 32–40.

Thylstrup, Nanna Bonde. *The Politics of Mass Digitization.* Cambridge, MA: MIT Press, 2019.

Tsing, Anna Lowenhaupt. "On Nonscalability: The Living World Is Not Amenable to Precision-Nested Scales." *Common Knowledge* 25, no. 1 (2019): 143–62.

Tuck, Eve. "Suspending Damage: A Letter to Communities." *Harvard Educational Review* 79, no. 3 (2009): 409–28.

Vergès, Françoise. "Memories of Struggles and Visual/Sonic Archives." Paper presented at the symposium "Archival Encounters. Colonial Archives, Care and Social Justice," University of Copenhagen, May 14, 2019.

Verhoeven, Deb. "As Luck Would Have It: Serendipity and Solace in Digital Research Infrastructure." *Feminist Media Histories* 2, no. 1 (2016): 7–28.

Virgin Islands Studies Collective (VISCO). "Ancestral Queendom. Reflections on the Prison Records of the Rebel Queens of the 1878 Fireburn in St. Croix, USVI (formerly the Danish West Indies)." *Nordisk Tidsskrift for Informationsvidenskab og Kulturformidling* 8, no. 2 (2019): 19–36.

Wadewitz, Adrienne. "Wikipedia's Gender Gap and the Complicated Reality of Systemic Gender Bias." HASTAC (2013). https://www.hastac .org/blogs/wadewitz/2013/07/26/wikipedias-gender-gap-nd-complicated -reality-systemic-gender-bias.

Wernimont, Jacqueline. *Numbered Lives: Life and Death in Quantum Media.* Cambridge, MA: MIT Press, 2019.

Wilson, Ara. "The Infrastructure of Intimacy." *Signs* 41, no. 2 (2016): 247–80.

III

Pedagogies

9

Walking Away from the Black Box of Social Media

MARK SAMPLE

Walking Away

There's a short story by Ursula Le Guin I think about constantly, "The Ones Who Walk Away from Omelas." If you don't know it, you should. Le Guin wrote it in 1975 as an allegory for the "American conscience,"[1] but it strikes me more and more as a prescient tale about the hidden costs of living our lives online, churning our way through endless streams of social media. Le Guin's Omelas is a paradise, a rapturous city of happy citizens, "bright-towered by the sea."[2] But there is a hidden cost to the sweet joy that blankets the citizens of Omelas. "Their happiness, the beauty of their city, the tenderness of their friendships, the health of their children" and so much more all depend upon the "abominable misery" of a small child locked in a basement somewhere in the city.[3] Out of the immense cruelty this child is subjected to—deprived of light, of food, of love and affection, imprisoned in a dark and putrid room—out of this abject callousness comes the success and splendor of Omelas. It is the deal its citizens live with. The happiness of an entire population in exchange for the misery of a single child. The city knows of this transaction. It is not a secret. Every schoolchild learns of the vile basement room with its wretched prisoner, and learns of the bargain. Should the miserable child be released, "all the prosperity and beauty and delight of Omelas would wither and be destroyed."[4] Occasionally—very occasionally—an adolescent from Omelas learns of the child, or even an older adult reflecting on the situation, and silently slips away from the city, turning their back on that awful paradox, and walks away from Omelas.

In my modern interpretation of "The Ones Who Walk Away from Omelas," we happy people on Facebook, Instagram, Twitter (now X),

Google, and everywhere else online are the citizens of Omelas, reaping a splendid bounty at incredible but conveniently overlooked costs. And what's locked in that dank, dark basement room? My analogy breaks down here because it's not a single entity. There's no one human child "hunched in the corner," covered with "festered sores" and sitting in "its own excrement."[5] The bargain we have struck is far more wide-ranging than that. What's locked in the basement room is everything the social media giants don't want us to see, everything that powers the constant flow of engagement, likes, clicks, comments. For every white-foamed heart cappuccino favorited there is a video of gut-wrenching animal abuse, flagged and taken down by poorly paid content moderators who suffer posttraumatic stress due to the inhuman cruelty they witness in eight-hour shifts.[6] For every beach vacation photo autotagged with the names of friends and family, facial recognition software misidentifies nonwhite people more than white people, with terrifying implications for policing and public safety.[7] For every on-the-mark advertisement in your Instagram stream, a ping from your phone's location history has been aggregated and sold, along with that of your friends and contacts.[8] For every algorithmically recommended TED Talk on YouTube that buttresses your faith in human enlightenment, another algorithm has determined that this or that loan application ought to be rejected because the applicant lives in the wrong zip code.[9]

There's a name for the hidden systems and mechanisms that power social media. Black boxes. There's an input, and there's an output. But what happens in between is a mystery. Think about the last search you performed on Google. There's your input, that question or phrase you type into Google's beckoning white page. Then there's Google's output, that long list of search results tailored to our own browsing history. But what happens in between? How does Google go from our input to its output? We simply don't know. That's the black box. Here's a decent definition of "black box": *what happens in between.* Another black box: you happen to mention to a friend that you like her new sandals, and a day later you start seeing ads for sandals on Instagram. You're not even surprised, this kind of coincidence is so common—and it's not a coincidence, by the way.[10] Lest we conflate black boxes with ubiquitous surveillance and automated algorithms, remember that black boxes are *what happens in between*, and sometimes humans, not machines, make the call about what happens in between. Bureaucracies are notorious black boxes, for example, with their hidden and inexplicable decision-making apparatus. Or this: to highlight the horrors of war, someone posts Nick Ut's Pulitzer Prize–winning photograph of a nude girl fleeing napalm during the Vietnam War, and Facebook mysteriously takes down the powerful photograph because it counts as pornography.[11]

Human content moderators made that decision. But from the Facebook user's perspective, it's a black box.

The dark basement in Le Guin's story and the black boxes of social media are both sites of exchange, of unfathomable transactions. Yet there is a significant distinction between them. In Omelas, people know about that basement room. Schoolchildren visit the cellar. Learning about the room and the neglected child within are part of the social pedagogy of Omelas. "They all know it is there," Le Guin tells us.[12] They've witnessed it, which makes their complicity with the system all the more sickening. Clearly Le Guin sides with the ones who walk away from Omelas, and wants her reader to as well. The black boxes that power social media, however, are not open to inspection. We are not invited to examine them. We are not asked to witness *what happens in between* so that we understand the horrible cost of our happiness, shallow though it might be on social media. This is not to say that people haven't tried to delve into the black boxes of social media. Lisa Nakamura has explored the cruel dynamics of trolling on gaming platforms.[13] Virginia Eubanks dives into algorithms behind public assistance programs to show how they confuse parenting while poor with poor parenting.[14] Sarah Roberts has documented the dehumanizing work of commercial content moderators, those Facebook subcontractors responsible for watching and removing hundreds of traumatic videos every day.[15] Safiya Noble has exposed the racist and sexist results of Google's search algorithm.[16] The work of these and other scholars is crucial in advancing our knowledge of what happens behind the scenes in social media and technology. But even work as widely acclaimed as Noble's can only reckon with the *results* of black boxes, because the techniques, algorithms, and protocols inside the box remain hidden from view, tightly held proprietary secrets, only occasionally and very selectively shared with others—for example, when Google gives its largest advertisers a heads-up regarding a change in its search algorithm.[17]

How strange, how cruel, how utterly American, that the sacrificial child that enables the paradise of Omelas is more public than the secret engines that power contemporary life. If, like Le Guin, we aspire for some segment of society to *walk away* toward what she calls "a place even less imaginable to most of us than the city of happiness,"[18] what is to be done? If turning away is an act of resistance, how do we start? Le Guin's self-imposed exiles know what they're walking away from. They've visited that windowless cellar. They're haunted by it, an unassimilable knowledge of the source of their well-being. There are analogs to this knowledge in our own world. If social media is its own devil's bargain, a sparkling seaside city of guiltless wonder made possible by unimaginable and hidden cruelty, then we must lead our citizens to that locked basement door and crack it open. Not merely by reading about it, or talking about it, but by visiting the cellar itself.

Gender and Technology

Visiting the cellar. This was the approach I adopted in Gender and Technology (DIG 340), a seminar in the Digital Studies program at Davidson College. The class explores the intersection of gender and technology, with a particular emphasis on contemporary algorithmic culture. The overarching goal of Gender and Technology is to defamiliarize the daily encounters and practices made possible by the internet, smart phones, social media, and AI. Perhaps "defamiliarize" isn't a strong enough characterization. Subvert is more like it. Or even better: *resist.* This is not an epistemological objective. It's ontological, existential. How do you teach students to resist the lure of social media and to walk away? Think of the pedagogy of Omelas. Introduce students to the black box. Show them the cellar door, awakening them to its very existence. One particular project in the Gender and Technology course specifically addresses this problem. I call this project the Social (Justice) Media Campaign. The official goal for the project as it appears on the syllabus is "to explore, critique, and undermine social media ad platforms."[19] Unofficially, the project is about getting ready to walk away.

Quite simply, the Social (Justice) Media Campaign asks students to hack social media advertising by placing social justice–oriented material in the timelines and search results of users who would normally not encounter that material. Inspired by the principles of culture jamming and what Carl DiSalvo calls "adversarial design,"[20] the assignment is an exercise in dissensus—in disagreeing with the status quo in order to advance democratic ideals, a process that DiSalvo points out is "intrinsically contentious."[21] The targets of our adversarial designs are as much social media platforms as the users of those platforms. Before there can be users, there must be platforms that draw those users. Platforms are the structural foundation for what happens on social media, shaping what's possible and what's not in visible and invisible ways. The Social (Justice) Media Campaign is an intervention into the digital infrastructure of what Michael Goldhaber long ago called the "attention economy," where "the goal is simply to get either enough attention or as much as possible."[22] Every social media platform measures its success in terms of user engagement. Engagement, of course, is Facebook's, Google's, and other online advertisers' euphemism for the efficient serving of ads—of reaching the largest target audience possible. If social media were Omelas, engagement is the Omelasian equivalent of the spectacular "Festival of the Summer," when everyone feels "a boundless and generous contentment."[23] In the attention economy, nothing matters more than grabbing users' attention. Countless news reports since 2016 have shown that the unintended consequences of an internet driven by advertising are dire. As Zeynep Tufecki memorably puts it, "we're building this infrastructure of surveillance authoritarianism merely to get people to click on ads."[24]

In Gender and Technology we study the way digital infrastructures reinforce, extend, and amplify racist, sexist, transphobic, and other hateful ideologies. In addition to the social hegemony of racist Google search results[25] and the troubling implications of the default settings on Facebook[26]—more about that later—we also study the way social media has been weaponized against marginalized and vulnerable groups. For example, the explosive *ProPublica* report that advertisers on Facebook could deliberately reach anti-Semitic audiences using keywords and demographics from Facebook's vast data-mining operations.[27] Or, as *Buzzfeed* reporters discovered, how racist advertisers could exploit Google's ad network.[28] My own institution experienced an unwelcome outcome with social media advertising when an inline ad for an alumni association event appeared on *Breitbart.com*. The display of promotional material for my academic institution next to the anti-immigration and nativist rhetoric of Breitbart was not only a jarring juxtaposition, but also completely inadvertent, an algorithmic outcome of Facebook's advertising platform.

These nefarious examples set the stage for the Social (Justice) Media Campaign. Working in groups of three to four, students managed a social justice–oriented ad campaign of their own design on either Facebook, Instagram, Twitter, or Google's ad platforms. Each team explored the contours, possibilities, and limits of social media advertising as they ran a series of campaigns with progressively larger budgets. Each group had a budget of $5 for their first campaign, which may have only lasted a day. The next campaign had a budget of $20. Groups fine-tuned their messaging and promotional strategy as they geared up for even bigger campaigns. The third campaign had a budget of $50 and students had $175 to work with for the final campaign.[29] Each ad campaign was tied to my institutional purchase card (e.g., credit card) so that students did not pay out of pocket. Google, Twitter, and Facebook each support budget limits, so that the campaigns automatically ended when they reached their designated dollar limit. For the sake of privacy, I hesitate to provide too much detail about the various social media campaigns students designed. In broad strokes, though, I can say that groups tackled issues such as commonsense gun laws, LBGTQI rights, women in STEM, and consent in sexual relationships. One group used Google Ads, the kind that appear in the right column of Google search results. Another group used Twitter, paying to promote their tweets so that they appeared in users' timelines. And two groups centered their ad campaigns on Facebook. In every case, the groups tried to confront users with material that those users were likely to disagree with or be hostile to. The projects truly were adversarial.

None of the students had ever run a social media promotional campaign before. At the outset of the project, the social media manager from my institution's communications office gave a workshop. He explained key principles of social media advertising, including how to hone a message, the importance of visuals, and subtle differences in the way various platforms measure engagement. He also walked students through the process of posting paid promotional content on Facebook, demonstrating the exacting precision with which advertisers can target audiences when they "boost" a post. In the early days of the project students also learned other practical matters that had deeper, meaningful implications. For example, students working on Facebook were astounded how easy it was—once they were logged in with their own credentials—to create new pages that appeared unaffiliated with their personal accounts. Students quickly realized that Facebook's insistence that every page on the platform be transparent was easily skirted. The Twitter group meanwhile discovered that, as Twitter puts it, "New accounts will be held in review for a period before they can begin advertising with Twitter Ads."[30] Again, students found that a rule designed to rein in spam or misinformation was easily sidestepped; students simply rebranded an old, unused Twitter account I gave them, and they were off to the races. These initial discoveries were like standing outside the cellar door in Omelas, about to confront the underlying truth of a system that up to this point they had profoundly misunderstood. And once they began their campaigns, it was like unlocking the door.

The hands-on work was complemented by a more theoretical and critical approach to social media advertising derived from Sara Wachter-Boettcher's revelatory work *Technically Wrong: Sexist Apps, Biased Algorithms, and Other Threats of Toxic Tech* (2017). Wachter-Boettcher exposes the underside of what she calls "toxic tech," looking at, for example, the way platforms like Twitter not only enable harassment and abuse but are in fact optimized for it.[31] She spends considerable time discussing gender and technology. Surveying default settings in a variety of apps and social media platforms, she finds avatars whose default gender is male, beauty standards whose defaults are white women, or smartphone assistants whose default voices are female. None of these observations will be surprising to most users of smartphones and social media. It's when Wachter-Boettcher delves deeper into the fundamental assumptions of tech culture that she starts to lead readers to that cellar door. Her discussion of default settings in online forms—say, when you sign up for a new social media service for the first time—especially fueled students' approach to their social media campaigns. "Forms inherently put us in a vulnerable position," argues Wachter-Boettcher.[32] Instead of allowing us to define ourselves, forms corral us into predefined and standardized slots, what the anthropologist Amber Case calls "templated selves."[33] Though Facebook made headlines in 2014 when it allowed users to select custom genders (such as transwoman or nonbinary), the platform still requires users to choose between male and female when first signing up for a Facebook account.[34] Why? Because Facebook is designed with advertisers in mind, not users, and advertisers want to be able to target either men, women, or both.[35]

When students launched their first campaigns, they discovered how templated selves work firsthand. For example, the groups working with Facebook must designate an "audience" for an ad campaign. The first three choices to make are the gender, age, and location of the desired audience. As I note above, no matter what gender a Facebook user selects for their profile, they are still limited to either male or female when first signing up. And indeed, male, female, or both are the only gender options available when building a target audience. Facebook's version of templated selves goes well beyond gender. Consider the five broad areas Facebook makes available for reaching desired audiences: location, demographics (which include age, gender, education, relationship status, and job title), interests, behavior, and connections.[36] While some of these characteristics may appear straightforward, such as age or location (see figure 9.1), others are functions of the templated selves that users have chosen, or quite frequently, that Facebook has chosen for users based on the vast amounts of data Facebook collects. Wachter-Boettcher introduces the concept of proxy data to explain how this works. As she describes proxy data, "when you don't have a piece of information about a user that you want, you use data you *do* have to infer that information.[37] Understanding proxy data is key to unlocking the cellar door—or opening the black box. Wachter-Boettcher encountered proxy data on a personal level when she tried to figure out why Google had specified in her Google ad preferences profile that she was a man. It turns out that her search history was "littered with topics like web development, finance, and sci-fi" and Google surmised, because of these interests, she must be a man.[38] Proxy data is a special kind of *what happens in between* because of the likelihood that the output bears little relationship to the input.

Going back to the five areas that Facebook uses to segment audiences (location, demographics, interests, behavior, and connections), we can see

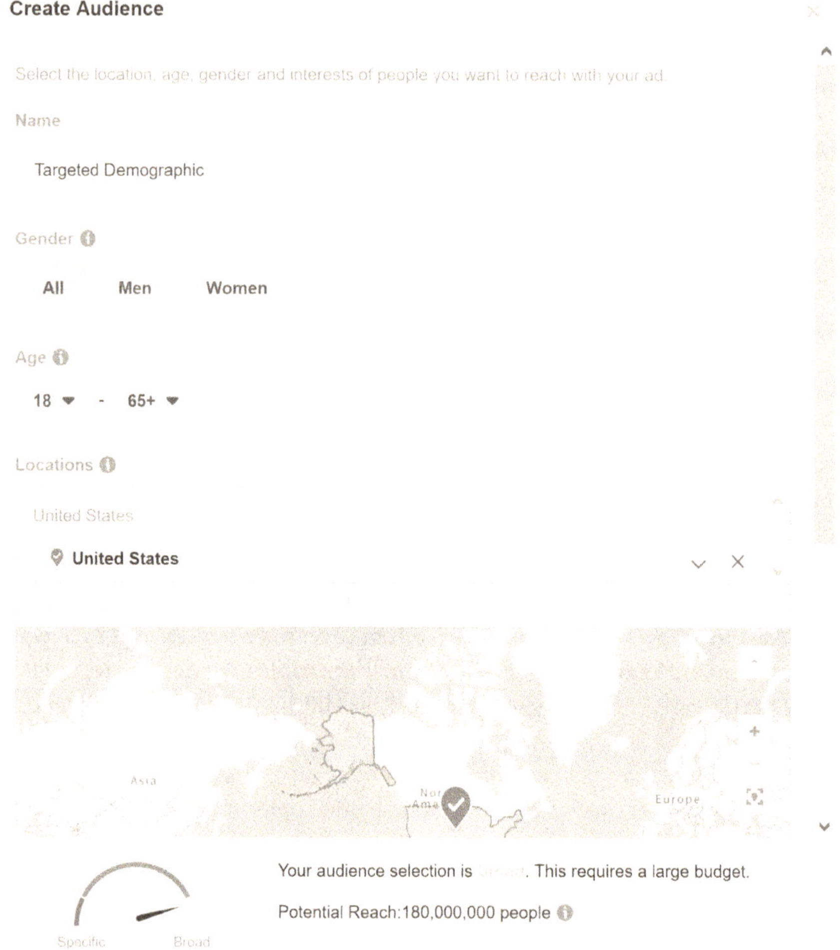

Figure 9.1. Creating an Audience on Facebook.

proxy data most at work with interests and behavior. Facebook determines "interests" by the pages and groups a user likes, the ads a user clicks on, the contents of the user's own posts, and so on. "Behavior," as Facebook understands it, boils down to "consumer behaviors such as prior purchases and device usage."[39] In other words, "interests" refers to actions that users have explicitly and actively taken on Facebook, while "behaviors" refers to actions that happen away from Facebook, often tracked with Facebook's hidden pixel technology, which can be quietly embedded on any website.[40] Students were shocked to discover the level at which Facebook relies on proxy data to surmise user interests.[41] Let's say one group wanted to promote commonsense gun laws. Using Facebook's fine-grained interest categories, students were able to narrowly target males in rural North Carolina between the ages of eighteen and forty whose interests included (and here I'm quoting Facebook's categories) Right to keep and bear arms, Conservatism, Country living, 2nd Amendment, Christian music, Fox News Channel, National Rifle Association, Homeschooling, and more.[42] Obviously, the students in this group relied on their own inferential power; they assumed this demographic would likely be less receptive to commonsense gun laws. The irony of using proxy data to subvert Facebook's use of proxy data was not lost upon the students.

After several weeks the assignment concluded with students writing a reflective synthesis of their experience. At the outset of the project, the ad campaigns themselves may have seemed to the students to be the point of the assignment. But the synthesis, an opportunity to debrief, analyze, and evaluate, was the real—by which I mean intended—takeaway from the project. I couldn't have cared less how successful any given campaign on Facebook, Google, or Twitter was. It's in the synthesis that space opened up for the students to ask that question: *what happens between?* It's in the synthesis that students had the chance to start pondering what it would mean to emulate that rare citizen of Omelas who "falls silent for a day or two, and then leaves home."[43]

The assignment included a set of wide-ranging prompts for students to consider in their syntheses. While some of the prompts focused on the nuts-and-bolts of designing adversarial promotional campaigns, other prompts asked students to zoom out and think more generally. For example, I asked students to compare their expectations about social media advertising with the reality of social media. A key prompt addressed the ethical dimensions of the project: "Think through the ethical concerns that came up in this assignment. This could be anything from the creep factor of Facebook's data to the deliberate deception that many groups attempted." Other prompts borrowed from feminist digital media scholar Tara McPherson's call to avoid "bracketing" aside gender and race (not to mention, sexuality, class, and ability) when analyzing technological platforms.[44] For instance: "Analyze the platform itself. How did Facebook/Twitter/Google make some things easy and other things difficult? Hypothesize about the way the technology 'used' you or forced you to conform to its protocols." And this complementary question: "Try to capture what you know now about social media, gender, and power that you did not know a month ago."[45]

Who Gets to Walk Away

This particular project was likely a one-time activity. Ongoing changes in the way social media platforms target users and monetize content means

I would have to make significant changes to the project if it were to run again. In the past two years Facebook has already altered its terms of services for advertisers, explicitly banning misleading or disruptive content.[46] Furthermore, faced with lawsuits from the ACLU and complaints from the US Department of Housing and Urban Development, Facebook now prohibits housing, job, or credit advertisers from targeting (or excluding) specific genders, races, or age groups.[47] Not expecting to run this particular project again or expecting others to duplicate it exactly, it's useful to zoom out and highlight overarching principles that might inspire other interventions into social media. What does the big picture look like when it comes to interventionist pedagogy, especially a *feminist* intervention? There are three broad principles of guerilla resistance at play in an interventionist project like mine:

1. Study the technological systems.
2. Exploit the technological systems.
3. Turn away from the technological systems.

But there are two important caveats here. First, what exactly do we mean when we use the phrase "technological systems"? What do we think about when we think about technology? What do we mean when we say the word "technology"? What does technology do for us? What does it do to us? How does it move us? How does it elude us? These questions lurk behind my interventionist pedagogy, and indeed, behind every Digital Studies course I teach. To help pin down some answers—or at least raise the questions—with my students, I build on an idea that the digital media scholar Elizabeth Losh mentioned in passing during a digital pedagogy roundtable at the 2017 Modern Language Association convention in Philadelphia. Losh was discussing FemTechNet, a collaborative network of feminist artists and scholars studying technology, and just briefly she displayed a slide summarizing the seven the theoretical touchstones of FemTechNet, transcribed here:

- Technology assumes competence in tacit knowledge practices (although it is often presented as *transparent*)
- Technology promotes particular values (although it is often presented as *neutral*)
- Technology is material (although it is often presented as *transcendent*)
- Technology involves embodiment (although it is often presented as *disembodied*)
- Technology solicits affect (although it is often presented as highly *rational*)

- Technology requires labor (although it is often presented as *labor-saving*)
- Technology is situated in particular contexts (although it is often presented as *universal*)[48]

These seven touchstones are incredibly generative, and I integrate them into nearly every course. The touchstones are clarifying in the sense that they give students the language to diagnose how technology actually functions without "bracketing" aside theories of difference (to quote McPherson). Losh's touchstones capture what we often already know in our bones about technology but have trouble articulating. I usually frame them in terms of what I call the "technological imaginary," that is, of how we imagine technology to be versus how it really is.

Before I introduce the Social (Justice) Media Campaign project to my students, I rework the seven touchstones into two lists, first what we imagine technology to be, and second how technology really functions. We imagine technology to be:

- transparent (it's easy to use and fades into the background)
- neutral (technology itself has no values)
- transcendent (it's intangible, beyond our senses)
- disembodied (it exists apart from our physical bodies)
- rational (it's logical, makes sense)
- labor-saving (it gives us free time)
- universal (it's the same everywhere)

But in truth, technology:

- assumes tacit knowledge (it's not transparent)
- promotes particular values (it's not neutral)
- is grounded in materiality (it's not transcendent)
- foregrounds human bodies (it's not disembodied)
- solicits emotional affect (it's not flat or detached)
- requires labor (it's not labor-saving)
- is situated in specific contexts (it's not universal)

It doesn't take long for us to name examples of the technological imaginary at work. The "cloud" comes up quite often as a disembodied, transcendent, and universal space that is actually a physical location, or rather, a series of physical locations, such as the server farms Apple, Facebook, Google, and others operate. In their analysis of the promotional rhetoric around data centers, Jennifer Holt and Patrick Vonderau astutely observe that "the notion of the cloud is a marketing concept that renders the physical, infrastructural realities of remote data storage into a palatable abstraction."[49]

The class also thinks about platforms themselves in terms of the technological imaginary. Users generally imagine platforms are neutral, and the platforms themselves tell us that they are. For example, in 2019 Mark Zuckerberg declared that Facebook would not remove political ads spreading misinformation.[50] At first blush this stance appears to demonstrate absolute neutrality, but in practice it ensures that the political campaign with the biggest war chest can go viral with falsehoods, drowning out truthful advertisements from other sources. The work of Wachter-Boettcher shows how the illusion of neutrality is perpetuated at even the smallest levels of the social network interface. Examining the way default settings shape our engagement with technology, Wachter-Boettcher says, "Default settings can be helpful or deceptive, thoughtful or frustrating. But they're never neutral. They're designed."[51] And more to the point, they are designed to keep us engaged, to keep us delighted. Social media is all about affect. Why else would, for example, Instagram withhold likes to a post so that it can release them in a burst, resulting in a bigger dose of dopamine than a slow trickle of likes what have achieved.[52]

What realities of the technological imaginary does the Social (Justice) Media Campaign project reveal? Students invariably remarked in their syntheses that running their campaigns exposed them to a deep network of tacit knowledge—that occult knowledge that allowed them to bend Facebook, Twitter, and Google to their wills. Many students were alarmed by the way the social media platforms allowed them to micro-target such detailed demographics, which they saw as hidden levers of manipulation that belied these platforms' claims of neutrality. Another revelation for students was how affective and embodied their projects turned out to be. Students described the physiological reaction of seeing strangers engage— frequently with hostility—with their social media campaigns in the comments on their pages. Students were thankful at last for the wide degree of anonymity Facebook allows its pages. The Social (Justice) Media Campaigns were affective too in the same way some people were affected by seeing the imprisoned child in Omelas, an encounter that blossomed into the desire to walk away.

Earlier I mentioned there were two caveats to my three principles of guerilla resistance. First was a deeper understanding of what we mean by "technological systems." The second caveat concerns the third principle of turning away from technological systems. And the caveat is this: turning away, walking away, it's extremely difficult to do. It's reasonable to describe my students' attraction—and mine, and likely yours—to social media in terms of what Lauren Berlant calls "cruel optimism." For Berlant, cruel optimism describes the "condition of maintaining an attachment to a significantly problematic object."[53] We *know* social media can make us edgy and miserable, yet still we turn to it, hoping beyond hope that our next engagement with it will be the one that fulfills the promise of connectivity, community, validation, and affinity we seek. Berlant doesn't prescribe a way out of our "magnetic attraction" to problematic objects so much as diagnose the symptoms of cruel optimism and the impasse in which we frequently find ourselves when it comes to our ambivalent relationship with the things we hate to love.[54] Other theorists, however, are more focused on detaching from those things we think we want that cause us anguish. In the early part of our semester the Gender and Technology students spend a considerable amount of time engaged with the work of Sara Ahmed, whose stunning incision and insight guided my approach to this project. As we zoom further out from the Social (Justice) Media Campaigns, we can see them as extended exercises in being what Ahmed calls a "feminist killjoy." A feminist killjoy, in Ahmed's formulation, is one "who gets in the way of other people's happiness."[55] In the final paragraph of "The Ones Who Walk Away from Omelas," Le Guin describes Omelas as "the city of happiness."[56] It's a happiness premised on not dwelling on the terrible arrangement that makes that happiness possible. In the same fashion, the smooth functioning of social media requires a willingness to look away from the black box. But what exactly is happiness? This is a question Ahmed takes up again and again in her work. For Ahmed—like Le Guin before her—"Happiness is used to justify social norms."[57] The ones who walk away from Omelas "walk ahead into the darkness."[58] It's not clear where they are heading. Even Le Guin acknowledges that regarding their destination—some, no, *any* alternative to Omelas—it's "possible that it does not exist."[59] But still they walk away. Similarly, there may not seem to be an alternative to the black boxes of social media, but one must at least consider the possibility. By playing in the domain of adversarial design, the Social (Justice) Media Campaign project sought to ruin happiness and, as a result, not only question social norms but to walk away from them entirely.

Notes

1. Le Guin, "The Ones Who Walk Away from Omelas," 275.
2. Le Guin, "The Ones Who Walk Away from Omelas," 276.
3. Le Guin, "The Ones Who Walk Away from Omelas," 282.
4. Le Guin, "The Ones Who Walk Away from Omelas," 282.
5. Le Guin, "The Ones Who Walk Away from Omelas," 281.

6. Newton, "Bodies in Seats"; Dwoskin, "Facebook Content Moderator Details Trauma That Prompted Fight for $52 Million PTSD Settlement."

7. Hao, "Making Face Recognition Less Biased Doesn't Make It Less Scary."

8. Thompson and Warzel, "Twelve Million Phones, One Dataset, Zero Privacy."

9. O'Neil, *Weapons of Math Destruction*, 145–46.

10. Graham, "Is Facebook Listening to Me?"

11. Scott and Isaac, "Facebook Restores Iconic Vietnam War Photo It Censored for Nudity."

12. Le Guin, "The Ones Who Walk Away from Omelas," 282.

13. Nakamura, "'I WILL DO EVERYthing That Am Asked.'"

14. Eubanks, *Automating Inequality*.

15. Roberts, "Commercial Content Moderation."

16. Noble, *Algorithms of Oppression*.

17. Grind et al., "How Google Interferes with Its Search Algorithms and Changes Your Results."

18. Le Guin, "The Ones Who Walk Away from Omelas," 284.

19. Sample, "Social (Justice) Media Campaign."

20. DiSalvo, *Adversarial Design*, 2.

21. DiSalvo, *Adversarial Design*, 4

22. Goldhaber, "The Attention Economy and the Net."

23. Le Guin, "The Ones Who Walk Away from Omelas," 280.

24. Tufekci, "We're Building a Dystopia Just to Make People Click on Ads."

25. Noble, *Algorithms of Oppression*.

26. Wachter-Boettcher, *Technically Wrong*.

27. Angwin and Varner, "Facebook Enabled Advertisers to Reach 'Jew Haters.'"

28. In response to these findings from investigative journalism, Facebook has updated its advertising policy to specifically ban advertising that discriminates against individuals (see "Discriminatory Practices," 2). Kantrowitz, "Google Allowed Advertisers to Target People Searching Racist Phrases."

29. The project was made possible thanks to funding from Davidson College's Justice, Equality, and Community grant from the Andrew W. Mellon Foundation.

30. "About Eligibility for Twitter Ads."

31. Wachter-Boettcher, *Technically Wrong*, 149–57.

32. Wachter-Boettcher, *Technically Wrong*, 51.

33. Case, "Why We All Need to Make the Internet Fun Again."

34. Wachter-Boettcher, *Technically Wrong*, 63–64.

35. Wachter-Boettcher, *Technically Wrong*, 65.

36. "Facebook Advertising Targeting Options."

37. Wachter-Boettcher, *Technically Wrong*, 110, emphasis in original.

38. Wachter-Boettcher, *Technically Wrong*, 109–10.

39. "Facebook Advertising Targeting Options."

40. Madrigal, "The Most Important Exchange of the Zuckerberg Hearing."

41. Students invariably checked what Facebook had decided their own interests were. Any Facebook user can sign into the platform and see what Facebook has determined to be their interests. Facebook frequently changes its menus, but the current URL to view one's advertising preferences is https://www.facebook.com/ads/preferences/. Note how Facebook calls them "preferences" as if one had actually made a deliberate decision to learn more about this or that product, when in fact, Facebook inferred these preferences. A more appropriate term for this page would be "advertising inferences."

42. It's worth noting that Facebook frequently updates its interface for creating and managing ads. The latest update consists of scrolling windows inside of scrolling windows, a fragmented view that makes it nearly impossible to document the process in screenshots. I can't help but wonder if this documentary elusiveness is by design an effort to thwart critiques such as this one.

43. Le Guin, "The Ones Who Walk Away from Omelas," 283.

44. McPherson, "Designing for Difference," 181.

45. Sample, "Social (Justice) Media Campaign."

46. "Advertising Policies."

47. Scheiber and Isaac, "Facebook Halts Ad Targeting Cited in Bias Complaints."

48. Losh, "#mla17 #s155 Sorry to Speed by Thispic," emphasis in the original.

49. Holt and Vonderau, "Where the Internet Lives," 72.

50. Isaac, "Dissent Erupts at Facebook Over Hands-Off Stance on Political Ads."

51. Wachter-Boettcher, *Technically Wrong*, 35.

52. "What Is 'Brain Hacking'?"

53. Berlant, *Cruel Optimism*, 24.

54. Berlant, *Cruel Optimism*, 48.

55. Ahmed, "Feminist Killjoys (And Other Willful Subjects)."

56. Le Guin, "The Ones Who Walk Away from Omelas," 284.

57. Ahmed, *Living a Feminist Life*, 254.

58. Le Guin, "The Ones Who Walk Away from Omelas," 284.

59. Le Guin, "The Ones Who Walk Away from Omelas," 284.

Works Cited

"About Eligibility for Twitter Ads." *Twitter*. Accessed March 4, 2020. https://business.twitter.com/en/help/overview/about-eligibility-for-twitter-ads.html.

"Advertising Policies." *Facebook*. Accessed June 30, 2019. https://www.facebook.com/policies/ads/prohibited_content.

Ahmed, Sara. "Feminist Killjoys (and Other Willful Subjects)." *The Scholar and Feminist Online* 8, no. 3 (Summer 2010). http://sfonline.barnard.edu/polyphonic/print_ahmed.htm.

Ahmed, Sara. *Living a Feminist Life*. Durham, NC: Duke University Press, 2017.

Angwin, Julia, and Madeleine Varner. "Facebook Enabled Advertisers to Reach 'Jew Haters.'" *ProPublica*, September 14, 2017. https://www.propublica.org/article/facebook-enabled-advertisers-to-reach-jew-haters.

Berlant, Lauren. *Cruel Optimism*. Durham, NC: Duke University Press, 2011.

Case, Amber. "Why We All Need to Make the Internet Fun Again." *Vox*, July 17, 2015. https://www.vox.com/2015/7/17/11614788/why-we-all-need -to-make-the-internet-fun-again.

DiSalvo, Carl. *Adversarial Design*. Cambridge, MA: MIT Press, 2015.

"Discriminatory Practices." *Facebook Advertising Policies*. Accessed June 29, 2019. https://www.facebook.com/policies/ads/prohibited_content/ discriminatory_practices#.

Dwoskin, Elizabeth. "Facebook Content Moderator Details Trauma That Prompted Fight for $52 Million PTSD Settlement." *Washington Post*, May 13, 2020. https://www.washingtonpost.com/technology/2020/05/12/ facebook-content-moderator-ptsd/.

Eubanks, Virginia. *Automating Inequality: How High-Tech Tools Profile, Police, and Punish the Poor*. New York: St. Martin's Press, 2017.

"Facebook Advertising Targeting Options." *Facebook Business*. Accessed June 29, 2019. https://www.facebook.com/business/ads/ad-targeting.

Goldhaber, Michael H. "The Attention Economy and the Net." *First Monday* 2, no. 4 (April 1997). https://doi.org/10.5210/fm.v2i4.519.

Graham, Jefferson. "Is Facebook Listening to Me? Why Those Ads Appear after You Talk about Things." *USA Today*, June 27, 2019. https://www.usa today.com/story/tech/talkingtech/2019/06/27/does-facebook-listen-to-your -conversations/1478468001/.

Grind, Kirsten, Sam Schechner, Robert McMillan, and John West. "How Google Interferes with Its Search Algorithms and Changes Your Results." *Wall Street Journal*, November 15, 2019. https://www.wsj.com/articles/how-google -interferes-with-its-search-algorithms-and-changes-your-results-11573823753.

Hao, Karen. "Making Face Recognition Less Biased Doesn't Make It Less Scary." *MIT Technology Review*, January 29, 2019. https://www.technology review.com/s/612846/making-face-recognition-less-biased-doesnt-make-it -less-scary/.

Holt, Jennifer, and Patrick Vonderau. "Where the Internet Lives: Data Centers as Cloud Infrastructure." In *Signal Traffic: Critical Studies of Media Infrastruc- tures*, edited by Lisa Parks and Nicole Starosielski, 71–93. Urbana: University of Illinois Press, 2015.

Isaac, Mike. "Dissent Erupts at Facebook Over Hands-Off Stance on Politi- cal Ads." *New York Times*, October 29, 2019. https://www.nytimes.com/ 2019/10/28/technology/facebook-mark-zuckerberg-political-ads.html.

Kantrowitz, Alex. "Google Allowed Advertisers to Target People Searching Racist Phrases." *BuzzFeed News*, September 15, 2017. https://www.buzzfeed news.com/article/alexkantrowitz/google-allowed-advertisers-to-target-jewish -parasite-black.

Le Guin, Ursula. "The Ones Who Walk Away from Omelas." In *The Wind's Twelve Quarters*, 275–84. New York: Harper & Row, 1975.

Losh, Elizabeth. "#mla17 #s155 Sorry to Speed by Thispic." Twitter *@lizlosh*, January 5, 2017. https://twitter.com/lizlosh/statuses/817169946463571972.

Madrigal, Alexis C. "The Most Important Exchange of the Zuckerberg Hearing." *The Atlantic*, April 2018. https://www.theatlantic.com/technology/archive/2018/04/the-most-important-exchange-of-the-zuckerberg-hearing/557795/.

McPherson, Tara. "Designing for Difference." *differences* 25, no. 1 (January 2014): 177–88. https://doi.org/10.1215/10407391-2420039.

Nakamura, Lisa. "'I WILL DO EVERYthing That Am Asked': Scambaiting, Digital Show-Space, and the Racial Violence of Social Media." *Journal of Visual Culture* 13, no. 3 (December 2014): 257–74. https://doi.org/10.1177/1470412914546845.

Newton, Casey. "Bodies in Seats." *The Verge*, June 19, 2019. https://www.theverge.com/2019/6/19/18681845/facebook-moderator-interviews-video-trauma-ptsd-cognizant-tampa.

Noble, Safiya Umoja. *Algorithms of Oppression: How Search Engines Reinforce Racism*. New York: New York University Press, 2018.

O'Neil, Cathy. *Weapons of Math Destruction: How Big Data Increases Inequality and Threatens Democracy*. New York: Crown, 2016.

Roberts, Sarah T. "Commercial Content Moderation: Digital Laborers' Dirty Work." In *The Intersectional Internet: Race, Sex, Class, and Culture Online*, edited by Safiya Umoja Noble and Brendesha M. Tynes, 147–60. New York: Peter Lang, 2016.

Sample, Mark. "Social (Justice) Media Campaign." DIG 340 (Gender and Technology) (February 2018). https://courses.digitaldavidson.net/gtech18/projects/social-justice-media-campaign/.

Scheiber, Noam, and Mike Isaac. "Facebook Halts Ad Targeting Cited in Bias Complaints." *New York Times*, March 19, 2019. https://www.nytimes.com/2019/03/19/technology/facebook-discrimination-ads.html.

Scott, Mark, and Mike Isaac. "Facebook Restores Iconic Vietnam War Photo It Censored for Nudity." *New York Times*, September 9, 2016. https://www.nytimes.com/2016/09/10/technology/facebook-vietnam-war-photo-nudity.html.

Thompson, Stuart A., and Charlie Warzel. "Twelve Million Phones, One Dataset, Zero Privacy." *New York Times*, December 19, 2019. https://www.nytimes.com/interactive/2019/12/19/opinion/location-tracking-cell-phone.html.

Tufekci, Zeynep. "We're Building a Dystopia Just to Make People Click on Ads." *TED Talk*, Accessed October 27, 2017. https://www.ted.com/talks/zeynep_tufekci_we_re_building_a_dystopia_just_to_make_people_click_on_ads.

Wachter-Boettcher, Sara. *Technically Wrong: Sexist Apps, Biased Algorithms, and Other Threats of Toxic Tech*. New York: W. W. Norton, 2018.

"What Is 'Brain Hacking'? Tech Insiders on Why You Should Care." *60 Minutes*, CBS, April 9, 2017. https://www.cbsnews.com/news/brain-hacking-tech-insiders-60-minutes/.

10

Teaching Feminist Text Analysis

LISA MARIE RHODY

The problem with gender is that it
prescribes how we should be rather
than recognizing how we are.
—Chimamanda Ngozi Adichie,
We Should All Be Feminists

We are experiencing a cultural sea change accelerated by the proliferation of computational text technologies. The rapid production of textual data combined with brisk technological and methodological developments has led to a fundamental shift in the way texts construct and reflect our individual and collective lives. Perhaps this strikes you as hyperbolic, but consider the hundreds of times each day we interact—often unaware—with computational text tools. From text prediction algorithms that help you efficiently swipe your finger across your phone's keyboard to shape words, to friends' posts queued up in your social media applications, to sorting junk email in your spam folder, to the directions you ask Siri to find while you are driving, to the search engine you may have used to find this book, computationally enabled collection, preparation, processing, and analysis of text mediates nearly all our modern-day activities. While our discomfort may be assuaged by the conveniences afforded by computational methods— like machine learning (ML) algorithms, large language models (LLMs), and generative text artificial intelligence (AI)—text algorithms are equally, if not more, efficient at extending and systematizing historic social inequities, stereotypes, and injustices.

The real and potential harms computational text methods present are hardly a surprise to feminist—especially Black and trans feminist—scholars, who have been vocal and prolific as they have been sounding the alarm. In *Race after Technology*, Ruha Benjamin writes of algorithmic biases: "While the gender wage gap and the "race tax" (non-Whites being charged more for the same services) are nothing new, the difference is that coded inequity makes discrimination easier, faster, and even harder to challenge, because there is not just a racist boss, banker, or shopkeeper to report. Instead, the public must hold accountable the very platforms and programmers that legally and often invisibly facilitate the New Jim Code."[1] Critiques of algorithmic practices represent an expanding area of contemporary scholarship, but they unable to keep pace with the production of tools and applications. Researchers like danah boyd have exposed how textual data voids are weaponized by white supremacist and hate groups on platforms like YouTube.[2] Virginia Eubanks has revealed the injustices in algorithmic sentencing in the justice system.[3] Safiya Noble has demonstrated the sexist and racist algorithmic assumptions that Google's search algorithm reproduces and circulates.[4] Joy Buolamwini's research uncovers the racial and gender bias in Artificial Agents that belong to corporations such as Microsoft, IBM, and Amazon.[5] Likewise, Sasha Costanza-Chock, Benjamin, and other feminist scholars in multiple fields have been calling into question the inequities that text technologies including ML, AI, LLMs, and natural language processing (NLP) have not only reinscribed but worsened.[6] Nevertheless, as Benjamin points out, more needs to be done to respond to and mitigate the damage such methods can perpetuate.[7]

While critique is valuable and necessary, even more pressing is the need to prepare students with a theoretical framework and computational literacies required to call out, resist, and change text-based tools of oppression. As humanities teachers and scholars, we have a responsibility to prepare students to navigate the social, political, economic, and academic futures shaped by ever-expanding algorithmic black boxes that process, analyze, and generate texts. Language, a fundamental currency for human exchange, is increasingly beholden to spectacular digital Infrastructures that simultaneously naturalize and erase social harms, and as text technologies increase in number and capacity the need for feminist scholars to confront such challenges directly, especially in the classroom, is even more urgent.

Historically, feminist scholars have been reluctant to venture into quantitative or empirical methods for understandable reasons, not the least of which is that women have not always been welcome or valued participants in what has become a male-dominated field, particularly when their work becomes inconvenient, exposing actual and potential collateral damage new technologies pose. "To live a feminist life," Sarah Ahmed writes, "is to live in very good company" with other feminist "killjoys"—those who are usually framed as making what seemed uncomplicated and easy a locus of friction or argument.[8] The feminist killjoy is someone who "stops the smooth flow of communication" until things become tense.

[W]hen you name something as sexist or as racist you are making that thing more tangible so that it can be more easily communicated to others. But for those who do not have a sense of the racism or sexism you are talking about, to bring them up is to bring them into existence.

When you expose a problem, you pose a problem. It might then be assumed that the problem would go away if you would stop talking about it or if you went away.[9]

Acting as the feminist killjoy can be a professionally precarious position. Take for example the situation of Timnit Gebru, who in 2019 was the co-lead of Google's ethical AI division and who was asked by executives to retract or to remove her name from a paper she had recently coauthored (and had been internally reviewed) on the dangers of LLMs. Fearing that the paper was not enthusiastic enough about the integration of GPT3 features into Google's search engine, executives sidelined and then fired her for refusing to comply with their request.[10] Only a few short months later, Margaret Mitchell, Gebru's supportive division co-lead, was also let go under questionable circumstances.

Beyond its social barriers, computational text analysis's reliance on empiricism—reducing words to numeric representations—seems particularly inhospitable territory for feminist inquiry, which values affect, experience, and intersectionality. In "The Ground Truth of DH Text Mining," Tanya Clement locates an inherent conflict for feminist scholars in text analysis's singular focus on the written word, traditionally the site of phallocentric, logocentric systems of authority and power. If, as Clement argues, analog text analysis is an *a priori* masculinized form of knowledge production and power, then pairing it with computation seems to redouble that concern. In "Gender and Cultural Analytics: Finding or Making Stereotypes?" Laura Mandell posits that feminist scholars are avoidant of what she defines as the "m/f," the conflation of biological sex assignments with gender in most data science. Such practice exposes a fundamental conflict between computational methods and our contemporary feminist understanding of sex and gender. Mandell warns that feminist scholars may refuse to engage with cultural analytics altogether—and by association text analysis. She goes on to insist that the temptation "to simply walk away" (a phrase that resonates with Mark Sample's chapter in this volume) is ill-advised and recounts how in the 1960s feminist sociologists focused exclusively on qualitative methods, "leaving the field susceptible to 'bad science' (Haraway, "Gender," 55) and 'bad description' (Marcus, Love, and Best, 6)."[11] In much the same way, refusing to engage with computational text analysis today leaves us vulnerable to an untold number of pseudoscientific studies at every turn because the methods used in quantitative social science, digital literary studies, and cultural analytics are similarly (and often much less critically) deployed by social media companies, ubiquitous corporations like Amazon, policing and court systems, publishing companies, and political campaigns. In other words, the stakes could be more far-reaching now than they were then.

I share Mandell's conviction that engaging with computational text analysis provides ample opportunities to reexamine feminist theory's own problematic histories, as well as to forge tangible connections between feminist scholarship and digital methods. These convictions inform my teaching, as well. In the chapter that follows, I argue that computational text analysis courses present opportunities for students to make feminist arguments with code and that feminist pedagogy courses have the potential to cultivate digital literacies[12] and computational competencies among students who otherwise may see themselves as outsiders in the fields of information and computer science.[13] Drawing on my experience teaching three semester-long, graduate-level introductions to text analysis, I share how foregrounding a feminist ethic of care in the quantitative methods classroom can empower students to craft their own definitions of feminist text analysis while learning digital skills, and by extension encourage them to imagine digital practices that mobilize theory toward social justice. Following a brief description of the course's institutional context and curricular design, I provide examples of in-class activities, weekly assignments, projects, and assessments that might be adapted for use in other digital humanities or women's and gender studies courses. With a brief acknowledgment of the challenges that the course presents, I conclude by demonstrating how students built upon their work in future semesters and beyond.

The Course

A core course in the CUNY Graduate Center's MA in Digital Humanities Program and cross-listed in the MS in Data Analysis and Visualization, "Methods of Text Analysis" provides a conceptual and practical introduction to the computational methods of text analysis, including NLP, ML, and AI, as well as other emerging tools and technologies. In 2019, I had the opportunity to develop the inaugural course in the program. Starting fresh without a local precedent afforded me creative license to reimagine what the purpose of an introduction to text analysis might be and to design a curriculum with the flexibility to respond to widely varied student skills, interests, and experiences, while pushing them to lean into the difficulty of making tangible connections between theory, lived experience, and digital methods.

Flexibility would be a necessity given the heterogeneous composition of the students who are inclined to take the course. The MA and MS programs boast a diverse student body and many of the students who register for the course are attuned to the potential hazards of unexamined implementations of computational methods. At the same time, students apply to the program with a sense of optimism about what text technologies offer them as educators, data scientists, librarians, educational technologists, museum curators, grant officers, lawyers, and journalists—just a few of types of full or part-time positions students may hold while they are taking classes. Although the hybridity of students' experience presented challenges for course development, it also proved fertile territory for feminist pedagogy as a liberatory classroom practice that values diversity of lived experience alongside traditional academic forms of knowledge production.[14] Informally renaming the course "Feminist Text Analysis," I established three core values in my development of the curriculum: creating a classroom atmosphere in which students could take risks while extending their digital skills and critical abilities, cultivating students' ability to enact feminist critique grounded in examples of code, and fostering students' confidence forming authentic arguments that respond to open-ended, scholarly conversations about digital methods.

Focusing the course objectives on building functional digital literacy that would allow students to make critical arguments with code alleviated the need for students to perform independent text analyses for their final projects, the typical final assignment in such introductory courses. Instead, class discussions, activities, assignments, and the final project were scaffolded for students to read, modify, and evaluate code in service of making informed arguments. Returning to a guiding question for the course each week—"Can there be such a thing as feminist text analysis?"—provided a conceptual throughline across the fifteen weekly two-hour meetings either in person (2019), online (2020), or both (2023).[15] Assignments in the class were designed to help students develop their own response to this question and to support their argument with code-based evidence.

After the first three weeks, which focus on developing a shared critical vocabulary and a baseline comfort with Jupyter notebooks,[16] the remainder of the semester proceeded in two-week units with topics that correspond to the steps in a typical text analysis workflow: forming research questions, data, conceptualization, operationalization, and analysis.[17] Each week, readings were paired with hands-on code-based activities in Jupyter (and later Google Colab) notebooks that I pre-populated with annotated, executable code. At a minimum, students were asked to read through each notebook and execute each code block, occasionally making minor adjustments to the code to see how it might impact the outcome. Routinely, students were asked to create text blocks in their notebooks and to write reflections that connect themes in the readings to the code activities. To keep assignments low-stakes and to encourage experimentation, notebooks were evaluated based on completeness rather than accuracy. Students also had the opportunity to write blog posts during the semester presenting a digital text analysis project and proposing a topic for the class's final activity, a public roundtable discussion on the course's guiding question about feminist text analysis. During the final class of the semester, we held a mock conference roundtable and invited members of the university community to join us for moderated five-minute presentations and discussions. Presentations gave students a chance to draft and receive feedback on writing that could be revised as part of the culminating assignment for the class: a portfolio of each week's Jupyter notebook assignment with a five-page position paper introducing the notebook assignments and making an original argument as to whether feminist text analysis is possible while drawing evidence from code activities.

Building a Shared Vocabulary

The first three weeks of the course focused on establishing a shared critical vocabulary that students could draw upon throughout the semester, on developing a comfortable workflow for completing notebook assignments, and on establishing a generous class environment where students support one another in taking risks. Introducing key and contested terms, like "feminist," "text," and "analysis," students with strong backgrounds in the humanities reported greater comfort during class conversations about Mary Beard's *Women and Power*, Adichie's *We Should All Be Feminists*, and Ahmed's *Living a Feminist Life*—the kind of academic work with which they were already familiar. Centering our discussion on the problematic history of US feminism in our search for a shared definition of what it means to "do feminism," readings on the history of feminist reading practice, such as Mae Gwendolyn Henderson's "Speaking in Tongues: Dialogics, Dialectics, and the Black Woman Writer's Literary Tradition" and Nancy K. Miller's "Rereading as Woman: The Body in Practice," formulated a collective awareness of the feminist tradition of textual analysis and established a sense of the analog feminist practice of "reading against the grain."[18] Early discussions around vocabulary foreshadowed future topics that would appear in code notebook assignments that contended with structured vocabularies, feature extraction, data cleaning, and generalizing functions.

Meanwhile, for students less familiar with coding and digital tools, the first three weeks of the course provided students with a gentle introduction Python, Jupyter notebooks, GitHub, and/or Google Colab, which they would need to complete future assignments.[19]

Figure 10.1 shows the first activities from the first notebook assignment. Students accessed the notebook from a GitHub repository and opened it with their own Google Colab accounts. The first activities of the notebook ask students to click into an existing text box and to edit the text. The second activity requires them to click inside a code block and execute the code. Where possible, I included additional information explaining each activity as they should find it and then how it should change after it has been executed.

In figure 10.2, the next activity in the same Google Colab notebook, students learn how to import a common Python package for text analysis called the Natural Language Toolkit (NLTK). Students would need to learn how to perform this process throughout the semester, but at this point, the assignment was designed to get students comfortable with the process of importing a package and reporting back through the notebook on their work.

Next, in figure 10.3, students begin a two-part exercise. First, they create a sample variable "sentence" from a *New York Times* article. Then they use the NLTK package they recently imported to divide the sentence into

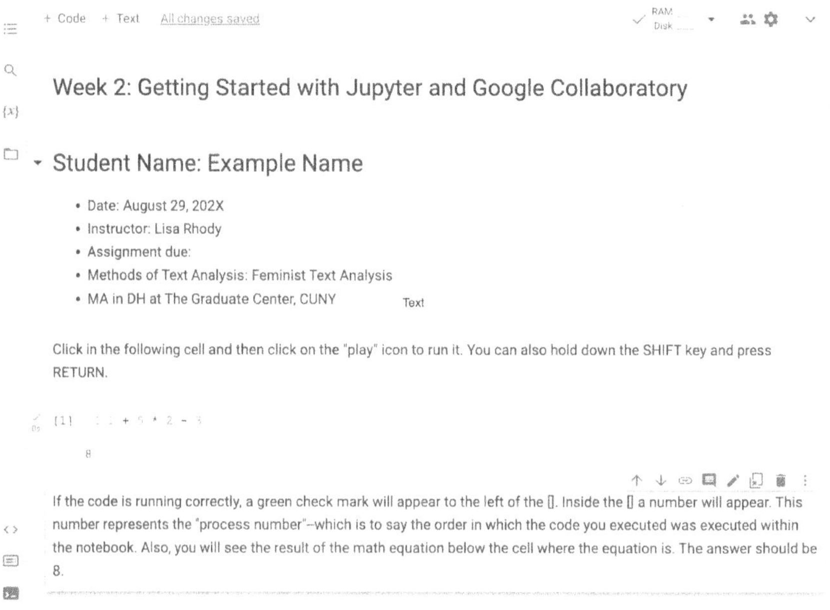

Figure 10.1. An example of the first Jupyter notebook assignment completed in Google Colab. Students are asked to click into a text block and edit the text. Then they are asked to run a code block that calculates an equation.

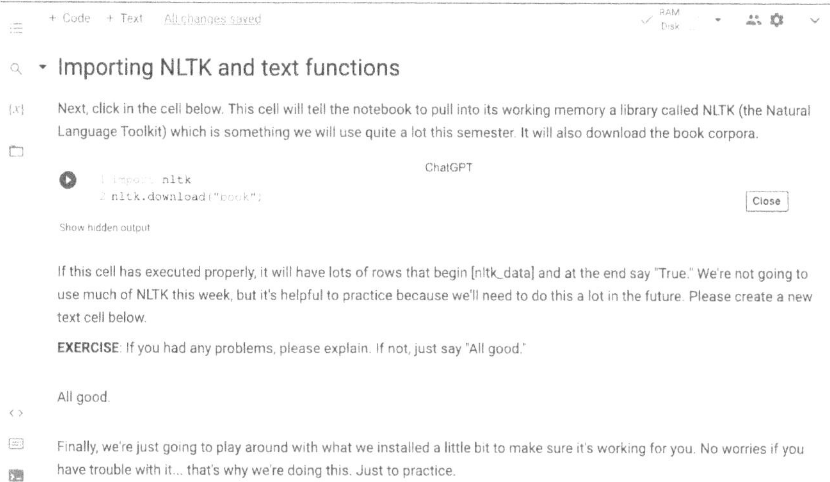

Figure 10.2. Using Google Colab, students run a code block that imports the Python package NLTK and then downloads the "book" corpus. The activity is designed to give students a low-stakes introduction to a common process when using Python to perform text analysis.

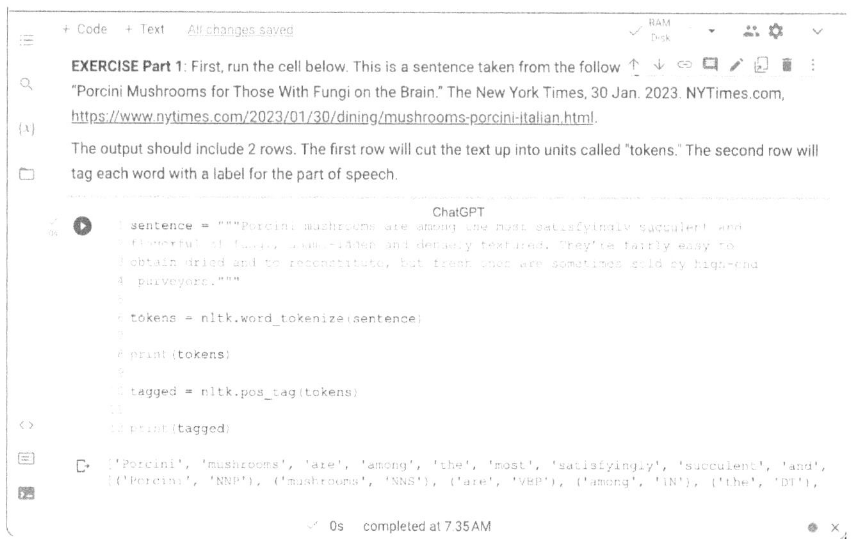

Figure 10.3. In the first of a two-part exercise, students are asked to run a code block that has been prefilled for them. The code takes a sample sentence and assigns it the variable "sentence." Then the sentence is tokenized and tagged with each word's part of speech. The results are displayed below the code block after the cell runs without error.

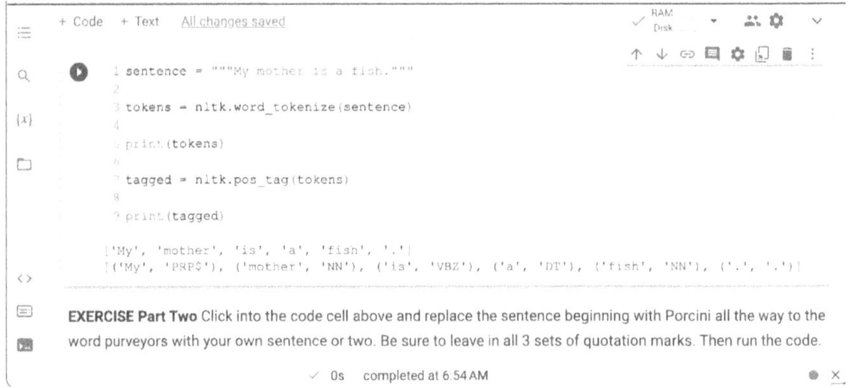

Figure 10.4. In the second of a two-part exercise, students replace the sentence provided in the text block with a sentence of their own. When they rerun the code block, the results will change to reflect the new sentence. This is an activity that students will repeat with greater sophistication in later assignments.

discrete units of words using a predefined method in NLTK and label each word with its part of speech using the "pos_tag" method. The results appear in the notebook below the code block. Finally, in figure 10.4, students are asked to go back to the sample sentence and to change it so that they can see how the results also change.

After completing the assignment, students saved the notebook in a folder in their Google Drive and shared the link with me. By the time students completed the first assignment, they have not only practiced the workflow for submitting weekly assignments, but they have also begun two activities that set the stage for in-class discussion about what a "text" is. In the following week's assignment, they extended their work with importing packages to download the NLTK book corpus, which includes eighteen prepared texts such as William Shakespeare's *Macbeth*, Jane Austen's *Emma*, and Walt Whitman's *Leaves of Grass*. The texts included in the NLTK corpus serve as a starting point for the following week's discussion about the structural inequities invisibly perpetuated by way text analysis is typically taught using corpora that are easy to find and out of copyright.

In combination with the notebook assignment, readings presented students with multiple disciplinary understandings of what a text is, drawing on feminist literary theory, textual criticism, philosophy, sociology, and economics.[20] During class, students were divided into groups, given a book, and asked to identify the "text" according to definitions in their readings and the notebook assignment. Books included: *Nox* by Anne Carson, an accordion-bound volume of poetry in a box that combines illustrations, drawings, and photos with a poem composed on a computer and printed;[21] *The Making of Samuel Beckett's Molloy*, a print descriptive catalog designed to accompany the genealogical edition of plays in the Samuel Beckett Digital Manuscript Project;[22] and a print edition of *Debates in the Digital Humanities*,[23] which also appears in an open-access, online version using Manifold.[24] Our earlier discussions of feminism's emphasis on an ethics of care, embodiment, affect, and context established a critical vocabulary that students could deploy to discuss the differences between expectations and reality in computational text analysis. By denaturalizing the concept of "text," students could articulate the way that computation and empirical analysis obscure or remove necessary context and could identify those moments as "sweaty concepts"—Ahmed's term for moments when the description of the conditions of oppression reorient our perspective of what is considered "natural."[25] By the end of the class period, we turned our conversation toward the topic of the following week—analysis—and considered how analysis might be grounded in an imperative to expose the ideological assumptions that make computational methods akin to "common sense." In the weeks to follow, we focused on each stage of the computational text analysis process, exposing the ways they naturalize ideological assumptions, which I suggest is a feminist practice of *reading against an algorithmic grain*.

Reading against an Algorithmic Grain

Throughout the remainder of the course, we returned to the question of whether feminist text analysis is necessarily or inherently reactionary—always having to respond to white, cis-male normativity—or can it intervene at the level of code to create new forms of knowledge production? In other words, can there be a feminist text analysis that is liberatory? Setting our sights on feminism's imperative to move us toward justice, we considered each stage of the computational text analysis process and what feminist practice might look like throughout the methodological life cycle. Organized into two-week units, the class tracked the text analysis pipeline as described in "How to Do Things with Words," a collaborative publication undertaken for the purpose of helping humanities scholars understand the text analysis project workflow: asking research questions, collecting and cleaning data, conceptualizing, operationalizing, and analyzing. Weighing an orientation toward a feminist ethic of care against the illegibility of messy results, students were pressed to consider what computational feminist text analysis might look like. Notebook assignments established a base technical vocabulary including terms like "tokenizing," "lemmatizing," and "stemming." Notebook assignments included prewritten code for students to execute so that learning can be scaffolded based on students' relative level of comfort with code. At a minimum, students develop a *functional* digital literacy as their ability to read, interpret, and describe what is happening at each stage improved, while more fluent coders can challenge themselves to extend the assignments.

During the units on forming research questions, collecting, and cleaning data, students split their time between case studies of projects, readings, and notebook activities, focusing on what question is being asked by the researcher, what dataset is in use, and then executing code that approximates similar collection and preparation practices in their own notebooks. By connecting across readings, group discussion, sample projects, and notebook assignments, students develop their practice of reading against the algorithmic grain. For example, students explored Ben Schmidt's data visualization of Rate My Professor faculty reviews.[26] Asked to identify Schmidt's research question, students considered the difference between asking whether faculty identified as female or faculty identified as male are better teachers or whether we can detect gender bias in the language students use to evaluate faculty or how language can be deployed to reproduce gendered stereotypes. In other words, is it true that male-identified faculty in every discipline are funnier than their female-identifying counterparts, as the visualization in figure 10.5 may suggest?[27]

Students explored how the orientation of the research question and the assumptions inherent in the data collection and cleaning practice impact the final visualization and viewers' interpretation of the experiment's results. Exploring the project was coupled with readings such as "The Numbers Don't Speak for Themselves" from *Data Feminism*, "Against Cleaning," a chapter that exposes how off-the-shelf data cleaning practices also remove valuable contextual information from the data, potentially perverting our interpretation of results; and "One-Size-Fits-Men."[28] In groups, students synthesized these readings with excerpts from data science and statistical publications on concepts like "tidy data" and worked with various data types to produce shared criteria for evaluating and preparing data.[29] In the week's notebook assignments, students imported, cleaned, and prepared sample text datasets from popular sources ranging from Kaggle to academic data repositories. As they organized and displayed the data in their notebooks, students evaluated the dataset using criteria they created based on their readings and lived experiences. As they did so, students encountered "sweaty concepts," places where assumptions made in the data are exposed as normalized cultural biases or poor data practice. In one case, students were asked to evaluate an IMDB dataset of 50,000 movie reviews that had

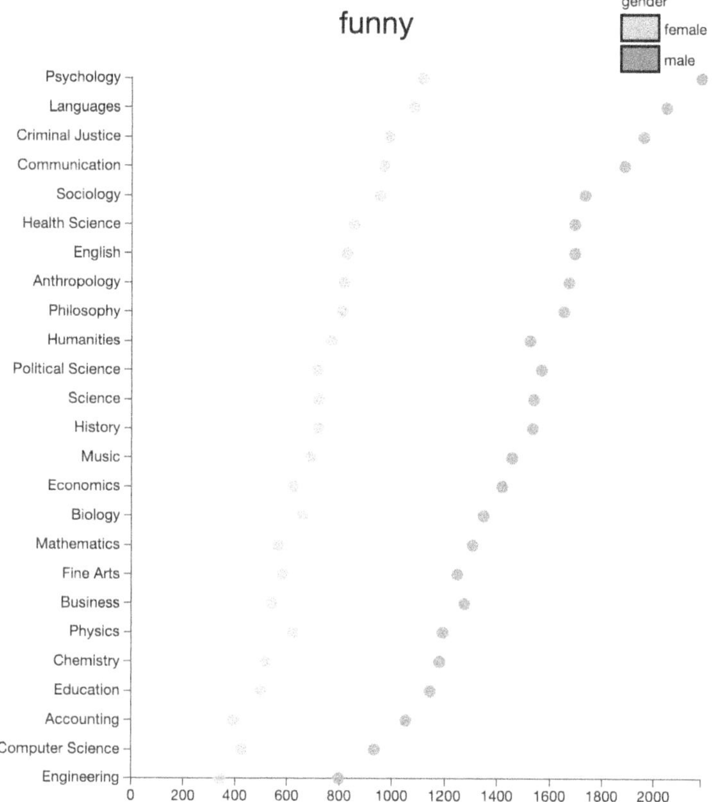

Figure 10.5. This is a graph of the frequency with which the word "funny" appears in reviews of faculty from Rate My Professor. The graph is ordered along the *y* axis according to academic department and data is separated by inferred gender. Reviews of male faculty (darker dots) include the word funny more frequently than their female (lighter dots) colleagues. See Ben Schmidt, "Rate My Professor," February 6, 2015, https://benschmidt.org/2015/02/06/rate-my-professor/.

been used to train ML algorithms for sentiment analysis. Their investigation not only included mechanical questions about data completeness, OCR errors, and missing labels, but also the ethical considerations, such as consent. For example, students found that the dataset had been shared with the IMDB user profile information intact.

When we addressed "conceptualization" (turning data and research questions into measurable quantities and formats) and "operationalization" (the processing of the data in ways that model the research question), students wrangled with empirical methods deployed by various text classification projects to ask questions about ways gender is functionally reinscribed as binary and oppositional—the "m/f" Mandell refers to. Pairing Joan Scott's "Gender: A Useful Category of Historical Analysis" with text classification exercises, conversation turned to the usefulness of Scott's articulation of gender as "a tactical term to talk about the conflation of gender as an assignment of sex and cultural identity" in contrast with the labeling of text required to perform supervised ML.[30]

During conversations about conceptualization and operationalization, students developed a deeper understanding of how structural inequities are technically instantiated in text analysis and first recognized the way that privileging what is easy over what is accurate or valued reproduces injustice. For example, many of the notebook assignments were based on the open-source book *Natural Language Processing with Python*; however, chapter six begins with an assertion that the *simplest* type of classification is by gender. The chapter begins by asking questions like: "How can we identify particular features of language data that are salient for classifying it? How can we construct models of language that can be used to perform language processing tasks automatically? What can we learn about language from these models?"[31]

Recalling Mandell's article, text classification assignments of gender could be considered "easy" because historically our data collection practices are based on a binary taxonomy that conflates sex-assignment with the social constructions of gender. Until relatively recently, data collection practices usually included a male/female category, even if gender is unrelated to the purpose of the data being collected in the first place. Nevertheless, supervised algorithmic classification algorithms (like *tf-idf*) at their least efficient have a 50 percent chance of accuracy (same as a coin toss) for random assignments. What makes the activity "easy" is that it is more likely to succeed even if the features selected have little efficacy. We looked at the process together in class, identifying the key factors that lead to expected results and how the temptation to learn how to train models on gender binaries is strong because it offers a high statistical likelihood of success. Instead, students worked on a more complex classification activity—assigning bug reports to one of five categories. Together the assignments rehearsed with students what it might mean to read *against the grain* of algorithmic simplicity as feminist killjoys. Meanwhile, students were learning the principles of algorithmic classification while actively working to avoid its harms.

At its most powerful, feminist DH pedagogy should reflect the type of text analysis we wish to see in the world and resist masculinist and normative stereotypes where possible. When placing the simplicity of gender classification against Adichie's framing of gender as a prescription for how to behave rather than a representation of who we are, students begin to ask of the methods whether algorithmic approaches to text yield insights or if they are using the past to prescribe our interpretation of the future. As we moved from operationalization to analysis, some characteristics of reading against the algorithmic grain began to form. Students would repeatedly ask: Are we valuing ease over care? What could be the affective result? What context has been removed or needs to be reintroduced during analysis? Whom does this method serve? Whose experience is erased? Can we imagine asking this question another way to be more representative? This practice began to shape their growing digital literacy and ground their interpretive practices in preparation for the final assignment.

Staying with the Trouble

Donna Haraway uses the phrase "staying with the trouble" (also the title of her book) to describe speculative feminism's resistance to what she describes as "a comic faith in technofixes, whether secular or religious: technology will somehow come to the rescue of its naught but very clever children, or what amounts to the same thing."[32] To "stay with the trouble" resists the bitter cynicism that on our way to environmental extinction there is no value in trying to make things better or that "only if things work do they matter." Staying with the trouble in the course, however, also meant creating conditions in which students could learn enough code to be able to make informed arguments—exposing a problem requires understanding the problem in the first place. To stay with the trouble requires that feminist practice tread into the field of empirical text analysis with all its flaws and continue to do the work of exposing systematic inequities, even if what it can offer is merely an imperfect better.

Introducing computational text analysis that relies on students' understanding code presents theoretical and technical challenges in the humanities classrooms. NLP and text mining can be mathematically and procedurally complex, requiring a rudimentary familiarity with a programming language, such as R or Python, as well as a general familiarity with linguistics, and a formative sense of statistics and algebra—skills not so common among graduate and undergraduate students in the humanities. Out-of-the-box tools, such as Voyant, can be used to make performing such analysis more accessible to novice computer users, and in introduction to digital humanities courses that cover a wide range of digital methods, graphical user interface (GUI) tools such as AntConc or JStor's Text Analyzer, or even HathiTrust's Research Center, make analyzing text corpora much more reasonable. However, if the purpose of the course is to help students understand the logic of computational methods, establishing a functional literacy in coding in languages such as Python or R allows students to engage more substantially with the choices and assumptions that happen invisibly with GUI tools.

Approaching text analysis this way, however, also shifts the work back to the instructor to create each notebook assignment in advance and to prepare datasets that demonstrate the values of feminist text analysis. Developing Jupyter notebook assignments—those that are not simply built on the easiest possible activity—with functional, prewritten code meant that the course took much more time to prepare and test. Each semester, notebooks would need to be updated, changed, or rewritten due to updates in Python or the various packages we were using, or even to try to stay current with best practices. Nevertheless, I was unable to find another way to introduce students to *enough* code to navigate between the feminist and computational imperatives of the course. As more feminist text analysis courses emerge, perhaps there will be greater sharing and availability of similar activities that makes lighter and more collaborative work of preparing to teach such a class.

Near the conclusion of his chapter in *Debates in the Digital Humanities 2019*, Andrew Goldstone makes what could be called a feminist DH claim. He writes: "I have argued that teaching quantitative methods is hard, but I am not suggesting that it needs to be made easy. On the contrary, the digital humanities should be wary of promises of ease in prepackaged tools, in well-meaning introductory tutorials and workshops that necessarily stop short of what a researcher would need to draw conclusions, and in rationalizations of inconclusive arguments as exploration, play, or productive failure." Borne out of a similar inclination, the weekly Jupyter notebook assignments were designed for students unfamiliar with coding to feel the productive discomfort of learning how to read and interpret code. Notebook assignments that make use of "readymade" processes, ones that can be repurposed for multiple kinds of research questions, rather than "custommades," more artisanal processes developed for a specific dataset and research question—a distinction Matthew Salganik offers in *Bit by Bit: Social Research in the Digital Age*—can help reduce the instructor's workload. Working with standardized activities allows students opportunities to see how various text analysis projects draw on similar statistical arguments to create categories and detect patterns, and accompanying reflections create space for questions that resist normative practice and at the same time encourage deeper learning. Nevertheless, through such activities, students develop familiarity with basic scripting skills but are unlikely to develop self-sufficiency. Making peace with the possibility that it is impossible to teach self-sufficiency in text analysis methods in a single semester is necessary if the goal is to begin from a place of critical agency.[33]

Introducing how to code in the introduction to text analysis course is only one of its challenges. Goldstone explains, "The available strategies for teaching literary data analysis under the 'DH' rubric, including my own, have so far been inadequate to the task of training scholars in research methods." Adequately studying methodology, Goldstone argues, requires better datasets for teaching and that a single-semester course is insufficient time for students to develop enough facility with computational methods to advance to the point of making arguments with literary data.[34] After my experiences teaching Feminist Text Analysis, I agree with Goldstone that DH continues to suffer from a dearth of teaching corpora that have enough complexity to demonstrate concepts like the value of cleaning data without overwhelming students. In other words, more needs to be done to figure out how we create *just enough* trouble.

Conclusion

Developing a methods of text analysis class grounded in feminist pedagogy allowed me to create a learning environment in which students could bring their full selves to class. Calling attention to the course as feminist in the title and course description seems to have led to a more diverse classroom than if it had been advertised as just "Methods of Text Analysis." Connecting lived experience to feminist data science principles reinforced the stakes at play in developing and utilizing methods of text analysis, including the potential harm inflicted through the common practice of collecting demographic information that insists on gender as analogous to one's biological sex, assigned at birth, and static. Insisting on students' embodied, unified experience of text analysis connected feminist pedagogy with course content by demonstrating the potential harmful impact of assumptions that undergird many text analysis methods. In our discussions of data collection, nonbinary students shared their experiences filling out data collection forms in which the only options for gender were binary male/female designations, erasing their experience from the historical record. We could connect these experiences to the Jupyter notebook activities in which students were required to identify stable categories of analysis and put them in conversation with readings, such as Klein and D'Ignazio's *Data Feminism*, which pronounces that a core feminist data science principle is that it "teaches us to value multiple forms of knowledge, including the knowledge that comes from people as living, feeling bodies in the world."[35] Lifting up the full range of students' academic and life experiences in the classroom allowed me to draw from a much wider range of academic disciplines, to connect classroom learning to current events, and to create a climate in which women and gender nonbinary students felt supported and able to thrive. If changing the way computational text analysis is deployed inside and outside of academia is a feminist goal, then creating a liberating classroom practice for students who are female-identifying and racialized minorities becomes a necessary measure of success.

The introduction to text analysis course is rich with opportunities to explore feminist theory, to connect cultural theory and social justice to current technologies, and to cultivate students' development of a functional computational literacy so that they may become advocates for themselves and others. A feminist approach to teaching text analysis can cultivate functional code literacy in text analysis while modeling how to read against the grain of such methods. By asking where in the research process we can inject social justice, students contextualize distant reading within a feminist tradition of literary and historical analysis akin to Henderson's "dialogic dialectics" or Judith Fetterley's "resistant reading." In other words, the outcomes of feminist pedagogy should be, as Haraway writes, to "stay with the trouble" rather than relinquishing the field and falling back to a position in which feminist approaches to text analysis are only ever reactionary. By teaching feminist text analysis, we expand students' practice as critical readers, scholars, and activists by reading against the invisible logic of algorithms and offer them a sense of what the resisting distant reader can do, including intervening in conversations that will lead to social change.

The success of such an approach was evident in students' final projects. For example, one student proposed that feminist text analysis might include something akin to a "Bechdal-Wallace test" that could measure representation of women in text data and could be used as a statistical measure of a text analysis projects' efficacy. Other students considered how feminist critique might challenge the use of "ownership" of language when labeling features for authorship attribution analysis. Meanwhile other students returned to the need to consider gender either as a vector or a scale and noted that at a minimum feminist text analysis would need to resist the urge to begin with a recognition that gender is complex but capitulate that since binary methods are all we have that is what we need to continue to use. The resulting conversations were generative and allowed students to practice how they might put what they had learned through the semester into active use as practicing scholars in digital humanities and in the public sphere. While discussions began by identifying strategies for resistance within the notebook assignments, they often grew much broader by the end of the roundtable presentation, pointing to current events, such as the public release of ChatGPT. Students from the course have gone on to create capstone projects that draw on NLP and ML to introduce readers to romance novels written by Caribbean authors and to display correlations between global events and the translation of Arabic-language novels by women.

If feminist pedagogy represents a persistent striving that is both an ideality and a necessity, then practicing feminist text analysis in the classroom means teaching computational methods as a fundamental contemporary skill for exposing and redressing cultural assumptions that have been naturalized through automation. In other words, there is space for productive feminist digital humanities to engage with methods of text analysis and to develop methods for reading against the grain of the determinism of algorithmic logic, extending its impetus to resist injustices. By extension, there is a valuable and necessary role to play for feminist pedagogy in the process. "Living a feminist life" for the feminist digital humanist means exposing methodological sites of structural inequity, including those embedded in complex and challenging algorithmic systems. By doing our work as humanists and by teaching students core technical competencies that refuse the easy solution in favor of more nuanced considerations of ethics, statistical biases, and historical challenges (like that of using gender as a category of analysis), we prepare students (and ourselves) to look with informed skepticism at the many ways in which our lives are shaped through the use of predictive natural language processing and empower them to become active citizens with the capacity to expose injustice and enact change.

Notes

Thank you to Filipa Callado, Tanya Clement, Lauren Klein, Stephen Ramsay, Jason Rhody, Susan Schreibman, and the external reviewers for their generous and thoughtful feedback and suggestions. I am grateful to the students of the Feminist Text Analysis classes who were willing to stay with me through the trouble of creating and revising the class and from whom I learned so much.

    1. Benjamin, *Race after Technology*.
    2. Golebiewski and boyd, "Data Voids."
    3. Eubanks, *Automating Inequality*.
    4. Noble, *Algorithms of Oppression*.
    5. Buolamwini and Gebru, "Gender Shades."
    6. Costanza-Chock, *Design Justice*; and Benjamin, *Race after Technology*.
    7. This list is a mere sampling of the excellent work currently done by women in fields like data journalism, critical code studies, science and technology scholarship, media studies, and more. Other examples might include *Data Feminism*

by Catherine D'Ignazio and Lauren Klein, *Algorithms of Oppression* by Safiya Umoja Noble, and *Artificial Unintelligence* by Meredith Brussard, among others.

8. Ahmed, *Living a Feminist Life*.

9. Ahmed, *Living a Feminist Life*, 37.

10. Simonite, "What Really Happened When Google Ousted Timnit Gebru."

11. Mandell, "Gender and Cultural Analytics." See also Brown and Mandell's discussion of the discussion of the m/f binary in this volume.

12. My use of the term *functional literacy* draws on UNESCO's definition of the term. See "What You Need to Know about Literacy." UNESCO's definition is based on work by Freire, *Pedagogy of the Oppressed*.

13. For demographic information about women in STEM, see Funk and Parker, "Women and Men in STEM Often at Odds Over Workplace Equity."

14. hooks, *Teaching to Transgress*, 28.

15. See the course syllabi from Fall 2019 (https://textmethods19.commons. gc.cuny.edu/), Fall 2020 (https://femethods2020.commons.gc.cuny.edu/), and Spring 2023 (https://femethods2023.commons.gc.cuny.edu/). Sample Jupyter notebooks from the course can be found on GitHub: https://github.com/ lmrhody/femethodsS23.

16. Jupyter and Google Colab notebooks provide a means of publishing executable Python code in a web browser alongside text blocks, images, and links.

17. Nguyen et al., "How We Do Things with Words." The article was first published on arxiv.org, which is the version students in 2019 read, but was subsequently published in *Frontiers in Artificial Intelligence* in August 2020, which is the version students in 2020 read.

18. Beard, *Women and Power*. Henderson, "Speaking in Tongues." Miller, "Rereading as a Woman."

19. While Google Colab notebooks were not a viable option for the first two iterations of the course, by 2023 it became students' preferred tool for text analysis.

20. See the assigned readings at https://femethods2023.commons.gc.cuny .edu/week-3-september-10-2019-text/.

21. Carson, *Nox*.

22. Beckett, *Molloy*.

23. Gold and Klein, eds., *Debates in the Digital Humanities 2019*.

24. "Manifold."

25. Ahmed, *Living a Feminist Life*, 12.

26. Schmidt, "Gendered Language in Teaching Evaluations."

27. Note: this is not the argument Schmidt is making, but a question students consider because of the way the information could be misleading out of context.

28. D'Ignazio and Klein, *Data Feminism*; Rawson and Muñoz, "Against Cleaning"; Criado-Perez, *Invisible Women*, 157–68.

29. Wickham, "Tidy Data."

30. Scott, "Gender as a Useful Category of Historical Analysis."

31. Bird, Klein, and Loper, "Learning to Classify Text," in *Natural Language Processing with Python*.

32. Haraway, *Staying with the Trouble*, 3.

33. Salganik, *Bit by Bit*. Salganik describes the difference between data science methods as readymades and custommades by comparing them to Marcel Duchamp's *Fountain* and Michelangelo's *David* in figure 1.2.

34. Goldstone, "Teaching Quantitative Methods."

35. D'Ignazio and Klein, *Data Feminism*, 48.

Works Cited

Adichie, Chimamanda Ngozi. *We Should All Be Feminists*. New York: Anchor Books, 2015.

Ahmed, Sara. *Living a Feminist Life*. Durham, NC: Duke University Press, 2016.

Beard, Mary. *Women and Power: A Manifesto*. New York: Liveright Publishing Corporation, 2017.

Beckett, Samuel. *The Beckett Digital Library: A Digital Genetic Edition*. The Beckett Digital Manuscript Project. Edited by Dirk Van Hulle, Mark Nixon, and Vincent Neyt. Brussels: University Press Antwerp (ASP/UPA), 2016. Accessed March 12, 2023. http://www.beckettarchive.org.

Benjamin, Ruha. *Race after Technology: Abolitionist Tools for the New Jim Code*. Medford, MA: Polity, 2019.

Bird, Steven, Ewan Klein, and Edward Loper. *Natural Language Processing with Python*. 1st ed. Beijing; Cambridge [MA]: O'Reilly, 2009.

Broussard, Meredith. *Artificial Unintelligence: How Computers Misunderstand the World*. Cambridge, MA: MIT Press, 2018.

Buolamwini, Joy, and Timnit Gebru. "Gender Shades: Intersectional Accuracy Disparities in Commercial Gender Classification." *Proceedings of Machine Learning Research, Conference on Fairness, Accountability, and Transparency* 81 (2018): 1–15.

Carson, Anne. *Nox*. New York: New Directions, 2010.

Clement, Tanya. "The Ground Truth of DH Text Mining." In *Debates in the Digital Humanities*, edited by Matthew K. Gold and Lauren F. Klein. Minneapolis: University of Minnesota Press, 2019.

Costanza-Chock, Sasha. *Design Justice: Community-Led Practices to Build the Worlds We Need*. Cambridge, MA: MIT Press, 2020.

Criado-Perez, Caroline. *Invisible Women: Data Bias in a World Designed for Men*. New York: Abrams Press, 2019.

D'Ignazio, Catherine, and Lauren F. Klein. *Data Feminism*. Strong Ideas Series. Cambridge, MA: MIT Press, 2020.

Eubanks, Virginia. *Automating Inequality: How High-Tech Tools Profile, Police, and Punish the Poor*. New York: St. Martin's Press, 2018.

Fetterley, Judith. *The Resisting Reader: A Feminist Approach to American Fiction*. Bloomington: Indiana University Press, 1978.

Freire, Paulo. *Pedagogy of the Oppressed*. Translated by Myra Bergman Ramos. 30th anniversary edition. New York: Bloomsbury Academic, 1998.

Funk, Cary, and Kim Parker. "Women and Men in STEM Often at Odds Over Workplace Equity." *Pew Research Center's Social & Demographic Trends Project* (blog), January 9, 2018. https://www.pewresearch.org/social-trends/2018/01/09/women-and-men-in-stem-often-at-odds-over-workplace-equity/.

Gold, Matthew K., and Lauren F. Klein, eds. *Debates in the Digital Humanities 2019*. Minneapolis: University of Minnesota Press, 2019.

Goldstone, Andrew. "Teaching Quantitative Methods: What Makes It Hard (in Literary Studies)." In *Debates in the Digital Humanities*, edited by Matthew K. Gold and Lauren F. Klein. Minneapolis: University of Minnesota Press, 2019. Accessed February 3, 2022. https://dhdebates.gc.cuny.edu/read/untitled-f2acf72c-a469-49d8-be35-67f9ac1e3a60/section/620caf9f-08a8-485e-a496-51400296ebcd#ch19.

Golebiewski, Michael, and Danah Boyd, "Data Voids: Where Missing Data Can Easily Be Exploited." *Data & Society*, October 29, 2019.

Haraway, Donna J. *Staying with the Trouble: Making Kin in the Chthulucene*. Durham, NC: Duke University Press, 2016.

Henderson, Mae G. "Speaking in Tongues: Dialogics, Dialectics, and the Black Woman Writer's Literary Tradition." In *Feminists Theorize the Political*, edited by Joan Scott and Judith Butler, 144–56. New York: Routledge, 1992.

hooks, bell. *Teaching to Transgress: Education as the Practice of Freedom*. New York: Routledge, 1994.

Mandell, Laura. "Gender and Cultural Analytics: Finding or Making Stereotypes?" *Debates in the Digital Humanities* (2019). https://dhdebates.gc.cuny.edu/read/untitled-f2acf72c-a469-49d8-be35-67f9ac1e3a60/section/5d9c1b63-7b60-42dd-8cda-bde837f638f4.

"Manifold," n.d. Minnesota University Press and CUNY Graduate Center. https://manifoldapp.org/.

Miller, Nancy K. "Rereading as a Woman: The Body in Practice." *Poetics Today* 6, no. 1/2 (1985): 291–99.

Nguyen, Dong, Maria Liakata, Simon DeDeo, Jacob Eisenstein, David Mimno, Rebekah Tromble, and Jane Winters. "How We Do Things with Words: Analyzing Text as Social and Cultural Data." *Frontiers in Artificial Intelligence* 3 (2020). https://www.frontiersin.org/article/10.3389/frai.2020.00062.

Noble, Safiya Umoja. *Algorithms of Oppression: How Search Engines Reinforce Racism*. New York: NYU Press, 2018.

Rawson, Katie, and Trevor Muñoz. "Against Cleaning." In *Debates in the Digital Humanities 2019*, edited by Matthew K. Gold and Lauren F. Klein. Minneapolis: University of Minnesota Press, 2019. https://dhdebates.gc.cuny.edu/read/untitled-f2acf72c-a469-49d8-be35-67f9ac1e3a60/section/07154de9-4903-428e-9c61-7a92a6f22e51#ch23.

Rhody, Lisa. "Methods of Text Analysis, Fall 2019." The Graduate Center, CUNY. https://textmethods19.commons.gc.cuny.edu/.

Rhody, Lisa. "Methods of Text Analysis, Fall 2020." The Graduate Center, CUNY. https://femethods2020.commons.gc.cuny.edu/.

Rhody, Lisa. "Methods of Text Analysis, Fall 2023." The Graduate Center, CUNY. https://femethods2023.commons.gc.cuny.edu/.

Salganik, Matthew J. *Bit by Bit: Social Research in the Digital Age*. Princeton, NJ: Princeton University Press, 2019.

Schmidt, Benjamin. "Gendered Language in Teaching Evaluations." Accessed September 18, 2023. https://benschmidt.org/profGender/.

Scott, Joan Wallach. "Gender as a Useful Category of Historical Analysis." In *Culture, Society and Sexuality*, 77–97. New York: Routledge, 2007.

Simonite, Tom. "What Really Happened When Google Ousted Timnit Gebru." *Wired*, June 8, 2021. https://www.wired.com/story/google-timnit -gebru-ai-what-really-happened.

UNESCO. "What You Need to Know about Literacy." June 29, 2023. https:// www.unesco.org/en/literacy.

Van Hulle, Dirk, Edouard Magessa O'Reilly, and Pim Verhulst, eds. *The Making of Samuel Beckett's "Molloy."* London: Bloomsbury Publishing, 2017. https://www .bloomsbury.com/uk/making-of-samuel-becketts-molloy-9781472532565/.

Wickham, Hadley. "Tidy Data." *Journal of Statistical Software* 59, no. 10 (2014): 1–23.

11

Dismantling the Code

A Liberatory Feminist Pedagogy for Teaching Digital Humanities

DHANASHREE THORAT

Awake, arise and educate
Smash traditions—liberate!
We will come together and learn.
—Savitribai Phule (1831–1897).
Translated by Sunil Sardar and
Victor Paul; in *A Forgotten Liberator*,
edited by Braj Ranjan Mani and
Pamela Sardar

During my high school years in Pune, India, my classmates and I walked over to the computer lab once a week for the newly launched computer literacy class. In a school where generations of footfalls had polished and smoothened wood and stone since 1908, the white air-conditioned lab and its steady hum of desktop computers was a novel space for us. Next door to the lab, we learned needlework and knitting, and in an upstairs classroom, we grappled with Shakespearean prose in *Julius Caesar*. In the computer literacy class, we progressed from learning how to switch on a computer to simple programming in BASIC. A programming language created in 1963 at Dartmouth, BASIC was intended to make programming accessible to beginners. My encounter with BASIC occurred during a concerted push for information technology (IT) literacy at the state level coinciding with the growth of IT parks in Indian cities as well as a jump in outsourcing in the early 2000s. IT classes for young women were premised on the techno-utopian notion that technological progress could empower women in the digital age—in pursuing careers or at home. The programming lessons at school, however, were an alienating experience for me—many of us did not have home computers to continue practicing these programming skills,[1] and the programming seemed to lack any connection to my life as a young woman growing into my identity and body. It was only later, many years after high school, that I could ask why we were not taught coding in Hindi or in Marathi (my native tongue), if coding could be a feminist act, and how inequitable access to IT training programs deepened caste, class, and gender hierarchies in India.

I remember still my bafflement when we were asked to draw a red square with BASIC and my program failed to render (or "print" as the command was labeled in BASIC) the promised shape. I had made a simple mistake. The code refused to acknowledge my British spelling of "colour" and required the American "color." As a lingering legacy of our colonial past, Indian education favors British English (when English is the medium of instruction), and all of us had spent years acquainting ourselves with its linguistic peculiarities and white canonical literature. But in this moment of banal programming failure, my colonized tongue was thrice rebuked: first denied the two Indian languages (Marathi and Hindi) I spoke and then asked to substitute the dialect of one empire for that of another. The techno-utopian vision of women's equality was conditioned on British and American knowledge systems and required access to a "good" education, which itself is a privilege and depends on variables like class, caste, gender, and geographical location in India.

My purported failure at programming in that moment, or more accurately, the failure of knowing the appropriate codes to access a hegemonic knowledge, has since become a cautionary tale as I now foster digital humanities initiatives in Pune, India. Serving as a founding executive member at the Center for Digital Humanities, Pune (CDH Pune),[2] I facilitate the biennial DH institute called the Digital Humanities Winter School. This Winter School was first held in December 2014 and concluded its third iteration in December 2018. Over the years we have witnessed a growing interest from Indian scholars in digital methods and platforms, studying digital spaces, and adopting digital pedagogies.[3] In 2019, the University Grants Commission, the regulatory body for higher education in India, acted on suggestions by Indian academics and designated the "digital humanities" as a thrust area with the following subspecialties: digital archiving, digital pedagogy, digital spaces and culture, and Indian Digital Humanities.[4]

This chapter addresses the liberatory feminist pedagogy that grounded the planning and facilitation of the DH Winter School in our specific postcolonial context and lived material realities. This pedagogical practice was predicated on the understanding that knowing the code, that is, accessing and participating in Western or even Indian dominant knowledge systems, is not the goal of a transformative education. A liberatory pedagogy, pre-mised on decolonial and feminist values, is committed to cultivating radical imaginations and fostering worldmaking where we can envision and work toward equitable futures, digital and otherwise, for our communities. As Sara Ahmed reminds us, "feminism is praxis" and feminist politics are a collective project to not simply transform ideologies but to dismantle systemic oppression in its entirety.[5] This liberatory feminist pedagogical approach frames digital humanities methods as a pathway to pursuing social justice commitments held by community members, drawing especially on the #transformDH movement, which has long insisted that digital humanities practitioners "must work collectively towards transformative, social justice–oriented engagements."[6] Moya Bailey and colleagues have argued too that a critical practice of DH implies that we "seek to understand the social, intellectual, economic, political, and personal impact of our digital practices as we develop them."[7] Critical digital humanities not only refers to the study of power relations, systemic oppressions, and identity (race, gender, sexuality, and more) in digital humanities but also attests to a research ethic of consent, collaboration, and self-reflexivity.

I explore three interlinked ideas as the basis of a liberatory feminist pedagogy for teaching digital humanities in India: decolonizing access through a place-based pedagogy, encouraging community-oriented collaborative learning that draws on feminist praxis, and practicing self-reflection. Enacting a feminist pedagogy in the postcolonial context of India meant acknowledging that issues of gender, sexuality, caste, class, and colorism are co-constituted, and we have to be accountable to the communities in which we are embedded. In the Indian context, conversations on coloniality, caste, gender, and sexuality are necessarily joined as matrices that have defined contemporary Indian society.[8] Feminist movements cannot be single issue struggles. The liberatory pedagogy I outline below draws on the community-oriented pedagogies that Savitribai Phule and bell hooks write about and the diasporic and postcolonial approach to digital pedagogy suggested by Roopika Risam.[9] By foregrounding place-based concerns and material realities for our communities, I sought to listen to and foster local inflections in digital humanities practices in India.

This chapter outlines a model for DH training institutes actively grounded in postcolonial and feminist principles and contextualized locally. I hope our emphasis on equity and justice in teaching digital humanities will be of interest for DH institutes in other disparate geopolitical locations grappling with their own issues of inequitable power relations and systemic injustices. DH training institutes have been held in many locations in the Global South (including Nigeria, India, Ghana, Lagos, Mexico, and more).

The DH Winter School held in Pune, like these DH institutes, shares the goal of introducing DH skills and research to new scholarly audiences. It also emphasizes, however, the necessity of foregrounding a critical digital humanities agenda and supporting local and minoritized scholars, activists, and teachers whose work might be rendered invisible due to the westernized locus of digital humanities publishing. I consider especially the importance of theorizing, teaching, and making based on space and place, local histories and sociopolitical conditions.

Decolonizing Access through Place-Based Learning

The Digital Humanities Winter School was initially launched in 2014 as an alternative to the DH training institutes in the West, which are largely inaccessible to Indian scholars because of their cost and the exclusionary visa processes. This was the first DH training institute to be held in India and it is the only recurring one. Other DH training institutes have been held in Indore, Kolkata, and Gandhinagar, and DH workshops are now offered all over India.[10] Each DH Winter School runs for two to three days, a shorter time span that makes it easier for faculty participants to obtain leave from their institutions. Our participants are mainly humanities graduate students and faculty, and everyone is given a certificate of attendance as institutional documentation. In my capacity as an organizer, I plan the program (including inviting speakers) and facilitate some of the sessions at each Winter School. While topics have varied over the years (based on suggestions from previous events and speaker availability), we offer a slate of introductory lectures and workshops on a variety of digital humanities topics such as digital archiving, visualization methods, postcolonial digital humanities, feminist approaches to digital culture, and game studies.

In Pune, where this DH Winter School is held, one of the earliest models of a liberatory education was offered by feminist visionaries Savitribai Phule and Jyotirao Phule, who championed formal schooling for women in the mid-1800s. For the Phules, access to education was critical in breaking the shackles of caste oppression because it enabled minoritized people to access knowledge that had been denied to them under Brahmanical patriarchy. Schooling was, however, more than learning subjects like English or becoming assimilated into dominant (and oppressive) ideologies. In her poetry, Savitribai Phule exhorts students to join together and learn together so they can "smash traditions—liberate."[11] Phule articulates a pedagogy oriented around ongoing processes of collaboration, co-learning, and dismantling oppressive systems. This history of an anticolonial and anticaste pedagogical practice in Pune speaks to the value of attending to and situating ourselves within localized genealogies of social justice work.

Thinking with and through local space is necessary so that communities can build critical digital projects that will sustain them, and we (as educators and community members) can advocate for and support such liberatory articulations. In his work on decolonizing the university, Achille Mbembe writes about developing a "pluriversity," a university that embraces epistemic diversity via a "horizontal strategy of openness to dialogue among different epistemic traditions."[12] This model challenges the epistemic colonization of higher education in the Third World by the Euro-American canon, including the privileging of English, of white Euro-American scholars and writers, and those forms of knowledge dissemination (conferences, publications, archives, etc.) that are inaccessible to those in the Global South. Indian history testifies to the many ways in which the white Eurocentric canon and Western modernity was transplanted to India by British colonial authorities operating on racist assumptions of native inferiority and technological backwardness. Thomas Macaulay's "Minute on Indian Education," for example, argued for reforming Indian education by disparaging native languages and literatures and making a case for defunding the teaching and printing of these so-called "false texts and false philosophy."[13]

This perspective has lingered on in Indian education even after independence (1947)—in the same year that I learned BASIC programming in high school, I was also reading Shakespeare, Wordsworth, and Twain while national and local writing (including by the Phules) was woefully absent on our high school and college syllabi. As Kush Patel has poignantly observed, anticolonial DH pedagogies in India have to "address with care the colonial histories and discursive practices pervading our digital and material networks" such that we can "engage lived histories locally."[14] Given this postcolonial context, creating a location-specific pedagogy for the first DH Winter School in 2014 thus began with the following questions: What canons and knowledges are privileged when the origin and development story of "digital humanities" is narrated within the geopolitical scope of Euro-America?

As Risam argues, the "hegemonic universal—the Global North—is taken as the basis for digital humanities scholarship" and this is reflected in bibliographies and syllabi reifying scholarship produced in the Global North and often by white male scholars.[15] What were the inequities in scholarly production that we needed to acknowledge within the scope of the DH Winter School? Would our participants have access to DH research, digital tools, and eventually, DH platforms (conferences, journals) to continue learning and eventually, for knowledge dissemination? How could we build local networks of collaboration and knowledge sharing so participants could extend their projects and inquiries beyond the training institute? Being accessible, creating a space for Indian scholars to gain new skills and network with each other, and orienting ourselves around local exigencies and interests drive how the Winter School program is assembled.

The decolonial, place-based framework I adopted drew upon what Risam has called the "diasporic logic of digital humanities."[16] This diasporic logic challenges the binary framing of digital humanities scholarship flowing from the Global North to the Global South by situating the field "rhizomatically in the many tangled roots and offshoots between national contexts, local scholarly practices, and overlapping histories of the digital humanities."[17] One way of unsettling the center-and-periphery model of digital humanities was by outlining humanistic, revolutionary, and cultural engagements with technology that can be located in India before this field came to be termed digital humanities. I wished to outline alternate, local, and radical genealogies for "digital humanities" different from the more commonly narrated one originating with Roberto Busa in the 1970s. In the American context, alternative trajectories of digital humanities can be traced to the data justice work by Black visionaries like Ida B. Wells and W.E.B. Du Bois.[18]

While digital humanities might be a new field, radical pedagogical practices and critical engagements with technology have a long-established presence in our communities. When the first National Conference on Women's Studies was held in 1981 in the nearby city of Mumbai, one of the nine working groups focused on the area of "science and technology" and advised further study of the impact of science and technology on women's "roles and status, especially in view of the fact that working-class women are, by and large, excluded from access to scientific and technological knowledge and equipment."[19] This conference would lead to the foundation of the Indian Association for Women Studies in 1982 and this early emphasis on science and technology in feminist studies in India offers both a genealogy and a call to action for digital humanities practitioners today. Similarly, the "prehistories of digital humanities in India," as I have noted elsewhere, can draw from the radical repurposing of Western modernity during Indian independence when colonial communication technologies and infrastructures (such as the railway and telegraph) were adopted by Indian nationalists.[20] These technologies were introduced in India for more efficient administration of the colony and yet, they were eventually repurposed by nationalists to foster a national independence movement.[21]

Locating this historical moment in the genealogy of DH in India highlights the messiness of working in postcolonial contexts—this revolutionary praxis for engaging technology was developed in a period when the very status of natives as humans was questioned under colonial ideologies. There is a cautionary tale here, too, that revolutionary praxis cannot be unequivocally celebrated—the Indian independence movement, despite its successful anticolonial goal, was rife with its own exclusionary caste and gender politics. See, for example, Vina Mazumdar's work on women's participation and the question of women's rights as it was raised during the independence movement.[22] Yet the continuing violence of neocolonialism and of caste-based and gender-based oppression points to the necessity of developing new strategies of digital resistance grounded in liberatory worldmaking. This is the kind of challenge that digital humanities practitioners can take up today. Opening with such examples can clear the space for our participants to ask and trace local and humanistic engagements of (digital) technology and bring their own expertise and knowledge to bear in situating DH in India.

Aside from such framing examples, my methodological and skill-building workshops "localized" digital humanities in India—showing, for example, how Indian scholars could draw on digital tools or platforms in their own humanities inquiries. Our practical workshops on digital tools and platforms have emphasized skill building, critical making, and theoretical interventions to ensure that participants can apply those skills more broadly and contextually. For example, a workshop on StorymapJS not only focused on the specifics of the platform but also introduced participants to digital mapping as a methodology. Over the years, I've found that the most useful workshops are the ones that show participants how digital tools can be embedded in research or teaching practices. In the workshops I offered, adapting or localizing digital platforms was also accomplished by highlighting how Indian communities had previously used these platforms, addressing their successes and pitfalls in our local contexts of use, and teaching by using local examples.

We have had workshops on Wikipedia (facilitated by Padmini Ray Murray in 2014), Wordpress, Twine, Omeka, and StorymapJS—open access digital platforms that have low technical skill requirements, and which are widely known in DH scholarship but can be adapted to the Indian context.[23] In another instance of local context, accessible platforms also need to be available on low internet bandwidth and on phones. Although most of these tools were developed in the West, using these platforms can also become a means of (re)claiming digital space by marginalized people to articulate their own voices and stories. Riddhima Sharma offers an important note in this regard when she writes that feminist digital humanities "explores the potential of leveraging existing frameworks and imagining new ones for articulating intersectional subjectivities and building radically inclusive communities for social justice."[24]

Wikipedia is a notable example in this regard as the digital platform has already been adopted by Marathi and other native language communities, and by Indian activists. Wikipedia does have a long and well-known history of editorial bias, and of centering knowledge created in and about privileged Western locations. Yet, the widespread accessibility of the platform has prompted Indian scholar-activists to stage interventions and diversify entries. CIS India, an Indian partner of the Wikimedia Foundation, and Feminism in India, a feminist media organization, are just two examples of groups that have organized regular edit-a-thons in India. Open access digital platforms can be leveraged by marginalized people when they have been historically denied traditional platforms for publishing. I find Risam's point on DH pedagogy particularly poignant in this regard as she notes that "digital humanities is not an attempt to teach students particular technical skills, applications, or platforms but a pedagogical approach that enables them to envision a relationship between themselves and knowledge production."[25]

Though I emphasized this kind of localization, I acknowledge that most of these tools and platforms were developed in Western contexts, and some are optimized for English. In other words, we might diversify the voices represented in an existing platform, space, or field but the overall infrastructure (systems, developers, policies, standards) within which liberatory thinking is enacted might stay in place. The development of DH tools and platforms in India will likely require more sustained training efforts as well as dedicated infrastructure and funding. Notably, though, the Bichitra platform (which I discuss below) is optimized for linguistic analysis in Bengali literature (albeit limited to Rabindranath Tagore's work) and a team of DH practitioners lead by Nirmala Menon at IIT Indore is developing a DH publishing initiative.[26] I take these two examples as indicative of another level of DH community building where we create infrastructures and platforms that are attuned to local needs and exigencies.

Community-Oriented Collaborative Learning

The place-based pedagogy that I have outlined thus far asks educators to be accountable to the communities in which we are located. Among other aspects, community accountability implies that we create an equitable learning space, center the voices and experiences of community members (especially historically marginalized voices), and connect scholarly work to the communities in which we are embedded. This learning space enables what bell hooks has called the "insurrection of subjugated knowledge"— where a learning community can share and practice liberatory thinking.[27] Creating such a learning space necessitates that we first acknowledge the asymmetrical power relations (including caste, class, gender, and sexuality) in the learning community of the DH Winter School. Discussions on these topics can become flashpoints and in 2018, we adopted a code of conduct (adapted from the Digital Library Federation Forum Code of Conduct) reiterating our commitment to a diverse and equitable learning environment. For this reason, we also try to keep fees as low as possible. The DH Winter School is currently funded by the Institute for Advanced Studies in English (IASE Pune). This funding covers travel, accommodation, and an honorarium for invited facilitators, and venue-related costs. We received a grant from Savitribai Phule Pune University in 2016 that allowed us to subsidize fees for participants that year. But grant funding for scholarships has not been easy to acquire given the lack of dedicated funding for DH at national or institutional level in India.

In planning sessions, I was especially cognizant of my own programming experiences in high school when I learned skills that most of us could not connect to our lived experiences or practice at home. As my high school programming classes illustrated, technical skills cannot be taught in a cultural vacuum, and should not be removed from broader sociopolitical questions and challenges. Donna Haraway's reminder that "we need to learn in our bodies" points to the importance of situated and embodied knowledge and locating ourselves in the complexities of our lived experiences.[28] What enables learners to unpack the ideological orientations embedded in technological systems, and transition from functional literacy to radical use and "critical making"?[29] Padmini Ray Murray, writing about critical making in India, offers "collaborative codesigning" as a pedagogical practice in this context.[30] Collaborative codesigning is a way of engaging and reading digital artifacts and activities that is also attentive to "different materialities and modalities of knowledge production."[31] This, in turn, enables students to "[challenge] the hegemonic, proprietary nature of our digital devices and begin to imagine alternative models by which to configure future iterations of knowledge universes."[32] Liberatory education, then, engages local epistemological frameworks and envision new modes of knowledge production that are equitable.

Local and experiential knowledge is prioritized in the Winter School by inviting Indian scholars or DH scholars working in India to facilitate some of the lectures and workshops.[33] (Invited scholars were offered travel, accommodation, and an honorarium.) Local scholars were most attuned to how the field was taking shape in India and to the conditions (disciplinary, academic, institutional, sociopolitical) in which our participants were learning, working, and living. The Center for Digital Humanities, Pune, co-organizer for this school, also emphasizes cultivating local expertise, and creating platforms for Indian scholars to share their expert knowledge has been one of the center's foundational goals.[34] Two examples below will illustrate how these DH scholars brought unique concerns to light, particularly aspects specific to Indian contexts.

In the first DH Winter School in 2014, for instance, Sukanta Chaudhuri introduced the Bichitra digital project to our participants.[35] He outlined that the project team had to diverge from the more commonly used text encoding standards for DH projects and create a local solution adapted to the project.[36] In explaining why the project team made this choice, Chaudhuri noted that "XML was not a viable option. Our primary corpus came to nearly 140,000 pages. Over a third was in manuscript, most of it in Bengali with its cumbersome keyboard. It was hard enough to find enough capable operators to make and check the transcriptions in the time available. It would have been unrealistic to demand training in XML markup and TEI encoding as well."[37] Chaudhuri's presentation opened up a conversation about multilingual computing and multilingualism in digital humanities as our participants began to question whether (and how) they could pursue digital projects in the different languages they spoke or worked in. Could the other platforms we had looked at support their native tongues? The overall presentation about Bichitra opened up space for us to ask how certain languages (e.g., English), sociotechnical standards, or platforms are reified in digital humanities, and how to develop technosocial solutions suited for our local audience. Similarly, in the 2018 DH Winter School, Maya Dodd and her students Anjali Chandavarkar, Kunjika Pathak, and Nidhi Prabhakar presented a digital pedagogy showcase highlighting how they were using digital tools and platforms in the humanities classroom. Such pedagogical conversations have highlighted local innovations that are known within the community but which an external invited speaker would be unfamiliar with—for instance, the use of Whatsapp in the classroom. Our participants and facilitators drew on their experiential knowledge and deepened our conversations about digital pedagogy in India.

Moreover, devising a program oriented around collaboration and rooted in local expertise was a key step in the planning process for the Winter School. I understand collaboration as a feminist practice here—participants engage in co-learning and co-production by balancing each other's skill sets and knowledge. Writing about collaboration as a feminist strategy, Geraldine Pratt notes that collaboration is a means of "achieving the kind of reflexivity necessary to recognize the limits of the knowledge that we produce."[38] In the DH Winter School, collaborative and critical making was undertaken as a means of affirming local epistemologies and lived experiences and sustaining and building our collective future. For example, in an Omeka workshop that I facilitated, participants worked in groups to create a digital exhibit of cultural sites related to marginalized histories in Pune. They drafted short writeups, located public domain images, and finally learned how to add these on an Omeka exhibit. This process gave participants an introduction to building digital exhibits, making collaboratively, and drawing on local and community histories in digital humanities. The familiar landscape of Pune was immensely generative for the teams and emphasized the value of their knowledge in critical digital making.

This sociotechnical knowledge could also be adopted to other sites of study. (I certainly don't want to suggest that Indian scholars are limited to Indian sites of study as that would be reinforcing another restrictive imaginary.) Such an exercise models collaborative work that joins theory and praxis, and cuts across traditional academic hierarchies. Finally, these exercises in making together also enabled us to have conversations about ethical collaborations in digital humanities. The collaborative and critical making we encouraged in the Winter School was intended as a forerunner for the kind of collaborative work often called upon in digital humanities projects. Drawing on his own experiences of collaborative making in the classroom, Souvik Mukherjee also points out the *joy* that participants derive from such activities as humanities curriculums in Indian universities don't typically call for group work.[39]

Discomfort and Self-Reflection

A key part of liberatory pedagogy involves the acknowledgment of risks (for participants belonging to minoritized groups) when systemic violence is challenged. The classroom space is not equally constituted for everyone, and multiple marginalizations exist even in postcolonial settings. In one of the DH Winter School's Smita Vanniyar facilitated a session on gender-based discrimination online and digital rights.[40] Their workshop sparked animated dialogue as Vanniyar created a learning environment where we could express our vulnerabilities about existing in hegemonic digital spaces and discuss how to transform these spaces. Such sessions, which issue a call for working toward social justice, can make some participants uncomfortable because they raise questions about the structures and systems we (or some of us) are implicated in and where our responsibilities lie in redressing harms. Yet, as Ahmed notes, discomfort holds the "promise of reorientation" when we challenge long-held assumptions and begin asking questions that can reshape how we perceive the social order.[41] These sessions are especially important because they show how virtual and real-world spaces and issues intersect and interact.[42]

In this line of thinking on personal responsibility and community accountability, it has also been important for me to reflect critically my own positionality, as the organizer, as a DH scholar and practitioner, and as a community member (located in particular matrices of caste, class, and gender that have material effects). In her discussion on teaching social justice, Toneisha Taylor writes that the first step is that "faculty have to be willing, and able, to acknowledge their privilege at all levels and access points" and then "turn that acknowledgement into action."[43] I am conscious that my placement in US academia affords me privileges that my Indian counterparts may lack in their institutions, including access to research/grant funding, publishing opportunities, libraries and archives, and Western scholarly networks. Chandra Talpad Mohanty and M. Jacqui Alexander note that the US academy is a privileged cultural location whose "spatiality of power" must be challenged and disrupted, and academic institutions should not be normalized as the "epitome of knowledge production."[44] In the context of my own role as organizer, disrupting privileged spatialities and social formations means that I must know when to step up and when to step aside. I have to determine what kind of role I can ethically hold in shaping liberatory spaces and creating collaborative opportunities—this involves knowing too when to give up the space that I am occupying.

White and diasporic scholars working in Western institutions need not be constantly positioned as experts in Global South contexts. One way of decentering my privileged position was by turning it over to support Indian scholars—for instance, leveraging potential resources for local participants or connecting Indian scholars (if they wish) to the American scholarly DH networks in which I participate. I also remain open to altering the training based on community suggestions, and to co-organizing with a local scholar who takes intellectual lead (while I handle logistics). As a student myself in this learning space, the varied explorations of critical digital humanities have enriched my work and my understanding of postcolonial and feminist subjectivities in relation to Western modernity. Many years after my short-lived encounter with BASIC programming, I find myself asking the question that really matters: How do digital technologies and the digital humanities support the liberatory projects that sustain our communities?

Challenges and Future

In this concluding section, I would like to offer some challenges and suggestions for future DH training institutes, in India and elsewhere, and then conclude with a short note on feminist digital pedagogy.

Over the years, some of the participants have stayed in touch with us and expressed interest in developing their DH portfolio. How best to support and sustain this interest after the DH Winter School has ended has been a vexing concern. One of the Winter Schools led to a special journal issue in *Asian Quarterly* on digital humanities in India (the first such journal issue in India) and this created an opportunity to continue scholarly conversations in a different form. Creating collaborative opportunities, either for scholarly publications or digital projects, might be ideal for participants who are just getting started in DH. Academic collaborative networks are tremendously valuable in professional development and career opportunities and have historically oriented around dominant subject positions. Organizers and speakers, particularly those who hold positions of relative privilege (sociopolitical or institutional) are likely to have access to DH networks and opportunities already. Drawing on our own networks to create collaborative opportunities and enabling junior or new scholars to access and tap into them is another way of disrupting the privilege some of us may hold in academic settings.

With more DH institutes now being held in the Global South in the last five years, we also have new opportunities for Global South–South collaboration in digital humanities. This offers another way to decenter the Euro-American locus of digital humanities and specifically, the more common model of a Global North–South collaboration. The unfortunate drawback is that scholarship produced in the Global South is often rendered invisible unless it is disseminated in Western scholarly venues or produced by diasporic or white scholars working in Euro-American contexts. Scholars in the Global South are often expected to keep up with research emerging in Euro-American institutions while the reverse is not always true. Part of our decolonial praxis must be to create alternate venues for Global South scholars to share their work and collaborate with each other without the mediating channels of Western academia.

In the Indian context, I hope that future training institutes will particularly account for the important critique that the disciplinary formation of DH in India is reproducing the caste-ist politics of Indian academia and society.[45] Those of us involved in the institutional apparatus of DH in India need to address this important call to action. Finally, we also have more work to do in promoting multilingualism—despite projects like Bichitra (which integrates Bengali alongside English), the language of digital humanities in India is English. But in Pune, for example, we have participants who teach and research in Marathi (the commonly spoken language in the state) and bilingual programs for training institutes would be a good start.

As this overall discussion indicates, the DH Winter School models a flexible, adaptive, and community-oriented program for teaching digital humanities to new audiences in postcolonial contexts. Pursuing a liberatory pedagogy drawing on feminist and postcolonial principles has highlighted the overlapping interests between these two lines of thinking, in particular opening up educational access for marginalized peoples, dismantling canonical forms of knowledge production, and sustaining movements for equity and justice as defined by community members. Far from outlining a static model to teaching digital humanities, this locational approach asks organizers to ground DH training institutes in their specific sociopolitical and institutional contexts. In a historical moment defined by digital activism, educators (as community members) have the opportunity to join with community partners in defining transformative practices and spaces for our collective futures.

Notes

1. Miriam Posner has addressed how the tacit favoring of coding in the digital humanities (to build digital projects) can reiterate gatekeeping along lines of gender, class, and race (Posner, "Some Things to Think about before You Exhort Everyone to Code").

2. CDH Pune was founded in 2013 with the goal of supporting Indian researchers pursuing digital humanities research. The center mainly offers skill-building opportunities, consultations on DH projects and program building, and small sponsorships for professional travel and the HASTAC Scholars Program.

3. Conversations and events about "digital humanities" organized specifically under that category have been ongoing since 2010. See Sneha, "Mapping Digital Humanities in India."

4. UGC STRIDE Report.

5. Ahmed, *Living a Feminist Life*, 255.

6. Cong-Huyen, "#mla13 'Thinking through Race' Presentation."

7. Bailey et al., "Reflections on a Movement."

8. This chapter doesn't delve into the important complications of each of these matrices separately, but I do wish to acknowledge the many fissures and erasures of caste-based oppression in savarna (upper caste) feminism and in strands of postcolonial thinking.

9. Mani and Sardar, eds., *A Forgotten Liberator*; hooks, *Teaching Community*; Risam, "Diasporizing the Digital Humanities"; Risam, *New Digital Worlds*.

10. Shanmugapriya and Menon, "Infrastructure and Social Interaction."

11. Mani and Sardar, eds., *A Forgotten Liberator*.

12. Mbembe, "Decolonizing the University," 37.

13. Macaulay, "Minute on Indian Education."

14. Patel, "Digital Humanities Pedagogy for Whom?"

15. Risam, *New Digital Worlds*, 68.

16. Risam, *New Digital Worlds*, 70.

17. Risam, *New Digital Worlds*, 70.

18. Gallon, "Data and the Recovery of Black Humanity in the Digital Humanities."

19. Velayudhan and Hydari, "Women's Studies in India."

20. Thorat, "Digital Humanities in India."

21. For a deeper dive in the history of the railway and telegraph in India and the complexities surrounding their introduction in India as techno-modern projects and their role in the nationalist movement, see Bear, *Lines of the Nation*; Choudhury, *Telegraphic Imperialism*; and Headrick, "A Double-Edged Sword."

22. Mazumdar, "Emergence of the Women's Question in India and the Role of Women's Studies."

23. Center for Digital Humanities, "DH Winter School."

24. Sharma, "Feminist Digital Humanities."

25. Risam, *New Digital Worlds*, 91.

26. Menon and Shanmugapriya, "Digital Humanities in India."

27. hooks, *Teaching Community*, 2.

28. Haraway, "Situated Knowledges," 582.

29. Ratto, "Critical Making," 253.

30. Murray, "Decolonising Design," 133.

31. Murray, "Decolonizing Design," 133.

32. Murray, "Decolonizing Design," 135.

33. In 2014 and 2018 we did have one external speaker each time from the Global North. This involvement was premised on the speaker bearing some or all of the international travel costs, and conversations beforehand on how their sessions would fit into the Winter School program goals for Indian participants.

34. CDH Pune website.

35. Chaudhuri, ed., *Bichitra*; *Bichitra: Online Tagore Variorum*.

36. Chaudhuri, "Managing a Literary Project and Electronic Editing."

37. Chaudhuri, ed., *Bichitra*.

38. Pratt, "Collaboration as a Feminist Strategy," 46.

39. Mukherjee, Digital Humanities; or What You Will," 119.

40. Vanniyar is a researcher at the Mumbai-based organization Point of View, which seeks to bring the "points of view of women into community, social, cultural, and public domains through media, art and culture" (POV website, https://pointofview.org/). Bringing them to the Winter School was particularly valuable because it allowed us to connect academic and nonprofit activist conversations (Center for Digital Humanities, Pune, "DH Winter School."

41. Ahmed, *Living a Feminist Life*, 133.

42. Gajjala, "Caring Archives of Subalternity?"

43. Taylor, "Social Justice."

44. Mohanty and Alexander, "Cartographies of Knowledge and Power," 27.

45. Ayyar, personal conversation; Singh, "Digital Humanities in India?"

Works Cited

Ahmed, Sara. *Living a Feminist Life.* Durham, NC: Duke University Press, 2017.

Ayyar, Varsha. Personal conversation. May 2020.

Bailey, Moya, Anne Cong-Huyen, Alexis Lothian, and Amanda Phillips. "Reflections on a Movement: #transformDH, Growing Up." In *Debates in the Digital Humanities 2016*, edited by Matthew K. Gold and Lauren F. Klein. Minneapolis: University of Minnesota Press, 2016.

Bear, Laura. *Lines of the Nation: Indian Railway Workers, Bureaucracy, and the Intimate Historical Self.* New York: Columbia University Press, 2007.

Bichitra: Online Tagore Variorum. School of Cultural Texts and Records, Jadavpur University. http://bichitra.jdvu.ac.in/index.php.

Center for Digital Humanities, Pune. "Aims and Objectives." https://cdhpune .com/about/aims-and-objectives/.

Center for Digital Humanities, Pune. "DH Winter School." https://cdhpune .com/dh-winter-school/.

Center for Internet and Society. "Search Results for Wikipedia." https://cis-india .org/@@search?SearchableText=wikipedia.

Chaudhuri, Sukanta. "Managing a Literary Project and Electronic Editing." Lecture, Digital Humanities Winter School, December 18, 2014, Pune, India.

Chaudhuri, Sukanta, ed. *Bichitra: The Making of an Online Tagore Variorum.* London: Springer, 2015.

Choudhury, Deep Kanta Lahiri. *Telegraphic Imperialism: Crisis and Panic in the Indian Empire, c. 1830.* London: Palgrave Macmillan, 2010.

Cong-Huyen, Anne. "#mla13 'Thinking through Race' Presentation." January 7, 2013. https://anitaconchita.wordpress.com/2013/01/07/mla13-presentation/.

Dodd, Maya, Anjali Chandavarkar, Kunjika Pathak, and Nidhi Prabhakar. "Digital Pedagogy." Workshop, Digital Humanities Winter School, 2018, Pune, India.

Gajjala, Radhika. "Caring Archives of Subalternity?" In *Debates in the Digital Humanities 2019*, edited by Matthew K. Gold and Lauren F. Klein. Minneapolis: University of Minnesota Press, 2019.

Gallon, Kim. "Data and the Recovery of Black Humanity in the Digital Humanities." Keynote address, Digital Humanities Forum 2017, Lawrence, KS.

Haraway, Donna. "Situated Knowledges: The Science Question in Feminism and the Privilege of Partial Perspective." *Feminist Studies* 14, no. 3 (1988).

Headrick, Daniel. "A Double-Edged Sword: Communications and Imperial Control in British India." *Historical Social Research/Historische Sozialforschung* 35, no. 1.131 (2010): 51–65.

hooks, bell. *Teaching Community: A Pedagogy of Hope.* New York: Routledge, 2003.

hooks, bell. *Teaching to Transgress: Education as the Practice of Freedom.* New York: Routledge, 1994.

Macaulay, Thomas Babington Macaulay, and G. M. Young. "Minute on Indian Education." In *Speeches by Lord Macaulay, with His Minute on Indian Education.* London, 1863.

Mani, Braj Ranjan, and Pamela Sardar, eds. *A Forgotten Liberator: The Life and Struggle of Savitribai Phule*. N.p.: Mountain Peak, 2008.

Mazumdar, Vina. "Emergence of the Women's Question in India and the Role of Women's Studies." Center for Women's Development Studies, New Delhi, 1985.

Mbembe, Achille. "Decolonizing the University: New Directions." *Arts & Humanities in Higher Education* 15, no. 1 (2016): 29–45.

Menon, Nirmala, and T. Shanmugapriya. "Digital Humanities in India: Pedagogy, Publishing, and Practices." In *Exploring Digital Humanities in India: Pedagogies, Practices, and Institutional Possibilities*, edited by Maya Dodd and Nidhi Kalra. New York: Routledge, 2020.

Mohanty, Chandra Talpade, and M. Jacqui Alexander. "Cartographies of Knowledge and Power: Transnational Feminism as Radical Praxis." In *Critical Transnational Feminist Praxis*, edited by Richa Nagar and Amanda Swarr. Albany, NY: SUNY Press, 2010.

Mukherjee, Souvik. "Digital Humanities; or What You Will: Bringing Digital Humanities to the Classroom." In *Exploring Digital Humanities in India: Pedagogies, Practices, and Institutional Possibilities*, edited by Maya Dodd and Nidhi Kalra. New York: Routledge, 2020.

Murray, Padmini Ray. "Decolonising Design: Making Critically in India." In *Exploring Digital Humanities in India: Pedagogies, Practices, and Institutional Possibilities*, edited by Maya Dodd and Nidhi Kalra. New York: Routledge, 2020.

Patel, Kush. "Digital Humanities Pedagogy for Whom?" Paper presented to the DHARTI Twitter Conference, January 19, 2020.

Pratt, Geraldine. "Collaboration as a Feminist Strategy." *Gender, Place & Culture* 17, no. 1 (2010): 43–48.

Posner, Miriam. "Some Things to Think about before You Exhort Everyone to Code." Blog. February 29, 2012.

Ratto, Matt. "Critical Making: Conceptual and Material Studies in Technology and Social Life." *The Information Society* 27 (2011): 252–60.

Risam, Roopika. "Diasporizing the Digital Humanities: Displacing the Center and Periphery." *International Journal of E-Politics* 7, no. 3 (2016): 65–78.

Risam, Roopika. *New Digital Worlds: Postcolonial Digital Humanities in Theory, Praxis, and Pedagogy*. Evanston, IL: Northwestern University Press, 2019.

Shanmugapriya T., and Nirmala Menon. "Infrastructure and Social Interaction: Situated Research Practices in Digital Humanities in India." *Digital Humanities Quarterly* 14, no. 3 (2020).

Sharma, Riddhima. "Feminist Digital Humanities." In *Introduction to Digital Humanities: A Textbook*. Center for Digital Humanities, Pune. Forthcoming.

Singh, Ravinder. "Digital Humanities in India?: A Few Preliminary Notes towards an Argument." Paper presented at Digital Humanities Alliance of India Conference, Indore, 2018.

Sneha, P. P. "Mapping Digital Humanities in India." Center for Internet and Society, India, 2016.

Taylor, Toniesha. "Social Justice." *Digital Pedagogy in the Humanities: Concepts, Models, and Experiments*. MLA Commons, 2016.

Thorat, Dhanashree. "Digital Humanities in India." *Asian Quarterly: A Journal of Contemporary Issues* 15, no. 4 (2017): 4–12.

University Grants Commission (UGC). "Operational Guidelines: Scheme for Transdisciplinary Research for India's Developing Economy (STRIDE)." July 2019.

Vanniyar, Smita. "A Feminist Internet." Workshop, Digital Humanities Winter School, 2018, Pune, India.

Velayudhan, Meera, and Vidya Hydari. "Women's Studies in India: A National Conference." *International Supplement to the Women's Studies Quarterly* 1 (1982): 32–33.

12

Reparatory Praxis

The Role of Intersectional Feminism in Digital Pedagogy

ANDIE SILVA

The COVID-19 pandemic not only forced us to work in precarious and inadequate conditions for teaching and learning, but also exacerbated racial and economic divides, prompting many of us in the classroom to push even harder for changes in academia—an environment that is still largely elitist and reliant on racist, exclusionary practices.[1] Despite (or perhaps precisely *because* of) all the physical and psychological challenges the pandemic brought on, we now face a moment ripe with opportunities for reaffirming the importance of careful, ethical digital pedagogy. What is the ideal balance between teaching digital literacy and teaching advocacy, citizenship, and activism, as is the goal of a humanist education? This chapter explores how an intersectional feminist framework may help address this question, ensuring a classroom environment centered on care and action in complimentary, rather than mutually exclusive, ways. Through a discussion of my digital pedagogy seminar (DHUM 74000) taught at the CUNY Graduate Center, I argue that feminist digital pedagogies encourage students to be more ethical digital humanities practitioners and teachers. Within public universities such as CUNY, as well as within institutions with a large contingent of first-generation students, digital humanities can play a vital role in social mobility and empower students to become well-informed critics and users of digital technologies. The digital modalities we experimented with during the pandemic can help us think more carefully about how to take advantage of informal spaces that center affect and community as starting points for equitable digital humanities practice.

Although there is hardly ever *one* feminist praxis that represents all learners and practitioners, at its heart I see the goal of liberatory feminist pedagogy as focused on decentering hegemonic structures of power and privilege in order to showcase perspectives from the margins (or, rather, marginalized spaces and voices). My pedagogical understanding of feminist praxis is grounded in the work of Audre Lorde, bell hooks, and Paulo Freire and their calls for a classroom committed to justice and advocacy. An intersectional approach to feminist pedagogy should begin with an ethics of inclusivity that removes whiteness as the default center and considers ways to teach social justice that offer practical solutions for liberation and equity.[2] As Sondra Hale argues, we must be leery of diversity approaches that "have often been imposed on the 'Other' in the name of egalitarianism and community" and where it appears as if "one group developed and learned the rules and doled them out to the 'invitees' and the 'newcomers.'"[3] Whether we are challenging the existing practices of current educators or preparing future ones, we should employ what Freire describes as a "co-intentional" praxis, whereby instructor and student uncover oppressive systems together and find new ways to use digital tools for representation and mutual support.[4] In order to avoid engaging in digital work that reifies structures of oppression, our syllabus should challenge methodologies we take for granted while offering models that resituate and improve our approach to teaching. Looking back at a year of emergency, reactive teaching, I reflect on useful pedagogy practices that focus on purposeful but slow academia, such as process- and discovery-based course prep; creating formal virtual discussion spaces to make room for emotions and community; and modeling caring critical scholarship in assignment and syllabus design.

Designing Collaborative Course Goals

"DHUM 74000: Digital Pedagogy I" caters to students enrolled in the master's in Digital Humanities Program at the CUNY Graduate Center. After taking a two-semester "Introduction to Digital Humanities," students are invited to explore courses in three tracks: Digital Textuality, Data Visualization and Mapping, and Digital Pedagogy. The DH master's program balances theory, practice, and curricular design to help students experience the many avenues that compose the field and consider the role of DH in a variety of professional spaces: the lab, the library, the classroom, and even virtual spaces like Twitter (now X) and Zoom. The two pedagogy courses, Digital Pedagogy I and II, model the Intro to Digital Humanities sequence by offering one semester of theory and criticism followed by a semester more focused on praxis and project development.[5]

My Spring 2020 digital pedagogy class was largely composed of individuals who were already practicing educators, including part-time faculty,

K–12 faculty, instructional technicians, and self-employed instructors. I therefore expressed to students that our course would be participatory and collaborative from the start, and I was open to suggestions for changes.[6] In part due to the pandemic, and also because this was my first time teaching this course, I intentionally left gaps in our schedule for suggested readings and designed assignments that would ask students to critique the syllabus design. Following hooks, our syllabus was a "site of resistance" where I asked students to evaluate what assignments or parts of the course needed critical attention.[7] For example, were the course materials actually accessible to a wide range of abilities? What percentage of the projects assigned require significant funding to build and high-speed internet to properly use? What kinds of assumptions did our digital tools or spaces make about their core audience, and what might it mean to ask students to use or even study a project that felt alienating? Through weekly blog assignments, students were invited to reflect on these potential critical blind spots and make suggestions for texts or approaches we should consider adding to the syllabus. Our two formal assignments, an annotated list of digital resources on a topic of their choice and a set of course materials for a future course, were designed to build a shared pedagogical philosophy and create a bank of tools and resources we could use in years to come.

Envisioning my syllabus as a model for intersectional praxis students might want to incorporate in their current or future classes, every project and article spoke to the interests of communities outside the white, male, cis-het normativities. In the first half of the semester, we considered the place of digital humanities at the intersection of race, gender, sexuality, and neurodiversity. In selecting our core readings, I privileged the work of women (especially women of color), Indigenous communities, and queer scholars to ensure we were exploring perspectives written about and *by* underrepresented communities in the field. The second half of the semester was deliberately more flexible, with weeks dedicated to looking at how specific digital tools and platforms could be effectively used to center and empower students and to promote social justice. Equitable, responsible, and responsive digital humanities labor often happens at the local level, and many of our students are likely to be teaching digital literacy with limited resources. As such, feminist digital pedagogy instructors may wish to focus on assigning medium- and small-scale projects as models for project development and criticism.

Some highlights from our DHUM 74000 syllabus included the Torn Apart/*Separados* project, Queering the Map, the Standing Rock Syllabus, and the Māori Video Games Database.[8] My goal was to seek projects that offered a diversity of digital humanities topics (in this case data viz, mapping, pedagogy, and gaming), and showcased scholars who were committed to using digital tools to respond to specific, often urgent, community needs such as the US immigration crisis (Torn Apart/*Separados*) and teaching activism and allyship with Indigenous groups (Standing Rock Syllabus). I also sought to include undergraduate student perspectives shared in places such as TED Talks and academic blogs to ensure our conversations about what students gain from participating in digital spaces was not based on outsider perspectives but on listening to and evaluating public-facing content built by students. Overall, it was important to me that students in my class saw how much intersectional feminist labor has been made available through and because of digital spaces. As Marcia Chatelain argues, social media (despite its perils) can help marginalized groups build "interdisciplinary cooperation" and earn a kind of visibility that seemed previously out of reach for nonwhite scholars.[9] This kind of labor is not easy if one is to keep a syllabus updated and socially relevant, but there is a growing community of scholars committed to building and sharing resources that help make our classrooms more representational while keeping materials free to access, reproduce, and even modify.

Through an open and collaborative course prep, instructors and students can work together to identify gaps in representation and equity. As one student observed in their blog about decolonizing the curriculum, even when one intentionally seeks to include more voices, we might be going to the same staid sources as always: award-winning projects, academic editions, canonized authors.[10] Although the solution might not necessarily be to avoid all large projects or formally edited texts, it is important to discuss the colonialist reasons why certain projects, authors, and institutions are more visible and seem more worthy of academic inquiry. As a resistance exercise, students may be invited to investigate social knowledge approaches such as collaboratively written documents and public minutes from workshops, and to design social editing assignments of new and underrepresented texts using annotating tools like Hypothesis.[11] Going to less traditionally academic sources like Instagram, TikTok, and YouTube can also help, but when using free intellectual labor in our course syllabus we must beware not to reproduce the kind of gatekeeping that frames feminist work (especially the work of women of color) as a "labor of love" while simultaneously marginalizing and underpaying it. Cassius Adair and Lisa Nakamura caution against this, reminding us that "merely making visible the invisibilized labor of digitization and circulation, even in the context of a larger academic conversation about the racialized and gendered aspects of this labor, does not sufficiently account for the knowledge work that groups of vernacular learners and teachers are doing."[12] When using work that is freely available online in our syllabus, we might also work "alongside content producers to develop an alternative model of citation and circulation, one based on a feminist politics of consent and safety, rather than on legalistic notions of 'fair use.'"[13] In turn, such negotiations can be brought into the digital pedagogy classroom when students are asked to produce content of their own for public consumption: What kinds of terms and conditions do they wish to establish for their work to be used and cited? What aspects of their identity may they wish to keep private when writing about sensitive or politicized topics? Aside from completing work for the course, how will their writing or digital labor be contributing to their academic careers? In cases where students feel reticent about having their names appear online, instructors may consider crediting work to the class without including individual names or hosting student blogs and works-in-progress behind password-protected sites.

Feminist Community in Capitalist Spaces

As many of us learned during the pandemic, collaboration and chat platforms like Slack or Discord can become useful spaces for peer-to-peer support. In my own emergency teaching, I experimented with both tools, electing to use Slack in my graduate seminar and Discord in my undergraduate "Intro to DH" course at York College.[14] There are benefits and challenges to both tools, but the main deciding factor for me was adopting a tool students were already likely to be using. The choice of Discord for the undergraduate course felt ideal: any casual user of online gaming (as are many of my students) has at least heard of Discord, and the platform balances an informal, community-driven environment with robust options for channel moderation and assigning of roles.[15] However, since Slack had become the go-to choice for DH collaboration,[16] I chose to use it in my seminar to avoid overloading students with another tool to monitor. Our Slack server was the site for formal student-led discussion as well as where the students and I communicated over official matters, shared additional readings, and destressed with memes and pet photos. This space provided an opening for mutual care: discussion threads grew into places where students could share frustrations with the classes they were teaching or help each other troubleshoot problems. Later in the semester, Slack also became a useful repository for the many projects and articles students brought up during class discussion, as well as for them to share unexpected connections between our class and other classes they were taking. Although online communication tools might not be able to replace the relative ease and human connection of face-to-face class discussions, research shows that computer-mediated social spaces provide a supportive environment that is designed for regular engagement, encouraging students to ask and answer questions and share ideas with minimal instructor interference.[17]

In hybrid or even fully in-person classes, virtual discussion tools may prove extremely productive for facilitating an equitable and collaborative classroom. Indeed, Slack and other platforms like it can provide a space for "flattened hierarchies, a shared horizontal community."[18] Since anyone can start or moderate a thread, these spaces become ideal for student-led discussion. In turn, face-to-face class time can be used for collaborative writing, brainstorming, and even silent reflection, as I discuss below. Using a chat tool for class discussion can additionally encourage students who normally feel uncomfortable speaking in class to participate more regularly. I also found that students often preferred sending me private messages than communicating over email. The community space provided by a chat platform can help disrupt power imbalances not only between the students and the instructor but also among students who may perceive one person as being more "knowledgeable" or confident in how they articulate their ideas. Finally, incorporating chat tools to our digital pedagogy praxis helps ensure equity in terms of access, since these platforms require very low internet bandwidth and can be used from a smartphone.[19]

Many of the pedagogical approaches we developed in a state of emergency—Slack groups, collaborative writing, virtual meetings—will remain valuable to supporting equitable classrooms. Yet, as we move past the emergencies of the pandemic, we may become leerier of proprietary programs that do not privilege user privacy and are not designed with the classroom in mind.[20] It has now become a cliché to say that if a digital tool is free, the user is often the product. Feminist, abolitionist praxis indeed demands that we acknowledge and, where possible, reject capitalist structures that seek to turn collective knowledge into a commodity. However, providing free and low-barrier access to tools in a course that is already likely to be costing students a lot of money (factoring in not only tuition but commuting and time away from work) is also a crucial component to a feminist pedagogy. Proprietary tools surround us in nearly all our digital learning spaces: as Andrew Bretz reminds us, "corporations like Blackboard, 2U, D2L, and TurnItIn, are either publicly traded companies or companies owned by venture capital partnerships . . . issues of privacy aside, these technologies integrate the university into a corporate ecosystem that extends well beyond the walls of the academy."[21] Where, then, does that leave us? There is no easy answer here; concerns about the use of proprietary tools cannot be taken for granted and instructors should be prepared to deal with students who may be reluctant to give away their data to a business outside the protections of our institution. At the same time, these spaces can be productive sites of resistance, and open conversations in the classroom will promote digital literacy and call attention to the difficulty of discussing and enacting social justice work through neoliberal tools. When using tools that collect student data or otherwise require private information, we must also design some contingency plans such as allowing anonymous posting through pseudonyms or using a shared account tied to an email address created for the class, which students can use to post assignments. The flexibility required of pandemic teaching will therefore be useful as we continue to design courses that support and protect vulnerable students.

Digital pedagogy courses must inevitably grapple with issues of surveillance and privacy. In my graduate seminar, we discussed how to avoid "cop pedagogy" (thus aptly named by Dorothy Kim),[22] and considered ways to teach students to recognize and critique how their data is stored online by using tools such as Me and My Shadow.[23] Looking ahead, I expect that hybrid or so-called "hyflex" models—where some students attend classes face-to-face while others call in or join via videoconference—will become a regular part of our postpandemic life. Using the tools around us, instructors and students may collaboratively deconstruct our tenuous relationship with surveillance: why do we need cameras in the (virtual or presential) classroom? What are the risks of this kind of exposure, especially for those of us who may be targets of prejudice and racism based on how we talk, dress, or what spaces we occupy? What do we give away when we acquiesce to working in these spaces? The choices we, as educators, must make to run our courses—from what course management system we choose or are required to use for hosting course readings, to the free, but proprietary platforms we assign for projects—can offer opportunities to reflect on our own complicity in perpetuating exclusionary systems and invite us to consider how the assigned materials might help us subvert and resist these systems.

(Self) Care and Emotional Labor

During and beyond a time of emergency, teaching (with) digital tools requires that we acknowledge the inevitable technological and psychological barriers digital spaces impose upon us—particularly upon marginalized communities and communities of color.[24] Although DH and digitally enhanced classrooms may have an advantage in that we tend to attract students who are more confident in their use of technology (or at least eager to learn), we cannot take for granted that students will have the appropriate tools, bandwidth, physical or mental space to conduct digital work outside the confines of the university. A feminist approach to online teaching and digital humanities teaching must therefore incorporate a "pedagogy of care" for both student and instructor. First espoused by Nel Noddings, this concept invites an approach "rooted in receptivity, relatedness, and responsiveness."[25] Although caring as originally framed in Noddings was described as a stereotypically feminine, gendered practice, Noddings herself later admitted terming this a "feminine approach" was inherently problematic.[26] Considerations of care and emotional labor need to be normalized in the classroom and seen not as feminine but as *feminist*, that is: as political and critical for a healthy, functional classroom. Digital tools can offer more opportunities for community-building, where students are assessed and rewarded for moments of self-guided discovery and empowered to participate in the classroom prep. Students in a DH or DH pedagogy classroom may be asked to collaborate on building bibliographies and course units to share resources and to disperse course prep labor by serving as notetakers, researchers, and editors. As Melinda Cro and Sarah Kearns argue, a process- and affect-oriented classroom need not eschew the goals of building and tinkering altogether; rather, we may conceptualize the DH classroom as "a series of experiences" where "the definition of building could be more widely and inclusively constructed to reflect an attention to design and experimentation."[27]

Care may take many shapes depending on the size and composition of one's class, but its key feature is a willingness to make space: whether that means ensuring there are plenty of opportunities for informal interactions; setting aside deliberately unstructured time; or allowing emotions to play a larger role in class discussion.[28] As someone who typically plans for every minute of in-class interaction, attempting a responsive and supportive classroom environment required a good deal of retooling of my course prep. At the start of term, I ran my synchronous class meetings like I would have conducted a face-to-face class, offering a prepared set of discussion questions designed to help us engage in the readings and respond to ideas brought up in the students' blogs. However, virtual meetings can become tiresome quickly, and I began to experiment with starting our classes with more open-ended questions: "What's on your mind today?" or "What do you want to talk about?" Rather than demand an immediate response, I used short instrumental jazz pieces to time our exercise as students worked on a shared Google Doc. This free-writing exercise (as we might call it in a composition classroom) helped me gauge what texts or tools had appealed most to the class, but most importantly they helped us a community take a moment to recenter, switch from whatever else held our attention earlier in the day, and begin a silent conversation without the pressure of a fully formed thought. While this process was especially helpful on high-anxiety days like the 2020 US elections, moments of silence and recentering can make our class accessible to students with social anxiety and neurodivergent students without requiring that those students out themselves.

Although our open-ended sharing moments sometimes completely shifted my goals for the class, being more flexible and opening up my course prep to be a collaborative effort with the students generated extremely positive outcomes. For instance, one week, instead of shifting from the "check-in" moment to a formal, instructor-led discussion of our assigned readings, I decided to delete my discussion questions altogether and leave a blank page for the class to propose questions and topics for discussion. Using the "unconference" model, I had students write ideas and then vote on one or two issues that interested them most. Although we were not due to discuss the topic of accessibility for another week, the topic was up-voted by a large number of students in the class as something they wanted to explore further. We realized the group had a lot of frustrations and concerns over accessibility, from the lack of training educators receive on rules and guidelines, to the fact that digital tools often curtail accessibility altogether (Zoom for instance did not have the option of closed captioning at first, and the autogenerated option is still quite unreliable). After a few minutes of sharing, I then broke up the class into small groups where they explored problems with accessibility not just in academic institutions, but in tech companies like Apple and Google, which dictate so much of the digital work we do in the classroom. We reflected on ways we could serve as advocates for more (and more effective) accessibility policies in our institutions but had to come to terms with the extent to which capitalism and power play a huge role in ensuring that the burden of making websites accessible be on the few who care about or need these technologies. Passionate about ways to make a concrete intervention, we agreed that we would return to the topic in a future classroom meeting and collaborate on drafting a document with links and useful questions to ask when using digital tools in the classroom.

In hindsight, I think the students were preoccupied with accessibility in part because they were experiencing firsthand how exhausting reading, writing, and communicating digitally can be even in the most ideal conditions. Their frustrations made a topic they already cared deeply about feel especially urgent. Since our classrooms always depend on the energy in the (virtual or physical) room, we should consider how digital spaces can help capture and potentialize students' emotional responses to scholarship. A number of our synchronous virtual meetings ended up in "venting" sessions where, for instance, we reflected on readings about decolonizing the curriculum by opening up about our past experiences with gatekeeping and discrimination (both personal and through our students). Courses that deal with sensitive subjects in general and that explore intersectionality in particular must make some room for students to share their experiences with Othering and gatekeeping. In order to move from personal frustration to communal liberation, the instructor or an assigned student mediator can respond with activities that repurpose these experiences into opportunities for action. For instance, students may break up into groups to research new projects that better represent their values, or write a checklist of inclusive practices digital projects must employ to be selected for classroom discussion.

Another productive take-away from our distanced-learning classroom is the reminder that there are limits to the amount of engagement any of us is able to offer, regardless of the course modality. Whether because their home lives do not lend themselves to quiet reflection, or because an evening class is the culmination of a full day of responsibilities, there are myriad reasons why a student might not be able to participate in measurable ways in class discussion. We can anticipate this by building in empathetic assignments and making space for moments of process—for instance, inviting students to sit in silence at the start of every class and use some of the down time to raise issues or admit to physical or mental hurdles that might be impacting their engagement that day. The class can discuss how to make use of their time productively by dividing tasks so those with creative energy can co-write while others research or edit. Megan Boler argues that digital pedagogies should privilege a "politics of emotion," centering feelings, reactions, and discomfort over patriarchal approaches that seek to divest reason from feeling. Boler cautions that online learning can often rely on what Freire calls the "banking model" of education, where the instructor deposits information in a virtual space and students simply receive and react to it. Instilling moments of discovery and collaborative learning into digital spaces "requires renewed dedication to delinking neoliberal discourses of efficiency and productivity from theories and practices of learning."[29] We may thus infuse intersectional feminist praxis into our syllabus not only by being mindful of the texts and projects we assign, but by using digital tools to expand where teaching happens (e.g., in blank documents, in memes and emoji, in collective course prep) and what counts as progress in the course. Assessing student participation may include, for example, giving credit to students who initiate topics and action plans in a shared document, acknowledging students who help moderate or maintain threads in the class chatroom, and citing students as syllabus or course-material coauthors in future iterations of the course. In this way, students are invited to become both "constructors and evaluators of their own learning."[30]

In the final project for the class, students were asked to direct the emotional momentum of our virtual debates toward designing a course unit or assignment sequence they might use in a future course. This assignment challenged students to think of the practical applications of our semester-long discussions and aimed to engage them in an active exercise in transformative justice. I asked students to begin by defining intersectionality as it applies to digital learning: "What is gained by developing a teaching philosophy that is, at its center, intersectional? What kinds of questions, values, and actions are instructors and students called upon to consider?" With this in mind, students were to think of a scaffolded set of materials—at least one low-stakes assignment and one high-stakes assignment—that either trained students in a particular digital tool or made use of a tool or platform to deliver content. These materials could take any shape, for example: a lesson plan, a course unit, a video series, or a project-based assignment prompt. In addition to serving as a way for students to think of practical applications of the readings and ideas that surfaced over the course of the semester, the goal here was also to challenge students to think about how their pedagogy would be impacted by a deliberately intersectional feminist approach.

Collectively, the final projects showcased students' deep understanding of the role of care and equity when teaching with digital technologies and their engagement with intersectional feminist praxis. Projects included exploring digitized materials about a seventeenth-century trans narrative; a free, virtual course for yoga instructors on digital pedagogy best practices; a course unit on global data feminisms; and a course aimed at reappropriating text analysis tools for TESOL. Students used a wide range of tools, many that were new to me, such as the website StoryCorps, which archives "stories from people of all backgrounds and beliefs."[31] What struck me most was the fact that intersectionality took on a very personal meaning for each student, reflecting issues they had been passionate about discussing throughout the semester as well as their own positionality in the classroom. Intersectional feminism is therefore an ideal fit for digital pedagogy not only because of the ways it privileges sharing, inclusion, and advocacy, but also because it challenges digital humanities students to interrogate their goals for teaching with technology.

With the growing popularity of digital humanities programs, we have a unique opportunity to conceive of digital pedagogy as the starting point where students build the necessary (digital and intellectual) tools needed to dismantle the patriarchal, racist, elitist practices that continue being reproduced across many higher education institutions. Intersectional feminism should therefore not be relegated to a course unit, but serve as a guiding principle for equitable community building. Institutional requirements typically demand a final project to assess students' learning and critical engagement with the content, and many DH courses (my own included) tend to culminate in work toward a finished product or a public-facing set of materials. These projects are excellent for teaching students about collaboration and project management—two values that are crucial to our field. Yet, when the goal is at least in part to reject neoliberal narratives of productivity and hierarchical power, final projects might broaden what counts as successful completion by rewarding slow planning, small-scale, and deeply personal interpretations of the prompt. Students may be called upon to demonstrate their application of the ethics and equity practices modeled in the syllabus by reflecting on how their pedagogy has changed over the course of the term. When teaching practicing educators, instructors might also craft prompts that help students balance the labor demands of being a full-time worker and graduate student. One student in my course, for instance, had concerns about how to complete the course while attending to pandemic emergencies in their role as a digital instructional design specialist. At the proposal stage we brainstormed ways the prompt could help them tackle stalled collaborative projects at their local institution, and the student ended up using their final project as an opportunity to finally write a grant proposal for an interdisciplinary pedagogical cooperation project.

Conclusion

Throughout this chapter, I have argued that digital pedagogy is most productive when anchored in a praxis of care, equity, and justice. If we normalize intersectional feminism as a tenet of digital pedagogy, we might end up with productive disruptions to a curriculum that is still very much in need of inclusive practices not just in strict boundaries of gender, sexuality, ability, and neurodiversity but at the various real-life intersections of these identities as we see them embodied in our students.[32] As José Esteban Muñoz has argued, when it comes to documenting minoritarian knowledge, "mechanisms ensure that the production of such knowledge 'misfires' insofar as it is misheard, misunderstood, and devalued."[33] Although we acknowledge this inherent failure, or coming up short, of pedagogy, we always strive for more, and do so with commitment and love. This, I would argue, is the largest contribution of feminism: it demands a praxis that is thoughtful and gentle, while also reparatory and subversive. Creating space for unplanned activities, student-centered course prep, and productive sharing of emotions offers graduate students a model for digital pedagogy that promotes compassionate scholarship and alternate modes of productivity. Aimée Morrison, Bill Hart-Davidson, and Rebecca Quintana and James DeVaney have referred to this approach as "resilient pedagogy," calling for educators to take the lessons of pandemic teaching as an opportunity for designing classrooms that do not simply adapt but thrive in the face of change.[34] Intersectional feminism in digital pedagogy encourages us to teach a form of digital literacy that empowers students at all levels to see themselves represented in the materials they study and to reject neoliberal approaches to teaching and learning. The digital pedagogy classroom can be a place to enact an inclusive praxis whose ultimate goal is not just envisioning a better digital scholarly community, but also actively shifting our thinking and actions toward an academic model that does not simply critique, but gives back.

Notes

1. Discussions of the neoliberal and colonialist practices in academia abound, from problems with unequal access to resources to lack of representation within the staff and faculty, to qualifying examinations such as the American SATs, which were founded upon racist principles. For DH in particular, Maha Bali perhaps puts it best: "[D]igital tools are largely Western products, dominated by American and Western European interests; as such, they can somewhat colonize the spaces and networks depending on them, including by making the 'other' invisible or tokenized, if not silenced or oppressed." See Bali, "The 'Unbearable' Exclusion of the Digital," 295. For some proposed solutions, see Brown et al., "Mechanized Margin to Digitized Center" and the chapter by Stringfield in this volume.

2. Any conversation about intersectionality is of course always indebted to Kimberlé Crenshaw. See Crenshaw, *On Intersectionality*.

3. Hale, "The Connections between Education and Power in the Liberatory Feminist Classroom," 382.

4. Freire, *Pedagogy of the Oppressed*, 69.

5. The Graduate Center also offers a certificate in "Interactive Technology and Pedagogy," which is available to students in all disciplines and programs. Although our introductory digital pedagogy courses share much in common, DHUM 74000 dives more critically into teaching and practicing digital humanities as a field as well as reflecting on the role of DH in high school and undergraduate education.

6. The final version of the syllabus is available here: https://bit.ly/DHUM 74000_Silva.

7. If "any classroom that employs a holistic model of learning will also be a place where teachers grow, and are empowered by the process," in a digital pedagogy class with feminist aims the instructor must allow for a certain degree of vulnerability and fallibility. hooks, *Teaching to Transgress*, 21.

8. Ahmad et al., *Torn Apart/Separados*; *Queering the Map*; NYC Stands with Standing Rock Collective, "#StandingRockSyllabus"; Andrews, "The Māori Video Games Database." Andrews's project has unfortunately been taken offline. An archived version is available through the Wayback Machine (see Works Cited).

9. Chatelain, "Is Twitter Any Place for a [Black Academic] Lady?" I discuss some potential downsides to this approach later in the chapter.

10. Instructors who have flexibility with their syllabus design may consider leaving one or two weeks in particular open to suggested topics, platforms, and projects as the collective interests of the class begin to take shape over the course of the term. Such an approach encourages students to begin actively thinking about their own future syllabus design and helps dispel the notion that the professor is the arbiter of what counts as worthwhile reading. For those who have to follow more strict requirements in how they plan and deliver their courses, low-stakes writing can similarly engage the class in a meta-analysis of what is included or left out when we choose texts and projects to discuss as examples of different kinds of digital humanities work.

11. See, for example, Morford and Jacob, "De-/Anti-/Post-Colonial DH Workshop"; and "Black Digital Humanities Projects and Resources."

12. See Adair and Nakamura, "The Digital Afterlives of *This Bridge Called My Back*," 269. See also Sample's chapter in this volume for a discussion of how to use social media in the classroom to interrogate the ways those spaces rely on dehumanizing and damaging labor intentionally hidden behind its "black box."

13. Adair and Nakamura, "The Digital Afterlives of *This Bridge Called My Back*," 274.

14. Like many professors in the CUNY system, I am an appointed faculty member of the CUNY Graduate Center but my contractual appointment is with York College, a four-year senior college at CUNY that caters largely to undergraduate students.

15. As an open-source tool Discord also has a transparency ethos that may better align with course goals to teach students about openness and collaboration. For more on their privacy policy, see https://discord.com/privacy. For a quick overview on how to set up a server, see Cordell, "Tips for Classroom Discord."

16. The Digital Humanities Slack group (https://digitalhumanities.slack.com), for instance, currently boasts of over 2,500 members.

17. See, for instance, Ross, "Slack It to Me"; Tuhkala and Kärkkäinen, "Using Slack for Computer-Mediated Communication to Support Higher Education Students' Peer Interactions during Master's Thesis Seminar"; Huang, "Exploring Students' Acceptance of Team Messaging Services"; see also Evalyn et al., "One Loveheart at a Time."

18. Evalyn et al., "One Loveheart at a Time."

19. Instructors considering nonproprietary platforms may want to look into Zulip as an alternative to Slack or Discord. Jonathan Reeve writes about this and other wonderful open-source alternatives in his blog. See Reeve, "Notes on My Teaching Methodology."

20. See Grandinetti, "Pandemic Pedagogy, Zoom, and the Surveillant Classroom." For broader discussions of the ways data use in education is becoming increasingly problematic, see Jarke and Breiter, eds., "The Datafication of Education."

21. Bretz, "The New Itinerancy."

22. Dorothy Kim talked about the pitfalls of "cop pedagogy"; see "Teaching with Digital Tools." Jeffrey Moro has similarly written about this idea, calling on instructors to abandon words like "rigor" and "discipline" in their thinking about students and student work. See Moro, "Against Cop Shit."

23. *Me and My Shadow.*

24. See Parolin and Lee, "Large Socio-Economic, Geographic, and Demographic Disparities Exist in Exposure to School Closures"; Katz, Jordan, and Ognyanova, "Digital Inequality, Faculty Communication, and Remote Learning Experiences during the COVID-19 Pandemic"; Dorn et al., "COVID-19 and Learning Loss"; Dubois, Bright, and Laforce, "Educating Minoritized Students in the United States during COVID-19."

25. Noddings, *Caring*, 2.

26. Noddings, *Caring*, xiii.

27. Cro and Kearns, "Developing a Process-Oriented, Inclusive Pedagogy," para. 3, 6. Cro and Kearns suggest that "particularly within a pedagogical context, DH project work might be conceived as *communal* in addition to or in contrast with *public-facing*" (para. 33; emphasis in original). Helping students see their work in the classroom as the foundation for future community-building and publication places emphasis on the often long and nonlinear process of DH project development both in and beyond the classroom.

28. For some discussions on the role of emotions in the classroom, see Day and Leitch, "Teachers' and Teacher Educators' Lives"; Burke, "Re/Imagining Higher Education Pedagogies"; Rosiek, "Emotional Scaffolding."

29. Boler, "Feminist Politics of Emotions and Critical Digital Pedagogies," 1495.

30. Fiore and Rosenquest, "Shifting the Culture of Higher Education: Influences on Students, Teachers, and Pedagogy." The authors highlight the importance of documentation as a way to record and assess self-guided discovery in the process of training educators.

31. StoryCorps.

32. For two examples, see Wernimont, "Whence Feminism?"; and Bailey, "All the Digital Humanists Are White, All the Nerds Are Men, but Some of Us Are Brave."

33. Muñoz, "Teaching, Minoritarian Knowledge, and Love," 120.

34. Morrison, "Resilient Pedagogy for Fragile Times"; Hart-Davison, "Imagining a Resilient Pedagogy"; Quintana and DeVaney, "Preparing for Future Disruption."

Works Cited

Adair, Cassius, and Lisa Nakamura. "The Digital Afterlives of *This Bridge Called My Back*: Woman of Color Feminism, Digital Labor, and Networked Pedagogy." *American Literature* 89, no. 2 (2017): 255–78.

Ahmed, Manan et al. *Torn Apart/Separados.* Accessed March 15, 2021. https://xpmethod.columbia.edu/torn-apart/volume/1/.

Andrews, Nicola. "The Maori Video Games Database." Accessed March 15, 2021. https://web.archive.org/web/20200331112401/http://nicolaandrews.net/maori-games-database.

Bailey, Moya. "All the Digital Humanists Are White, All the Nerds Are Men, but Some of Us Are Brave." *Journal of Digital Humanities* 1, no. 1 (2011). http://journalofdigitalhumanities.org/1-1/all-the-digital-humanists-are-white-all-the-nerds-are-men-but-some-of-us-are-brave-by-moya-z-bailey/.

Bali, Maha. "The 'Unbearable' Exclusion of the Digital." In *Disrupting the Digital Humanities*, edited by Dorothy Kim and Jesse Stommel, 295–321. Goleta, CA: Punctum Books, 2018.

"Black Digital Humanities Projects and Resources." www.bit.ly/Black-DH-List=.

Boler, Megan. "Feminist Politics of Emotions and Critical Digital Pedagogies: A Call to Action." *PMLA* 130, no. 5, *Special Topic: Emotions* (October 2015): 1489–96.

Bretz, Andrew. "The New Itinerancy: Digital Pedagogy and the Adjunct Instructor in the Modern Academy." *Digital Humanities Quarterly* 11, no. 3 (2017).

Brown, Nicole M., Ruby Mendenhall, Michael L. Black, Mark Van Moer, Assata Zerai, and Karen Flynn. "Mechanized Margin to Digitized Center: Black Feminism's Contributions to Combatting Erasure within the Digital Humanities." *International Journal of Humanities and Arts Computing* 10, no. 1 (2016): 110–25.

Burke, Penny Jane. "Re/Imagining Higher Education Pedagogies: Gender, Emotion, and Difference." *Teaching in Higher Education* 20, no. 4 (2015): 388–401.

Chatelain, Marcia. "Is Twitter Any Place for a [Black Academic] Lady?" In *Bodies of Information: Intersectional Feminism and Digital Humanities*, edited by Elizabeth Losh and Jacqueline Wernimont. Minneapolis: University of Minnesota Press, 2018.

Cordell, Ryan. "Tips for Classroom Discord." https://ryancordell.org/teaching/classroom-discord/.

Crenshaw, Kimberlé. *On Intersectionality. Essential Writings*. New York: New Press, 2014.

Cro, Melinda, and Sarah Kearns. "Developing a Process-Oriented, Inclusive Pedagogy: At the Intersection of Digital Humanities, Second Language Acquisition, and New Literacies." *Digital Humanities Quarterly* 14, no. 1 (2020).

Day, Christopher, and Ruth Leitch. "Teachers' and Teacher Educators' Lives: The Role of Emotion." *Teaching and Teacher Education* 17 (2001): 403–15.

Dorn, Emma, Bryan Hancock, Jimmy Sarakatsannis, and Ellen Viruleg. "COVID-19 and Learning Loss—Disparities Grow and Students Need Help." McKinsey & Company, December 8, 2020. https://www.mckinsey.com/industries/public-and-social-sector/our-insights/covid-19-and-learning-loss-disparities-grow-and-students-need-help#.

Dubois, Elizabeth, Dara Bright, and Salimah Laforce. "Educating Minoritized Students in the United States during COVID-19: How Technology Can be Both the Problem and the Solution." *IT Professional* 23, no. 2 (2021): 12–18.

Evalyn, Lawrence, C.E.M. Henderson, Julia King, Jessica Lockhart, Laura Mitchell, and Suzanne Conklin Akbari. "One Loveheart at a Time: The Language of Emoji and the Building of Affective Community in the Digital Medieval Studies Environment." *Digital Humanities Quarterly* 14, no. 3 (2020). http://digitalhumanities.org/dhq/vol/14/3/000474/000474.html.

Fiore, Lisa, and Barbara Rosenquest. "Shifting the Culture of Higher Education: Influences on Students, Teachers, and Pedagogy." *Theory into Practice* 49, no. 1 (2009): 14–20.

Freire, Paulo. *Pedagogy of the Oppressed*. Translated by Myra Bergman Ramos. New York: Continuum, 2005.

Grandinetti, Justin. "Pandemic Pedagogy, Zoom, and the Surveillant Classroom: The Challenges of Living Our Advocacies in a Pandemic." *Communication, Culture & Critique* 14, no. 2 (2021): 347–50.

Hale, Sondra. "The Connections between Education and Power in the Liberatory Feminist Classroom: Appreciating and Critiquing Freire." In *The Wiley Handbook of Paulo Freire*, edited by Carlos Alberto Torres, 379–88. Hoboken, NJ: John Wiley and Sons, 2019.

Hart-Davison, Bill. "Imagining a Resilient Pedagogy." *Medium*, April 5, 2020. https://billhd.medium.com/imagining-a-resilient-pedagogy-40a9622d5678.

hooks, bell. *Teaching to Transgress: Education as the Practice of Freedom*. New York: Routledge, 1994.

Huang, Yong-Ming. "Exploring Students' Acceptance of Team Messaging Services: The Roles of Social Presence and Motivation." *British Journal of Educational Technology* 48 (2017): 1047–61.

Jarke, Juliana, and Andreas Breiter, eds. "The Datafication of Education." *Learning, Media, and Technology* 44, no. 1 (2019).

Katz, Vikki S., Amy B. Jordan, and Katherine Ognyanova. "Digital Inequality, Faculty Communication, and Remote Learning Experiences during the COVID-19 Pandemic: A Survey of U.S. Undergraduates." *PLOS ONE*, February 10, 2021. https://journals.plos.org/plosone/article?id=10.1371/journal.pone.0246641.

Kim, Dorothy. "Teaching with Digital Tools." Arizona Center for Medieval and Renaissance Studies (ACRMS). https://www.youtube.com/watch?v=OqLkJ-iG8W4&ab_channel=ACMRS.

Me and My Shadow: Take Control of Your Data. Accessed March 15, 2021. https://myshadow.org/.

Morford, Ashley Caranto, and Arun Jacob. "De-/Anti-/Post-Colonial DH Workshop." June 10, 2018. https://goo.gl/8MwQsP.

Moro, Jeffrey. "Against Cop Shit." https://jeffreymoro.com/blog/2020-02-13-against-cop-shit/.

Morrison, Aimée. "Resilient Pedagogy for Fragile Times," *Hook & Eye: Fast Feminism, Slow Academe*, December 9, 2020. https://hookandeyeca.wordpress.com/2020/12/09/resilient-pedagogy-for-fragile-times/.

Muñoz, José Esteban. "Teaching, Minoritarian Knowledge, and Love." *Women & Performance: A Journal of Feminist Theory* 14, no. 2 (2005): 117–21.

Noddings, Nel. *Caring: A Feminine Approach to Ethics and Moral Education.* Berkeley: University of California Press, 1984.

NYC Stands with Standing Rock Collective. "#StandingRockSyllabus." 2016. Accessed March 15, 2021. https://nycstandswithstandingrock.wordpress.com/standingrocksyllabus/.

Parolin, Zachary, and Emma K. Lee. "Large Socio-Economic, Geographic, and Demographic Disparities Exist in Exposure to School Closures." *Nature Human Behavior* 5 (2021): 522–28.

Queering the Map. Accessed March 15, 2021. https://www.queeringthemap.com/.

Quintana, Rebecca, and James DeVaney. "Preparing for Future Disruption: Hybrid, Resilient Teaching for a New Instructional Age." *Inside Higher Ed,* April 15, 2020. https://www.insidehighered.com/blogs/learning-innovation/preparing-future-disruption-hybrid-resilient-teaching-new-instructional.

Reeve, Jonathan. "Notes on My Teaching Methodology." September 8, 2020. https://jonreeve.com/2020/09/teaching-online/.

Rosiek, Jerry. "Emotional Scaffolding: An Exploration of the Teacher Knowledge at the Intersection of Student Emotion and the Subject Matter." *Journal of Teacher Education* 54, no. 5 (2003): 399–412.

Ross, Spencer M. "Slack It to Me: Complementing LMS With Student-Centric Communications for the Millennial/Post-Millennial Student." *Journal of Marketing Education* 41, no. 2 (2019): 91–108.

StoryCorps. Accessed March 15, 2021. https://storycorps.org/.

Tuhkala, Ari, and Tommi Kärkkäinen. "Using Slack for Computer-Mediated Communication to Support Higher Education Students' Peer Interactions during Master's Thesis Seminar." *Education and Information Technologies* 23 (2018): 2379–97.

Wernimont, Jacqueline. "Whence Feminism? Locating Critical Sites in Digital Literary Archives." *Digital Humanities Quarterly* 7, no. 1 (2013). http://www.digitalhumanities.org/dhq/vol/7/1/000156/000156.html.

Contributors

DANIELA AGOSTINHO is an assistant professor in the Department of Digital Design and Information Studies at Aarhus University, Denmark. Her areas of research and teaching are cultural theory; visual culture; feminist, postcolonial, and decolonial studies; and digital culture. She is coeditor of the books *Uncertain Archives: Critical Keywords for Big Data* (2021) and *(W)archives: Archival Imaginaries, War, and Contemporary Art* (2020).

MONIKA BARGET is an early modern historian and digital humanist specializing in the political history of the eighteenth century, visual cultures, and spatial history. From 2017 to 2018, she contributed to the Letters 1916–1923 and Ignite projects at the National University of Ireland, Maynooth. Following postdoctoral work in Mainz, she joined the History Department of Maastricht University as an assistant professor in August 2021.

JENNY BERGENMAR is a professor of comparative literature at the University of Gothenburg, Sweden. She is a literary history scholar who has previously worked with digital scholarly editing and archival materials through digitization and crowdsourcing. She is currently principal investigator of the research infrastructure project QUEERLIT database: Metadata Development and Searchability for LGBTQI Literary Heritage (2021–2023).

NANNA BONDE THYLSTRUP is an associate professor in the Department of Arts and Cultural Studies, University of Copenhagen. Her research explores the ethics and politics of digital infrastructures, data collections, and machine learning practices and models. She is author *of The Politics of Mass Digitization* (MIT Press 2019) and coeditor of *Uncertain Archives: Critical Keywords for Big Data* (MIT Press 2021) and *(W)archives: Archival*

Imaginaries, War, and Contemporary Art (Sternberg Press 2021). She is part
of the editorial collective of Cambridge Forum on AI: Culture and Society.

SUSAN BROWN, a professor of English at the University of Guelph, holds
a Canada Research Chair in Collaborative Digital Scholarship. Her research
explores semantic technologies, critical infrastructure studies, and, through
the Orlando Project, feminist literary history. She leads the Canadian Writing Research Collaboratory, a virtual research environment for literary and
cultural studies in Canada, and the Linked Infrastructure for Networked
Cultural Scholarship.

TANYA E. CLEMENT is an associate professor in the Department of English
at the University of Texas at Austin. Her primary areas of research are textual
studies, sound studies, and infrastructure studies. She leads High Performance Sound Technologies for Access and Scholarship (HiPSTAS) for the
development and interrogation of sociotechnical infrastructures to increase
access to and scholarship with audiovisual cultural heritage collections. She
is the author of *Dissonant Records: Close Listening to Literary Archives* (2024).

KATRINE DIRCKINCK-HOLMFELD's artistic research practice centers
on developing "reparative critical practices." Working across media and in
collaboration with various communities, she uses video installation, performance, and text to explore the reparative critical practice as a communal,
dense exploration of fragments from (broken) histories, and making them
into new assemblages. As part of Uncertain Archives Research Collective,
she explores the politics and aesthetics of digitization of colonial archives.

JAIME LEE KIRTZ is an assistant professor of media studies and algorithmic culture in the School of Art, Media, and Engineering at Arizona
State University. Her work lies at the intersections among new materialism,
feminist theory, science and technology studies, and media archaeology.
She is also the founding codirector of the TechnoMaterials Lab and affiliate
faculty at the Center for Strategic Communication and the Lincoln Center
for Applied Ethics.

CECILIA LINDHÉ holds a PhD in comparative literature, and she is director
of GRIDH: Gothenburg Research Infrastructure in Digital Humanities.
Lindhé has extensive experience in building humanities research infrastructures and digital humanities research projects. Her current research
spans ancient/medieval rhetorical and aesthetic theory in relation to digital
materiality and digital representation of cultural heritage.

LAURA MANDELL is a professor of English at Texas A&M University where she founded, and for twelve years directed, the Center of Digital Humanities Research. She has written *Breaking the Book: Print Humanities in the Digital Age* (2015), *Misogynous Economies: The Business of Literature in Eighteenth-Century Britain* (1999), and numerous articles. She is general editor of the Poetess Archive (poetessarchive.org) and founding director of the Advanced Research Consortium (ar-c.org).

LISA MARIE RHODY is deputy director of Digital Initiatives at the CUNY Graduate Center and affiliated faculty in the MA in Liberal Studies and Digital Humanities, MS in Data Analysis and Visualization, and Interactive Technology and Pedagogy Certificate programs. Her work has been supported by the Andrew W. Mellon Foundation, the Alfred P. Sloan Foundation, the National Endowment for the Humanities, and the Institute of Museum and Library Services.

ASTRID VON ROSEN is a professor of art history and visual studies and the director of CCHS: Centre for Critical Heritage Studies at the University of Gothenburg. She specializes in critical performing arts historiography and is principal investigator of the cross-disciplinary research project Expansion and Diversity funded by the Swedish Research Council. Recent publications include "Affect and Digital Caregiving," *Archives and Records* (2022).

MARK SAMPLE is a professor of film, media, and digital studies at Davidson College. His teaching and research focus on digital culture, creative coding, and videogames. He is also coauthor of *10 PRINT CHR$ (205.5+RND(1)); : GOTO 10*, an exploration of the Commodore 64 and creative computing in the 1980s. His most recent work uses the procedural rhetoric of videogames to comment on twenty-first-century America and can be found at sample reality.itch.io.

SUSAN SCHREIBMAN is a professor of digital arts and culture at Maastricht University, the Netherlands. She works at the intersections of computationally based teaching and research in the interplay of the digital archive, cultural innovation, and participatory engagement processes. She is the series editor of the Topics in the Digital Humanities (University of Illinois Press). Her current research projects include: PURE3D, Contested Memories: The Battle of Mount Street Bridge, and #dariahTeach.

ANDIE SILVA is an associate professor of English, York College, and digital humanities, Graduate Center, CUNY. She is the author of *The Brand* *of Print: Marketing Paratexts in the Early English Book Trade* (2019) and coeditor (with Scott Schofield) of *Digital Pedagogy in Early Modern Studies: Method and Praxis* (2023). You can read more about her at https://andiesilva.commons.gc.cuny.edu/.

NIKKO L. STEVENS is a critical technology researcher, software engineer, and open-source contributor. Stevens researches the ways that systems of oppression, like white supremacy and transphobia, are both foundational to and re-created within data modeling and database creation practices. They are currently a postdoc at MIT where they are writing a book about the role of software in the contemporary American prison abolition movement.

RAVYNN K. STRINGFIELD recently earned her PhD in American Studies from William & Mary. Her work lies at the intersection of Black digital humanities, media studies, and literary studies. Her dissertation project centered on Black women and girls in fantasy new media narratives. She is formerly a visiting assistant professor of media studies in the University of Richmond's Department of Rhetoric and Communication Studies.

DHANASHREE THORAT is an assistant professor of English at Mississippi State University. Her research is situated at the intersection of Asian American studies, postcolonial studies, and digital humanities and focuses on how colonial and racial ideologies shape internet infrastructures. She is a founding Executive Council member of the Center for Digital Humanities, Pune, in India.

KRISTIN VEEL is an associate professor, Department of Arts and Cultural Studies, University of Copenhagen. Her research focuses on the integration of digital technologies into everyday life and its impact on cultural imagination. She is coauthor (with Henriette Steiner) of *Tower to Tower: Gigantism in Architecture and Digital Culture* (2020) and *Touch in the Time of Corona: Reflections on Love, Care, and Vulnerability in the Pandemic* (2021).

JACQUELINE WERNIMONT is a digital media scholar who specializes in mathematical and computational media and their histories. She is the Distinguished Chair of Digital Humanities and Social Engagement and an associate professor of film and media studies at Dartmouth. In her making practice, Wernimont creates "data visceralizations," working with sound and haptics to render information. Her scholarship includes *Numbered Lives: Life and Death in Quantum Media* (2019) and the coedited (with Elizabeth Losh) *Bodies of Information: Intersectional Feminism and Digital Humanities* (2018).

Index

Abbas, Ackbar, 84
academic credit, 109, 112–13, 241–42, 247
academic infrastructures: and Black scholars, 143–54; and cooperatives, 9, 102–14; and embodiment, 80; funding for, 83–84; and gender, 83–84; and labs, 103–6, 108, 114, 149, 154; and service, 80, 83
accessibility: and colonial archives, 166; and infrastructures, 9, 80, 83, 85–86, 89–91, 124, 125, 166; and minimal computing, 84, 86, 90; and Nordic projects, 124, 125, 127–33; in overview, 2, 9; and pedagogy, 221, 223–27, 231–33, 240–43, 246; and scale, 171
accountability, 89, 227, 231
Adair, Cassius, 241
Adams, Alison, 69
adaptation to infrastructures, 80–81
Adichie, Chimamanda Ngozi, 198, 211
Adler, Melissa, 132, 164
Advanced Research Consortium (ARC), 85, 88
adversarial design, 10, 184
advertising and social media, 182, 183, 184–90, 192
affective labor: and Black women scholars, 145; and infrastructure projects, 163; in overview, 7–8; and pedagogy, 244–49; and social media, 148. *See also* emotions
"Against Cleaning" (Muñoz), 3, 208
agency: and audiation, 18, 20–22, 28, 29; and cooperatives, 111; and infrastructures, 81, 82, 87, 88, 91–92; and Irish women's WWI letters, 37–42, 46–51; and labs, 104; and pedagogy, 213
agential realism, 18, 21–22
Agostinho, Daniela, 159–72
Ahmed, Sarah: on care work, 148; on challenge of transforming institutions, 102, 114; on discomfort, 230; on feminism as a practice, 5, 222; on feminist killjoys, 5, 193, 199–200, 210; overview of scholarly engagement with, 2; on screening techniques, 62; on sweaty concepts, 207
AIDS quilt, 87
Alexander, Brian, 103
Alexander, M. Jacqui, 231
Algorithms of Oppression (Noble), 2, 151
Alliance for Networking Visual Culture (ANVC), 105
Alliance of Digital Humanities Organizations (ADHO), 123
Allman, Katherine, 47, 48

Analytical Engine, 61, 65
Anderson, Susan, 107
anti-Semitism and social media, 185
Apollo spacecraft, 61, 64
apparatus and audiation, 20–21, 28–29
Archives and Library of the Queer Movement (QRAB). *See* QRAB (Archives and Library of the Queer Movement)
Archives That Matter, 166, 168–69
Arizona State University. *See* Nexus Digital Co-op
Art+Feminism, 163
artificial intelligence, 69, 198–99, 200
arts and crafts and gender, 69
"As Luck Would Have It" (Verhoven), 2
attention economy, 184–85
Audacity, 22–23, 27–28
audiation, 6, 17–29
AudioSet, 31n21
Autonets, 90–91

Babbage, Charles, 65
background noise, 27–28
Bailey, Moya Z., 105–6, 144, 222
Bali, Maha, 250n1
Balsamo, Ann, 8, 87
Barad, Karen: and agential realism, 18, 21–22; and Balsamo, 87; on change, 8; on constraints, 92; on mattering, 18; overview of scholarly engagement with, 2; on tools, 20
Barget, Monika, 6, 7, 35–51
Belfast War Hospital Supply Committee, 44
Belle, La Vaughn, 168, 171
Bengali literature and Bichitra platform, 227, 229, 232
Benjamin, Ruha, 3, 198–99
Berg, David, 168–69
Bergenmar, Jenny, 7, 8, 9, 121–35
Berlant, Lauren, 193
Between the Dusk and Dawn (how to navigate an unsettled empire) (Belle), 171
bias: addressing in pedagogy, 230; in algorithmic text processing, 198–99; in criminal justice system, 199; in Google search, 183, 185, 199; in machine learning, 60; in social media, 151, 182, 183, 185, 186, 199; in visualizations, 208, 209; and Wikipedia, 162–65, 227
bibliographies, LGBTQ+, 128–34
Bichitra platform, 227, 229, 232
binaries: and algorithmic text processing, 10, 200, 210–11; avoiding binaries as principle of data feminism, 8, 137n27; and core rope memory, 61; and Expansion and Diversity project, 126; and infrastructures, 8, 79, 82, 84, 85, 88, 89–90, 92, 123; and pedagogy, 10, 200, 210–11, 213–14, 225; and relationships, 88
birth defects, 71n22
Bishop, Elizabeth, 23
black boxes: algorithmic text processing as, 199; bureaucracies as, 182; Google search as, 182, 183; social media as, 10, 181–93
Black Girl Does Grad School (BGDGS) blog, 144–45, 146, 147, 148
Black Gotham Archive, 3
Blacklight, 94n55
Black women scholars, 9, 143–54
Bleier, Roman, 39
blogs: archiving, 133, 152–53; and Black scholars, 144–48; and care work, 147; pedagogical use, 203, 240, 241, 245
Bodies of Information (Losh and Wernimont, eds.), 3
Bodies That Matter (Butler), 2
body. *See* embodiment and body
Bohr, Niels, 30n17
Bojsen, Heidi, 174n47
Boler, Megan, 247
Bomis, 165
boundary objects, recordings as, 20–21
boyd, danah, 199
Boyd, Jason, 130
bracketing, 189, 191
Branch Out Alternative Break (William & Mary), 150–51
Bratton, Benjamin, 82, 86
Breitbart.com, 185
Bretz, Andrew, 243
Brock, André, Jr., 154n4

Brown, Susan, 8, 9, 79–92
Buechley, Leah, 86
"Building a Legacy" project, 150–51
Buolamwini, Joy, 199
Busa, Roberto, 3, 63, 65, 225
Butler, Judith, 2, 30n17
Byron, Jennifer, 109

Campbell, Grant D., 130
Campt, Tina, 161, 166
Canadian Writing Research Collaboratory (CWRC), 85, 90
"Can Digital Humanities Mean Transformative Critique?" (Lothian and Philips), 122
Capuchin archives in Ireland, 42
cárdenas, micha, 85, 91
care work and reproductive labor: and Black women scholars, 9, 143–54; and conferences, 148; and COVID-19 pandemic, 91; described, 69; and editing Wikipedia projects, 163; as feminine, 62, 69, 90; as feminist value, 2, 70, 90, 201; and infrastructures, 7, 83, 91, 92, 146–48, 162, 170–71; invisibility of, 161–62; and labs, 105; and manufacturing, 62–63; and mentoring, 145, 146, 148; in overview, 2, 7–8; and pedagogy, 9, 11, 201, 207, 238, 242, 244–49; and scale, 170–71; scholarship and ethics of care, 9, 201, 207; and self-care, 147, 244; and social media, 146–48; and textiles, 62, 69; as third shift, 148
Caribbean Digital, 105
Carson, Anne, 206–7
Case, Amber, 187
caste, 11, 221, 222, 223, 226, 228, 231, 232
categories. *See* interest categories and social media; tagging
Center for Digital Humanities, Pune, 221, 228–29. *See also* Digital Humanities Winter School (Pune, India)
Centre for Solutions to Online Violence, 84

Chandavarkar, Anjali, 229
CHANT (Crucian Heritage and Nature Tourism), 168–69
Charlie Daly collection, 37, 41, 46–51
Chatelain, Marcia, 241
Chat GPT3, 200
Chaudhuri, Sukanta, 229
Chicana por mi Raza, 105
Christen, Kimberly, 90
ciné-geography, 174n63
circuit boards, compared to textiles, 61
CIS India, 227
Civic Laboratory for Environmental Action Research (CLEAR), 104–5
CLARIN (Common Language Resources and Technology Infrastructure), 83, 121
class: and distribution of space, 114n2; and Irish WWI letters, 39, 43; and pedagogy in India, 221, 222, 228, 231
classification and classification systems: binaries in, 210–11; and hierarchies, 60; as infrastructures, 131; and neutrality, 130
Clement, Tanya E., 5–6, 17–29, 200
climate change and textile projects, 59, 66–69
Lady Clonbrock (Augusta Caroline Dillon), 45–46, 51, 52n13
close reading, 37, 46, 50
clothing and wearables, 60, 86, 91, 109
cloud computing, materiality of, 65–66, 191–92
codes of conduct, 228
coding: English as dominant language of, 221; and gatekeeping, 233n1. *See also* computational text analysis
Colab notebooks, 202, 203–4
collaboration: collaborative codesign, 228; and collectives, 105–6, 152, 168; and cooperatives, 102–14; and editing Wikipedia, 163–65; as feminist practice, 4, 229; and infrastructures, 85, 86, 87, 91; and Irish women's WWI letters, 36, 51; and labs, 149, 154; and Nordic recovery projects, 125–35; and pedagogy, 212, 222–25, 227–32, 238–47, 249; and textile projects, 59, 67; valuing of, 7

collecting and preserving materials: and gender, 36, 39, 42; by individuals, 133; and LGBTQ+ archives, 127–28, 133
Collective Biographies of Women, 3
collectives, 105–6, 152, 168
COLLEX, 94n55
Collins, Patricia Hill, 127
colonialism: and academic recognition, 241; colonial archives and infrastructures, 160, 162, 165–72; and digital tools, 250n1; and language, 221; and pedagogy, 11, 220–27; and technology, 225. *See also* postcolonialism
Colored Conventions Project, 105
colorism, 222
communication tools and pedagogy, 242–44
community: and cooperative model, 110, 113; and feminist labs, 105; and pedagogy, 11, 222, 224–30, 231, 233, 242–44, 245, 248–49; and recovery projects, 8, 121, 125–26, 128–29, 132, 150, 169; and social media, 147; and Wikipedia projects, 163
computational text analysis: and pedagogy, 11, 198–215; and queer readings, 131
conceptualization and operationalization in text analysis pedagogy, 209–10
conferences: and Black women scholars, 148–49; and care, 148; mock conferences, 203; and social media, 145, 146–47; topics in Nordic, 9, 121, 122–23, 134
Connacht Rangers, 52n13
content moderation, 173n17, 182–83
context: and data cleaning, 10, 208; and modularization, 164; and pedagogy, 10, 207, 214, 220–27, 229, 231–33; as principle of data feminism, 8, 125, 207; and recovery projects, 124–27, 134–35, 165–71; of technology, 191; and textile projects, 64, 67, 68, 70
control and labs, 104
controlled vocabularies vs. tagging, 132

cooperatives, 9, 102–14
cop pedagogy, 244
core rope memory, 61
correspondence, WWI Irish, 6, 35–51
Costanza-Chock, Sasha, 199
COVID-19 pandemic, viii, 91, 238, 240
Cowen, Deborah, 169
craft: and gender, 69; vs. technology, 86
credit, academic, 109, 112–13, 241–42, 247
criminal justice system, 199
critical race theory, 2, 84, 143
critique: challenges of infrastructure critique, 79, 81, 82, 83–84; and classification, 131; feminist infrastructure as critique, 82; as feminist principle, 89, 92; and labs, 149; and middle-distance reading, 37; and pedagogy, 11, 199, 202, 232, 240, 250
Cro, Melinda, 245
cruel optimism, 192–93
Crunk Feminist Collective, 3
Cuboniks, Laboria, 79, 92, 102
CUNY Graduate Center, 201–15, 238–50
custommades, 212
Cvetkovitch, Ann, 128
"Cyborg Manifesto" (Haraway), 2
cyborgs, 85

Daly, Charlie, 37, 46, 47, 48
Daly, Charlie, collection, 37, 41, 46–51
Daly, Cornelius, 47, 48
Daly, Ellen, 47, 48, 50
Daly, Mary (May), 47, 48, 50
Danbolt, Mathias, 128
"Danger, Jane Roe!" project (Knight), 60
Danish West Indies colonial archives, 165–72
Dannenberg, Roger, 31n23
DARIAH (Digital Research Infrastructure for the Arts and Humanities), 83, 121
data: access to, 89; cleaning, 10, 133–34, 208; datafication of Black

and brown bodies, 167; and embodiment, 61, 68–70; and exposure of assumptions, 208–9; as framed, 59–60; as masculine, 59, 60; materiality of, 61, 65–70, 191–92; proxy data and social media, 187–88; quality of, 89; and reproduction of historic inequities, 60, 64

data cleaning: indexing as, 133–34; and loss of context, 10, 208

Data Feminism (D'Ignazio and Klein), 3, 125

data feminism, principles of, 8, 125, 127. *See also* care work and reproductive labor; collaboration; recovery projects; repair and reparative practices; visibility and invisibility

data-geography, 171

data modeling as conference topic, 123, 134

Davis, Rebecca Frost, 103

Debates in the Digital Humanities, 133, 207, 212

de Beauvoir, Simone, 84

decolonization: and pedagogy, 10, 11, 222, 223–27, 231, 232; and Wikipedia, 162–65, 226, 227

The Defense of a Madman (Strindberg), 131

Delmont, Matthew, 108–9, 154n2

Depression Quest, 87

design: adversarial design, 10, 184; collaborative codesign, 228; feminist interface design principles, 89; game design, 86–87; geodesign, 82; iterative design and participants, 87; value-sensitive design, 93n9

DeVaney, James, 249–50

Dewey Decimal Classification, 130

DH in the Nordic Countries (DHN), 121, 122–23, 134

Dickinson Electronic Archive, 3

Difference Engine, 65

DIGARV (Digitization and Accessibility of Cultural Heritage), 121

Digital Black Feminism (Steele), 2, 3, 146

digital humanities: and Black women scholars, 9, 143–54; English as

dominant language of, 221, 227, 229, 232; labs, 9, 103–6, 154; multilingual, 229, 232; Nordic conferences in, 9, 121, 122–23, 134; overview of approaches to, 1–5; responsibility of, 2; self-identification in, 144–45; and self-reflection/inquiry, 143–44, 152, 230–31, 243, 247, 248; volume's approach to, 1. *See also* infrastructures; pedagogy; readings

Digital Humanities in the Nordic and Baltic Countries (DHNB), 121, 122–23

Digital Humanities Quarterly, 103

Digital Humanities Summer Institute (DHSI), 9, 151–52

Digital Humanities Winter School (Pune, India), 11, 221–33

Digital Library Federation Forum Code of Conduct, 228

digital literacy and pedagogy, 202, 208, 213, 214–15

D'Ignazio, Catherine: and binaries, 8, 79; and feminist principles, 89, 125, 213; and making labor visible, 62; overview of scholarly engagement with, 3; and visualizations, 127

Dillon, Augusta Caroline (Lady Clonbrock), 45–46, 51, 52n13

Dirckinck-Holmfeld, Katrine, 159–72

DiSalvo, Carlo, 184

discomfort, 230

Discord, 242

discourse theory, 30n17

dissensus, 184

distant reading, 37, 46

diversity: diversity stack, 8, 82; efforts in technology sector, 84; imposed by the majority, 238; and pluriversity concept, 224; work as third shift of labor, 148

Documenting the American South, 3

Dodd, Maya, 229

domesticity of textiles and fiber arts, 60, 61–62, 63, 69

Drift, 22–27, 28

Drucker, Johanna, 124, 127

Duffin family, 52n13

Earhart, Amy, 3, 133, 151
Early Caribbean Digital Archive, 3
economy: attention, 184–85; plantation, 170–71
edit-wars, 163
Eichmann-Kalwara, Nickoal, 123
18thConnect.org, 88
Electric Marronage project, 152–53
Ellis, Dan, 31n21
embodiment and body: and care work, 69; and data, 61, 68–70; elevating embodiment as principle of data feminism, 127, 137n27; and Expansion and Diversity project, 126, 127; and gender, 63, 69; and infrastructures, 80, 81, 85; and knowledge, 79, 168; and labor of Black women scholars, 143; and materiality, 63; and pedagogy, 207, 213, 228; and recordings and listening, 6, 19; and social media, 192; and technology, 61, 68–70, 190, 191; and textiles and fiber arts, 61, 67, 68; and visualizations, 127; and wearables, 86
Emerson, Lori, 85, 86, 103, 104, 105
emotions: elevating emotions as principle of data feminism, 127, 137n27; and pedagogy, 200, 207, 239, 244–49; and recovery projects, 126, 127, 128; and social media, 192; and technology, 190, 191; and textiles, 67, 69. *See also* affective labor
engagement: and cooperative model, 110, 113; and infrastructures, 88, 91–92; and materiality, 67, 68–69; and Nordic recovery projects, 125–26
England, Jonathan, 108
English, dominance of, 221, 224, 227, 229, 232
epistemic violence, avoiding, 8, 125, 159–60, 165
Equality Lab, 9, 105, 149
Eshun, Kodwo, 174n63
Eubanks, Virginia, 183
evaluation and pedagogy, 247, 248–49
Ewing, Eve L., 155n11
Expansion and Diversity project, 121, 123–27, 133–34

expropriation and open-access publishing, 90
Extensible Markup Language (XML), 85, 229

Facebook, 10, 181, 184–89, 190–92
faculty: collaboration with students in pedagogy, 238–42, 246, 247, 249; privilege, 231, 232; ratings, 208, 209; student/staff interactions and co-op model, 107, 108, 109, 111–12, 114; teacher-student/student-teacher structure, 111
Fairchild Semiconductor Corporation, 62–63
Fauci, Anthony, 94n52
feminism: collaboration as feminist practice, 229; critique as principle of, 89, 92; and decentering privilege, 239; intersectional feminist framework for pedagogy, 11, 238–50; and killjoys, 5, 193, 199–200, 210; overview of approaches to digital humanities, 1–5; and pluralism, embracing, 8, 91, 125, 213–15; as a practice, 5, 222; principles of data feminism, 8, 125, 127; and shared vocabulary, 203, 207; and "staying with the trouble" concept, 211, 214; terms and definitions, 1, 2; use of term in course titles, 213
Feminism in India, 227
Feminist in a Software Lab (McPherson), 3, 105
Feminist Principles of the Internet, 84
FemTechNet: and care work, 148; as collective, 3–4, 105; as labor-centric, 83; and online violence, 84; and privacy, 90; touchstones of, 190–91
fiber arts. *See* textiles and fiber arts
fiction: indexing of, 129, 130–31; LGBTQ+ bibliographies, 128–34
Figueroa, Yomaira C., 152–53
Fireburn Queens, 168
Fitzpatrick, Kathleen, 91
Flanagan, Mary, 86–87
Florini, Sarah, 109
folksonomies, 85, 132
forms and vulnerability, 187

Foucault, Michel, 30n17, 54n51
"The Freak Show" (Sexton), 19–20
free trade zones, 173n17
Freire, Paulo, 104, 111, 239, 247
French and Irish women's WWI letters, 39, 40
funding: cooperatives, 107–8; infrastructures, 83–84

Gallon, Kim, 151
GamerGate, 87, 90, 163–64
Gamer Trouble (Phillips), 3
games: harassment on gaming platforms, 87, 90, 163–64, 183; and infrastructures, 86–87; Māori Video Games Database, 240–41
gatekeeping: and Black women scholars, 145; and coding, 233n1; and Nordic conferences, 134; and pedagogy, 241, 246–47
Gebru, Timnit, 200
gender: and arts and crafts, 69; and bracketing, 189, 191; and care work, 62, 69, 90; and classification, 210–11; and collecting and preserving materials, 36, 39, 42; and embodiment, 63, 69; gender-based hiring practices, 62–63, 65; and Indian independence movement, 226; and infrastructure labor, 83–84; Irish WWI letters, gender ratio in, 36, 39, 42, 46–47; Irish WWI letters, topics in, 37–42, 48–50; man as "neutral" form of humanity, 84; materiality of gendered body, 63; norms and gender identity, 62; and reparative practices, 90; and service, 80, 83; and social media settings, 187; and textiles and fiber arts, 59–70
"Gender" (Scott), 210
gender and academia: and distribution of space, 114n2; and infrastructure labor, 83–84; and labs, 104; and pedagogical course design, 240, 249; and pedagogy in India, 221, 222, 228, 230, 231; and perceptions of scholarliness, 144; and quantitative methods in digital humanities pedagogy, 199–201, 213; and topics

in digital humanities scholarship, 122–23, 134
"Gender and Cultural Analytics" (Mandell), 2
gender and technology: bias in Google search, 183, 199; bias in visualizations, 208, 209; and machine learning, 60; and open source, 84; and punch cards, 63; and quantitative methods in digital humanities pedagogy, 199–201, 213; technology/data as masculine, 59, 60, 62, 65; and text processing, 198–201, 210, 213
General Department of Voluntary Organisations, 43
Gentle, 23
geodesign, 82
geography: ciné-geography, 174n63; and colonial archives, 171; datageography, 171; and networks in Irish women's WWI letters, 36, 42–46; and pedagogy in India, 221, 223–27
Gerard, Frandelle, 169
German language and Irish women's WWI letters, 39, 40
gestures and infrastructures, 80, 81
Gethen, Pax Ahimsa, 164
Girls Lost (Schiefauer), 129
GitHub, use in pedagogy, 203, 204
Global North: and pedagogy events in India, 234n33; and scholarly interactions with South, 224, 225, 231, 232; as "universal," 224
Global South: and digital humanities training institutes, 222–23; and editing Wikipedia projects, 162, 227; and pedagogy in India, 220–33; and scholarly interactions with North, 224, 225, 231, 232
Goldberg, David Theo, 84
Goldhaber, Michael, 184
Goldstone, Andrew, 212, 213
Google: and advertising, 185–89, 192; and artificial intelligence, 200; Colab notebooks, 202, 203–4; and proxy data, 187; search, bias in, 183, 185, 199; search as black box, 182, 183

Gothenburg, Sweden and Expansion and Diversity project, 121, 123–27, 133–34
Gray, Ros, 174n63
Griffin, Gabrielle, 122
Group for Experimental Methods in Humanistic Research, 105
Grumbach, Elizabeth, 103, 107, 109–11, 113

Hacker, Sally, 111
Hale, Sondra, 238
Hammerschmidt, Soren, 109
Hanish, Carol, 143
happiness and norms, 193
Haraway, Donna, 2, 85, 211, 214, 228
hard drive disks, materiality of, 66
hardware and infrastructures, 85–86, 91
Harney, Stefano, 114n2, 161
Hart-Davidson, Bill, 249–50
Hartman, Saidiya, 161
HASTAC Commons, 3, 83, 105
Hatcher, Erik, 94n55
Hawkins, Max, 31n21
hero scientist trope, 87
hetereogeneity: and open source, 84; of students, 202
hierarchies: and classification, 60; and cooperatives, 9, 107–8, 111–14; and Expansion and Diversity project, 124–25; and labs, 104, 106; and pedagogy, 221, 230, 243, 249; and power in flat hierarchies, 111; questioning of in digital humanities, 4, 8; rethinking hierarchies as principle of data feminism, 126, 137n27
High Performance Sound Technologies for Access and Scholarship (HiPSTAS), 23
Hollerith, Herman, 65
Holt, Jennifer, 191–92
homogenization and standards, 84
Homosaurus, 131
hooks, bell: and autoethnographic research, 143; on labor, 106, 111; overview of scholarly engagement with, 2; and pedagogy, 222, 227, 239, 240

Howe, Jason, 130
Humanities Networked Infrastructure (HuNI), 83–84, 88

identity: digital humanities and self-identification, 144–45; Irish language and Irish identity, 48–49; norms and gender identity, 62; and social media, 144–45, 187
ideology: and infrastructures, 8, 81; and pedagogy, 11, 207, 222, 223, 228
IIT Indore, 227
IMDB, 208–9
Immersive Reality Lab for the Humanities, 105
indexing, 128, 129–32, 133–34
Index Thomisticus, 3, 63, 65
India: education of women in, 223; feminist pedagogy in, 220–33; independence movement, 225, 226
Indian Association for Women Studies, 225
Indigenous people: expropriation of Indigenous knowledge, 90; and gender-based hiring practices, 62–63; and online harassment and violence, 90; reading and interpretive strategies, 6
inequities: and cooperatives, 111; and infrastructures, 81, 86; and labs, 104; and machine learning bias, 60; and networks, 86; and New Jim Code, 199; and NLTK book corpus, 206; technology/data as reproducing, 60, 64
infrapolitics, 159–72
infrapuncture concept: and cooperatives, 105, 106, 113–14; described, 9, 91, 102; and labs, 105
infrastructures: and accessibility, 9, 80, 83, 85–86, 89–91, 124, 125, 166; and agency, 81, 82, 87, 88, 91–92; binaries, avoiding, 8, 79, 82, 84, 85, 88, 89–90, 92, 123; and Black women scholars, 9, 143–54; and care work, 7, 83, 91, 92, 146–48, 162, 170–71; challenge of critiquing, 79, 81, 82,

83–84, 92; and colonial archives, 160, 162, 165–72; and cooperatives, 9, 102–14; described, 79–80; and ecosystems, 82, 91–92; and embodiment, 80, 81, 85; feminist approaches to building, 79–92; feminist infrastructure as critique, 82; funding for, 83–84; and ideology, 8, 81; illusion of accessibility, 83; illusion of neutrality, 83, 124, 166–67; indexing and classification terms as, 131, 132; and infrapolitics, 159–72; labor of, 7–9, 83–84, 91, 92; and labs, 9, 103–6, 114, 149, 154; and materiality, 85, 86, 87, 191–92; and mattering, 21–22, 29; and modularity, 164, 170; and networks, 85–86, 91; and Nordic projects, 121–35; in overview, 1–5, 7–9; and relationships, 88, 105; and reparative practices, 7, 8, 90; role of users, 80–81, 88, 91, 184; smoothness/invisibility of, 80–81, 92, 102, 161–62; and the stack, 8, 79, 82; and standards, 84–85; and Underground Railroad, 169; and waste, 9, 123, 133–34. *See also* academic infrastructures; infrapuncture concept; infrastructures and technology

infrastructures and technology: and hardware, 85–86; and interfaces, 88, 89; and metadata, 88; and software, 86–87, 91

Inniss, Tara A., 166

Instagram, 10, 181, 182, 185–89, 192, 241

Institute for Advanced Studies in English (IASE Pune), 228

Institute for Humanities Research (Arizona State University). *See* Nexus Digital Co-op

Intentionally Digital, Intentionally Black conference, 9, 148

interest categories and social media, 187–89, 192

interfaces and infrastructures, 88, 89

intersectional feminist framework for pedagogy, 11, 238–50

invisibility. *See* visibility and invisibility

Ireland: Irish language and Irish identity, 48–49; Irish language in WWI letters, 39, 40, 48–49; Irish nationalism and correspondence, 36, 39, 41; Knitting Map, 6, 67–68, 69–70; WWI Irish letters, 6, 35–51

Irish War Hospital Supply Organisation (IWHSO), 37, 42–46, 51

Jacquard, Jacques Marie, 64

Jacquard looms, 61, 64–65

Jemielniak, Dariusz, 163

Jesuit archives in Ireland, 42

Johnson, Jessica Marie, 105, 144, 145, 152–53, 167

Jones, Stevens, 103

Jorgensen, Jeana, 123

Jupyter notebooks, 202, 203–4, 212, 213

justice: and algorithmic text processing, 198, 199; criminal justice system, 199; and open-access publication, 90; in overview, 2, 4; and tools, 28–29, 244

justice and pedagogy: and Black women scholars, 9, 151–53; and digital tools, 244; in India, 222, 224, 225, 226, 230–33; and intersectional feminist approach, 238, 239, 240, 244, 248; in overview, 4, 9, 11; and social media as black box, 181–93; and text analysis, 11, 198, 199, 201, 207, 210, 214, 215

Kaldi, 31n21

Kawahara, Hideki, 31n22

Kearns, Sarah, 245

killjoys, 5, 193, 199–200, 210

Kim, Dorothy, 151–52, 244

Kirtz, Jaime Lee, 4, 6–7, 59–70

Klein, Lauren F.: and binaries, 8, 79; and feminist principles, 89, 125, 213; and making labor visible, 62; overview of scholarly engagement with, 3; and visualizations, 127

Knight, Kim Brilliante, 60, 86

Knitting Map, 6, 67–68, 69–70

knowledge: embodied knowledge, 228;
    knowledge dissemination between
    Global North and South, 224, 225;
    local knowledge and pedagogy, 10,
    11; minoritarian, 5, 249; subjugated,
    227
Korn, Jennifer, 146
Krabbe Meyer, Mette Kia, 166, 169

The Lab Book (Wershler et al.), 103, 104
labor: assumption that technology
    saves labor, 191; and cooperatives,
    108, 111, 112; and gender-based
    hiring practices, 62–63, 65; gender
    divisions between skilled and
    unskilled labor, 63–64; of infrastruc-
    tures, 7–9, 83–84, 91, 92; and labs,
    103, 108, 114; of marginalized groups
    in academia, 241–42; and men-
    toring, 145, 146, 148; of students
    and designing pedagogical course,
    241–42, 249; visibility of labor and
    COVID-19 pandemic, viii; visibility
    of labor as principle of data femi-
    nism, 137n27; by wives, sisters, and
    assistants, 115n10; women's invisible
    labor, 43. *See also* affective labor;
    care work and reproductive labor
labs, 9, 103–6, 108, 114, 149, 154
language: and colonial archives, 166;
    and colonialism, 221; English, domi-
    nance of, 221, 224, 227, 229, 232;
    and Irish women's WWI letters, 39,
    40; local languages and pedagogy,
    10, 227, 229, 232; and multilingual
    digital humanities, 229, 232; Sexton
    on, 20–21
Latent Dirichlet Allocation (LDA), 39
Latent Semantic Analysis (LSA), 38
Le Guin, Ursula, 10, 181–82, 183–85,
    189, 193
"Lemon Project," 149–50
Leonard, Ellen, 47
Letters 1916–1923, 35–51
Levi, Amalia S., 166
LGBTQ+ people: bibliographies,
    128–34; collecting and preserv-
    ing materials by, 127–28, 133; and
    indexing of LGBTQ+ materials,

128, 129–32; and infrastructural
    resistance, 8; and online harass-
    ment and violence, 90, 91, 164; and
    pedagogy, 213–14, 228, 240, 249;
    Queerlit project, 121, 123, 127–34;
    and queer readings, 130–31; as
    receiving less academic credit, 113;
    and social media settings, 187; terms
    in archives and bibliographies, 128,
    129–30, 131, 132
Liboiron, Max, 105, 113
Library of Congress Classification, 130
Library of Congress Subject Headings,
    130, 132
The Library of Missing Datasets (2016),
    167
LibraryThing, 132
Libris (National Union Catalog,
    Sweden), 128, 131–32, 133
LilyPad Arduino, 86
Lindhé, Cecilia, 7, 8, 9, 121–35
Linked Infrastructure for Networked
    Cultural Scholarship (LINCS),
    83–84
listening: and audiation, 6, 17–29; and
    embodiment, 6, 19; and race, 29n3
Liu, Alan, 8, 79, 80, 81, 82, 124
Living a Feminist Life (Ahmed), 2, 203
Local Autonomy Networks (Autonets),
    90–91
LOL memory, 64
Lorde, Audre, 239
Losh, Elizabeth, 3, 90–91, 105, 149,
    190–91
Lothian, Alexis, 122
Lovelace, Ada, 61
LSA (Latent Semantic Analysis), 38
Lucy, Con, 48
Lynn, Kathleen, 42

MacArthur, Marit, 30n20
Macaulay, Thomas, 224
MacCarron, Pádraig, 43
machine learning and bias, 60. *See also*
    computational text analysis
magnetic-core memory, 61
maker-space movement, 90
The Making of Samuel Beckett's Molloy,
    207

Malta, and Irish women volunteers in WWI, 45–46

Mandell, Laura: and Advanced Research Consortium, 88; on binaries, 10, 79, 200, 210; and feminist infrastructure building, 7, 8, 9, 79–92; overview of scholarly engagement with, 2

Mandiberg, Michael, 163

Māori Video Games Database, 240–41

mapping: and Expansion and Diversity project, 126–27; of Irish women's WWI letters, 43–46; and middle-distance readings, 43; in pedagogy in India, 226

Marathi language, 232

Marchant, Claude, 125, 133

Martin, Marie, 52n13

materiality: of cloud computing, 65–66, 191–92; of data, 61, 65–70, 191–92; and engagement, 67, 68–69; of gendered body, 63; and infrastructures, 85, 86, 87, 191–92; and technology, 60, 61, 65–68, 85, 86, 190; of textiles, 61, 65–70

mattering and audiation, 18, 20–22, 29

Mazumdar, Vina, 226

Mazzoni, Dominic, 31n23

Mbembe, Achille, 224

McGonigal, Jane, 87

McKinney, Cait, 128, 132

McPherson, Tara: and bracketing, 189, 191; and collaboration, 85, 87; and infrastructures, 85, 86, 87, 105; and modularity, 164, 170

Me and My Shadow, 244

Media Archeology Lab, 105

Meeting the Universe Halfway (Barad), 2

memory, 61, 64

memory planes, 64

men: and Irish WWI letters, 36, 39, 42, 44, 46–47; man as "neutral" form of humanity, 84; and open-source technology, 84; technology/data as masculine, 59, 60, 62, 65; and textile jobs, 71n15. *See also* gender

Menon, Nirmala, 227

mentoring: and Black women scholars, 145, 146, 148–49, 153–54; as care work, 145, 146, 148

mesa-medieval.org, 88

metadata: Advanced Research Consortium categories, 85, 88; and colonial archives, 166, 167; evolution of, 88; Irish women's WWI letters, 37, 38, 40–41, 42, 47; and queer bibliographic projects, 131–32. *See also* Queerlit

Middlebrook, Diane, 30n9

middle-distance readings, 6, 7, 36–51

Milowski, Daniel, 108

minimal computing, 84, 86, 90

minoritarian knowledge, 5, 249

"Minute on Indian Education" (Macaulay), 224

Mitchell, Margaret, 200

modnets.org, 88

modularity, 164, 170

Mohanty, Chandra Talpad, 231

Mondragón (cooperative), 111

Moro, Jeffrey, 167, 252n22

Morrison, Aimée, 249–50

Moten, Fred, 114n2, 161

mourning, 145

Mukherjee, Souvik, 230

Mukurtu, 90

Muñoz, José Esteban, 249

Muñoz, Trevor, 3, 133–34

Murray, Padmini Ray, 226, 228

Museum of Gothenburg, 133

Nakamura, Lisa, 183, 241

NASA, 61, 64

National Conference on Women's Studies, 225

National Norwegian Archive for Queer History (Skeivt Arkiv), 128

National Union Catalog (Libris) [Sweden], 128, 131–32, 133

natural language processing: and gender, 210; NLTK, 39, 48, 204–6; and pedagogy, 210, 211–12; prominence of in Nordic conferences, 123, 134

Natural Language Processing with Python, 210

Navarro, Tami, 168
Navarro-McElhaney, Kristine, 108
Nelson, Diane, 162
networks: and infrastructures, 85–86, 91; and Irish women in WWI, 36, 42–46, 47; and middle-distance readings, 36, 43; and power, 85–86, 91; and scholarly collaboration, 232
neurodiversity and pedagogy, 240, 249
neutrality: and indexing, 130; and infrastructures, 83, 124, 166–67; man as "neutral" form of humanity, 84; and platforms, 192; and technology, 83, 190, 192
New Digital Worlds (Risam), 2
New Jim Code, 199
Newsom, Leah, 109
Nexus Digital Co-op, 9, 103, 106–14
Nieves, Angel David, 151–52
NINES.org, 85, 88
NLTK (Natural Language Toolkit), 39, 48, 204–6
NMF (Non-Negative Matrix Factorization), 39
Noble, Safiya Umoja, 2, 151, 183, 199
Noddings, Nel, 245
noise, background, 27–28
Non-Negative Matrix Factorization (NMF), 39
Nordic digital humanities conferences, 9, 121, 122–23, 134
Nordic infrastructure projects, 121–35
norms: and feminist critique, 81, 82; and gender identity, 62; and happiness, 193; and infrastructures, 82; racist, 151; and textiles, 61–62
notebooks and text analysis course, 202–9, 212, 213
Notick, Samantha, 108
Nowviskie, Bethany, 88
Nox (Carson), 206–7
Nyhan, Julianne, 63
Nyröp, Marii, 90

Ochshorn, Robert, 31n21
Odumosu, Temi, 166
Oiva, Mila, 103

Omeka, 226, 230
"The Ones Who Walk Away from Omelas" (Le Guin), 10, 181–82, 183–85, 189, 193
Onuoha, Mimi, 167
open-access publication, 90
Open Source Diversity project, 84
open source software, 84
optimism, cruel, 192–93
Orlando Project, 3
Orne, Martin, 19, 22
O'Sullivan, Katie Maria, 47
Othering and pedagogy, 239, 247

Parham, Marisa, 153
Parikka, Jussi, 103, 104
Park Central Mall project, 108–9, 113
Patel, Kush, 224
Pathak, Kunjika, 229
pauses, measuring, 6, 22–28
Pawlicka-Deger, Urszula, 103
pedagogy: and accessibility, 221, 223–27, 231–33, 240–43, 246; and adversarial design, 10, 184; banking model, 247; and Black women scholars, 9, 151–53; and care work, 9, 11, 201, 207, 238, 242, 244–49; and codes of conduct, 228; and collaboration, 212, 222–25, 227–32, 238–47, 249; and colonialism and postcolonialism, 11, 220–27, 230–33; communication tools in, 242–44; and context, 10, 207, 214, 220–27, 229, 231–33; cop pedagogy, 244; core values, 202; and COVID-19 pandemic, 238, 240; and education role of cooperative model, 110–11; and embodiment, 207, 213, 228; and emotions, 200, 207, 239, 244–49; and evaluation, 247, 248–49; feminist pedagogy in India, 220–33; and gatekeeping, 241, 246–47; intersectional feminist framework for, 11, 238–50; in overview, 4, 5, 10–11; resilient, 249–50; and self-reflection, 230–31, 243, 247, 248; and shared vocabulary,

203–8; and social media, 10, 181–93;
and "staying with the trouble"
concept, 211–13, 214; teacher-stu-
dent/student-teacher structure, 111;
and text analysis, 10, 198–215; and
unstructured time, 240, 245–46,
247, 249. *See also* justice and
pedagogy
performativity, 30n17
performing arts recovery projects, 121,
123–27, 133–34
Phillips, Amanda, 3, 122
Phule, Jyotirao, 223
Phule, Savitribai, 220, 222, 223
pitch, measuring, 25, 26, 31nn21–22
place-based learning and pedagogy in
India, 223–27
plantation economy, 170–71
Plath, Sylvia, 23
pluralism, embracing: and infrastructures, 8, 91, 92, 134, 135; and pedagogy, 213–15; as principle of data
feminism, 8, 91, 125, 213–15
Point of View, 234n40
Pojkarna (Schiefauer), 129
politics: infrastructures and infrapolitics, 159–72; political ads and social
media, 192
Pollicy, 84
poor theory, 84
positionality, 18–20, 29
Posner, Miriam, 82, 233n1
postcolonialism: and Irish identity,
48–49; and labs, 105; and pedagogy, 11, 222, 224–27, 230–33; and
Wikipedia editing, 162, 164. *See also*
colonialism
power: challenging/examining power as
principles of data feminism, 137n27;
and distribution of space in academia, 114n2; and infrastructures,
82, 91; and labs, 104, 106; and mattering, 18; and networks, 85–86, 91;
and pedagogical communication,
243; and tools, 18; unnamed power
in flat hierarchies, 111; of US academics, 231

Prabhakar, Nidhi, 229
Pratt, Geraldine, 229
privacy: and digital communication
tools in pedagogy, 243–44; and
open-access publishing, 90
privilege: and Indian pedagogy, 221,
224, 231, 232, 239; and Wikipedia,
227
proxy data, 187–88
publishing: and academic credit, 109,
112–13, 241–42, 247; and author
order, 113; and feminist labs, 105;
open-access models, 90
punch cards, 63, 64–65
puppetry, 126
Pussyhat Project, 69
Python: NLTK, 39, 48, 204–6; and
text analysis courses, 203–6, 211–12;
and text analysis of Irish women's
WWI letters, 39, 43, 49

QRAB (Archives and Library of the
Queer Movement), 128, 131, 133
quantitative methods: and digital
humanities pedagogy, 199–201, 212,
213; in heterogenous data sources,
36–37, 48; in Nordic recovery
projects, 126–27; prominence of in
Nordic conferences, 123; and textile
projects, 36, 37
Queering the Map, 240–41
Queerlit, 121, 123, 127–34
queer readings, 130–31
queer theory, 130
Quinn, Zoë, 87
Quintana, Rebecca, 249–50
Quissell, Christin, 107

race: Black feminism term, 2; and
Black women scholars, 9, 143–54;
and bracketing, 189, 191; critical
race theory, 2, 84, 143; datafication
of Black and brown bodies, 167;
decentering whiteness in pedagogy,
239; and distribution of space in
academia, 114n2; and feminist labs,
105; and "Lemon Project," 150;

race (*continued*): and listening, 29n3; and online harassment and violence, 90; and perceptions of scholarliness, 144; and readings in pedagogical course design, 240; and reproductive labor, 162; and search, 183, 185, 199; and technology, 154n4, 199; and textiles, 60; and visualizations, 208, 209; and Wikipedia editing, 162–65

"Race, Memory, and the Digital Humanities and My Mother Was a Computer" symposium, 149

Race after Technology (Benjamin), 3, 198

Radzikowska, Milena, 89

Rate My Professor, 208, 209

Rawson, Katie, 2–3, 132, 133–34

readings: against the grain, 10, 203, 207–11, 214, 215; and audiation, 6, 17–29; close reading, 37, 46, 50; distant reading, 37, 46; and meaning vs. aboutness, 131; middle-distance, 6, 7, 36–51; and multiple forms of texts, 19; in overview, 5–7; in pedagogical course design, 240; queer, 130–31; reparative reading, 170; symptomatic vs. surface, 130–31; and textiles, 6, 59–70; WWI Irish letters, 6, 35–51

readymade processes, 212

recordings: analysis of Sexton's therapy sessions, 6, 17–29; as boundary objects, 20–21

Recovering the U.S. Hispanic Literary Heritage, 105

recovery projects: colonial archives and infrastructures, 165–72; as devalued work in digital humanities, 151; Expansion and Diversity project, 121, 123–27, 133–34; focus on in early digital humanities, 3–4; Nordic projects, 121–35; Queerlit project, 121, 123, 127–34; role of, 6; and William & Mary projects, 150–51; women in Ireland (1914–1923), 6, 35–51. *See also* repair and reparative practices; visibility and invisibility

reflection. *See* self-reflection

relationships: and alternative lab and collaboration models, 105–6; and infrastructures, 88, 105; and mentors, 145, 146, 148–49, 153–54; social media and Black women scholars, 144–48, 149, 153–54

Renegade Runners, 162

repair and reparative practices: and colonial archives, 159, 160, 170–72; as feminine, 7, 83, 90; in overview, 7, 8; reparative reading, 170. *See also* care work and reproductive labor; recovery projects

reproductive labor. *See* care work and reproductive labor

rerouting, 167–69, 171

resistance: and algorithmic text processing, 200–201; principles of guerrilla resistance, 190; and "staying with the trouble" concept, 211–13, 214; walking away from social media, 10, 183–84, 189–93

Resource Description Framework, 85

resource-sharing and cooperative model, 110

responsibility: of digital humanities scholarship, 2, 18, 28, 50–51, 240; and infrastructures, 91–92; and pedagogy, 199, 230–31

RFSL (Swedish Federation for Lesbian, Gay, Bisexual, Transgender, Queer and Intersex Rights), 131

Rhody, Lisa Marie, 1–11, 198–215

Rich, Adrienne, 23

Risam, Roopika: on Global North/South, 224, 225; overview of scholarly engagement with, 2; and pedagogy, 222, 226, 227; and violence of digital archive, 145

risks and pedagogy, 202

R language, 211–12

Roberts, Sarah, 183

Rogoff, Irit, 169

Rosen, Astrid von, 7, 8, 9, 121–35

Rouse, Joseph, 104

Royal College of Physicians, 42

Rozsika, Parker, 62

Ruberg, Bonnie, 130

Sadler, Elizabeth, 94n55
Salganik, Matthew, 212
Samlaska, Daniel, 108
Sample, Mark, 10, 181–93
Savitribai Phule Pune University, 228
Scalar platform, 86, 87, 105, 108
scale, 170–71
Schiefauer, Jessica, 129
Schmidt, Ben, 208
scholarship: and academic credit, 109, 112–13, 241–42, 247; Black women scholars, 143–54; and blogs, 144–48; and conferences, 148–49; and distribution of space in academia, 114n2; and ethics of care, 9, 201, 207; and hero scientist trope, 87; and information distribution, 67–68; knowledge dissemination between Global North/South, 224, 225, 231, 232; and mattering of subjects, 18; perceptions of scholarliness and gender/race, 144; and positionality, 18–20, 29; responsibility of, 2, 18, 28, 50–51, 240. *See also* academic infrastructures; gender and academia; pedagogy
Schreibman, Susan, 1–11, 35–51
Sciences Po MediaLab, 106
Scott, James C., 160–61
Scott, Joan, 210
SCRAM, 105
search: bias in, 183, 185, 199; as black box, 182, 183; and colonial archives, 166
Sedgwick, Eve, 170
self-care, 147, 244
self-making: online, 144–45; Sexton and therapy recordings, 6, 19
self-reflection: on digital humanities, 143–44, 152, 230–31; and pedagogy, 230–31, 247, 248; reflection time in class, 243
semiconductor industry, 62–63
serendipity, 54n51
service and academic infrastructures, 80, 83. *See also* care work and reproductive labor
Sewer, Hadiya, 168
Sex and Slavery Lab, 105

Sexton, Anne, 6, 17–29
Sexton, Linda Gray, 30n8
Sharma, Riddhima, 226
silence, measuring, 23, 27, 28
Silva, Andie, 10, 11, 238–50
Silva, Stephanie, 107
Singh, Rianka, 161
Skeivt Arkiv (National Norwegian Archive for Queer History), 128
Slack, 242, 243
slavery, 150, 167, 169, 170–71
smuggling, 169
social media: and affective labor, 148; bias in, 151, 182, 183, 185, 186, 199; as black box, 10, 181–93; and Black women scholars, 144–48, 149, 153–54; and conferences, 145, 146–47; and content moderation, 173n17, 182–83; and cooperation between marginalized groups, 241; and infrastructure of care, 146–48; and pseudoscience, 201; resisting/walking away from, 10, 183–84, 189–93
software and infrastructures, 86–87, 91
solid state drives and materiality, 66
sonic color line, 29n3
spaces: and Black women scholars, 9, 145, 146, 149; and cooperatives, 102–14; creation of, in overview, 6–7; and Expansion and Diversity project, 124–25, 126; and feminist labs, 105; and pedagogy, 10, 11, 245; and safety, 90–91
sphagnum moss, 43–46
Spivak, Gayatri, 8, 125
stack, 8, 79, 82
staff/student/faculty interactions and co-op model, 107, 108, 109, 111–12, 114
standards and infrastructures, 84–85
Standing Rock Syllabus, 240–41
Star, Susan Leigh, 80, 102, 161
Staying with the Trouble (Haraway), 2, 211
"staying with the trouble" concept, 211–13
Steele, Catherine Knight, 2, 3, 146, 148

Stenum, Helle, 174n47

Stevens, Nikki (Nikko) L., 7, 8, 9, 102–14

Stoever, Jennifer Lynn, 29n3

Stokes, Carla, 144

stop-word lists, 39, 48

StoryCorps, 248

Storymap, 226

Strindberg, August, 131

Stringfield, Ravynn K., 7, 8–9, 143–54

students: collaboration with faculty in pedagogy, 238–42, 246, 247, 249; staff/faculty interactions and co-op model, 107, 108, 109, 111–12, 114; teacher-student/student-teacher structure, 111

studiesinradicalism.org, 88

subject headings, 130, 132

Suchman, Lucy, 87, 91–92

suffragettes, 39

Superbetter app, 87

surface reading, 130–31

surveillance, 244

Sutherland, Tonia, 167

sweaty concepts, 207, 208

Sweden: Expansion and Diversity project, 121, 123–27; Queerlit project, 121, 123, 127–34

Swedish Federation for Lesbian, Gay, Bisexual, Transgender, Queer and Intersex Rights (RFSL), 131

Swedish Library Association, 132

symptomatic reading, 130–31

tagging: vs. controlled vocabularies, 132; Expansion and Diversity project, 126; Irish women's WWI letters, 37–38, 40

Tagore, Rabindranath, 227

Tallbear, Kim, 105–6

TANDEM-STRAIGHT, 31n22, 31n27

Taylor, Toneisha, 231

Teaching to Transgress (hooks), 2

Technically Wrong (Wachter-Boettcher), 186–87

technological imaginary, 191–92

technology: assumptions about, 190–91; and colonialism, 225; vs. craft, 86; diversity efforts in, 84; and embodiment, 61, 68–70, 190, 191; faith in technofixes, 211; illusion of accessibility, 83; illusion of neutrality, 83, 190, 192; and inequities, 60, 64; and labor of infrastructures, 83–84; as masculine, 59, 60, 62, 65; and materiality, 60, 61, 65–68, 85, 86, 190; and race, 154n4, 199; technological imaginary, 191–92; and textiles, 60–65; toxic tech, 186; and transparency, 124, 190, 191; wearables, 60, 86, 91, 109. *See also* infrastructures and technology

Tempestry Project, 6, 59, 66–69

templated selves, 187

Terras, Melissa, 63

text and text analysis: and audiation, 6, 17–29; binaries in, 10; computational analysis, 10–11, 131, 198–215; focus on written word, 200; Irish women's WWI letters, 35–51; and literature as cultural memory, 128; and pedagogy, 10–11, 198–215; Queerlit project, 121, 123, 127–34; and reading against the grain, 10, 203, 207–11, 214, 215

Text Encoding Initiative (TEI), 85

textiles and fiber arts, 6–7, 59–70

therapy sessions and audiation, 6, 17–29

Thorat, Dhanashree, 10, 11, 220–33

Thylstrup, Nanna Bonde, 7, 8, 159–72

"Time Will And Should Tell All" project, 150

tools: and apparatus concept, 20–21, 28–29; and audiation, 17–29; communication tools and pedagogy, 242–44; text analysis tools and pedagogy, 203–4, 211–12

topics and topic analysis: Irish women's WWI letters, 37–42, 48–50; and research selection in cooperatives, 110, 111; topic modeling, 37–42, 48–49

Torn Apart/Separados project, 240–41

"Toward a Diversity Stack" (Liu), 8

toxic tech, 186

Traces of the Old, Uses of the New
    (Earhart), 3
Traditional Knowledge Labels, 90
traffic and textile projects, 67–68
transcription and colonial archives, 166
transformation: and infrastructures,
    169; and pedagogy, 10; and recovery
    projects, 122, 133–35; role of digital
    humanities in, 122; spatial, 102. *See
    also* infrapuncture concept
#transformDH, 3
translation and colonial archives, 166,
    174n47
transparency: and cooperatives, 106,
    110; as feminist interface design
    principle, 89; of infrastructures, 79,
    80–81, 86; and scholarship, 144–45,
    147; and social media, 186; of tech-
    nology, 124, 190, 191
transportation and network mappings,
    44
Tsing, Anna, 170–71
Tufecki, Zeynep, 185
Twine, 87, 153, 226
Twitter (X), 60, 145–46, 147, 149, 181,
    185–89, 192

Uncertain Archives, 159, 162, 166,
    168–69
Underground Railroad, 169
University Grants Commission (India),
    221
Unstraight Museum, 128
US National Parks, 67
US Virgin Islands colonial archives,
    165–72

values: and games, 87; and infrastruc-
    tures, 86, 87; value-sensitive design,
    93n9
Vanniyar, Smita, 230
Vectors platform, 87, 105
Veel, Kristin, 159–72
Vergès, Françoise, 165
Verhoven, Deb: binaries in rela-
    tionships, 88; and infrapuncture
    concept, 9, 91, 102, 113; overview of
    scholarly engagement with, 2

Verma, Neil, 30n20
Victorian Women Writers Project, 3
violence: addressing in pedagogy,
    230; and algorithmic text process-
    ing, 198–99, 200–201; of archives,
    confronting, 159; of archives, coun-
    tering with rerouting and repurpos-
    ing, 167–69, 171; of archives, and
    cultural translations, 145; avoiding
    repeating (epistemic violence) in
    infrastructures, 8, 125, 159–60, 165;
    and content moderation, 182–83;
    datafication of Black and brown
    bodies as, 167; and harassment in
    editing Wikipedia projects, 163–64;
    online, 84, 90, 91, 164; and social
    media, 182–83, 186
Virgin Islands Studies Collective
    (VISCO), 168
virtual beauty shop, 146
visibility and invisibility: of assistive
    labor by women, 115n10; of Black
    women scholars, 9, 145; and femi-
    nist interface design principles, 89,
    92; and gender-based hiring prac-
    tices, 62–63; and indexing, 132; and
    infrapolitics, 161; of infrastructure
    labor, 83, 91, 92; of infrastructures,
    80–81, 92, 102, 161–62; and Irish
    women (1914–1923), 35–51; of labor
    and COVID-19 pandemic, viii;
    making labor visible, and credit,
    241–42; making labor visible as
    principle of data feminism, 137n27;
    and materiality, 67, 68; and Nordic
    recovery projects, 121, 123–35; in
    overview, 6–7, 9; of reproductive
    labor and care work, 161–62; and
    William & Mary projects, 150–51.
    See also recovery projects
visualizations: assumptions in, 124; bias
    in, 208, 209; and embodiment, 127;
    and emotions, 127; and Expansion
    and Diversity project, 126–27; in
    Sexton recordings analysis, 23, 27;
    and textiles, 60, 66–69; and wear-
    ables, 109; and WWI Irish letters, 7,
    45, 51

vocabulary: controlled vocabularies vs. tagging, 132; and text analysis course, 203–8
"Voice of the Shuttle" (website), 3
Vonderau, Patrick, 191–92
Voyant, 211

Wachter-Boettcher, Sara, 186–87, 192
Wales, Jimmy, 165
Walpole, Horace, 54n51
waste, 9, 123, 133–34
Watkins, S. Craig, 149
Wax, 90
wearables, technology, 60, 86, 91, 109
weather data and textile projects, 67–68
weaving: and reading, 6. *See also* textiles and fiber arts
Weinberg, Ari, 150
Weingart, Scott B., 123
Wernimont, Jacqueline: and Autonets, 90–91; and cooperatives, 7, 8, 9, 102–14; and interface as relationship, 88; overview of scholarly engagement with, 3
Wershler, Darren, 103, 104
Whelan, Elizabeth "Lily," 48
Wikipedia, 8, 162–65, 226, 227
William & Mary digital humanities projects, 9, 105, 149–51
Wilson, Ara, 88, 161

Wilson, Shawn, 105–6
witnessing, 145
women: association with service, 80, 83; Black women scholars, 9, 143–54; and diversity efforts in tech culture, 84; and online harassment and violence, 90; as receiving less academic credit, 113; role in early digital humanities, 3–4; textiles and fiber arts as feminine, 59–70; and Wikipedia editing, 162–65; women writers and early recovery projects, 3–4; WWI Irish letters, 6, 35–51. *See also* gender
"Women's Studies Database" (website), 3
Women Writers Project, 3, 85
Wordpress, 226
WoundPerson project, 109, 112–13
WWI Irish letters, 6, 35–51

X. *See* Twitter (X)
XML (Extensible Markup Language), 85, 229

Yanique, Tiphanie, 168
YouTube, 199, 241

Zoom, 246
Zulip, 251n19

The University of Illinois Press
is a founding member of the
Association of University Presses.

____

Composed in 11.5/13 Adobe Garamond Pro
with Gotham display
by Lisa Connery
at the University of Illinois Press

University of Illinois Press
1325 South Oak Street
Champaign, IL 61820-6903
www.press.uillinois.edu